HACKERS TOEFL
READING Intermediate 활용법

토플 보카 외우기
이용방법 고우해커스(goHackers.com) 접속 ▶
상단 메뉴 [TOEFL → 토플보카외우기] 클릭하여 이용하기

토플 스피킹/라이팅 첨삭 게시판
이용방법 고우해커스(goHackers.com) 접속 ▶
상단 메뉴 [TOEFL → 스피킹게시판/라이팅게시판] 클릭하여 이용하기

토플 공부전략 강의
이용방법 고우해커스(goHackers.com) 접속 ▶
상단 메뉴 [TOEFL → 토플공부전략]
클릭하여 이용하기

토플 자료 및 유학 정보
이용방법 고우해커스(goHackers.com)에
접속하여 다양한 토플 자료 및
유학 정보 이용하기

고우해커스 바로 가기 ▶

지문녹음 MP3
이용방법 해커스인강(HackersIngang.com) 접속 ▶
상단 메뉴 [토플 → MP3/자료 → 무료 MP3/자료] 클릭하여 이용하기

MP3/자료 바로 가기 ▶

단어암기 MP3
이용방법 해커스인강(HackersIngang.com) 접속 ▶
상단 메뉴 [토플 → MP3/자료 → 무료 MP3/자료] 클릭하여 이용하기

MP3/자료 바로 가기 ▶

iBT 리딩 실전모의고사
이용방법 해커스인강(HackersIngang.com) 접속 ▶
상단 메뉴 [토플 → MP3/자료 → 무료 MP3/자료] 클릭 ▶ 본 교재의 실전모의고사 프로그램 이용하기

HACKERS

TOEFL
READING
Intermediate

해커스 어학연구소

무료 토플자료·유학정보 제공
goHackers.com

최신 토플 경향을 반영한
Hackers TOEFL Reading Intermediate (iBT)을 내면서

◇

해커스 토플은 토플 시험 준비와 함께 여러분의 영어 실력 향상에 도움이 되고자 하는 마음에서 시작되었습니다. 해커스 토플을 처음 출간하던 때와 달리, 이제는 많은 토플 책들을 서점에서 볼 수 있지만, 그럼에도 해커스 토플이 여전히 **독보적인 베스트셀러**의 자리를 지킬 수 있는 것은 늘 **처음과 같은 마음으로** 더 좋은 책을 만들기 위해 고민하고, 최신 경향을 반영하기 위해 끊임없이 노력하기 때문입니다.

이러한 노력의 결실로, 새롭게 변경된 토플 시험에서도 학습자들이 영어 실력을 향상하고 토플 고득점을 달성하는 데 도움을 주고자 **최신 토플 경향을 반영한** 『Hackers TOEFL Reading Intermediate (iBT)』을 출간하게 되었습니다.

토플 리딩 고득점의 발판을 확실히 마련하기 위한 중급 교재!
『Hackers TOEFL Reading Intermediate (iBT)』은 학습자들이 중급 실력을 완성하고 나아가 상급 독해 실력으로 발돋움하기 위한 중급용 학습서입니다.

유형별 학습을 통한 완벽한 실전 대비!
학습자들이 실제 시험에 출제되는 문제 유형별로 체계적으로 학습함으로써 보다 수준 높은 독해 실력을 쌓을 수 있도록 구성하였습니다. 또한, 다양한 문제 유형을 가장 확실하게 풀어낼 수 있는 공략법을 제공하고, 문제 유형을 누적식으로 구성하여 학습자들이 모든 문제 유형을 골고루 공부할 수 있도록 하였습니다.

『Hackers TOEFL Reading Intermediate (iBT)』이 여러분의 토플 목표 점수 달성에 확실한 해결책이 되고 영어 실력 향상, 나아가 **여러분의 꿈을 향한** 길에 믿음직한 동반자가 되기를 소망합니다.

David Cho

Hackers TOEFL

Reading

Intermediate

CONTENTS

TOPIC LIST   6

iBT TOEFL Reading 고득점의 발판, 해커스 토플 리딩 인터미디엇!   8

iBT TOEFL 소개   12

iBT TOEFL Reading 소개 및 학습전략   14

iBT TOEFL Reading 화면 구성   16

해커스 학습플랜   18

Diagnostic Test   21

Chapter 01 Fact & Negative Fact   33

Chapter 02 Vocabulary   55

Chapter 03 Reference   77

Chapter 04 Sentence Simplification   99

Chapter 05 Rhetorical Purpose   123

Chapter 06 Inference   145

Chapter 07 Insertion   167

Chapter 08 Summary   189

Chapter 09 Category Chart   217

Actual Test 1   246

Actual Test 2   256

온라인 실전모의고사 (HackersIngang.com)
* 실제 시험과 동일한 환경에서도 Actual Test 1, 2를 풀어볼 수 있습니다.

정답 · 해석 · 정답단서 [책속의 책]   269

TOPIC LIST

다음의 TOPIC LIST는 교재에 수록된 모든 지문을 주제별로 구분하여 목록으로 구성한 것이다.

교재에 수록된 모든 지문은 실제 iBT 토플 Reading 시험의 주제별 출제 경향을 충실히 반영하여 구성되었다. 따라서 교재를 처음부터 끝까지 학습하면서 많이 출제되는 주제가 무엇인지, 자신이 취약한 주제가 무엇인지 파악할 수 있다. 특히 취약하다고 생각되는 주제만 골라 다시 한번 풀어보고, 해당 주제의 단어를 외워서 취약점을 보완한다.

Humanities	Anthropology	Ch 4 HP 02	Ch 5 HP 12
		Ch 6 HP 01, 09	Ch 8 HP 04
		AT 1 [1]	
	Archaeology	Ch 2 HP 07, 14, 15	Ch 3 HP 01
		Ch 6 HP 11	Ch 7 HP 05, HT [1]
		Ch 8 HT [2]	
	Architecture	Ch 4 HP 10	Ch 9 HT [2]
	Art	DT [2]	Ch 2 HP 02, 10
		Ch 3 HP 12	Ch 4 HP 07
		Ch 6 HP 12	Ch 7 HP 14
	Education	Ch 2 HP 01	
	Film	Ch 1 HP 08, 10	
	History	Ch 1 HT [1]	Ch 3 HP 11
		Ch 3 HP 14, HT [3]	Ch 4 HP 04, 06, 12
		Ch 5 HP 01	Ch 6 HP 03, HT [1], [3]
		Ch 7 HP 03, 09, 13, HT [3]	Ch 8 HP 01, 07
		Ch 9 HP 03	AT 2 [2]
	Literature	Ch 1 HT [2]	
	Music	Ch 1 HP 01	Ch 5 HT [2]
	Theater	Ch 1 HP 09	Ch 4 HP 15
		Ch 5 HP 04	Ch 6 HP 07
		Ch 8 HT [3]	

Social Science	Communication	Ch 3 HP 06	Ch 8 HP 02
	Economics	Ch 3 HP 07	Ch 7 HP 15
	Sociology	Ch 2 HP 04	Ch 3 HT [2]
		Ch 4 HT [3]	Ch 5 HP 02
		Ch 7 HP 07	Ch 9 HP 02
	Psychology	Ch 2 HP 05, HT [3]	Ch 5 HP 05, 09
		Ch 6 HP 05	Ch 7 HP 01
		Ch 9 HP 06, I IT [3]	
Natural Science	Astronomy	Ch 4 HP 03	Ch 6 HP 08
		Ch 7 HP 11	Ch 8 HP 05
		Ch 9 HP 07	AT 2 [1]
	Biology	DT [1]	Ch 1 HP 02, 05, 07, 11
		Ch 2 HP 03, 08, 13, 16, HT [2]	Ch 3 HP 02, 05, 08, HT [1]
		Ch 4 HP 11, 14, HT [1]	Ch 5 HP 03, 08, 11, 13, HT [1]
		Ch 6 HP 04	Ch 7 HP 04, 06, 10, 12, 16, HT [2]
		Ch 8 HP 03, 06	Ch 9 HP 04, HT [1]
	Chemistry	Ch 1 HP 03, HT [3]	Ch 4 HP 01
	Earth Science	Ch 1 HP 06, 12	Ch 2 HP 06, 11, HT [1]
		Ch 3 HP 03, 04, 10, 13	Ch 4 HP 05, 09, 13, HT [2]
		Ch 5 HP 06, 07, 10, HT [3]	Ch 6 HP 02, 06, 10, HT [2]
		Ch 7 HP 02	Ch 9 HP 01
		AT 1 [2]	
	Environmental Science	Ch 2 HP 09, 12	Ch 7 HP 08
	Physiology	Ch 1 HP 04	Ch 3 HP 09
		Ch 4 HP 08	Ch 8 HT [1]
		Ch 9 HP 05	

*DT: Diagnostic Test   HP: Hackers Practice   HT: Hackers Test   AT: Actual Test

iBT TOEFL Reading 고득점의 발판,
해커스 토플 리딩 인터미디엇!

01. 전략적인 학습으로 토플 리딩 정복!

최신 출제 경향 완벽 반영 및 TOPIC LIST

이 책은 iBT 토플 리딩의 **최신 출제 경향**을 철저히 분석하여 모든 지문과 문제에 **반영**하였다. 또한, 교재에 수록된 **모든 지문의 TOPIC을 목록으로 제공**하여 학습자가 특히 취약한 주제만 골라 공부하는 등 다양하게 활용할 수 있도록 하였다.

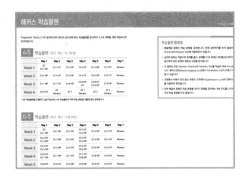

Diagnostic Test 및 4주/6주 학습플랜

실제 토플 시험의 구성 및 난이도로 제작된 Diagnostic Test를 통해 학습자가 자신의 실력을 스스로 점검할 수 있도록 하였으며, 이 결과에 따라 수준에 맞는 **학습플랜을 활용**하여 효과적으로 학습할 수 있도록 4주/6주 학습플랜을 제시하였다.

02. 체계적인 학습으로 실력 다지기!

학습자가 단계별 학습을 통해 각 챕터의 문제 유형을 확실하게 체득할 수 있도록 구성하였다.

문제 살펴보기 & 문제 공략하기

문제에 대하여 간략히 소개하고 실제 시험에서는 어떤 형태로 출제되는지 제시하였다. 또한, 각 문제 유형마다 가장 효과적인 공략법을 제공하고 적용 사례를 보여주어 실제 문제 풀이에 쉽게 활용할 수 있다.

Hackers Practice & Hackers Test

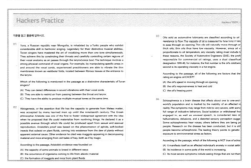

앞서 배운 문제 유형과 공략법을 실제 문제 유형과 유사한 연습 문제에 적용하여 풀어봄으로써 유형별 집중 학습이 가능하며, 실제 시험에 대한 적응력을 키울 수 있다.

Vocabulary List

각 챕터의 모든 지문으로부터 토플 필수 어휘를 선별하고 발음 기호와 뜻, 동의어를 함께 수록하여, 어휘 실력을 효율적으로 쌓을 수 있다.

Actual Test

실제 시험과 유사한 구성과 난이도로 제작된 문제를 제공하여, iBT 토플 리딩 학습을 효과적으로 마무리할 수 있다.

03. 정확한 해석과 정답단서로 실력 UP!

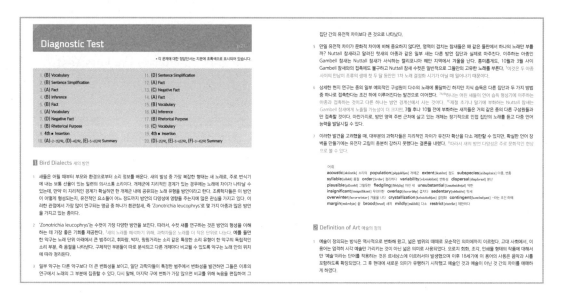

해석 및 어휘

교재에 수록된 **모든 지문의 매끄러운 해석과 중요 어휘**를 제공하여 학습자가 보다 정확하게 지문의 흐름을 이해하고 어휘 실력까지 함께 향상할 수 있도록 하였다.

정답단서

교재에 수록된 실전 형태의 문제에 대한 정답단서를 해석과 함께 제공하여 **정답과 오답의 근거를 학습자 스스로 파악**할 수 있도록 하였다. 이를 통해, 학습자들은 보다 능동적이고 효과적인 학습을 할 수 있다.

04. 해커스만의 다양한 학습자료 제공!

해커스인강(HackersIngang.com)

해커스인강 사이트에서 해커스 어학연구소에서 자체 제작한 **실전모의고사 프로그램**을 무료로 제공한다. 이 프로그램을 통해 교재에 수록된 2회분의 Actual Test를 실제 iBT TOEFL Reading 시험과 동일한 환경에서 풀어볼 수 있다. 또한, **교재에 수록된 지문과 Vocabulary List의 어휘가 녹음된 무료 MP3**를 다운로드 받아 학습 효과를 극대화할 수 있으며, 본 교재에 대한 유료 **동영상강의**를 통해, 선생님의 상세한 설명과 함께 토플 리딩 문제 유형을 체계적으로 학습할 수 있다.

고우해커스(goHackers.com)

온라인 토론과 정보 공유의 장인 **고우해커스 사이트**에서 다른 학습자들과 함께 교재 내용에 대하여 서로 의견을 교류하고 문제를 토론할 수 있으며, **다양한 무료 학습자료와 TOEFL 시험 및 유학에 대한 풍부한 정보**도 얻을 수 있다.

iBT TOEFL 소개

■ iBT TOEFL이란?

iBT(Internet-based test) TOEFL(Test of English as a Foreign Language)은 종합적인 영어 실력을 평가하는 시험으로 읽기, 듣기, 말하기, 쓰기 능력을 평가하는 유형의 문제 외에도, 듣기-말하기, 읽기-듣기-말하기, 읽기-듣기-쓰기와 같이 각 능력을 연계한 통합형 문제가 출제된다. iBT TOEFL은 Reading, Listening, Speaking, Writing 영역의 순서로 진행되며, 4개의 시험 영역 모두 노트테이킹을 허용하므로 문제를 풀 때 노트테이킹한 내용을 참고할 수 있다.

■ iBT TOEFL 구성

시험 영역	출제 지문 및 문항 수	시험 시간	점수 범위	특징
Reading	· 2개 지문 출제 지문당 길이: 약 700단어 지문당 10문항 출제	36분	0~30점	· 지문 길이가 길고, 다양한 구조의 지문이 출제됨 · 사지선다 형태, 지문 클릭(지문에 문장 삽입하기) 형태, 또는 정보를 분류하여 요약표나 정보 분류표에 넣는 형태 등이 출제됨
Listening	· 2개 대화 출제 대화당 길이: 약 3분 대화당 5문항 출제 · 3개 강의 출제 강의당 길이: 3~5분 강의당 6문항 출제	41분	0~30점	· 대화 및 강의의 길이가 길고, 실제 상황에 가까움 · 사지선다 형태, 다시 듣고 푸는 형태, 정보를 분류해 표 안에 넣거나 순서대로 배열하는 형태 등이 출제됨
Speaking	· 독립형 1문항 출제 · 통합형 3문항 출제	17분 준비: 15~30초 답변: 45~60초	0~30점	· 독립형 문제(1번) 특정 주제에 대한 의견 말하기 · 통합형 문제(2~4번) 읽고 들은 내용에 기초하여 말하기
Writing	· 통합형 1문항 출제 · 토론형 1문항 출제	35분	0~30점	· 통합형 문제 읽고 들은 내용에 기초하여 글쓰기 · 토론형 문제 토론 주제에 대한 글쓰기
		2시간 내외	총점 120점	

iBT TOEFL 접수 및 성적 확인

실시일	ETS Test Center 시험은 1년에 60회 이상 실시되며, 홈에디션 시험은 일주일에 약 4~5일 정도 실시됨
시험 장소	ETS Test Center에서 치르거나, 집에서 홈에디션 시험으로 응시 가능 (홈에디션 시험 응시 가능한 장비 및 환경 요건은 ETS 토플 웹사이트에서 확인 가능)
접수 방법	ETS 토플 웹사이트 또는 전화상으로 접수
시험 비용	(2024년 현재 기준이며, 가격 변동 있을 수 있음) · 시험 접수 비용 US $220 　　　　　· 추가 리포팅 비용 US $25 (대학당) · 시험일 변경 비용 US $60 　　　　　· 취소한 성적 복원 비용 US $20 · 추가 접수 비용 US $40 　　　　　· Speaking/Writing 재채점 비용 US $80 (영역당) 　(응시일로부터 2~7일 전에 등록할 경우)
시험 당일 주의사항	· 공인된 신분증 원본 반드시 지참하며, 자세한 신분증 규정은 ETS 토플 웹사이트에서 확인 가능 · 홈에디션 시험에 응시할 경우, 사전에 ProctorU 프로그램 설치하여 정상 작동 여부 확인 · 홈에디션 시험에 응시할 경우, 휴대폰 또는 손거울, 화이트보드 또는 투명 시트와 지워지는 마카 지참(일반 종이와 필기구, 헤드폰 및 이어폰은 사용 불가)
성적 및 리포팅	· 시험 응시 후 바로 Reading/Listening 영역 비공식 점수 확인 가능 · 시험 응시일로부터 약 4~8일 후에 온라인으로 성적 확인 가능 · 시험 접수 시, 자동으로 성적 리포팅 받을 기관 선택 가능 · MyBest Scores 제도 시행 (최근 2년간의 시험 성적 중 영역별 최고 점수 합산하여 유효 성적으로 인정)

iBT TOEFL Reading 소개 및 학습전략

iBT TOEFL Reading 영역에서는 대학 교재 수준의 학술적인 지문에 대한 학생들의 이해도를 평가한다. 다양한 분야의 지문이 등장하지만, 문제에 답하기 위해 해당 지문에 관한 특별한 전문 지식이 필요하지는 않으며 문제를 푸는 데 필요한 모든 정보는 지문에서 찾을 수 있다. 그러나 짧은 시간 내에 긴 지문을 읽고 많은 문제를 풀어야 하므로 지문을 빨리 읽고 정확하게 이해하며 정리하는 능력이 요구된다.

■ iBT TOEFL Reading 구성

· 지문 구성

시험은 총 2개의 지문으로 구성되며, 지문당 10문항이 출제된다. 지문당 길이는 약 700단어이다.

· 문제 형식

크게 사지선다, 지문 클릭(지문에 문장 삽입하기), 또는 주요 정보를 분류하여 요약표(Summary)나 정보 분류표(Category Chart)에 넣기 등 3가지 형식의 문제가 출제된다.

■ iBT TOEFL Reading 특이사항

· 노트테이킹이 허용된다.
· 지문의 제목이 주어진다.
· 전문 용어나 해당 토픽 내에서 특별한 의미를 가지고 있는 어휘의 뜻을 보여주는 Glossary 기능이 있다.
· 현재 풀고 있는 모든 문제의 답 체크 여부를 한눈에 확인할 수 있는 Review 기능이 있다.

■ iBT TOEFL Reading 문제 유형 소개

문제 유형		유형 소개	배점	지문당 문항 수
Identifying Details 지문 내용에 대한 기본적인 이해를 요하는 문제	Fact & Negative Fact	지문과 일치 또는 불일치하는 내용을 찾는 유형	1점	2~5개
	Vocabulary	주어진 표현과 가장 유사한 의미의 어휘를 찾는 유형	1점	1~2개
	Reference	지시어가 가리키는 대상을 찾는 유형	1점	0~1개
	Sentence Simplification	주어진 문장을 간략화하는 유형	1점	0~1개
Making Inference 지문 내면의 기저에 놓인 실질적인 의미를 파악하는 문제	Rhetorical Purpose	작가의 수사적 의도를 묻는 유형	1점	0~3개
	Inference	제시된 정보로 추론이 가능한 내용을 선택하는 유형	1점	0~2개
Recognizing Organization 지문 전체 또는 일부 내용을 종합해서 풀어야 하는 문제	Insertion	주어진 문장을 적절한 위치에 삽입하는 유형	1점	1개
	Summary	지문 요약을 완성시키는 유형	2점 (부분 점수 있음)	0~1개
	Category Chart	정보를 각 범주에 맞게 분류하는 유형	3~4점 (부분 점수 있음)	0~1개

■ iBT TOEFL Reading 학습전략

1. 토플에 자주 출제되는 토픽에 관한 배경지식을 쌓는다.
배경지식을 많이 알고 있을수록 글의 내용을 이해하는 것이 수월하므로 시험에 자주 출제되는 토픽과 관련된 내용을 많이 알아 두는 것이 좋다. 교재에 수록된 지문들과 함께, 평소에 다양한 분야의 학술·시사적인 영어 지문들을 많이 읽어 두도록 한다.

2. 어휘력을 기른다.
어휘력이 풍부하면 글을 읽는 데 막힘이 없으므로, 평소에 교재에 수록된 어휘를 비롯해 다양한 어휘를 외워 두도록 한다. 어휘 암기 외에도 글에 사용된 어휘 중 익숙하지 않은 것은 주위 문맥을 이용하여 그 뜻을 추측해 보는 연습을 병행하는 것이 좋다.

3. 글의 구조를 파악하며 지문을 읽는다.
각 단락의 주요 내용만 빠르게 훑는 skimming으로 큰 주제를 신속하게 파악하고, scanning을 통해 지문의 keyword를 찾는 연습을 하는 것은 독해에 있어 매우 중요하다. 또한, 문장 및 문단 간의 관계를 확인하는 구조 파악 훈련은 글 전체의 흐름을 이해하는 데 많은 도움이 된다.

4. Paraphrase 연습을 한다.
시험에 출제되는 거의 모든 문제와 답은 paraphrase되어 있으므로 한 단어부터 시작해 한 문장, 한 단락 전체를 paraphrase하는 연습을 해보는 것이 좋다. 교재에 수록된 지문들을 활용하여 paraphrase해보되, 단순히 어휘만 동의어로 바꾸어 쓰는 것이 아니라 문장 구조까지 바꾸어서 표현해 보도록 한다.

5. 요약 연습을 한다.
글을 읽고 글 전체의 내용을 이해한 후 요약(summary)하는 연습을 해보도록 한다. 교재에 수록된 지문들을 활용하여 중심 정보만을 추려내어 글의 주제를 정리해 본다. 이때, 글에 사용된 표현을 그대로 쓰지 말고 paraphrase하여 자신의 표현으로 정리해 보는 것이 좋다.

iBT TOEFL Reading 화면 구성

1. Reading Direction 화면

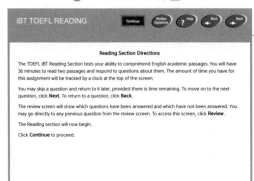

리딩 영역 시험 진행 방식에 대한 전반적인 디렉션이 주어지고, **Tool Bar** 이용에 관한 간단한 설명이 이어진다.

■ 시험 도중에 **Help 버튼**을 누르면 시험 진행 과정과 관련된 정보를 볼 수 있다. 이때 시험 시간은 계속해서 카운트된다.

2. 지문과 문제 화면

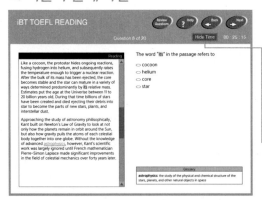

처음에는 지문만 화면에 등장하며, 스크롤을 내려 지문 전체를 한 번 읽은 후 **Next 버튼**을 눌러야 문제로 넘어갈 수 있다. 문제 간에 이동하려면 **Next 버튼**과 **Back 버튼**을 사용한다. 또한, 지문에 파란색으로 밑줄이 그어져 있는 단어를 클릭하면 우측 하단에 **Glossary**로 해당 단어의 의미가 나타난다.

■ **Hide Time 버튼**을 누르면 시간 카운트가 창에서 사라지고 **Show Time 버튼**이 나타나며, **Show Time 버튼**을 누르면 시간 카운트가 Hide Time 버튼과 함께 창에 다시 나타난다.

3. Summary 문제 화면

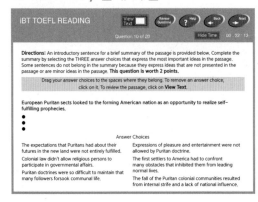

Summary 문제가 나오면 지문이 사라지고 문제만 화면에 나온다. 상단의 **View Text 버튼**을 누르면 지문이 나오고, **View Question 버튼**을 누르면 문제로 돌아간다. 답을 선택할 때는 Answer Choices 아래에 있는 보기를 정답 자리에 끌어오고, 답을 바꿀 때는 선택한 보기를 한 번 더 클릭하면 정답 자리에서 사라진다.

4. Category Chart 문제 화면

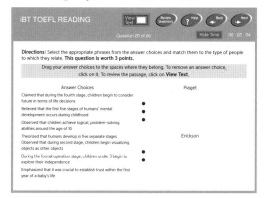

Category Chart 문제가 나올 때 역시 화면에서 지문이 사라지고, 문제가 화면 전체에 나타난다. Summary 문제와 동일하게, 지문을 보기 위해서는 View Text 버튼을, 문제를 보기 위해서는 View Question 버튼을 클릭해야 하며, 답을 선택할 때는 Answer Choices 아래에 있는 보기를 정답 자리에 끌어오면 된다.

5. Review 화면

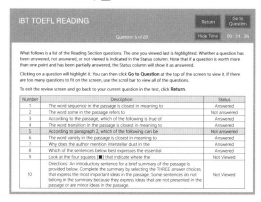

문제 화면에서 Review Questions 버튼을 누르면 현재 풀고 있는 문제 목록이 나타나며 문제별로 답을 체크했는지 여부가 다음과 같은 3가지 형태로 나타난다.

· 문제의 답을 클릭하고 넘어갔을 경우 – Answered
· 문제의 답을 클릭하지 않고 넘어갔을 경우 – Not Answered
· 문제를 아직 보지 않았을 경우 – Not Viewed

목록에 있는 각 문제를 클릭한 상태에서 Go To Question 버튼을 누르면 해당 문제로 바로 이동하며, Return 버튼을 누르면 직전의 화면으로 이동한다.

6. 시험이 끝났을 때 나오는 화면

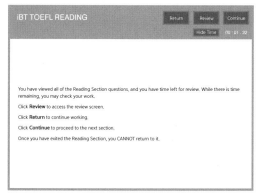

시험이 끝나고 나오는 디렉션 화면에서 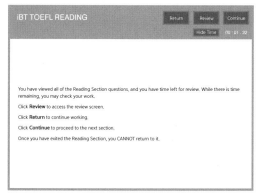 Continue 버튼을 누르면 다음 영역으로 넘어가고, 리딩 영역으로 **다시 되돌아갈 수 없다.** 따라서 다음 영역으로 넘어가기 전에 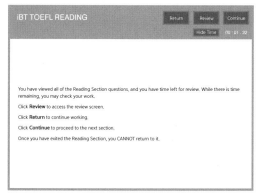 Review 버튼을 활용하여 리딩 영역의 모든 문제에 답했는지를 반드시 확인해야 한다.

해커스 학습플랜

Diagnostic Test(p.21)의 결과에 따라 본인의 점수대에 맞는 학습플랜을 참고하여 스스로 계획을 세워 학습하시면 효과적입니다.

4주 학습플랜 (맞은 개수: 14~20개)

	Day 1	Day 2	Day 3	Day 4	Day 5	Day 6	Day 7
Week 1	DT Ch 1 HP	Ch 1 HT	Ch 2 HP	Ch 2 HT	Ch 3 HP	Ch 3 HT	Review
Week 2	Ch 4 HP	Ch 4 HT	Ch 5 HP	Ch 5 HT	Ch 6 HP	Ch 6 HT	Review
Week 3	Ch 7 HP	Ch 7 HT	Ch 8 HP	Ch 8 HP HT	Ch 8 HT Ch 9 HP	Ch 9 HP	Review
Week 4	Ch 9 HT	DT Review	AT 1	AT 1 Review	AT 2	AT 2 Review	Review

* 8주 학습플랜을 진행하고 싶은 학습자는 4주 학습플랜의 하루 학습 분량을 이틀에 걸쳐 공부합니다.

6주 학습플랜 (맞은 개수: 13개 이하)

	Day 1	Day 2	Day 3	Day 4	Day 5	Day 6	Day 7
Week 1	DT Ch 1 HP	Ch 1 HP	Ch 1 HT	Ch 1 HT Ch 2 HP	Ch 2 HP	Ch 2 HT	Review
Week 2	Ch 2 HT Ch 3 HP	Ch 3 HP	Ch 3 HT	Ch 3 HT Ch 4 HP	Ch 4 HP	Ch 4 HT	Review
Week 3	Ch 4 HT Ch 5 HP	Ch 5 HP	Ch 5 HT	Ch 5 HT Ch 6 HP	Ch 6 HP	Ch 6 HT	Review
Week 4	Ch 6 HT Ch 7 HP	Ch 7 HP	Ch 7 HT	Ch 7 HT Ch 8 HP	Ch 8 HP	Ch 8 HT	Review
Week 5	Ch 8 HT	Ch 8 HT	Ch 9 HP	Ch 9 HP	Ch 9 HT	Ch 9 HT	Review
Week 6	Ch 9 HT	DT Review	AT 1	AT 1 Review	AT 2	AT 2 Review	Review

* **DT**: Diagnostic Test　　**HP**: Hackers Practice　　**HT**: Hackers Test　　**AT**: Actual Test

학습플랜 활용법

1. 매일매일 정해진 학습 분량을 공부합니다. 문제 공략하기를 먼저 꼼꼼히 학습한 후 이를 Hackers Practice와 Hackers Test에 적용하면서 익힙니다.

2. 실전에 임하는 마음으로 문제를 풀고, 문제를 다 푼 후에는 해석을 참고하여 지문을 정독하고 정답단서를 참고하여 모든 문제의 정답과 오답을 분석합니다.

3. 각 챕터의 모든 Hackers Practice와 Hackers Test를 학습한 후에 Vocabulary List를 통해 마무리합니다. 해커스인강(HackersIngang.com)에서 Vocabulary List의 어휘가 녹음된 무료 MP3를 다운로드할 수 있습니다.

4. 교재에서 이해가 되지 않는 부분은 고우해커스(goHackers.com)의 [해커스 Books > 토플 리딩 Q&A]를 이용하여 확인합니다.

5. 만약 매일의 정해진 학습 분량을 마치지 못했을 경우에는 계속 진도를 나가되 일주일이 지나기 전에 해당 주의 학습 분량을 모두 끝냅니다.

Hackers TOEFL

Reading

Intermediate

Diagnostic Test

Diagnostic Test

1 Bird Dialects

Biology

1 Birds learn acoustic information from their parents and environment from an early age. The most complex form of avian vocalization is the birdsong, an often melodic series of communicative sounds produced primarily during breeding. In cases where populations have geographical boundaries, differences in song may appear, and if these geographical limits are distinct, the shared song types within a population are referred to as dialects. Ornithologists are keenly interested in how these dialects form and to what extent genetic factors contribute to dialectical variation. One of the best-studied songbirds in this regard is the white-crowned sparrow, *Zonotrichia leucophrys*, a species with several subspecies and many dialects.

2 ➡ In *Zonotrichia leucophrys*, males demonstrate the greatest dialectical diversity. Therefore, studying male birds offers the best opportunity for understanding dialect formation. In order to make sense of birdsongs, scientists break them into smaller units. A phrase, for example, is a large category below the level of song, and specific sound types like whistles, pulses, and buzzes reflect the individual speech parts, or syllables, of a phrase. The phrases are ordered according to their position in the song so that specific parts can be analyzed separately and compared across different individuals.

3 Some phrases show more variability than others, and once scientists detect variability in a specific category, they can focus on that section of the songs in future studies. ■ In other words, if the terminal phrase shows the greatest inconsistency, recordings can be edited to single it out for comparisons. ■ Most white-crowned sparrow songs begin similarly with one or two whistles; consequently, the initial sequence is generally the most consistent component across subgroups. ■ In addition, a convenient feature of male white-crowned sparrows is that individual adults generally sing a single song, making analysis across groups a relatively simple task in comparison to other bird species that routinely learn multiple songs, such as song sparrows (*Melospiza melodia*). ■

4 ➡ Variations present among groups led some scientists to wonder whether there might be a genetic basis for dialectical uniqueness. Perhaps through the evolutionary isolation of some populations (for example, female preference for males of their own dialect), dispersal of the gene pool has been slowed to the point that differences in song reflect expressions of varying genetic compositions. Though a genetic explanation seems plausible, laboratory experiments have found that white-crowned sparrow chicks of particular dialect groups can learn the songs of other groups in their own subspecies in addition to dialects of other subspecies. Using recordings of adults, scientists have been able to train fledglings to reproduce multiple dialects, although the maximum number is approximately seven. In addition, comparisons of genetic material taken from blood sample DNA have revealed unsubstantial differences. In some instances,

genetic variation among individuals of a dialect group was found to be greater than genetic variation among larger groups, such as subspecies.

5 ➡ If genetic differences are insignificant in comparison to cultural influences, why do sparrows with overlapping territories sing only one song in the field? Some, such as those of the sedentary subspecies known as Nuttall's sparrow, do encounter other dialect groups. Gambell's sparrow, a migratory subspecies, overwinters in the coastal California area that Nuttall's sparrow inhabits. Interestingly, despite contacts between October and March with Gambell's sparrow, male Nuttall's sparrows typically sing their own distinct songs. This is because the encounters between the two subspecies occur outside the primary song crystallization period, which occurs during the first two months of a bird's life.

6 ➡ Detailed field research led to the discovery that some exceptional members of the species do master multiple songs, but their knowledge acquisition is contingent on contact with other groups in one of two ways. Either young birds come in contact with migratory subspecies during the formative period of language learning or they live on the margins of dialect borders. Nuttall's sparrows hatching early or late in the season are more likely to be exposed to Gambell's sparrows, but broods hatching after March or before October will mostly only interact with other members of their own kind. In like fashion, individuals living near the peripheries of their dialectic range may regularly hear the songs of an adjacent group and develop multilingual abilities.

7 ➡ In light of these findings, most scientists have concluded that geographic differences may mildly restrict gene flow, but that genetic isolation has not been strong enough to create a rigid linguistic barrier. Dialectical variety in birds can thus be viewed as primarily a cultural phenomenon.

1 The word "primarily" in the passage is closest in meaning to

(A) abundantly

(B) mainly

(C) loudly

(D) commonly

2 Which of the sentences below best expresses the essential information in the highlighted sentence in the passage? *Incorrect* choices change the meaning in important ways or leave out essential information.

(A) Dialects are those song types within a population that are shared by the group.

(B) Shared song types within a population with clear geographical boundaries are called dialects.

(C) Geographical boundaries may result in differences in song between distinct populations.

(D) Populations having clear dialects result from the shared song types within the group.

3 According to paragraph 2, scientists attempt to understand birdsongs by

(A) dividing them into smaller categories

(B) analyzing them as a single unit

(C) listening to phrases in reverse order

(D) labeling them as male or female

Paragraph 2 is marked with an arrow [➡].

4 What can be inferred from paragraph 4 about white-crowned sparrow chicks?

(A) The simplest dialects are the ones they learn first.

(B) The number of songs they can be trained to learn is limited.

(C) They learn songs of their own subspecies faster than those of other subspecies.

(D) They learn more easily from laboratory recordings than in the wild.

Paragraph 4 is marked with an arrow [➡].

5 According to paragraph 5, which of the following is true of Nuttall's sparrows?

(A) They migrate to the same overwintering locations that Gambell's sparrows do.

(B) They do not often encounter Gambell's sparrows during the initial period of song formation.

(C) They only have contact with Gambell's sparrows during the breeding season.

(D) They do not have the same inherent vocalization abilities that Gambell's sparrows do.

Paragraph 5 is marked with an arrow [➡].

6 The word "exceptional" in the passage is closest in meaning to

(A) extraordinary

(B) perceptual

(C) intelligent

(D) capable

7 According to paragraph 6, which of the following does NOT contribute to multilingualism in Nuttall's sparrows?

(A) Living on the edges of dialectical boundaries

(B) Interacting with other subspecies

(C) Hatching early or late in the season

(D) Mating between March and October

Paragraph 6 is marked with an arrow [➡].

8 Why does the author include paragraph 7 in the passage?

(A) To argue that genetic factors have nothing to do with linguistic ability in birds

(B) To offer a concluding argument for why birds have a variety of dialects

(C) To introduce a new issue that has emerged in research on bird dialects

(D) To suggest that language acquisition in birds is still poorly understood

Paragraph 7 is marked with an arrow [➡].

9 Look at the four squares [■] that indicate where the following sentence could be added to the passage.

Single adult males of this species have been recorded singing eleven different songs.

Where would the sentence best fit?

Click on a square [■] to add the sentence to the passage.

10 Directions: An introductory sentence for a brief summary of the passage is provided below. Complete the summary by selecting the THREE answer choices that express the most important ideas in the passage. Some sentences do not belong in the summary because they express ideas that are not presented in the passage or are minor ideas in the passage. **This question is worth 2 points.**

> Drag your answer choices to the spaces where they belong.
> To remove an answer choice, click on it. To review the passage, click on **View Text**.

In some bird populations, there are regional dialects in the birds' songs.

- ●
- ●
- ●

Answer Choices

(A) White-crowned sparrows are useful subjects for studying bird dialects because they usually only learn a single song and have many dialects.

(B) Using recordings in a laboratory setting, scientists have demonstrated that white-crowned sparrow chicks are capable of learning multiple dialects.

(C) Research conducted on Nuttall's sparrows and Gambell's sparrows suggests that the two subspecies have developed different dialects because one is sedentary while the other is migratory.

(D) Scientists thought that genetic factors may have contributed to dialectical diversity, but research has shown that genetic factors are limited.

(E) Field studies of two *Zonotrichia leucophrys* subspecies revealed that multilingualism is dependent upon the timing and nature of interactions between dialectical group members.

(F) One thing that is clear about the various subspecies of *Zonotrichia leucophrys* is that they all seem to begin learning songs for the first time after two months of age.

2 Definition of Art

1   How art is defined has varied throughout history, leading to a wide range of sometimes-contradictory meanings. In the ancient world, the term was used in a broad sense that was not strictly related to visual arts. The application of the word "art" exclusively to works in the form of paintings, sculptures, and prints came about only in the Renaissance, and later, in the eighteenth century, the use of the term expanded to include music and poetry. Subsequently, in modern times, a new meaning came into fashion, obscuring the distinction between what is art and what is not.

2   ➡ In the ancient world, there was no clear difference between art and crafts. In Greek and Latin, the terms *techne* and *ars* both translated as "art," and they stood for any activity that had rules and required expertise. They were thus used in reference to a wide range of fields, from medicine and law to blacksmithing. Those engaged in the production of art were viewed as craftsmen, more similar to manual laborers than artists. To the ancients, art was a pursuit necessitating skills that were learned according to rules, but that were believed to require no unique inspiration. Painting and sculpture had no special place in higher learning, as only music and poetry were taught as academic subjects. The visual arts were viewed simply as manual crafts, and because the ancients looked down on manual labor, artisans occupied the bottom of the social hierarchy.

3   ➡ The medieval world inherited this view of art, but things began to change during the Renaissance. At the forefront of this transformation was the elevated position of painters, sculptors, and architects. Renaissance artists increasingly employed scientific methods, and mathematics became central to their trade. Because their work was not simply mechanical but also intellectual, artists argued that they were superior to mere craftsmen, and their call for respect began to sway public opinion. Artists gradually gained acceptance as creative geniuses, and their reputation rose to be on par with that of poets. Painting, sculpture, and architecture were given their own place in academies, and art became synonymous with the label "classical art." During the 1700s, the definition was slightly expanded as the concept of fine art emerged. Collectively, the classical arts, along with music and poetry, came to represent the fine arts.

4   ➡ It was also in the Renaissance that the term "artisan" first appeared. ■ The word was used to clearly distinguish between arts and crafts. ■ Art required academic training, and its goal was to create perfect and idealized representations of reality that followed established principles of beauty. ■ This is in contrast to crafts, like beadwork or basket making, which were fashioned largely for everyday purposes. ■ Craftsmen whose production consisted of such practical, or merely decorative, items were called artisans. They often learned their trade from master craftsmen, but they did not study art in the academies. The clear division between arts and crafts saw its peak in the eighteenth century.

5   ➡ In the nineteenth century, modernists sought to promote the idea of "art for art's sake" and rejected classical definitions. Artists felt hindered by the conventions of classicism and began to ignore form in favor of stylistic expression. At the same time, they

rejected the convictions of some of their contemporaries, who claimed that art should be fundamentally utilitarian and beneficial to society. Modernists denied that purpose, whether moral or political, was an important criterion for art to have merit. Accordingly, they believed all art had an intrinsic value of its own. In addition, artists experimented with new techniques and subject matter. They began to include more impressionistic and abstract designs, emphasizing experimental over learned techniques.

6 ➡ This new perception of art as an end in itself eventually erased the fragmentation between artist and artisan. In a clear mockery of the classical tradition, the notion of art was extended to include anything a person creates. Therefore, it effectively eliminated the distinction between crafts and the so-called fine arts. A person who produced a basket and a person who painted a canvas in classical style were no different; they were both using their skills to create something. This meant that any creative work could be viewed as genuine and prestigious. Further, art moved beyond the realm of productive creativity. Some artists randomly collected everyday objects and displayed them, completely unmodified, as "creative sculpture."

7 Conceptions of art have changed remarkably and created much confusion. Today there is no consensus on the meaning of the term, and it is applied very subjectively. Evidence can be seen in art museums and galleries devoted to everything from primitive artifacts to video productions to commercial graphics. Certainly, the question of what constitutes art has become largely subjective.

11 Which of the sentences below best expresses the essential information in the highlighted sentence in the passage? *Incorrect* choices change the meaning in important ways or leave out essential information.

(A) Only in the Renaissance did the word "art" begin to refer exclusively to works such as paintings, sculptures, and prints.

(B) The use of the word "art" to refer to visual art declined following the Renaissance, after which the term referred exclusively to music and poetry.

(C) Music and poetry were not included in the definition of the word "art" until the eighteenth century, but the term itself had existed since the Renaissance.

(D) The word "art" was not applied exclusively to visual art until the Renaissance, and use of the term later grew to accommodate music and poetry.

12 Which of the following is consistent with the ancient view of art as described in paragraph 2?

(A) Visual art was not an undertaking worthy of esteem.

(B) Art was an activity that required special inspiration.

(C) Visual art occupied a special place in higher learning.

(D) Art applied to any pursuit involving formal education.

Paragraph 2 is marked with an arrow [➡].

13 Which of the following is NOT listed as an example of fine art in paragraph 3?

(A) Sculpture

(B) Architecture

(C) Mathematics

(D) Music

Paragraph 3 is marked with an arrow [➡].

14 Which of the following is a distinguishing feature of crafts according to paragraph 4?

(A) They were made for decoration.

(B) They were produced in large quantities.

(C) They were produced by artisans in the academies.

(D) They were made to closely follow aesthetic principles.

Paragraph 4 is marked with an arrow [➡].

15 The word "convictions" in the passage is closest in meaning to

(A) intense oppositions

(B) strong beliefs

(C) wrong assumptions

(D) feeble suggestions

16 What can be inferred from paragraph 5 about artists in the nineteenth century?

(A) Some of them thought that the primary value of art was in its social purpose.

(B) Most of them approached art as an academic discipline that required learning.

(C) They placed a greater emphasis on aesthetics than did classical artists.

(D) They viewed moral and political art as having no intrinsic value.

Paragraph 5 is marked with an arrow [➡].

17 What is the purpose of paragraph 6 in the passage?

(A) To introduce the reasons for the changes outlined in the preceding paragraphs

(B) To describe the resulting outcome of the ideas described in the previous paragraph

(C) To offer supporting evidence for the ideas introduced in the previous paragraph

(D) To provide a transition between the preceding paragraphs and the final paragraph

Paragraph 6 is marked with an arrow [➡].

18 The word "prestigious" in the passage is closest in meaning to

(A) obscure

(B) ubiquitous

(C) reputable

(D) credulous

19 Look at the four squares [■] that indicate where the following sentence could be added to the passage.

Other examples of crafts included studio pottery and metalworking.

Where would the sentence best fit?

Click on a square [■] to add the sentence to the passage.

20 **Directions**: An introductory sentence for a brief summary of the passage is provided below. Complete the summary by selecting the THREE answer choices that express the most important ideas in the passage. Some sentences do not belong in the summary because they express ideas that are not presented in the passage or are minor ideas in the passage. **This question is worth 2 points.**

Drag your answer choices to the spaces where they belong.
To remove an answer choice, click on it. To review the passage, click on **View Text**.

The term "art" has changed so much that its meaning has become rather subjective.

- ●
- ●
- ●

Answer Choices

(A) In the Latin and Greek worlds, art was looked down upon as a form of manual labor.

(B) Artists of the modern period began to experiment by combining classical and abstract techniques in their art.

(C) After the medieval period, the number of artists attending academies rose due to increased prestige in the arts.

(D) The ancients applied the term in a broad manner to any rule-based activity that required skill.

(E) Modernists, hoping to revolutionize the way art was conceived, completely redefined the term.

(F) As artists began to gain status, the distinction between arts and crafts became more apparent.

정답·해석·정답단서 p.270

* 채점 후 p.18을 보고 본인의 맞은 개수에 해당하는 학습플랜을 참고하세요.
* 진단고사 무료 해설 강의가 해커스 동영상강의 포털 해커스인강(HackersIngang.com)에서 제공됩니다.

CHAPTER 01

Fact & Negative Fact

Fact & Negative Fact

Fact & Negative Fact 문제는 지문의 내용을 묻는 질문에 대해 가장 정확하게 답을 한 보기를 선택하는 유형이다. 지문에서 설명된 세부 정보와 질문의 내용이 일치하는지 또는 일치하지 않는지를 묻는다. Fact & Negative Fact 문제는 한 지문당 2~5개가 출제되는데, Fact 문제의 출제 비중이 더 높다.

Fact 문제의 경우 지문의 내용과 일치하는 보기를, Negative Fact 문제의 경우 지문의 내용과 일치하지 않는 보기를 답으로 선택해야 한다. 따라서 Fact & Negative Fact 문제를 풀기 위해서는 지문에서 문제 해결에 필요한 정보를 바르게 찾아내고 그 정보가 보기에 적절하게 바뀌어 쓰여 있는지 확인하는 연습을 해야 한다.

▌ 문제 살펴보기

Fact & Negative Fact 문제는 보통 특정 단락을 지정해 주며, 해당 단락은 화면에 화살표로 표시된다. 특정 단락을 지정하지 않는 경우 전체 지문의 내용을 종합적으로 판단해서 세부 정보의 사실 여부를 판단해야 한다. 4개의 단어, 구 또는 문장이 보기로 주어지며, 지문의 내용이 그대로 나오거나 같은 의미의 다른 단어나 구로 바뀌어 (paraphrase) 나오기도 한다. 전형적인 질문 형태는 아래와 같다.

Fact

- According to paragraph #, which of the following is true of _____?
  단락 #에 의하면, 다음 중 _____에 관해 사실인 것은?
- According to paragraph #, what/how/why _____?
  단락 #에 의하면, 무엇이/어떻게/왜 _____ 했는가?
- According to the passage, which of the following is true of _____?
  지문에 의하면, 다음 중 _____에 관해 사실인 것은?

Negative Fact

- According to paragraph #, all of the following are mentioned EXCEPT . . .
  단락 #에 의하면, 다음은 …만 제외하고 모두 언급되었다.
- According to paragraph #, which of the following is NOT true of _____?
  단락 #에 의하면, 다음 중 _____에 관해 사실이 아닌 것은?

문제 공략하기

다음은 Fact & Negative Fact 문제의 공략법이다. 실전 고득점을 위해 이를 꼼꼼히 학습하고 Hackers Practice 와 Hackers Test를 풀면서 반드시 적용해 본다.

1 지문에서 질문의 키워드 찾기

질문의 핵심 내용인 키워드를 확인한 후 지문에서 키워드가 언급된 부분을 찾는다. 이때 키워드는 지문의 단어나 구가 그대로 나오거나 같은 의미의 다른 단어나 구로 바뀌어(paraphrase) 나온다.

2 찾은 정보를 제대로 바꾸어 쓴 보기 찾기

키워드 주변에서 찾은 내용과 보기를 비교하여, 지문 내용을 제대로 바꾸어 쓴 (paraphrase) 보기를 찾는다. 원문의 의미는 그대로 살리되 문장 구조를 바꾸거나 비슷한 단어나 구를 사용한 보기가 정답이다.

Amphibians are of great importance throughout the world. These relatively small animals are crucial members of the food chain, and their survival is vital to the overall health of ecosystems. Their large appetites help keep insect populations in check, and they serve as prey for a number of larger predators. Consequently, the loss of amphibians like frogs and salamanders is perceived as a critical threat to global biodiversity. In addition, their ability to regenerate limbs is of great interest in the study of cell function and genetics.

Which of the following is an example of the importance of amphibians?

(A) Their presence in most of the world's ecosystems
(B) Their role as specimens for scientific research
(C) Their place at the top of the food chain
(D) Their capacity to survive in difficult environments

지문해석 p.273

1 질문의 키워드인 the importance of amphibians(양서류의 중요성)를 지문에서 찾아보면 같은 의미의 Amphibians are of great importance(양서류는 아주 중요하다)가 언급되어 있다.

2 키워드 주변 내용을 살펴보면 In addition, their ability to regenerate limbs is of great interest in the study of cell function and genetics(게다가, 그들의 팔다리를 재생산하는 능력은 세포 기능과 유전학 연구에 큰 흥미를 불러 일으킨다)라고 언급되어 있다. 보기 (B) '과학 연구를 위한 표본으로서의 역할'은 지문 내용을 알맞게 바꾸어 썼으므로 정답이다.

TIP Fact 문제의 경우 지문의 내용과 일치하지 않거나 지문에서 언급되지 않은 내용의 보기가 오답이다.

CHAPTER 1
CH 2
CH 3
CH 4
CH 5
CH 6
CH 7
CH 8
CH 9
Hackers TOEFL Reading Intermediate

Hackers Practice

지문을 읽고 물음에 답하시오.

01

Tuva, a Russian republic near Mongolia, is inhabited by a Turkic people who exhibit considerable skill in harmonic singing. Legendary for their distinctive musical abilities, Tuvan singers have mastered the art of vocalizing more than one tone simultaneously. They achieve this by constricting their throats and carefully controlling certain regions of their vocal anatomy as air passes through the larynx(voice box). The technique involves a strong physical command of vocal organs. For example, by manipulating specific areas in and around the vocal cords, experienced practitioners are able to vibrate the thin membranes known as vestibular folds, located between fibrous tissues at the entrance to the larynx.

Which of the following is mentioned in the passage as a distinctive characteristic of Tuvan singers?

(A) They can detect differences in sound vibrations with their vocal cords.

(B) They are able to restrict air from passing between the throat and larynx.

(C) They have the ability to produce multiple musical tones at the same time.

02

Abiogenesis, or the assertion that life has the capacity to generate from lifeless matter, was accepted by many learned men up until the nineteenth century. The Greek philosopher Aristotle was one of the first to foster widespread agreement with the idea when he proposed that life could materialize from nonliving things. He declared it as a possible avenue through which life could be produced apart from sexual and asexual reproduction. Aristotle's proof was based on the phenomenon of aphids, soft-bodied insects that subsist on plant fluids, coming into existence from the dew of plants without apparent external cause. Other evidence he cited was maggots appearing in decomposing material and mice emerging from old bales of hay, both as if by magic.

According to the passage, Aristotle's evidence was founded on

(A) the capacity of some animals to breed in different ways

(B) the occurrence of organisms coming to life from abiotic material

(C) the formation of maggots and mice from plant fluids

---

01 inhabit[inhǽbit] 살다 distinctive[distíŋktiv] 특유의 vocalize[vóukəlàiz] 노래하다 constrict[kənstríkt] 수축시키다
anatomy[ənǽtəmi] 조직 larynx[lǽriŋks] 후두 manipulate[mənípjulèit] 조작하다 vocal cords 성대
vibrate[váibreit] 진동하다 membrane[mémbrein] 막 vestibular fold 가성대

02 abiogenesis[èibaioudʒénəsis] 자연 발생론 assertion[əsə́ːrʃən] 주장 foster[fɔ́ːstər] 조성하다
materialize[mətíəriəlàiz] 나타나다 avenue[ǽvənjùː] 방법 aphid[éifid] 진디 subsist[səbsíst] 생활하다 dew[djúː] 이슬
cite[sait] 언급하다 maggot[mǽgət] 구더기 decompose[dìːkəmpóuz] 부패하다 bale[beil] 더미 abiotic[èibaiátik] 비생물적인

03

Oils sold as automotive lubricants are classified according to oil viscosity, or an oil's resistance to flow. The viscosity of oil is measured by how long it takes a set volume of oil to pass through an opening. Thin oils will naturally move through an opening faster than thick oils; thin oils thus have low viscosity. However, since oil viscosity is inversely proportionate to oil temperature, any viscosity rating must include temperature data. For these reasons, the Society of Automotive Engineers (SAE), the professional organization responsible for commercial oil ratings, uses a dual classification system. In the designation 10W-40, for instance, the first number is the oil's cold(winter) viscosity and the second is its operating viscosity in a hot engine.

According to the passage, all of the following are factors that the SAE considers when rating an engine oil EXCEPT

(A) the oil's speed in moving through an opening

(B) the oil's responsiveness to heat and cold

(C) the oil's freezing point

04

Schizophrenia is a brain disease that affects about one to one-and-a-half percent of the world's population and is marked by the inability of an affected individual to perceive reality. The symptoms may range from mild to very severe, with some cases exhibiting the full range of indicative behaviors. Social isolation or withdrawal from activities normally engaged in, as well as unusual speech, is considered less obvious signs, while hallucinations, delusions, and a distorted sensory perception suggest an acute disorder. Some schizophrenics hear voices; others believe they are being persecuted by unseen people. Research on the disease has been conducted, but it is still unclear why some people become schizophrenic. The leading theory points to genetic inclination and early exposure to environmental stress as factors.

According to the passage, which of the following is NOT true of schizophrenia?

(A) It manifests itself as an affected individual's anxiety in social settings.

(B) Its incidence in some parts of the world is increasing.

(C) Its most severe symptoms include seeing things that are not there.

---

03 lubricant[lúːbrikənt] 윤활유 viscosity[viskásəti] 점도 inversely[invə́ːrsli] 반대로 proportionate[prəpɔ́ːrʃənət] 비례하는
   commercial[kəmə́ːrʃəl] 상업용의 designation[dèzignéiʃən] 표시 operate[ápərèit] 운전하다

04 schizophrenia[skìtsəfríːniə] 정신 분열증 mark[mɑːrk] 특징짓다 perceive[pərsíːv] 인식하다
   indicative[indíkətiv] 암시하는 hallucination[həlùːsənéiʃən] 환각 delusion[dilúːʒən] 망상
   distorted[distɔ́ːrtid] 왜곡된 acute[əkjúːt] 심각한 schizophrenic[skìtsəfrénik] 정신 분열증 환자
   persecute[pə́ːrsikjùːt] 학대하다 inclination[ìnklənéiʃən] 경향

05

Microbial bacteria sometimes face conditions unsuitable for optimal growth. If temperatures are too extreme or if nutrient, oxygen, and moisture levels are inadequate, these microorganisms adjust by developing hardened cell walls and entering a stage known as *microbial cyst*. The hardening process interrupts the metabolic activities of microbial cells, sending them into a period of dormancy, only to become active again when conditions appropriate for growth are restored. While at rest, the microbe neither feeds nor moves, reducing its nutrient intake requirements. Meanwhile, the hard coating protects the resting organism from inhospitable circumstances. Destruction of the coating is initiated by the return of favorable conditions, such as an end to a prolonged period of desiccation. As long as a microorganism remains dormant, it is protected; once it enters an active phase, however, it immediately becomes vulnerable. This explains why antibiotic medicines are only effective when pathogenic bacteria are active.

According to the passage, the destruction of the hard protective coating is initiated by

(A) the increased energy provided by nutrient intake

(B) the end of adverse environmental conditions

(C) the return of conditions unsuitable for active growth

(D) the interruption of metabolic activities

06

Gravity is the force of attraction between two objects that possess mass. Although it is a weak force, it exerts influence on all of the matter in space. Its extensiveness makes it the most dominant force in the universe. The strength of the gravitational force on two objects is dependent on the distance between the objects and their respective masses. The farther away two bodies are from each other, the weaker the force exerted upon them. In addition, the larger the mass of the object, the greater the gravitational force it exercises. Mass, which is the amount of matter in an object, stays the same no matter where the object is located. However, because the weight of an object is the measure of the force of gravity acting upon it, that object will weigh differently depending on its location. For example, an individual's weight is greater on Earth than on the Moon because Earth has a larger mass and exerts a stronger gravitational force than the Moon.

Select the TWO answer choices in the passage that describe the effects gravitational force has on objects that possess mass. **To receive credit, you must select TWO answers**.

(A) The force is more dominant when the distance between two objects is considerable.

(B) The attraction between the two bodies is stronger when their masses are larger.

(C) The heaviness of an object is dependent on the amount of gravity operating on it.

(D) The mass of an object increases as the gravitational force acting on it increases.

---

05 **microbial bacteria** 세균성 미생물　**optimal**[ɑ́ptəməl] 최적의　**inadequate**[inǽdikwət] 불충분한　**intake**[íntèik] 섭취　**inhospitable**[inhɑ́spitəbl] 황폐한　**desiccation**[dèsikéiʃən] 건조　**vulnerable**[vʌ́lnərəbl] 취약한　**antibiotic**[æ̀ntibaiɑ́tik] 항생의　**pathogenic**[pæ̀θədʒénik] 병원성의

06 **force**[fɔːrs] 힘　**mass**[mæs] 질량　**exert**[igzə́ːrt] 행사하다　**dependent**[dipéndənt] ~에 좌우되는　**respective**[rispéktiv] 각각의　**exercise**[éksərsàiz] 발휘하다

07

The biological concept of fitness in the context of natural selection is not merely an ability to compete for resources. It is an individual's ability to contribute its genetic makeup, or genotype, to the next generation relative to other members of its species. Therefore, fitness is closely connected with reproductive success. Certainly, an individual's ability to survive affects its chances of producing offspring. An individual that matures quickly and lives long has more opportunities to pass on its genetic information than organisms that die young. Then again, a sterile individual will have a poor relative fitness level regardless of its lifespan. As a point of comparison, let's consider three pigeons: one purple, one white, and one sterile. Let's assign the purple pigeon a fitness value of 1. If the white pigeon produces half the offspring of the purple pigeon, it would receive a relative fitness value of 0.5. Given that the sterile pigeon will never have progeny, its fitness value is 0.

According to the passage, a long lifespan influences an organism's evolutionary fitness because

(A) it allows the organism to spend time with its offspring

(B) it indicates the overall health of the organism

(C) it demonstrates the organism's capacity to survive

(D) it affords the organism more chances for reproduction

08

During the 1930s and 1940s, regimes in the United States and Europe expanded the use of documentary films to support political aims and instill a sense of patriotism in their citizens. Known as documentary propaganda, the films used actual footage of real events while twisting the content to invoke a desired response in the viewers. Perhaps the most famous example in American history was a series of seven films collectively titled *Why We Fight*, a production by American director Frank Capra. Commissioned by the United States government, Capra chronicled military activities and campaigns during WWII. His film included clips of speeches by military leaders interspersed with scenes of military gatherings, animated maps, and occasional written text displaying statistics and brief messages. The first episode, which was used to mobilize support for the war among soldiers and to recruit people for military service, was incredibly successful. President Franklin D. Roosevelt found it so moving that he requested it be made available for public viewing, and by 1945, more than fifty million Americans had seen the documentary.

According to the passage, the documentary's initial episode was used to

(A) change the minds of people opposed to the war

(B) recruit soldiers and generate military support for the war

(C) gain official approval from the nation's president

(D) attract as many viewers to the film as possible

---

07 **fitness**[fítnis] 적응도 **genotype**[dʒénətàip] 유전자형 **reproductive**[rìːprədʌ́ktiv] 번식의 **offspring**[ɔ́ːfsprìŋ] 자손
sterile[stéril] 불임의 **progeny**[prádʒəni] 자손

08 **regime**[rəʒíːm] 정권 **instill**[instíl] (서서히) 주입시키다 **patriotism**[péitriətìzm] 애국심
propaganda[prɑ̀pəgǽndə] 선전 **footage**[fútidʒ] 영상 **invoke**[invóuk] 불러내다 **commission**[kəmíʃən] 주문하다
chronicle[kránikl] 기록하다 **intersperse**[ìntərspə́ːrs] 중간중간 배치하다, 사이에 흩뿌리다 **statistic**[stətístik] 통계
recruit[rikrúːt] 모집하다

지문을 읽고 물음에 답하시오.

09

Theatrical performances frequently involve *blocking*, which is a term used to describe the positioning of actors and their movements on stage. The concept was originally applied to nineteenth-century plays where directors literally blocked out sections of a stage in miniature. Today, however, the concept of blocking has come to embody any activity or gesture a character uses and, in particular, the connection between those actions and the physical stage set. Stage motions often require clear instruction, as they may not reflect natural movements used in everyday life. Therefore, close collaboration on the part of actors and directors, as well as consistent awareness of the audience, is essential elements in blocking. A simple blocking rule might be to never turn one's back to the audience, for example. On the other hand, rigid adherence to blocking guidelines can result in an overly artificial performance. Consequently, an experienced stage actor who has mastered the fundamentals of blocking may be given some freedom to incorporate unplanned movements within a scene, even if those movements contradict established blocking standards. This freedom allows accomplished actors to become creative participants in the direction of a stage performance.

1. According to the description of stage blocking in the passage, which of the following is a reason given for the close cooperation between actors and directors?

   (A) Actors sometimes need help remembering their lines.
   (B) Directors know how to ensure that stage movements seem natural.
   (C) Movements performed on stage necessitate clear instruction.
   (D) Awareness of the audience requires more than one perspective.

2. According to the passage, which of the following is true of blocking rules?

   (A) They typically take years of practice to master.
   (B) Experienced actors are not always forced to follow them.
   (C) They are sometimes overlooked by the audience.
   (D) Actors implement them to add creativity to their performances.

---

09 **literally**[lítərəli] 문자 그대로 **embody**[imbádi] 포함하다 **collaboration**[kəlæ̀bəréiʃən] 협동
consistent[kənsístənt] 일관된 **adherence**[ædhíərəns] 고수 **overly**[óuvərli] 지나치게 **artificial**[à:rtəfíʃəl] 인위적인
fundamental[fʌ̀ndəméntl] 기초 **incorporate**[inkɔ́:rpərèit] 포함하다, 넣다 **contradict**[kàntrədíkt] 모순되다
accomplished[əkámpliʃt] 뛰어난

10

In the 1920s, the technology for synchronizing recordings with motion pictures had not yet been developed, so films were silent. Any ideas that made up a story were communicated to the viewer through facial expressions or actions on the part of the actors, but some linguistic information was also transmitted in the form of intertitles. Intertitles were images of printed text cards which were displayed on the screen at various points throughout a film. They were used most frequently to identify characters or to establish context by providing dates or locations. In some cases, spoken lines were represented in the text; but unlike modern subtitles, which include everything actors say in a performance, intertitles reflected only major themes, especially those that were difficult to convey to the audience using on-screen actions alone. This was because inserting text cards after each conversation or after each actor finished a line was too time consuming and would have slowed the pace of the film considerably. Though useful for some audience members, intertitles had the disadvantage of only being helpful to people who were literate. By the 1930s, sound films, or talkies, helped filmmakers communicate more effectively, and to a wider audience.

1. According to the passage, which of the following is true of intertitles?

   (A) They were no longer produced after the 1920s.

   (B) They were less comprehensive than modern subtitles.

   (C) They were communicated to the audience by actors.

   (D) They were primarily used to represent spoken lines.

2. According to the passage, why were intertitles not used after each conversation?

   (A) The ideas were easier to convey through on-screen actions.

   (B) It would have interrupted the tempo of the film.

   (C) It would have distracted the audience from the main story.

   (D) The dialogues were too long to fit on the text cards.

---

10 synchronize[síŋkrənàiz] (음성을) 화면과 일치시키다   communicate[kəmjúːnəkèit] 전달하다
linguistic[liŋgwístik] 언어의   transmit[trænsmít] 전달하다   represent[rèprizént] 나타내다   subtitle[sʌ́btàitl] 자막
convey[kənvéi] 전달하다   on-screen[ánskrìːn] 배역상의   time consuming 많은 시간이 걸리는
literate[lítərət] 글을 쓰고 읽을 줄 아는

CHAPTER 1

CH 2

CH 3

CH 4

CH 5

CH 6

CH 7

CH 8

CH 9

Hackers TOEFL Reading Intermediate

11

In early spring, frogs emerge from hibernation and make their way to aquatic breeding grounds. The males are the first to arrive and attract the females by uttering loud mating calls to announce and advertise their presence. Successful males engage with females in a mating embrace known as an amplexus, and they fertilize the eggs once they are deposited into shallow, still water by the females. These eggs, of which there can be thousands, are covered with a jelly-like substance that swells in the water to protect the fragile embryos. The collective mass of eggs and jelly is called frogspawn. As the embryos grow, they turn into tadpoles and emerge from the soft encasements. They feed on the frogspawn in the first few days before graduating to a diet of algae. Tadpoles have gills that allow them to breathe underwater and a tail that enables them to swim. A few weeks later, the tadpoles begin to undergo metamorphosis. Their fish-like gills disappear, and in their place lungs develop. Around the same time, legs begin to form and their tail is absorbed by the growing body. They then resemble miniature adults and can leave the water.

1. Which of the following is true of frogs according to the passage?

   (A) The males and females hibernate together.

   (B) The females reach the breeding grounds after the males.

   (C) They mate with the same partners year after year.

   (D) They deposit their eggs after fertilization.

2. According to the passage, tadpoles undergo all of the following physical changes EXCEPT

   (A) their tail drops off

   (B) they grow legs

   (C) they develop lungs

   (D) their gills disappear

---

11 hibernation[hàibərnéiʃən] 동면 aquatic[əkwǽtik] 수생의 breeding ground 번식지 utter[ʌ́tər] (소리를) 내다
amplexus[æmpléksəs] 포접 fertilize[fə́:rtəlàiz] 수정하다 still[stil] 흐르지 않는 swell[swel] 부풀다
fragile[frǽdʒəl] 약한 embryo[émbriòu] 배아 frogspawn[frɔ́:gspɔ̀:n] 개구리 알 tadpole[tǽdpòul] 올챙이
graduate[grǽdʒuèit] 시작하다 alga[ǽlgə] 조류, 해조 (pl.algae) gill[gil] 아가미 metamorphosis[mètəmɔ́:rfəsis] 변태
lung[lʌŋ] 폐 resemble[rizémbl] 닮다 miniature[míniətʃər] 작은

12

The Atacama Desert is a coastal desert located on the western side of tropical South America in Chile. Precipitation rarely falls on the high plateau, and two geographic phenomena combine to make the Atacama the driest place on Earth. As cool ocean currents from the poles pass along the continent's western coast, they cool the air above, inhibiting the air from rising and forming rain clouds. This process keeps fog and moist air near the edge of the coast because they are unable to move up and over the western Chilean Coast Range. There is also a rain shadow effect at the desert's eastern extremities. The high Andes Mountains block warm moist air from the east, and as the warm, easterly air rises and cools, moisture condenses and falls as rain in the eastern slopes and rain forests. By the time air approaches the western side of the Andes, it has shed virtually all of its moisture and is incapable of producing precipitation. Due to the extreme geography, only fauna adapted to life in arid conditions populate the Atacama, making the diversity of its wildlife very low. Even organisms like bacteria, which are known for their resilience, are scarce.

CHAPTER 1

CH 2

CH 3

CH 4

CH 5

CH 6

CH 7

CH 8

CH 9

Hackers TOEFL Reading Intermediate

1. **Select the TWO answers** that are mentioned in the passage as contributing to the Atacama's low precipitation levels. **To receive credit, you must choose TWO answers.**

   (A) Dry air blowing in off the coast

   (B) The cooling of air by polar currents

   (C) The warming of easterly air

   (D) A rain shadow effect

2. According to the passage, the extreme geography of the Atacama has which of the following effects?

   (A) It creates rain forests at its eastern extremities.

   (B) It causes animal populations to decline.

   (C) It produces resilient strains of bacteria.

   (D) It limits the abundance of wildlife in the area.

정답·해석·정답단서 p.273

---

12 coastal[kóustəl] 해안의   locate[lóukeit] 위치시키다   precipitation[prisìpətéiʃən] 강수량   plateau[plætóu] 고원
geographic[dʒì:əgrǽfik] 지리적인   combine[kəmbáin] 결합하다   current[kə́:rənt] 해류   cool[ku:l] 차갑게 하다
inhibit[inhíbit] 억제하다   extremity[ikstréməti] 끝   easterly[íːstərli] 동쪽의   condense[kəndéns] 응결하다
shed[ʃed] 떨어뜨리다   virtually[və́ːrtʃuəli] 사실상   fauna[fɔ́ːnə] 동물군   arid[ǽrid] 건조한   populate[pápjulèit] 살다
resilience[rizíljəns] 복원력   scarce[skɛərs] 드문

Hackers Test

1 Venetian Salt Trade

1 Salt was an important source of revenue for the Venetians. Venice began producing salt at least by the sixth century AD and for the first few centuries seemed content to use the saltworks in its own lagoons. However, Venice later directed its sights to its neighbors and began asserting control over the regional salt market.

2 ➡ Venice was initially founded as a salt-producing province, but problems later surfaced that affected production. The geographic layout of the immediate area was such that the lagoons were frequently exposed to storms, and hence, rough waters. Stormy waters made it difficult to build saltworks and also could temporarily halt output. More importantly, the constant flow of fresh water into the lagoons via the Po and Piave rivers gradually decreased the salinity of portions of the lagoons. By the thirteenth century, many of the saltworks in the northern and central parts of the lagoons ceased salt production completely. Most of Venice's salt production became confined to the southern port of Chioggia, and the town's output was insufficient to meet the demand of Venice's inland customers. These productivity concerns provided the impetus for Venice to seek ever-increasing control over the exchange of salt to avoid profit losses to rival producers.

3 ➡ Venice shifted its concentration from production to controlling the salt trade in the towns of the Po River Valley, a drainage basin stretching from the river's mouth in the Adriatic across northern Italy. It ultimately won rights to the region through a war with a southern rival, Ravenna, ending in a legal ban on northern shipments of salt from Ravenna not first passing through Venice. In 1238, Ravenna agreed to export salt only to Venice. Consequently, only salt produced by Venice, or salt passing through Venice, could be exchanged in northern Italy, and Venice was thus able to raise prices by as much as eighty percent. Realizing that monopolizing trade was more profitable than producing, the Venetian government sought to expand its control of salt shipments to the entire Adriatic, and it did so masterfully: profits from trade were invested in military operations, creating a mutually reinforcing arrangement that allowed Venice to extend its often ruthless command over the regional transport of salt. By the mid-fourteenth century, no vessel could transport salt in the Adriatic unless it was a Venetian ship. At its height, Venice is estimated to have handled more than thirty thousand tons of salt per year.

CHAPTER 1

CH 2

CH 3

CH 4

CH 5

CH 6

CH 7

CH 8

CH 9

Hackers TOEFL Reading Intermediate

1   According to paragraph 2, what was the main problem affecting salt production in Venice?

    (A) Its rivals had begun to produce a higher grade of salt.

    (B) The demand for salt among its customers had increased.

    (C) The salt content of its lagoons had changed.

    (D) Its salt-producing facilities had been damaged by storms.

    Paragraph 2 is marked with an arrow [➡].

2   The word "impetus" in the passage is closest in meaning to

    (A) suggestion

    (B) drive

    (C) method

    (D) avenue

3   The word "ultimately" in the passage is closest in meaning to

    (A) steadfastly

    (B) eventually

    (C) immediately

    (D) convincingly

4   According to paragraph 3, how did Venice gain regional control of the salt market?

    (A) It made alliances with salt producers in other countries.

    (B) It won the rights to manage salt production in Ravenna.

    (C) It upgraded its shipping fleet to reduce shipping times.

    (D) It devoted its commercial earnings to military activities.

    Paragraph 3 is marked with an arrow [➡].

1 ➡ Imagine if poetry were broadcast daily from the radio, or published in virtually every magazine and newspaper. This was precisely the situation in America resulting from the advent of modern mass media in the nineteenth century until the midpoint of the twentieth century. Rather than being confined to universities, literary magazines, or private discussions among groups of intellectuals, poetic verse was part of mainstream culture. The mass media presented an outlet for aspiring poets and a platform from which they could gain name recognition and popularize their work. In some cases, publication could launch relatively unknown poets into stardom.

2 ➡ An example is the case of Edgar Allan Poe, who submitted his 1845 poem "The Raven" to *the New York Evening Mirror*. The poem was accepted for publication and was reprinted in numerous periodicals throughout the country. The highlight of Poe's writing career and his most famous work, "The Raven" is a poem with which anyone educated in America should be familiar. Written in a lyrical narrative style, it exploits lively and entertaining language from literature and folklore to tell a story of devotion, loss, and mournful remembrance. The poem's emotional content appeals to the sensitivities of a wide audience, and the character of a talking raven offers a comic balance to the often dreary tone and subject matter.

3 ➡ Poe's style did not abandon the academics, however, and the poem's structure was constructed with a great deal of care, complexity, and attention to detail. Poe incorporated internal rhyme techniques and allegorical language in order to appeal to more urbane tastes. The poem's eighteen stanzas of six lines was, Poe believed, a length that literary scholars would also view as adequate. Poe turned out to be correct because, upon its publication in 1845, the poem received high remarks among many critics. Poe's goal of creating a work to satisfy the tastes of both a popular and critical audience had been successful.

4 ➡ Acclaim for "The Raven" went well beyond Poe's contemporaries and even the realm of literature itself, a testament to how a poet can alter the course of history. Scores of later poets imitated Poe, but his impact was felt in other areas of culture as well, for example, in movies. The 1963 Hollywood thriller *The Birds*, directed by Alfred Hitchcock, conjures up similar imagery with its ravens perched before a stark backdrop, presenting the audience with an eerie scene. Hitchcock once even credited Poe with stimulating his original interest in making suspense films. Poe was held in high regard by producers and directors who recognized the potential his writings had in film-making; well over one hundred and fifty productions made for television and film were adaptations of his works. "The Raven" is also one of the most parodied works in the history of American literature.

5 ➡ After the mid-twentieth century, the popularity of poetry as a genre dropped sharply. Although there are still some specialist periodicals to which poets can submit their work, these publications have a very limited circulation and readership. The decline in popular poetry in America has resulted from a combination of factors,

but most significantly from the replacement of poetry with other popular forms of entertainment in the mass media. Pop music, fiction novels, and television programs have all experienced tremendous gains in popularity since 1950. America still has popular art, music, and dance in the twenty-first century, but it has a very small conventional media outlet for poetry; radio and televisions stations, magazines, and newspapers mostly abandoned poetry after the 1960s. On a positive note, the presence of the Internet has recently created unprecedented access to a huge collection of popular and conventional verse, and this technological development offers a bright possibility for the future.

Glossary

stanza a unit of a poem containing a series of lines

1 Which of the following statements about poetry in nineteenth-century America is supported by paragraph 1?

(A) It was confined to discussions on college campuses.

(B) It was broadcast on the radio more often than it was printed in newspapers and magazines.

(C) It was dispersed by media outlets to a broad audience.

(D) It was a means through which unknown writers could become wealthy.

Paragraph 1 is marked with an arrow [➡].

2 According to paragraph 2, which of the following is true of "The Raven"?

(A) Poe submitted it to multiple sources before its eventual publication.

(B) It uses an amusing and lively linguistic style to convey its message.

(C) Poe wrote it in commemoration of a personal loss that he suffered.

(D) It remains Poe's most famous attempt to boost his writing career.

Paragraph 2 is marked with an arrow [➡].

3 The word "exploits" in the passage is closest in meaning to

(A) presents

(B) reinforces

(C) selects

(D) utilizes

CHAPTER 1

CH 2

CH 3

CH 4

CH 5

CH 6

CH 7

CH 8

CH 9

Hackers TOEFL Reading Intermediate

4   The word "urbane" in the passage is closest in meaning to

(A) inert
(B) specific
(C) professional
(D) sophisticated

5   According to paragraph 3, Poe chose the particular length of the poem in order to

(A) attract readers who normally do not read poetry
(B) make it more appealing to a popular audience
(C) leave a lasting mark on literary history
(D) meet the standards of the scholastic literary community

Paragraph 3 is marked with an arrow [➡].

6   The word "realm" in the passage is closest in meaning to

(A) respite
(B) instance
(C) foundation
(D) domain

7   The author's description of the legacy of Poe's poem in paragraph 4 mentions all of the following EXCEPT

(A) its popularity among movie directors
(B) its depiction of American literature
(C) its influence on the television industry
(D) its impact on other writers of poetry

Paragraph 4 is marked with an arrow [➡].

8   According to paragraph 5, all of the following are true of popular poetry after the mid-twentieth century EXCEPT:

(A) The number of poets writing it is fewer than before.
(B) The quantity of media outlets for it has diminished.
(C) The periodicals printing it have a limited readership.
(D) The Internet has made it more widely available.

Paragraph 5 is marked with an arrow [➡].

3 Natural Gas

1   Natural gas is a fossil fuel, meaning it is present in fixed amounts and cannot be quickly replenished. As with other mineral fuels like oil, natural gas forms in impermeable layers of rock as organic material becomes trapped through sedimentation and subjected to heat and pressure over thousands of years. Some of the most common gas pockets occur in shale and sandstone beds in the earth's crust. In order for humans to use the natural gas, it must be brought to the surface.

2   ➡ Gas is typically extracted by drilling. The location and depth of a gas pocket determines what sort of drilling process and equipment are necessary. Deposits located beneath the land's surface can be accessed by placing drilling rigs directly above the spots for onshore wells, but those located offshore beneath oceans require the construction of floating platforms, which must be anchored and secured to account for oceanic currents. To reach shallow reservoirs of natural gas, engineers use a technique called cable, or percussion, drilling. Cable drilling works by dropping a heavy metal bit attached to a cable repeatedly to break through rock, the bit digging deeper each time it is dropped. For reservoirs at greater depths, the usual method is to use a rotary drill, which spins a sharp metal drill bit into the soil. Huge rotary drills are able to drill wells deep into the Earth's crust, and can reach depths of thousands of feet. Once a reservoir is reached, powerful pumps are used to draw the gas up toward the surface. If a reservoir is found to be prolific, an investor may build multiple drills on-site to maximize extraction.

3   ➡ The gas then must be transported from the site to processing facilities, and ultimately to the intended customer market. In most cases, the gas is moved great distances to its eventual point of use. The first stage is to pump the raw gas from the extraction site to a nearby processing plant, where operators must remove impurities in the gas. Though its common name indicates a single gas, raw natural gas is actually made up of several hydrocarbons, including crude oil, methane, propane, ethane, and butane. It can also be found mixed with water vapor, helium, nitrogen, and carbon dioxide. Methane—a colorless, odorless gas that makes up nearly ninety percent of natural gas—is the principal constituent of natural gas used in people's homes and automobiles. Consequently, the other components are typically removed. Removal of the various items involves multiple processes depending on the chemical composition of the materials being separated. The process of isolating methane and disposing of other elements adds to the expense of producing natural gas. However, some by-products may be sold off to offset the costs. Propane, crude oil, and butane, for example, all have value as fuels.

4   ➡ After processing, the gas is then moved along a main pipeline made of hard carbon steel and often must cross state, provincial, or even international boundaries. Vast and expensive transportation networks are necessary to efficiently distribute the refined gas. The most common method is to build a main pipeline with a series of connecting pipelines to pump the gas from one place to another. Metering stations are built along the length of the pipeline to allow companies to meticulously monitor and measure the flow of gas. Large valves are also placed every ten kilometers or so. These valves can be opened or closed to control the flow of gas through the pipeline. In the event that maintenance needs arise,

CHAPTER 1
CH 2
CH 3
CH 4
CH 5
CH 6
CH 7
CH 8
CH 9

Hackers TOEFL Reading Intermediate

valves can be shut off to provide safe access for maintenance crews to enter the interior of the pipe. Finally, the gas is deflected into distribution pipes, which carry the gas to local sources where it is used in heating, electricity, and as a power source for automobiles.

Glossary
bit the part of a tool that does the drilling

1 The word "replenished" in the passage is closest in meaning to

(A) renovated

(B) reused

(C) redistributed

(D) restored

2 According to paragraph 2, which of the following dictates the type of drilling that is required?

(A) The deepness of the gas

(B) The condition of the equipment

(C) The stability of the land surface

(D) The direction of ocean currents

Paragraph 2 is marked with an arrow [➡].

3 All of the following are mentioned in paragraph 2 as tools for extracting natural gas EXCEPT

(A) vibration drills

(B) powerful pumps

(C) rotary drills

(D) percussion drills

4 The word "prolific" in the passage is closest in meaning to

(A) productive
(B) diminutive
(C) usable
(D) stable

5 According to paragraph 3, what happens to the by-products of natural gas?

(A) They are recycled for use in fueling the purification process.
(B) They are either disposed of or sold to counterbalance costs.
(C) They are separated according to fuel efficiency.
(D) They are mixed together to yield marketable products.

Paragraph 3 is marked with an arrow [➡].

6 All of the following are mentioned in paragraph 3 as profitable by-products found in natural gas EXCEPT

(A) crude oil
(B) propane
(C) helium
(D) butane

7 According to paragraph 4, which of the following is true about the transport of natural gas?

(A) It is regulated by state, provincial, and international laws.
(B) It is carefully monitored at different places along the pipeline.
(C) It costs more to distribute refined gas than unrefined gas.
(D) It creates dangerous conditions for maintenance crews.

Paragraph 4 is marked with an arrow [➡].

8 The word "meticulously" in the passage is closest in meaning to

(A) adequately
(B) finally
(C) carefully
(D) truthfully

정답·해석·정답단서 p.275

CHAPTER 1

CH 2

CH 3

CH 4

CH 5

CH 6

CH 7

CH 8

CH 9

Hackers TOEFL Reading Intermediate

VOCABULARY LIST

Chapter 01에서 선별한 다음의 토플 필수 어휘를 단어암기 음성파일을 들으며 암기한 후 퀴즈로 확인해보세요.

*해커스 동영상강의 포털 해커스인강(HackersIngang.com)에서 단어암기 음성파일을 무료로 다운로드할 수 있습니다.

inhabit[inhǽbit] 살다 (=dwell)

distinctive[distíŋktiv] 특유의 (=characteristic)

constrict[kənstríkt] 수축시키다

manipulate[mənípjulèit] 조작하다 (=control)

vibrate[váibreit] 진동하다

assertion[əsə́:rʃən] 주장 (=declaration)

foster[fɔ́:stər] 조성하다

materialize[mətíəriəláiz] 나타나다

subsist[səbsíst] 생활하다 (=survive)

cite[sait] 언급하다 (=mention)

decompose[dì:kəmpóuz] 부패하다 (=decay)

proportionate[prəpɔ́:rʃənət] 비례하는

commercial[kəmə́:rʃəl] 상업용의

designation[dèzignéiʃən] 표시

mark[ma:rk] 특징짓다

perceive[pərsí:v] 인식하다 (=notice)

indicative[indíkətiv] 암시하는

distorted[distɔ́:rtid] 왜곡된

acute[əkjú:t] 심각한 (=crucial)

persecute[pə́:rsəkjù:t] 학대하다 (=oppress)

inclination[ìnklənéiʃən] 경향 (=trend)

optimal[áptəməl] 최적의

intake[íntèik] 섭취

inhospitable[inháspitəbl] 황폐한 (=desolate)

desiccation[dèsikéiʃən] 건조

vulnerable[vʌ́lnərəbl] 취약한 (=susceptible)

exert[igzə́:rt] 행사하다 (=wield)

respective[rispéktiv] 각각의 (=individual)

reproductive[rì:prədʌ́ktiv] 번식의

sterile[stéril] 불임의 (=unproductive)

progeny[prádʒəni] 자손

regime[rəʒí:m] 정권

instill[instíl] 서서히 주입시키다

invoke[invóuk] 불러내다

intersperse[ìntərspə́:rs] 사이에 흩뿌리다

recruit[rikrú:t] 모집하다

literally[lítərəli] 문자 그대로

embody[imbádi] 포함하다 (=contain)

collaboration[kəlæ̀bəréiʃən] 협동 (=cooperation)

consistent[kənsístənt] 일관된 (=compatible)

adherence[ædhíərəns] 고수

overly[óuvərli] 지나치게

artificial[à:rtəfíʃəl] 인위적인 (=synthetic)

fundamental[fʌ̀ndəméntl] 기초

incorporate[inkɔ́:rpərèit] 넣다 (=include)

contradict[kàntrədíkt] 모순되다

accomplished[əkámpliʃt] 뛰어난 (=proficient)

transmit[trænsmít] 전달하다 (=send)

represent[rèprizént] 나타내다 (=express)

convey[kənvéi] 전달하다

literate[lítərət] 글을 쓰고 읽을 줄 아는

hibernation[hàibərnéiʃən] 동면 (=dormancy)

Quiz

각 단어의 알맞은 뜻을 찾아 연결하시오.

01	foster	ⓐ	최적의
02	optimal	ⓑ	나타나다
03	acute	ⓒ	인식하다
04	designation	ⓓ	조성하다
05	materialize	ⓔ	심각한
		ⓕ	표시

각 단어의 알맞은 동의어를 찾아 연결하시오.

06	perceive	ⓐ	control
07	subsist	ⓑ	survive
08	exert	ⓒ	notice
09	manipulate	ⓓ	wield
10	inhospitable	ⓔ	dwell
		ⓕ	desolate

ⓙ 01 ⓐ 02 ⓔ 03 ⓕ 04 ⓑ 05 ⓒ 06 ⓑ 07 ⓓ 08 ⓐ 09 ⓕ 10

CHAPTER 1

CH 2
CH 3
CH 4
CH 5
CH 6
CH 7
CH 8
CH 9

Hackers TOEFL Reading Intermediate

resemble[rizémbl] 닮다 (=take after)

locate[lóukeit] 위치시키다 (=situate)

combine[kəmbáin] 결합하다 (=incorporate)

inhibit[inhíbit] 억제하다 (=prohibit)

extremity[ikstréməti] 끝

condense[kəndéns] 응결하다

shed[ʃed] 떨어뜨리다 (=discard)

virtually[vɔ́ːrtʃuəli] 사실상 (=practically)

resilience[rizíljəns] 복원력

revenue[révənjùː] 수익

assert[əsə́ːrt] 주장하다 (=allege)

immediate[imíːdiət] 인접한 (=nearest)

halt[hɔːlt] 멈추게 하다 (=stop)

impetus[ímpətəs] 동기 (=stimulus)

ruthless[rúːθlis] 무자비한 (=harsh)

advent[ǽdvent] 도래 (=arrival)

outlet[áutlèt] 배출구

aspiring[əspáiəriŋ] 포부가 있는

submit[səbmít] 제출하다

periodical[pìəriádikəl] 정기 간행물

lyrical[lírikəl] 서정적인

devotion[divóuʃən] 헌신

abandon[əbǽndən] 버리다 (=relinquish)

allegorical[ǽligɔ́(ː)rikəl] 우의적인

urbane[əːrbéin] 세련된 (=elegant)

adequate[ǽdikwət] 적절한 (=sufficient)

testament[téstəmənt] 증거

alter[ɔ́ːltər] 바꾸다 (=modify)

imitate[ímətèit] 모방하다 (=mimic)

conjure[kándʒər] 그리다

perch[pəːrtʃ] (새가) 앉다

stark[stɑːrk] 황량한

eerie[íəri] 오싹한 (=weird)

tremendous[triméndəs] 엄청난 (=huge)

unprecedented[ʌnprésədèntid] 전에 없던

replenish[ripléniʃ] 다시 채우다 (=restore)

impermeable[impə́ːrmiəbl] 불침투성의

extract[ikstrǽkt] 추출하다 (=withdraw)

anchor[ǽŋkər] 정박하다 (=hold in place)

secure[sikjúər] 고정하다 (=fasten)

account for 감안하다

spin[spin] 돌리다 (=rotate)

intend[inténd] 의도하다 (=design)

eventual[ivéntʃuəl] 최후의 (=final)

impurity[impjúərəti] 불순물

indicate[índikèit] 나타내다 (=suggest)

principal[prínsəpəl] 주요한 (=main)

constituent[kənstítʃuənt] 성분 (=element)

dispose[dispóuz] 처리하다

offset[ɔ́ːfsèt] 상쇄하다 (=balance)

meticulously[mətíkjuləsli] 꼼꼼하게 (=carefully)

deflect[diflékt] 방향을 바꾸다 (=avert)

Quiz

각 단어의 알맞은 뜻을 찾아 연결하시오.

01 submit   ⓐ 고정하다

02 advent   ⓑ 제출하다

03 secure   ⓒ 다시 채우다

04 devotion   ⓓ 도래

05 replenish   ⓔ 결합하다

                       ⓕ 헌신

각 단어의 알맞은 동의어를 찾아 연결하시오.

06 locate   ⓐ practically

07 intend   ⓑ huge

08 meticulously   ⓒ design

09 tremendous   ⓓ allege

10 assert   ⓔ carefully

                       ⓕ situate

ⓓ 01   ⓓ 02   ⓐ 03   ⓕ 04   ⓒ 05   ⓕ 06   ⓒ 07   ⓔ 08   ⓑ 09   ⓓ 10

CHAPTER 02

Vocabulary

CHAPTER 02

Vocabulary

Vocabulary 문제는 지문에 음영 처리된 단어와 가장 유사한 뜻을 가진 단어를 선택하는 유형이다. 주로 단어의 뜻을 묻지만, 간혹 구의 뜻을 묻는 문제가 출제되기도 한다. Vocabulary 문제는 한 지문당 1~2개가 출제된다.

Vocabulary 문제를 풀기 위해서는 단어의 뜻을 정확하게 익히고 동의어를 많이 외워둬야 한다.

▶ 문제 살펴보기

Vocabulary 문제는 가장 유사한 뜻을 파악해야 하는 단어 또는 구를 지문과 질문에 음영으로 표시한다. 4개의 단어 또는 구가 보기로 주어진다. 전형적인 질문 형태는 아래와 같다.

- The word "⬛⬛⬛⬛⬛⬛⬛" in the passage is closest in meaning to . . .
  지문의 단어 "⬛⬛⬛⬛"은 의미상 …와 가장 가깝다.

- The phrase "⬛⬛⬛⬛⬛⬛⬛" in the passage is closest in meaning to . . .
  지문의 구 "⬛⬛⬛⬛"은 의미상 …와 가장 가깝다.

문제 공략하기

다음은 Vocabulary 문제의 공략법이다. 실전 고득점을 위해 이를 꼼꼼히 학습하고 Hackers Practice와 Hackers Test를 풀면서 반드시 적용해 본다.

1 동의어 추려내기

4개의 보기 중에서 음영 처리된 단어의 동의어로 예상되는 보기를 사전적 의미를 바탕으로 추려낸다.

2 문맥에 맞는 보기 찾기

지문에 대입하여 문맥에 맞는 보기가 정답이다.

In the United States, Central and South America, and Australia, dozens of species of stream-dwelling frogs have recently experienced a sudden decline in numbers or have completely vanished. Observers of this phenomenon have suggested several possible causes, including the well-documented issue of loss of habitat brought on by human activity.

The word "vanished" in the passage is closest in meaning to

(A) disappeared

(B) diminished

(C) decimated

(D) denied

지문해석 p.279

2 vanished의 자리에 disappeared를 대입하여 해석해 보면, '미국, 중남미, 호주에서는 개울에 사는 개구리 수십 종이 최근 갑작스런 개체수의 감소를 겪거나 완전히 사라졌다'와 같이 문맥에 맞으므로 보기 (A)가 정답이다.

1 음영 처리된 단어 vanished(사라지다)의 동의어로 예상되는 보기 (A) disappeared(사라지다)를 추려낸다.

TIP 질문의 단어와 뜻은 유사하나 지문에 대입하였을 때 문맥상 의미가 통하지 않는 보기 또는 반의어는 오답이다.

Hackers Practice

지문을 읽고 물음에 답하시오.

01

Although most educational professionals accept the idea that children learn at different paces, they generally agree that common deadlines and incentives can enhance overall student achievement.

The word "enhance" in the passage is closest in meaning to

(A) control   (B) exaggerate   (C) improve

02

The earliest form of pottery made by rudimentary man was fashioned with coils of clay that were built up around a base and then fired in ground ovens or pit kilns.

The word "rudimentary" in the passage is closest in meaning to

(A) compound   (B) antique   (C) primitive

03

Marsupials give birth to their young long before the newborns are capable of surviving outside in the elements of their natural environments. To account for this, adult females have pouches that provide ample shelter for their newborn offspring.

The word "ample" in the passage is closest in meaning to

(A) sufficient   (B) necessary   (C) moderate

04

Having grown up in isolation from human contact, feral children are of interest to psychologists because they provide insights into early human development regarding which behaviors are instinctive and which are acquired from the environment.

The word "acquired" in the passage is closest in meaning to

(A) ingested   (B) obtained   (C) created

---

01 incentive[inséntiv] 유인, 포상 enhance[inhǽns] 높이다 overall[óuvərɔ̀:l] 전반적인

02 rudimentary[rùːdəméntəri] 원시의 pit[pit] 구덩이 kiln[kiln] 화로

03 marsupial[mɑːrsúːpiəl] 유대류 ample[ǽmpl] 충분한, 넓은 shelter[ʃéltər] 거처

04 feral[fíərəl] 야생의 instinctive[instíŋktiv] 본능적인 acquire[əkwáiər] 습득하다, 획득하다

CH 1

CHAPTER 2

CH 3

CH 4

CH 5

CH 6

CH 7

CH 8

CH 9

Hackers TOEFL Reading Intermediate

05

Personality tests use questionnaires to reveal how people perceive the world and how they make decisions. Some tests attempt to describe a general overview of a personality, while others focus on specific characteristics of an examinee's psychology.

The word "reveal" in the passage is closest in meaning to

(A) show   (B) hint   (C) secure

06

The aridity and extreme temperatures in a desert make living conditions severe for plants and animals that reside there. Living organisms that cannot adapt to the desert or escape from it expire.

The word "aridity" in the passage is closest in meaning to

(A) altitude   (B) terrain   (C) dryness

07

As with other Paleolithic cave paintings, the Chauvet Cave in France includes figures of common animals like horses and reindeer depicted on the cave walls, but the site is unique in its inclusion of predatory animals, such as lions and hyenas, which are virtually absent in all other known ice age paintings.

The word "depicted" in the passage is closest in meaning to

(A) mounted   (B) pictured   (C) exposed

08

Herbivores do not normally have to forage for food because vegetation is usually abundant. Unlike herbivores, carnivores must employ tactics to obtain prey or remains of animals. They are not as plentiful as plants, must often be hunted and caught, and may have to be shared with other predators.

The word "forage" in the passage is closest in meaning to

(A) maneuver   (B) search   (C) excavate

---

05 questionnaire[kwèstʃənɛ́ər] 질문지 perceive[pərsíːv] 지각하다 examinee[igzǽməníː] 피험자

06 aridity[ərídəti] 건조함 severe[səvíər] 어려운 reside[rizáid] 거주하다 expire[ikspáiər] 죽다

07 site[sait] 유적지 inclusion[inklúːʒən] 포함 predatory[prédətɔ̀ːri] 육식성의

08 vegetation[vèdʒətéiʃən] 초목 abundant[əbʌ́ndənt] 풍부한 employ[implɔ́i] 쓰다 tactics[tǽktiks] 전략

지문을 읽고 물음에 답하시오.

09

Hydroelectric plants use turbines and a generator to convert the energy of flowing water into electricity. Plant construction typically costs hundreds of millions of dollars, a considerable investment, but this is offset by the plant's relatively low operating costs and the use of an abundant, free, and renewable energy source. Turbines do not produce carbon emissions because coal or oil is not required for production. The drawbacks, however, include detrimental effects to the physical environment and the organisms in it, and the necessity of relocating residents in the area. A hydroelectric plant occupies much land space, resulting in the destruction of animal habitats in the area where it is constructed.

1. The word "convert" in the passage is closest in meaning to

(A) reduce   (B) induce

(C) reverse   (D) change

2. The word "detrimental" in the passage is closest in meaning to

(A) useless   (B) harmful

(C) unknown   (D) profitable

10

Indigenous people in North America began crafting visual works soon after their appearance on the continent some 11,000 years ago. These included clothing, beadwork, blankets and rugs, pottery, baskets, figurines, masks, and totem poles. Despite being appreciated by museums and art galleries, the objects were originally conceived for functional and symbolic purposes rather than as works of art. A spiral motif, for instance, signified the nature and shape of the universe, whereas totem poles were often carved to illustrate sacred myths or cultural beliefs. Objects were also required in ceremonies and rituals carried out to make requests of the spirit world. Masks, for example, were not viewed merely as art objects but as integral spiritual parts of a tribe's religious existence.

1. The word "Indigenous" in the passage is closest in meaning to

(A) native   (B) rustic

(C) municipal   (D) foreign

2. The word "appreciated" in the passage is closest in meaning to

(A) embellished   (B) displayed

(C) valued   (D) kept

---

09 **hydroelectric**[hàidrouiléktrik] 수력 발전의 **generator**[dʒénərèitər] 발전기 **convert**[kənvə́ːrt] 전환하다
typically[típikəli] 보통 **renewable**[rinjúːəbl] 재생 가능한 **emission**[imíʃən] 배출 **detrimental**[dètrəméntl] 해로운
relocate[rìːloukéit] 이전시키다 **occupy**[ákjupài] 차지하다 **induce**[indjúːs] 권유하다

10 **indigenous**[indídʒənəs] 토착의 **continent**[kántənənt] 대륙 **figurine**[fìgjuríːn] 작은 입상 **spiral**[spáiərəl] 나선형의
signify[sígnəfài] 의미하다 **sacred**[séikrid] 신성한 **integral**[íntigrəl] 없어서는 안될

11

When the temperature of rock, soil or sediment remains at or below 0°C for a period of two years or more, the material is called permafrost. Ground temperature is the only relevant component in the formation of permafrost. The atmospheric temperature, soil moisture content, and snow cover are negligible. Permafrost develops when the net heat balance of the Earth has been negative for years. This means there is less incoming solar heat than the Earth's surface is radiating.

1. The word "component" in the passage is closest in meaning to

(A) relationship   (B) factor

(C) trace   (D) equivalent

2. The word "negligible" in the passage is closest in meaning to

(A) common   (B) external

(C) insignificant   (D) impressive

12

Scientists ascribe the gradual rise in global temperatures to atmospheric pollution generated by human activity. Manufacturing, construction, and the use of appliances and products are some activities that burn fossil fuels and add pollutants to the atmosphere. One pollutant, carbon dioxide, plays a major role in the increase in global temperatures. Carbon dioxide from fossil-fuel burning collects in the atmosphere, increasing in density and capturing the sun's heat. This causes the air to become warmer. China has emerged as the biggest source of carbon dioxide pollution in the twenty-first century, generating as much as 6.2 billion tons in 2006.

1. The word "generated" in the passage is closest in meaning to

(A) produced   (B) combined

(C) designated   (D) offered

2. The word "capturing" in the passage is closest in meaning to

(A) refining   (B) losing

(C) isolating   (D) trapping

---

11 permafrost[pə́ːrməfrɔ̀ːst] 영구 동토층 relevant[réləvənt] 관련 있는 formation[fɔːrméiʃən] 형성
radiate[réidièit] 방출하다 insignificant[ìnsignífikənt] 중요하지 않은

12 ascribe[əskráib] ~에 돌리다 generate[dʒénərèit] 발생시키다 manufacture[mænjufǽktʃər] 제조하다
appliance[əpláiəns] 전기제품 pollutant[pəlúːtnt] 오염 물질 carbon dioxide 이산화탄소 collect[kəlékt] 쌓이다
density[dénsəti] 밀도 emerge[imə́ːrdʒ] 드러나다

CH 1

CHAPTER 2

CH 3

CH 4

CH 5

CH 6

CH 7

CH 8

CH 9

Hackers TOEFL Reading Intermediate

지문을 읽고 물음에 답하시오.

13

Many organisms blend in with their natural surroundings using camouflage, a method of hiding that aids in their survival. Predators like sharks and dolphins have grayish-blue skin, which is similar in color to the ocean environments they inhabit. Their coloration allows them to approach potential prey without being noticed. Likewise, bottom-dwelling fish like flounder have markings that resemble the sea floor. That their bodies are hard to distinguish from the background helps these fish easily refrain from being detected by predators. Some animals can even modify their colors. Arctic foxes, for example, have a white coat that matches the snowy landscape in winter, but in summer, their outer layer takes on earth tones.

1. The word "Likewise" in the passage is closest in meaning to

   (A) supposedly
   (B) actually
   (C) similarly
   (D) in addition

2. The phrase "refrain from" in the passage is closest in meaning to

   (A) aspire
   (B) adjust to
   (C) allow for
   (D) avoid

3. The word "landscape" in the passage is closest in meaning to

   (A) path
   (B) climate
   (C) disguise
   (D) scenery

---

13 **camouflage**[kǽməflɑ̀ːʒ] 위장 **inhabit**[inhǽbit] 서식하다 **potential**[pəténʃəl] 잠재적인 **flounder**[fláundər] 도다리
refrain[rifréin] 피하다 **modify**[mɑ́dəfài] 바꾸다 **arctic**[ɑ́ːrktik] 북극의 **similarly**[símələrli] 비슷하게
disguise[disɡáiz] 위장하다

14

The ancient Aztecs did not possess bronze or iron tools and used stone or copper blades set in handles as their primary cutting tools. Despite this lack of complex tools, the Aztecs were versatile craftsmen and were able to construct a wide variety of temples, pyramids, civic buildings, and luxurious palaces. Most Aztec buildings served religious purposes and were deemed as holy centers by the population. On top of the pyramids were temples, where human sacrifices and different religious ceremonies were conducted. The Aztecs erected these very tall structures in a direct attempt to be closer to the gods.

1. The word "versatile" in the passage is closest in meaning to

(A) admirable

(B) reliable

(C) navigable

(D) adaptable

2. The word "deemed" in the passage is closest in meaning to

(A) regarded

(B) highlighted

(C) described

(D) revered

3. The word "erected" in the passage is closest in meaning to

(A) constructed

(B) destroyed

(C) planned

(D) worshipped

14 possess[pəzés] 소유하다 bronze[brɑnz] 청동의 blade[bleid] (칼붙이의) 날 complex[kəmpléks] 복잡한
versatile[və́:rsətl] 융통성 있는, 다재다능한 craftsman[kræftsmən] 장인 human sacrifice 인신 공양
conduct[kəndʌ́kt] 수행하다 attempt[ətémpt] 시도

15

The city of Atlantis is generally viewed as a myth created by Plato. Plato wrote about an advanced utopian society, which, due to natural disasters, was swallowed by the ocean in the interval of one day and one night. However, some scholars claim that Plato may have based his account on actual events. One of the more widely discussed ideas put forth is the idea that Atlantis was a city located on the island of Santorini. A volcanic eruption on the island could have caused the damage mentioned by Plato, and the island itself matches characteristics and descriptions of Atlantis. Archaeological evidence discovered on the island also revealed that its dwellers, the Minoans, had developed a complex system of engineering, including multi-storied buildings, plumbing systems and earthquake-resistant walls, which were technologically far ahead of their time.

1. The word "interval" in the passage is closest in meaning to

   (A) period
   (B) extension
   (C) supplement
   (D) addition

2. The word "account" in the passage is closest in meaning to

   (A) material
   (B) fable
   (C) idea
   (D) report

3. The word "dwellers" in the passage is closest in meaning to

   (A) inhabitants
   (B) founders
   (C) discoverers
   (D) immigrants

---

15 generally [dʒénərəli] 일반적으로, 대체적으로 utopian [juːtóupiən] 이상향의 description [diskrípʃən] 묘사
archaeological [àːrkiəládʒikəl] 고고학적인 engineering [èndʒəníəriŋ] 토목 기술 multi-storied [mʌ́ltistɔ̀ːrid] 다층의
extension [iksténʃən] 확장

16

Scientists know that the forked tongue of snakes is used in conjunction with the vomeronasal organ (VNO), which is involved in the sense of smell. The tongue's forked structure is believed to facilitate predation, but its specific function is obscure. A 1994 hypothesis suggested that the forked tongue is used to detect the lateral edge of a scent by using each prong to separately collect chemical data. According to this theory, one prong stays on the scent and the second sends sensory data to the VNO when it has moved off the scent trail. In a later study, scientists tested the proposition by severing only one of the vomeronasal nerves of a rattlesnake and observing the animal in a predatory context. They noticed no difference in trailing behavior and deduced that the unilateral severing had no effect on prey location success. Therefore, the forked structure may simply increase the chemical sampling area and serve to disturb chemicals in the air when a snake flicks its tongue.

1. The phrase "in conjunction with" in the passage is closest in meaning to

   (A) along with
   (B) in opposition to
   (C) according to
   (D) constant with

2. The word "obscure" in the passage is closest in meaning to

   (A) distinct
   (B) false
   (C) unclear
   (D) arbitrary

3. The word "deduced" in the passage is closest in meaning to

   (A) theorized
   (B) denounced
   (C) requested
   (D) concluded

정답·해석·정답단서 p.279

---

16 forked[fɔːrkt] 갈래 진 in conjunction with ~와 함께 facilitate[fəsílətèit] 용이하게 하다 hypothesis[haipáθəsis] 가설
scent[sent] 냄새 prong[prɔːŋ] 뾰족한 끝 trail[treil] 흔적 proposition[prὰpəzíʃən] 주장 sever[sévər] 절단하다
unilateral[jùːnəlǽtərəl] 일면적인 flick[flik] (혀 등을) 날름거리다

Hackers Test

1 Mapping the Ocean Floor

Earth Science

1   Unlike terrestrial geologists, marine geologists rarely get to study their subjects directly. Undersea mountain ranges, valleys, and basins lie beneath a vast amount of water. The depths are often so great that no natural light penetrates, and the pressure is so immense that diving with scuba equipment is impossible. Fortunately, however, other technologies make it possible for geologists to study the ocean floor.

2   ➡ Submarines are effective tools that scientists can use to collect information. Traveling in pressure-proof and insulated submarines, scientists can maneuver through the ocean depths and, with the aid of electronic lights, directly observe rocks and undersea surface features. A problem with manned undersea missions is that they require a great deal of time investment. The deepest dive ever undertaken was in 1961 in the Swiss-designed *Trieste*. Its descent and ascent took nearly eight hours, but the battery-powered craft only spent thirty minutes at the ocean's bottom. Although theoretically some nuclear submarines can remain submerged for several decades without refueling, remaining underwater for long periods can be uncomfortable for the crew. Consequently, robotic submersibles are sometimes used in place of manned submarines. Equipped with cameras and mechanical arms, submersible robots can take photographs of the ocean floor while collecting soil and rock samples for later study.

3   ➡ Submersible vehicles and robots provide glimpses of the undersea surface, but in order to gain a thorough understanding of the seabed's shape, a tremendous amount of territory must be covered. Sonar(an acronym for Sound Navigation and Ranging), a remote sensing technique that uses sound waves to measure depth, is one option for achieving this. Since sound waves move rapidly through water (at 1,500 meters per second), a ship moving across the surface can quickly send and receive sound signals, which are bounced off the ocean floor. The roundtrip time of the "echo" is then measured, and mathematical calculations are used to determine the distance traveled. Though less expensive than launching submersibles, sonar mapping includes no imagery and requires accumulating and interpreting a huge collection of data. It is estimated that using sonar mapping alone would require more than a century of work to produce an accurate map of the entire seabed.

4   In addition, computer and satellite technology gives scientists the means to examine the sea floor in extraordinary detail. Scientists are able to see in an instant what would have taken years of concentrated study only decades earlier. Satellite maps give us clear images of the undersea surface, as well as indications of how the ocean floor changes due to sedimentation, tectonics, and thermal processes.

1 The word "maneuver" in the passage is closest in meaning to

(A) transfer

(B) trespass

(C) gravitate

(D) move

2 The word "require" in the passage is closest in meaning to

(A) deny

(B) demand

(C) advise

(D) adjoin

3 According to paragraph 2, using manned submarines for underwater exploration is challenging because

(A) creating craft that can remain underwater for long periods is impossible

(B) nuclear-powered craft require continual maintenance

(C) the extreme pressure of the deep sea leads to health concerns

(D) staying below the surface for long intervals can create discomfort

Paragraph 2 is marked with an arrow [➡].

4 According to paragraph 3, which of the following is true of sonar?

(A) It is able to collect a large amount of data through imagery.

(B) It is not as costly as submarine exploration.

(C) It produces more accurate maps than other methods.

(D) It creates an echo that disrupts the sound signal.

Paragraph 3 is marked with an arrow [➡].

2 The Auditory System of Fish Biology

1   At first glance, fish appear to have poorly developed hearing. Their absence of external ears and lack of an eardrum or tube connecting the auditory organs with the outside world would seem to indicate that fish have ears that are not well-equipped to detect sound vibrations moving through water. However, biologists have found the auditory system of fish to be remarkably sensitive.

2   ➡ Many higher vertebrates like mammals have outer and middle ears, but fish do not. Fish only have inner ears. The fish ear is divided into upper and lower sections. The upper, or dorsal, section is the *pars superior*, which is subdivided into three semicircular canals. Filled with fluid and sensory hairs, these canals detect gravity and also give fish their sense of balance. Without the pars superior, fish would be confined to judging their vertical orientation in the water on the basis of light coming from the surface. However, ichthyologists believe the upper portion of the ear serves only a minor role in sound detection. It is the lower section, the *pars inferior*, which serves as the integral instrument in receiving auditory signals. Sound waves that reach the pars inferior pass through a solid receptive structure called an *otolith*, or "ear stone," which is lined with tissue connecting the otolith with sensory hair cells. Sound waves cause the otolith to vibrate, thus exciting sensory hair cells and activating sensory neurons of the auditory nerve. Fish interpret signals sent along the auditory nerve as "hearing" once the signals reach the brain.

3   All known fish species can detect the motion of sound particles in the ear, but some have developed peripheral specializations that enhance their auditory capacities. Fishes with these specializations are called hearing specialists, and fishes without such specializations are called hearing generalists. Most hearing generalists detect sound in a low-frequency range, from below 30 Hz to around 1,000 Hz. Specialists can detect sound in a much greater range. The American shad, for instance, can sense ultrasonic frequencies of up to 180,000 Hz. This is significantly more sensitive than human hearing, where 20,000 Hz is the approximate upper limit for natural sound detection in the average adult.

4   ➡ A notable example of a hearing specialization is in fishes that have a gas bladder adjacent to the ears. The gas bladder is an organ used to control a fish's buoyancy that has a density far below that of the body or the surrounding water. The American shad has gas tubes that directly connect the gas bladder to the ear. In catfish and carp, the gas bladder is indirectly connected to the ear by modified vertebrae. Due to the density variances, sound pressure waves can easily compress the gas within the bladder, causing the bladder to rhythmically expand and contract. These pulsations can then be transmitted to the ear. The gas bladder is thus believed to play a central role in sound reception in many fishes. Studies of Atlantic cod have clearly shown that the presence of the gas bladder results in heightened sensitivity to sound, especially at high frequencies. Using a hypodermic needle to deflate the gas bladder, and audiograms to chart the results, scientists were able to confirm that the cod's sensitivity to sound pressure was reduced, and the frequency range of audible

sounds was limited, when the bladder was emptied.

5 ➡ Understanding that fish have a more sensitive auditory system than was previously thought, marine scientists have begun to discuss the potential effects of increased noise in the oceans. Since the 1970s, the noise level in the Earth's waters has risen by more than ten percent. Boats, barges, and oil drills all inject sound vibrations into the water, and recent studies have shown that the noises can damage the ears of fish. In response to the findings, scientists have begun to urge people to be cautious when making sounds in marine environments.

1 The word "remarkably" in the passage is closest in meaning to

(A) intensively
(B) forcibly
(C) surprisingly
(D) basically

2 According to paragraph 2, all of the following have a major influence on a fish's ability to hear EXCEPT

(A) the otolith
(B) the *pars inferior*
(C) semicircular canals
(D) the sensory hair cells

Paragraph 2 is marked with an arrow [➡].

3 The word "interpret" in the passage is closest in meaning to

(A) bemoan
(B) facilitate
(C) dispense
(D) decipher

4 The word "significantly" in the passage is closest in meaning to

(A) considerably
(B) seemingly
(C) superficially
(D) marginally

CH 1
CHAPTER 2
CH 3
CH 4
CH 5
CH 6
CH 7
CH 8
CH 9
Hackers TOEFL Reading Intermediate

5   The phrase "adjacent to" in the passage is closest in meaning to

(A) posterior to

(B) nearby

(C) distant from

(D) beneath

6   According to paragraph 4, which of the following is true of the gas bladder?

(A) Its density is greater than a fish's body and the surrounding water.

(B) It helps fish distinguish between sounds at different frequencies.

(C) It compresses sound waves while expanding and contracting.

(D) Its rhythmic pulsing aids in the transfer of sounds to the ear.

Paragraph 4 is marked with an arrow [➡].

7   According to paragraph 5, what is a possible impact of noise in oceans?

(A) It disrupts the migratory patterns of fish.

(B) It harms the ability of fish to detect background noise.

(C) It interferes with the sensitivity of fish to changes in pressure.

(D) It injures the auditory organs of fish.

Paragraph 5 is marked with an arrow [➡].

8   The word "urge" in the passage is closest in meaning to

(A) encourage

(B) coerce

(C) recruit

(D) amass

3 Attribution Theory

Psychology

1   Psychologists have developed a theory of how people explain, make excuses about, and justify their behaviors. Known as attribution theory, it postulates that people are motivated to attribute their own or other people's behavior to either internal or external causes, depending on the circumstances of an event. According to this view, perceptions about causality can affect how a person interprets degrees of success and failure.

2   ➡ First put forth by the Austrian psychologist Fritz Heider in his 1958 book *The Psychology of Interpersonal Relations*, attribution theory presumes that all human behavior is motivated by internal or external factors. Accordingly, human judgments about causality will reflect this internal-external paradigm and result in a perceived dichotomy between the individual and the world. When a person feels like a situation is outside his or her control, he or she will feel a diminished sense of responsibility. For instance, if a typically punctual employee shows up at work late due to a random traffic jam, the tendency is to project causal responsibility outward. This external attribution of cause is referred to as *situational attribution*. On the other hand, if a person feels he or she has direct influence on the outcome of some event, the person is likely to feel a sense of responsibility. Studying hard for an exam, training diligently for a soccer match, and doing one's best to be a good parent all may be viewed as stemming from a person's internal characteristics. In such cases, people will describe their own efforts and personalities as the cause of their behaviors. Psychologists refer to this explanation as *dispositional attribution*.

3   ➡ While it is easy to attribute unexpected events to external forces, the line between a situational and dispositional attribution is often not so clear. Imagine a situation in which a person is seen engaged in a passionate dispute. If the person, or actor, is speaking in a raised voice or taking on an aggressive posture, a casual observer is likely to think the actor is prone to anger, or even naturally irrational or mean-spirited. Such an attribution often happens instantaneously without consideration for the overall framework in which the argument arose. The observer assumes that the observed behavior is the sole result of the actor's personality. This tendency for observers to emphasize the dispositional, as opposed to the situational, reasons for behavior is known as *correspondence bias*. Now imagine the same scenario from a first-person perspective. The actor may feel as if he or she has been the victim of some extreme injustice, and that his or her behavior is a justified reaction of self-defense. The discrepancy between how people interpret their own behavior and that of others is known as *actor-observer bias*.

4   ➡ A similar tendency, termed *self-serving bias*, can also be seen in the different reactions people have to their own positive and negative experiences. When individuals have a positive experience—for example, getting a promotion, publishing a book, or achieving goals—people view themselves as agents and are inclined to associate success with their own efforts. In contrast, when people undergo negative experiences, the bias is inverted, and they are likely to ascribe unsuccessful results to situational factors. Rather than assigning failure to personality faults, lack of ability, or insufficient effort, people magnify the factors outside their control. By mentally casting responsibility outward, people are able to blame the environment or others for their misfortunes and maintain the perception of themselves

Chapter 02 Vocabulary 71

as victims of circumstance.

5 ➡ Although psychologists still have a fragmentary understanding of attribution, they believe attributing causes helps people feel better by instilling a sense of optimism. Offering internal and external reasons for our behaviors allows us to emphasize our positive aspects, which can boost self-esteem and create favorable emotions, while justifying our negative characteristics, thus avoiding feelings of discouragement.

1 The word "postulates" in the passage is closest in meaning to

(A) proposes
(B) underlines
(C) instigates
(D) regulates

2 According to paragraph 2, what is NOT true about *dispositional attribution*?

(A) It is an explanation of why people feel no obligation to explain their actions.
(B) It is a phenomenon whereby people attribute outcomes to their personalities.
(C) It is an explanation of why people might feel a sense of responsibility.
(D) It is a phenomenon in which people credit results to their own efforts.

Paragraph 2 is marked with an arrow [➡].

3 The word "engaged" in the passage is closest in meaning to

(A) enlisted
(B) interested
(C) entrusted
(D) involved

4 According to paragraph 3, which of the following is true of *correspondence bias*?

(A) It describes the tendency to ignore the distinction between just and unjust behavior.
(B) It explains the inclination to take an overly aggressive stance in arguments.
(C) Its presence demonstrates inexperience in the realm of interpersonal relations.
(D) It indicates a failure to recognize the circumstances behind individual behavior.

Paragraph 3 is marked with an arrow [➡].

5   The word "magnify" in the passage is closest in meaning to

(A) clarify
(B) pacify
(C) identify
(D) amplify

6   According to paragraph 4, people demonstrate a *self-serving bias* when they

(A) blame situational factors for their negative experiences
(B) assign their lack of success to flaws in their personalities
(C) focus on the importance of personal effort in overcoming failure
(D) ignore the link between the environment and their problems

Paragraph 4 is marked with an arrow [➡].

7   The word "fragmentary" in the passage is closest in meaning to

(A) legitimate
(B) traditional
(C) incomplete
(D) naive

8   According to paragraph 5, which of the following do psychologists believe about attributing causes?

(A) It helps people cope with grief.
(B) It increases feelings of self-worth.
(C) It instills sentiments of negativity.
(D) It fosters unreasonable expectations.

Paragraph 5 is marked with an arrow [➡].

정답·해석·정답단서 p.281

VOCABULARY LIST

Chapter 02에서 선별한 다음의 토플 필수 어휘를 단어암기 음성파일을 들으며 암기한 후 퀴즈로 확인해보세요.

* 해커스 동영상강의 포털 해커스인강(HackersIngang.com)에서 단어암기 음성파일을 무료로 다운로드할 수 있습니다.

enhance [inhǽns] 높이다 (=upgrade)

overall [óuvərɔ̀:l] 전반적인 (=total)

ample [ǽmpl] 넓은 (=large)

acquire [əkwáiər] 획득하다 (=earn)

aridity [ərídəti] 건조함

severe [səvíər] 어려운 (=harsh)

reside [rizáid] 거주하다

expire [ikspáiər] 죽다

employ [implɔ́i] 쓰다 (=use)

convert [kənvə́:rt] 전환하다

typically [típikəli] 보통 (=usually)

detrimental [dètrəméntl] 해로운 (=harmful)

relocate [rì:loukéit] 이전시키다

relevant [réləvənt] 관련 있는 (=pertinent)

insignificant [ìnsignífikənt] 중요하지 않은

ascribe [əskráib] ~에 돌리다 (=refer)

generate [dʒénərèit] 발생시키다 (=produce)

manufacture [mæ̀njufǽktʃər] 제조하다 (=construct)

emerge [imə́:rdʒ] 드러나다 (=appear)

camouflage [kǽməflà:ʒ] 위장

inhabit [inhǽbit] 서식하다 (=live)

potential [pəténʃəl] 잠재적인 (=possible)

refrain [rifréin] 피하다

modify [mádəfài] 바꾸다 (=change)

similarly [símələrli] 비슷하게

avoid [əvɔ́id] 피하다 (=prevent)

disguise [disgáiz] 위장하다 (=conceal)

possess [pəzés] 소유하다

complex [kəmpléks] 복잡한 (=complicated)

craftsman [krǽftsmən] 장인

sacrifice [sǽkrəfàis] 희생

conduct [kəndʌ́kt] 수행하다

generally [dʒénərəli] 대체적으로 (=mainly)

utopian [ju:tóupiən] 이상향의

description [diskrípʃən] 묘사

in conjunction with ~와 함께

unilateral [jù:nəlǽtərəl] 일면적인

beneath [biní:θ] 아래의 (=below)

vast [væst] 굉장한 (=huge)

penetrate [pénətrèit] 통과하다 (=pierce)

immense [iméns] 막대한 (=enormous)

maneuver [mənú:vər] 이동하다 (=move)

aid [eid] 도움

observe [əbzə́:rv] 관찰하다 (=watch)

descent [disént] 내려감 (=falling)

ascent [əsént] 오름

determine [ditə́:rmin] 알아내다 (=figure)

accumulate [əkjú:mjulèit] 축적하다 (=collect)

entire [intáiər] 전체의 (=whole)

examine [igzǽmin] 관찰하다 (=inspect)

extraordinary [ikstrɔ́:rdənèri] 굉장한 (=exceptional)

in an instant 즉시

Quiz

각 단어의 알맞은 뜻을 찾아 연결하시오.

01 modify   ⓐ 통과하다
02 possess   ⓑ 바꾸다
03 penetrate   ⓒ 관찰하다
04 reside   ⓓ 드러나다
05 emerge   ⓔ 거주하다
     ⓕ 소유하다

각 단어의 알맞은 동의어를 찾아 연결하시오.

06 enhance   ⓐ earn
07 acquire   ⓑ use
08 manufacture   ⓒ conceal
09 disguise   ⓓ below
10 beneath   ⓔ upgrade
     ⓕ construct

01 ⓑ 02 ⓕ 03 ⓐ 04 ⓔ 05 ⓓ 06 ⓔ 07 ⓐ 08 ⓕ 09 ⓒ 10 ⓓ

indication[ìndikéiʃən] 징조

at first glance 얼핏 보기에

absence[ǽbsəns] 부재

lack[læk] 결핍

indicate[índikèit] 나타내다 (=imply)

detect[ditékt] 감지하다

remarkably[rimáːrkəbli] 매우

serve[səːrv] 역할을 하다

integral[íntigrəl] 없어서는 안 될

excite[iksáit] 자극하다 (=stimulate)

interpret[intəːrprit] 해석하다 (=explain)

peripheral[pərífərəl] 주변적인 (=exterior)

approximate[əpráksəmət] 대략의

notable[nóutəbl] 유명한 (=outstanding)

adjacent[ədʒéisnt] 가까운, 인접한

expand[ikspǽnd] 팽창하다 (=swell)

contract[kəntrǽkt] 수축하다

presence[prézns] 존재 (=existence)

previously[príːviəsli] 이전에

urge[əːrdʒ] 촉구하다

cautious[kɔ́ːʃəs] 조심하는 (=careful)

excuse[ikskjúːs] 핑계

justify[dʒʌ́stəfài] 정당화하다

postulate[pástʃulèit] 주장하다 (=claim)

presume[prizúːm] 추정하다

reflect[riflékt] 반영하다

perceive[pərsíːv] 지각하다 (=notice)

diminished[dimíniʃt] 감소된

punctual[pʌ́ŋktʃuəl] 시간을 잘 지키는

tendency[téndənsi] 경향 (=trend)

diligently[dílidʒəntli] 부지런히 (=industriously)

stem[stem] 비롯하다

engage[ingéidʒ] 참여하다

aggressive[əgrésiv] 공격적인 (=offensive)

posture[pástʃər] 자세

prone[proun] ~하기 쉬운 (=susceptible)

irrational[irǽʃənl] 비이성적인

instantaneously[ìnstəntéiniəsli] 즉시에

emphasize[émfəsàiz] 강조하다 (=stress)

perspective[pərspéktiv] 시점 (=view)

injustice[indʒʌ́stis] 불평등

discrepancy[diskrépənsi] 모순

incline[inkláin] ~하는 경향이 있다

associate[əsóuʃièit] 연관시키다

invert[invə́rt] 전도하다

ascribe[əskráib] 탓하다 (=attribute)

insufficient[ìnsəfíʃənt] 불충분한

magnify[mǽgnəfài] 확대하다

instill[instíl] 스며들다

boost[buːst] 돋우다 (=increase)

favorable[féivərəbl] 호의적인

discouragement[diskə́ːridʒmənt] 낙심

Quiz

각 단어의 알맞은 뜻을 찾아 연결하시오.

01 lack　　　　　ⓐ 팽창하다
02 excuse　　　　ⓑ 결핍
03 approximate　ⓒ 추정하다
04 detect　　　　ⓓ 핑계
05 expand　　　　ⓔ 감지하다
　　　　　　　　　ⓕ 대략의

각 단어의 알맞은 동의어를 찾아 연결하시오.

06 emphasize　ⓐ outstanding
07 indicate　　ⓑ stress
08 notable　　　ⓒ claim
09 postulate　　ⓓ offensive
10 aggressive　ⓔ imply
　　　　　　　　ⓕ attribute

ⓓ 01 ⓓ 02 ⓕ 03 ⓔ 04 ⓐ 05 ⓑ 06 ⓔ 07 ⓐ 08 ⓒ 09 ⓓ 10

CHAPTER **03**

Reference

Reference

Reference 문제는 지문에 음영 처리된 지시어가 가리키는 대상을 선택하는 유형이다. 지시어란, 글의 간결성과 응집성을 확보하기 위해 똑같은 단어를 반복해서 사용하지 않는 대신 사용된 대명사를 일컫는 말이다. Reference 문제는 한 지문당 1개가 출제되기도 하고 아예 출제되지 않기도 한다.

Reference 문제를 풀기 위해서는 지시어로 자주 쓰이는 여러 표현을 익히고, 문맥 속에서 문장의 의미를 정확히 이해하기 위해 그 지시어가 지칭하는 대상이 무엇인지 파악하는 연습을 해야 한다.

문제 살펴보기

Reference 문제는 지시어를 가리키는 대상을 파악해야 하는 지문과 질문에 음영으로 표시한다. 지시어 앞에 등장하는 4개의 단어 또는 구가 보기로 주어진다. 전형적인 질문 형태는 아래와 같다.

- The word "▢▢▢▢▢▢" in the passage refers to . . .
  지문의 단어 "▢▢▢▢"은 …을 가리킨다.
- The phrase "▢▢▢▢▢▢" in the passage refers to . . .
  지문의 구 "▢▢▢▢"은 …을 가리킨다.

▶ 문제 공략하기

다음은 Reference 문제의 공략법이다. 실전 고득점을 위해 이를 꼼꼼히 학습하고 Hackers Practice와 Hackers Test를 풀면서 반드시 적용해 본다.

1 문맥을 통해 지시 대상 추려내기

지시어 주변 문맥을 통해 지시대상을 역추적하여 보기에서 예상 답을 추려낸다. 지시어가 가리키는 대상을 지시대상이라고 하며 지시어보다 앞에 언급된다. 지시대상은 지시어와 같은 수, 의미 등을 가진다.

자주 출제되는 지시어

인칭대명사	it, its, they, their, them	부정대명사	some, others, one, another
지시대명사	this, that, these, those	관계대명사	who, which, that

2 문맥에 맞는 보기 찾기

지문에서 찾은 지시대상을 지시어 문장에 대입하여 문맥에 맞는 보기가 정답이다.

Since amphibian eggs have a soft coating but no hard shell, they are vulnerable to ultraviolet rays and tend to hatch prematurely or result in offspring with poor immune systems. Additionally, as cold-blooded creatures, (frogs) are affected by thinning ozone because they must use sunlight to regulate their body temperatures.

The word "their" in the passage refers to

(A) rays
(B) systems
(C) creatures
(D) frogs

지문해석 p.285

1 음영 처리된 지시어 their 주변 문맥을 살펴보면, regulate their body temperatures 그들의 체온을 조절한다)라고 언급되어 their의 지시대상은 생물임을 알 수 있다. 생물을 나타내는 보기 (C), (D)를 예상 답으로 추려낸다.

2 their에 frogs를 대입해보면 '개구리는 체온을 조절하기 위해 햇빛을 사용해야 하기 때문에 얇아지는 오존층의 영향을 받는다'가 되어 문맥에 맞으므로 보기 (D)가 정답이다.

지문을 읽고 물음에 답하시오.

01

> By the seventh century BC, Greeks had learned the art of carving stone from the Egyptians and were making statues from marble, known as kouroi. These life-size sculptures depicted nude, male youths with fists at their sides and left foot put forward.

The word "their" in the passage refers to

(A) Egyptians

(B) sculptures

(C) youths

02

> Trout are a popular food and game fish that belong to the salmon family. Although most are known to live entirely in fresh waters and streams, several varieties, known as sea trout, enter the ocean when they are about a year old and return upstream to spawn in their original freshwater habitats about two to five years later.

The word "most" in the passage refers to

(A) trout

(B) game fish

(C) salmon family

03

> Rare minerals, such as gemstones, have great commercial value due to their beauty and limited supply. Since the demand for gemstones is high but their availability is finite, exploration companies must work diligently to find new deposits before their competitors. The most successful of them draw upon a wide array of elaborate technologies to aid in their quest.

The word "them" in the passage refers to

(A) companies

(B) deposits

(C) competitors

---

01 **marble**[máːrbl] 대리석 **life-size**[láifsàiz] 실물 크기의

02 **trout**[traut] 송어 **game fish** 낚싯고기 **spawn**[spɔːn] 산란하다

03 **gemstone**[dʒémstòun] 원석 **finite**[fáinɑit] 제한된 **diligently**[díləgʒəntli] 부지런히 **deposit**[dipázit] 매장물
   elaborate[ilǽbərət] 정밀한

04

> Tornadoes are violent and destructive windstorms that occur more frequently in the United States than in any other country. Striking predominantly in Tornado Alley, a stretch of land from Texas to North Dakota, twisters are powerful enough to toss vehicles into the air and collapse structures. They average about sixty meters in diameter, but can stretch as far as 1.6 kilometers wide.

The word "They" in the passage refers to

(A) twisters
(B) vehicles
(C) structures

05

> Bat parasites are organisms that primarily feed off of bat blood but will bite humans, birds, and rodents if the usual hosts are unavailable. The places most likely to be infested are the roosting sites of bats. Some are located in attics, unused chimneys, and empty wall spaces. If these sites are destroyed, the parasites will seek other food sources.

The word "Some" in the passage refers to

(A) hosts
(B) roosting sites
(C) bats

06

> The first electric form of communication was the telegraph, a simple machine developed in 1828 by Harrison Dyar, which sent electrical sparks through wires that would burn a series of dots and dashes on chemically treated paper. These dots and dashes were a basic code that could be translated into a message. Later, in 1837, Samuel F. B. Morse created and patented a new telegraph which used electromagnetism rather than common electricity.

The word "which" in the passage refers to

(A) form
(B) communication
(C) telegraph

04 destructive[distrʌ́ktiv] 파괴적인 collapse[kəlǽps] 무너뜨리다 diameter[daiǽmətər] 지름
05 parasite[pǽrəsàit] 기생충 host[houst] 숙주 infest[infést] 창궐하다 roost[ruːst] 보금자리에 들다
06 code[koud] 부호 patent[pǽtnt] ~의 특허를 얻다 electromagnetism[ilèktroumǽgnətizm] 전자기

07

A free market economy has always existed in practice where people have exchanged goods or services without government intervention, but it was in the eighteenth century when free market ideology first became a part of political theory. Based closely on the French slogan *laissez-faire*, which means "allow to do," it was centered on the belief that governments should not attempt to control markets, but allow buyers and sellers to determine prices on their own.

The word "it" in the passage refers to

(A) government intervention

(B) free market ideology

(C) political theory

(D) *laissez-faire*

08

Considered one of the most intelligent animals on Earth, dolphins are studied to determine the nature of their mental abilities. Researchers are drawn to this marine mammal because it engages in behaviors that appear to have no clear purpose—leaping above the water surface in an acrobatic spin, for example. Scientists do not know if this is functional or for recreational enjoyment. Another unusual behavior is the dolphin's tendency to act in a social way toward other living beings. They often interact playfully with human swimmers in the ocean or in a pool.

The word "this" in the passage refers to

(A) marine mammal

(B) purpose

(C) water surface

(D) acrobatic spin

---

07 intervention[ìntərvénʃən] 간섭 determine[ditɔ́ːrmin] 결정하다
08 mental[méntl] 지적인 mammal[mǽməl] 포유동물 leap[liːp] 뛰어오르다 acrobatic[æ̀krəbǽtik] 곡예의
tendency[téndənsi] 성향 interact[ìntərǽkt] 상호작용하다

82 토플 인강·단어암기 MP3 HackersIngang.com

09

Infants are quick to distinguish their mothers' voices from the voices of other people. This was determined in a 1980 study conducted by developmental psychologists DeCasper and Fifer, who observed that an infant's response to familiar and unfamiliar voices is, in fact, learned even before birth. Canadian nursing professor Dr. Barbara Kisilevsky reached this conclusion in 2003 after testing how fetuses responded to an audiotape of their own mother reading a poem and another of a female stranger reading the same poem. Their heart rates accelerated faster when they heard their mothers' voices, indicating their ability to differentiate between the two.

The word "another" in the passage refers to

(A) response

(B) audiotape

(C) mother

(D) poem

10

Whereas the arctic tundra encircles the North Pole and extends to the coniferous forests of the upper northern latitudes, the alpine tundra may be found all around the world in areas of high altitudes. Both are characterized by harsh conditions: the arctic tundra is cold and desert-like; the alpine is dry and windy. Surprisingly, a large variety of animals is able to survive in both types of tundra, developing additional layers of fat to do so. Hundreds of kinds of plants also thrive in the tundra, but none are taller than a few feet.

The word "none" in the passage refers to

(A) animals

(B) layers

(C) kinds

(D) plants

---

09 quick[kwik] 영리한 fetus[fíːtəs] 태아 accelerate[æksélərèit] 가속하다 differentiate[dìfərénʃieit] 구분하다

10 arctic[áːrtik] 북극의 encircle[insə́ːrkl] 둘러싸다 coniferous[kounífərəs] 침엽수의 latitude[lǽtətjùːd] 위도
   alpine[ǽlpain] 고산성의 altitude[ǽltətjùːd] 고도 thrive[θraiv] 잘 자라다

지문을 읽고 물음에 답하시오.

11

The Tang Dynasty was influential in spreading Chinese traditions throughout the Far East, particularly in Japan, Korea, and Vietnam. Inspired by the empire's wealth and power, neighboring countries began to study and borrow cultural elements in the hopes of using them to their own advantage. For example, literary Chinese and its script became the language of government used by elites in all three countries. In the religious sphere, Buddhist beliefs and practices based on Indian texts and mixed with Chinese native philosophies, which included Taoism, were also imported. In addition, Confucian thought and values became the prevailing social and political force in the region.

1. The word "them" in the passage refers to

   (A) traditions
   (B) neighboring countries
   (C) cultural elements
   (D) hopes

2. The word "which" in the passage refers to

   (A) beliefs
   (B) practices
   (C) texts
   (D) philosophies

---

11 dynasty[dáinəsti] 왕조 inspire[inspáiər] 고취하다 element[éləmənt] 요소 literary[lítərèri] 문어의
elite[ilíːt] 최상류층 사람들 text[tekst] 원본 philosophy[filásəfi] 철학 Taoism[táuizm] 도교 Confucian[kənfjúːʃən] 공자의
prevailing[privéiliŋ] 지배적인

12

The first paintings were murals. Murals could not be detached, but later, the technique of painting on panels was developed. Panel paintings were done on single pieces of wood or thin strips that were pieced together. These creations were portable and could thus be easily moved. In the fourteenth century, painters began using canvases. Made of fabric, canvases were lightweight, so they were easy to work with and transport. The surface of canvases held paint much better than did wood, and it was not prone to warping and cracking. However, the woven fabric affected the texture of the painting in a way that Renaissance artists disliked. Therefore, they went to great lengths to smooth the surface of the painting so that it had a glossy finish, much like that of a photograph.

1. The phrase "These creations" in the passage refers to

   (A) murals

   (B) panel paintings

   (C) pieces of wood

   (D) thin strips

2. The word "it" in the passage refers to

   (A) fabric

   (B) surface

   (C) paint

   (D) wood

12 mural[mjúərəl] 벽화   detach[ditǽtʃ] 떼어내다   panel[pǽnl] 패널(캔버스 대용의 화판)   strip[strip] 가느다란 조각
portable[pɔ́ːrtəbl] 들고 다닐 수 있는   warp[wɔːrp] 휘다   go to great lengths 모든 노력을 다하다   finish[fíniʃ] 윤내기

13

A timberline is the line or elevation at which trees are unable to grow on mountains. From a distance, these tree lines may appear easily distinguishable, but upon closer examination, observers can clearly discern that the transitions are actually gradual. Trees closer to the line are shorter or even stunted, and those closest to the line look like clumps of bushes. Environmental conditions such as temperature, amount of sunlight, the direction of the wind, air pressure, and absence of moisture determine the location of the upper and lower timberlines. However, some mountains are not uniformly subject to the same conditions. One side of a mountain may have greater exposure to sunlight and thus have a higher timberline; the one in the shaded area will be lower.

1. The word "those" in the passage refers to

   (A) tree lines
   (B) observers
   (C) transitions
   (D) trees

2. The word "one" in the passage refers to

   (A) side
   (B) mountain
   (C) exposure
   (D) timberline

---

13 **timberline**[tímbərlàin] 수목한계선(=tree line) **elevation**[èləvéiʃən] 고도 **discern**[disə́ːrn] 알아보다
transition[trænzíʃən] 변화 **gradual**[grǽdʒuəl] 점진적인 **stunted**[stʌ́ntid] 왜소한 **clump**[klʌmp] 덤불
uniformly[júːnəfɔ̀ːrmli] 동일하게

14

In 1808, US Secretary of the Treasury Albert Gallatin recommended that the government provide funds for the construction of roads and other transport systems across the nation, but the proposition failed to get enough votes in Congress. It was not until the War of 1812 with Britain that officials realized the country was in desperate need of roads. Troops stationed in the West were needed at the battlefront, but because of the lack of adequate transportation networks, military leaders found moving them to be a painfully slow process. A solution came in the form of privately built roadways called turnpikes, which were maintained by private companies hoping to earn big profits by charging a toll for their use. These early toll roads, often established along stagecoach routes, were predecessors to modern highways and interstate systems, and most were eventually taken over by state highway departments in the twentieth century.

1. The word "their" in the passage refers to

(A) leaders

(B) turnpikes

(C) companies

(D) profits

2. The word "most" in the passage refers to

(A) toll roads

(B) stagecoach routes

(C) modern highways

(D) interstate systems

정답·해석·정답단서 p.285

14 the Treasury 재무부 proposition[prɑ̀pəzíʃən] 제안 Congress[kɑ́ŋgris] 의회 station[stéiʃən] 배치하다
battlefront[bǽtlfrʌ̀nt] 최전선 roadway[róudwèi] 도로 부지 turnpike[tə́ːrnpàik] 유료 고속도로 toll[toul] 요금
stagecoach[stéidʒkòutʃ] 역마차 predecessor[prédəsèsər] 전형 interstate[ìntərstéit] 주간의

CH 1
CH 2
CHAPTER 3
CH 4
CH 5
CH 6
CH 7
CH 8
CH 9

Hackers TOEFL Reading Intermediate

Hackers Test

1 Avian Navigation

1   Some birds are permanent residents and either have adapted to survival in winter habitats or inhabit areas where temperatures are relatively stable, such as near the equator. Nonetheless, many bird species living in seasonally inhospitable environments are seasonal residents. As winter is often the most challenging time for birds to access indispensable needs like food, shelter, and water, many escape the conditions by migrating to more suitable habitats as the days become shorter and temperatures drop in autumn. Interestingly, migratory birds often return to the same nesting grounds year after year and follow similar navigational paths to their winter homes.

2   Scientists have proposed two interrelated hypotheses for how this navigation may be achieved. The first is the theory that birds have internal star compasses. According to the theory, birds use the locations and spacing of stars, as well as their regular movements, to determine direction. Experimenting with indigo buntings in the 1970s, American ornithologist Stephen Emlen used a planetarium to simulate the night sky. Emlen put the birds in funnel-shaped cages so that the only visible direction was up. At the bottom of the cages he placed a wet ink pad and covered the walls with paper. By later removing and studying the paper, Emlen was able to trace the movements of the birds within the enclosures and confirm that the buntings altered their courses consistently in relation to the movement of stars.

3   ➡ Complicating this theory, however, is the fact that birds continue to navigate effectively at night under cloud cover, when no stars are clearly visible. Magnetic-compass theory, which asserts birds use magnetic fields to determine their location, is an attempt to explain how birds can continue to navigate without visual clues. Recent research indicates that birds have minute quantities of iron oxides in their heads and beaks. These magnetic crystals align north like needles of a compass regardless of changes in a bird's orientation, giving birds a constant flow of directional information to the brain.

4   In studying how birds navigate, scientists also unwittingly received cues about the inclination of birds to migrate. When nocturnal migrants were kept in cages at night, they demonstrated restless behavior, as if they were involuntarily being pulled in their normal migratory direction. Ornithologists refer to this migration stimulus of birds as *zugunruhe*, a term derived from the German roots meaning migration and anxiety. It is believed that birds have an innate impulse to migrate, which is universal among bird species, though much subdued in non-migratory populations.

1 The word "inhospitable" in the passage is closest in meaning to

(A) unfavorable

(B) indeterminate

(C) unremarkable

(D) incessant

2 The word "many" in the passage refers to

(A) environments

(B) residents

(C) birds

(D) needs

3 According to paragraph 3, iron oxides in the heads and beaks of birds enable them to

(A) determine when magnetic fields are optimal for migrating

(B) realign their flight directions in relation to the stars

(C) tell which way is north no matter what direction they are facing

(D) resume navigation routes after cloud cover has cleared

Paragraph 3 is marked with an arrow [➡].

4 The word "which" in the passage refers to

(A) behavior

(B) migration

(C) anxiety

(D) impulse

2 Population in Europe: The Great Transformation Sociology

1 ➡ Throughout the early modern period, Europe underwent demographic cycles, which included population upswings fostered by favorable political and economic conditions, and mortality crises triggered by harvest failures, disease, and war. These short-term variations in mortality rates created great panic among Europe's inhabitants. In his introduction to *The Decameron*, a medieval work on the Black Plague, the Italian writer Boccaccio described a chaotic scene in which the citizens of Florence thought the end of the world was near. Believing they would all die soon and that the plague-related deaths were of divine origin, people cared nothing of laws, or even of rites of mourning, and began living every day as if it were their last.

2 Such dismal images can be found throughout European literature of the fourteenth century, a period ravaged by plague and severe population decline. Similar circumstances returned in the seventeenth century: Europe endured a resurgence of plague, and extensive wars devastated lives, damaged agricultural industries, and interrupted transportation networks. Some of the most severe endured for several decades. As a result of these difficulties, the population of Europe managed only to gradually increase during the period 1300-1800. This cyclical demographic pattern, with its extreme swings, along with associated fears about population subsistence crises, came to an end in the nineteenth century. Between 1800 and 1914, Europe witnessed a dramatic rise in population, from 188 to 458 million.

3 ➡ Historians refer to this period as *the Great Transformation*, a span in which the prior demographic network transitioned into a modern form, marked by a decreased average mortality rate combined with a steady fertility rate. For hundreds of years, the average life expectancy for a European had been less than forty years, but the number began to rise as major improvements in agricultural production were implemented. Better tools, widespread use of machinery, and selection of productive seed varieties all contributed to greater yields for farmers, which could then be distributed to offset famines. These developments, along with the introduction of new crops from the Americas, led to diversification of the European diet and more balanced nutrition. In addition, enhanced medical knowledge toward the end of the nineteenth century factored into extending lives and reducing infant mortality. Biological research revealed the relationship of carriers to contagious diseases (e.g. lice for typhus, mosquitoes for malaria, and humans for tuberculosis), as well as a better understanding of contagion and the need to isolate infected people.

4 Overall, most European countries saw a fifteen- to twenty-year rise in life expectancy at birth during the nineteenth century. In contrast, fertility rates during the period declined, in part due to an unlikely source. Despite his objection to contraception, English demographer Thomas Malthus indirectly gave rise to a movement for birth control with his 1798 paper, *An Essay on the Principle of Population*. In it, Malthus blamed overpopulation for threatening the world's resources—a complete reversal of the views of earlier writers, who, like Boccaccio, painted visions of catastrophe not from overpopulation, but *under* population. Later advocates of birth control would

draw on the Malthusian hypothesis to promote voluntary contraception, a practice that had been traditionally exercised only by isolated communities or individual families. Their work eventually paid off. Between 1870 and 1910, people began to increasingly invoke personal choice on when and whether to have children, and consequently, the average female fertility rate decreased by thirty percent in a matter of decades.

5   ➡ The combination of longer life spans and fewer births has become the standard in modern industrialized Europe. With the exception of the period involving the two World Wars, the twentieth century saw continual medical advances, improved nutrition, and ever-declining birth rates in Europe. In the first decade of the twenty-first century, the population of Europe experienced negative natural growth for the first time in the modern era. In a period of relative peace and stability on the continent, fertility rates actually dipped below death rates. Legal changes during the decade, including widespread access to abortion, also contributed to the demographic shift. Negative natural growth is expected to continue indefinitely. The population of Europe was around 728 million in 2005; the United Nations Population Division projects that the figure will dip below 665 million by 2050.

1   According to paragraph 1, how did people respond to mortality from plague?

(A) They abandoned their homes.

(B) They took refuge in religious establishments.

(C) They lost all concern for legal norms.

(D) They performed mass funerals.

Paragraph 1 is marked with an arrow [➡].

2   The word "their" in the passage refers to

(A) deaths

(B) people

(C) laws

(D) rites

3   The word "Some" in the passage refers to

(A) wars

(B) lives

(C) industries

(D) networks

4 According to paragraph 3, all of the following contributed to the population incline in Europe EXCEPT

(A) innovations in agriculture

(B) advances in medical science

(C) increased fertility rates

(D) reduced mortality rates

Paragraph 3 is marked with an arrow [➡].

5 The word "which" in the passage refers to

(A) tools

(B) varieties

(C) yields

(D) farmers

6 The phrase "gave rise to" in the passage is closest in meaning to

(A) spawned

(B) created dissent in

(C) reinstated

(D) shed light on

7 The phrase "a practice" in the passage refers to

(A) overpopulation

(B) thinking

(C) promotion

(D) contraception

8 According to paragraph 5, which of the following is true about negative natural population growth in Europe?

(A) It reversed in times of war and instability.

(B) It occurred after the twentieth century.

(C) It stimulated labor shortage concerns.

(D) It caused changes in the legal system.

Paragraph 5 is marked with an arrow [➡].

⧉ Brazilian Independence (History)

1   In 1500, Portuguese explorer Pedro Álvares Cabral landed in Brazil and claimed the territory as part of the Portuguese empire. Over the next few hundred years, Portuguese migrated to their new colony and established settlements using indigenous and African slave labor. By the early 1800s, the native people of Brazil represented only around five percent of the total population. Thus, it was Portuguese colonists themselves who played the primary role in creating a sense of independent national identity in Brazil, and ultimately a new nation.

2   Indeed, the first emperor of Brazil, Dom Pedro I, was born in Portugal. His 1822 independence speech "O Grito do Iparanga," given on horseback to cavalry troops during a military exercise, has become symbolic of the Brazilian independence movement, which succeeded with comparatively little bloodshed. Some minor battles did occur, but independence came to Brazil largely through economic and political channels. Many of the economic and political foundations for Brazilian independence were laid by Dom Pedro's father, Dom Joao, who was prince and heir to the Portuguese throne.

3   The first major boost for the independence of Brazil came in 1808 when France, led by Napoleon, invaded via Spain, and the entire royal court of Portugal was forced to flee the kingdom. The government relocated to its South American colony, transferring Portugal's capital from Lisbon, in Portugal, to Rio de Janeiro, in Brazil. When the Portuguese officials arrived, they found a colony with immense natural resources but with only rudimentary economic and industrial infrastructure. Witnessing the poor state of the colony, the new government under Dom Joao embarked upon an ambitious development project in Brazil.

4   ➡ Over the next thirteen years, the Portuguese initiated a number of infrastructural improvements. Roads were built, ports widened, and banks established—developments essential to promoting commercial activities. Other additions included a botanical garden, a national library, a naval academy, and a national museum, all of which were located in Rio de Janeiro. Elaborate colonial architecture was also constructed, complete with paintings and sculptures. These infrastructure upgrades contributed significantly to the power and prestige of Brazil in the Americas, as well as in the Portuguese empire. They were also very influential in creating a sense of Brazilian nationality among the colonists living in Brazil.

5   ➡ After the defeat of Napoleon in Europe, however, pressure mounted from elites in Portugal to move the power base back to Lisbon, which led to a series of events that further catalyzed the Brazilian independence movement. In 1815, the same year of Napoleon's defeat, Dom Joao elevated Brazil's status to kingdom, putting it politically on par with Portugal. He was then named ruler of Portugal in 1816, but chose to remain in Brazil. Dom Joao's decision met with disapproval among some Portuguese. Since the populace of Brazil was mixed between natives, African Americans, and descendants of Europeans, people living in Portugal still viewed Brazil merely as a colony, an inferior people to be exploited for the gain of the empire. Such attitudes offended many of the people living in Brazil and created revolutionary ideas among some local political and intellectual leaders. In 1821, loyalists who were committed to Lisbon confronted Dom Joao and demanded that he relocate to Portugal if he wanted to remain king. Reluctant to give up his crown, Dom Joao consented and went to Lisbon. He

left behind his son, Dom Pedro, to serve as regent in Brazil.

6 → Following Dom Joao's return, Lisbon aggressively sought to restore Brazil's status as a colony even though Rio de Janeiro had ruled the Portuguese empire since 1808. The *Cortes Gerais*, Portugal's parliamentary assembly, approved a measure to reestablish monopoly control over Brazilian trade. It wanted to officially restore Lisbon's direct authority over Brazil and undermine the growing independence movement. As part of the plan, the assembly ordered Dom Pedro to return to Portugal; yet nationalists who supported independence encouraged him to resist Lisbon's demands, and on January 9, 1822, Dom Pedro formally declared his plans to stay in Brazil. In September of the same year, when Lisbon sent Dom Pedro orders curtailing his power, Dom Pedro announced Brazil's independence and gave himself the title of emperor. After a brief period of denial, Portugal recognized Brazil's independence in 1825.

1 The word "which" in the passage refers to

(A) independence speech

(B) cavalry troops

(C) military exercise

(D) independence movement

2 The phrase "the kingdom" in the passage refers to

(A) Brazil

(B) France

(C) Spain

(D) Portugal

3 The word "immense" in the passage is closest in meaning to

(A) miscellaneous

(B) luminous

(C) scant

(D) vast

4   The word "all" in the passage refers to

    (A) additions
    (B) developments
    (C) activities
    (D) improvements

5   According to paragraph 4, all of the following were improvements made to Brazil's infrastructure EXCEPT

    (A) the construction of manufacturing centers
    (B) the expansion of harbors
    (C) the addition of elaborate architecture
    (D) the establishment of financial institutions

    Paragraph 4 is marked with an arrow [➡].

6   According to paragraph 5, which of the following contributed to the rise of revolutionary ideas in Brazil?

    (A) Napoleon's exile from Europe
    (B) Dom Joao's refusal to remain in Brazil
    (C) Political conflict over royal succession in Portugal
    (D) Discriminative attitudes in Portugal toward Brazil

    Paragraph 5 is marked with an arrow [➡].

7   The word "It" in the passage refers to

    (A) Portuguese empire
    (B) *Cortes Gerais*
    (C) monopoly control
    (D) Brazilian trade

8   According to paragraph 6, which of the following is true of Brazilian independence?

    (A) It led to the creation of a parliamentary assembly.
    (B) It was supported by the majority of Brazilians.
    (C) It was officially acknowledged by Lisbon in the end.
    (D) It caused turmoil between Dom Pedro and Dom Joao.

    Paragraph 6 is marked with an arrow [➡].

정답·해석·정답단서 p.287

CH 1
CH 2
CHAPTER 3
CH 4
CH 5
CH 6
CH 7
CH 8
CH 9

Hackers TOEFL Reading Intermediate

VOCABULARY LIST

Chapter 03에서 선별한 다음의 토플 필수 어휘를 단어암기 음성파일을 들으며 암기한 후 퀴즈로 확인해보세요.

*해커스 동영상강의 포털 해커스인강(HackersIngang.com)에서 단어암기 음성파일을 무료로 다운로드할 수 있습니다.

finite[fáinɑit] 제한된

diligently[dílədʒəntli] 부지런히 (=industriously)

elaborate[ilǽbərət] 정밀한 (=intricate)

destructive[distrʌ́ktiv] 파괴적인

collapse[kəlǽps] 무너뜨리다

infest[infést] 창궐하다

patent[pǽtnt] ~의 특허를 얻다

intervention[intərvénʃən] 간섭 (=influence)

mental[méntl] 지적인

leap[li:p] 뛰어오르다

interact[intərǽkt] 상호작용하다

accelerate[æksélərèit] 가속하다 (=hasten)

differentiate[dìfərénʃieit] 구분하다 (=distinguish)

encircle[insə́ːrkl] 둘러싸다

thrive[θraiv] 잘 자라다 (=prosper)

inspire[inspáiər] 고취하다 (=motivate)

detach[ditǽtʃ] 떼어내다 (=separate)

portable[pɔ́ːrtəbl] 들고 다닐 수 있는

discern[disə́ːrn] 알아보다

transition[trænzíʃən] 변화 (=alteration)

gradual[grǽdʒuəl] 점진적인

station[stéiʃən] 배치하다

stable[stéibl] 고정적인 (=constant)

seasonally[síːzənli] 계절적으로

inhospitable[inhɑ́spitəbl] 황폐한 (=desolate)

indispensable[ìndispénsəbl] 필수적인

escape[iskéip] 벗어나다 (=avoid)

migrate[máigreit] 이동하다 (=travel)

suitable[súːtəbl] 적절한 (=appropriate)

propose[prəpóuz] 제안하다 (=proffer)

interrelated[ìntərriléitid] 관련된

hypothesis[hɑipáθəsis] 가설

simulate[símjulèit] 만들다 (=imitate)

visible[vízəbl] 보이는

enclosure[inklóuʒər] 가두기

confirm[kənfə́ːrm] 확인하다

alter[ɔ́ːltər] 변경하다 (=modify)

consistently[kənsístəntli] 끊임없이

complicate[kámpləkèit] 복잡하게 하다

assert[əsə́ːrt] 주장하다 (=claim)

align[əláin] 정렬시키다

unwittingly[ʌnwítiŋli] 우연히 (=unintentionally)

inclination[ìnklənéiʃən] 경향 (=preference)

nocturnal[nɑktə́ːrnl] 야행성의 (=active at night)

involuntarily[inváləntèrəli] 무의식적으로

stimulus[stímjuləs] 자극 (=motivation)

term[təːrm] 용어

derive[diráiv] 파생하다 (=originate)

innate[inéit] 선천적인 (=natural)

impulse[ímpʌls] 충동

subdued[səbdʒúːd] 완화된 (=reduced)

demographic[dìːməgrǽfik] 인구의

Quiz

각 단어의 알맞은 뜻을 찾아 연결하시오.

01 interact	ⓐ 상호작용하다
02 station	ⓑ 뛰어오르다
03 interrelated	ⓒ 가설
04 term	ⓓ 배치하다
05 leap	ⓔ 용어
	ⓕ 관련된

각 단어의 알맞은 동의어를 찾아 연결하시오.

06 diligently	ⓐ hasten
07 accelerate	ⓑ imitate
08 stable	ⓒ industriously
09 simulate	ⓓ preference
10 inclination	ⓔ constant
	ⓕ intricate

01 ⓐ 02 ⓓ 03 ⓕ 04 ⓔ 05 ⓑ 06 ⓒ 07 ⓐ 08 ⓔ 09 ⓑ 10 ⓓ

upswing [ʌ́pswìŋ] 증가

foster [fɔ́:stər] 촉진하다

mortality [mɔːrtǽləti] 사망률

divine [diváin] 신성의

rite [rait] 의식

mourn [mɔːrn] 애도하다

dismal [dízməl] 음울한

ravage [rǽvidʒ] 황폐화하다

resurgence [risə́:rdʒəns] 부활

devastate [dévəstèit] 유린하다

subsistence [səbsístəns] 생존 (=survival)

implement [ímpləmənt] 이행하다

offset [ɔ́:fsèt] 상쇄하다 (=balance)

diversification [divə̀:rsəfikéiʃən] 다양화

factor in ~을 요인의 하나로 넣다

contagious [kəntéidʒəs] 전염성의 (=communicable)

isolate [áisəlèit] 격리하다 (=segregate)

infected [inféktid] 감염된

unlikely [ʌ̀nláikli] 믿기 어려운

objection [əbdʒékʃən] 반대

indirectly [ìndəréktli] 간접적으로

give rise to 발생하게 하다

reversal [rivə́:rsəl] 반대

advocate [ǽdvəkèit] 지지자

promote [prəmóut] 장려하다

voluntary [váləntèri] 자발적인

exception [iksépʃən] 예외 (=exclusion)

stability [stəbíləti] 안정

dip [dip] 내려가다

legal [lí:gəl] 법적의

indefinitely [indéfənitli] 무기한으로

indigenous [indídʒənəs] 토착의 (=aboriginal)

primary [práimeri] 주요한

ultimately [ʌ́ltmətli] 결국 (=eventually)

indeed [indí:d] 실제로 (=in fact)

independence [ìndipéndəns] 독립

symbolic [simbálik] 상징적인

comparatively [kəmpǽrətivli] 상대적으로 (=relatively)

flee [fli:] 도망하다 (=evade)

witness [wítnis] 목격하다

embark [imbá:rk] 시작하다

ambitious [æmbíʃəs] 야심적인

initiate [iníʃièit] 시작하다 (=originate)

contribute [kəntríbju:t] 기여하다

influential [ìnfluénʃəl] 영향력 있는 (=potent)

defeat [difí:t] 패배시키다

disapproval [dìsəprú:vəl] 반대

offend [əfénd] 감정이 상하다

restore [ristɔ́:r] 복원하다

resist [rizíst] 저항하다 (=withstand)

declare [diklɛ́ər] 공표하다

denial [dináiəl] 부인

Quiz

각 단어의 알맞은 뜻을 찾아 연결하시오.

01 ambitious   ⓐ 도망하다
02 objection   ⓑ 야심적인
03 flee   ⓒ 이행하다
04 declare   ⓓ 반대
05 implement   ⓔ 부활
     ⓕ 공표하다

각 단어의 알맞은 동의어를 찾아 연결하시오.

06 exception   ⓐ exclusion
07 ultimately   ⓑ aboriginal
08 indigenous   ⓒ relatively
09 initiate   ⓓ segregate
10 isolate   ⓔ originate
     ⓕ eventually

ⓓ 01 ⓓ 02 ⓐ 03 ⓕ 04 ⓒ 05 ⓔ 06 ⓕ 07 ⓑ 08 ⓔ 09 ⓓ 10

CHAPTER 04

Sentence Simplification

CHAPTER 04
Sentence Simplification

Sentence Simplification 문제는 지문에 음영 처리된 문장의 핵심 정보를 간결하게 가장 잘 바꾸어 쓴 문장을 선택하는 유형이다. Simplification이란, 주어진 문장에서 부가 정보를 제외한 핵심 정보를 추려내어 간략하게 바꾸어 쓰는(paraphrase) 것을 의미한다. Sentence Simplification 문제는 한 지문당 1개가 출제되기도 하고 아예 출제되지 않기도 한다.

Sentence Simplification 문제를 풀기 위해서는 주어진 문장의 핵심 정보를 정확하게 이해하고 이와 같은 뜻으로 간략하게 바꾸어 쓴 문장을 파악하는 연습을 해야 한다.

▶ 문제 살펴보기

Sentence Simplification 문제는 간략화해야 할 문장을 지문에 음영으로 표시한다. 음영 처리된 문장을 재진술한 문장 4개가 보기로 주어진다. 전형적인 질문 형태는 아래와 같다.

- **Which of the sentences below best expresses the essential information in the highlighted sentence in the passage?** *Incorrect* **choices change the meaning in important ways or leave out essential information.**
  아래 문장 중 어떤 것이 지문 속의 음영된 문장의 핵심 정보를 가장 잘 표현하고 있는가? 오답은 문장의 의미를 현저히 왜곡하거나 핵심 정보를 빠뜨리고 있다.

CHAPTER 4

CH 1
CH 2
CH 3
CH 5
CH 6
CH 7
CH 8
CH 9

Hackers TOEFL Reading Intermediate

문제 공략하기

다음은 Sentence Simplification 문제의 공략법이다. 실전 고득점을 위해 이를 꼼꼼히 학습하고 Hackers Practice와 Hackers Test를 풀면서 반드시 적용해 본다.

1 핵심 정보 추려내기

음영 처리된 문장에서 가장 중요한 내용으로 생각되는 부분을 핵심 정보로 추려낸다. 동격이나 예시와 같이 추가적이거나 세부적인 내용은 부가 정보이므로 제외한다.

2 핵심 정보를 간략화한 보기 찾기

핵심 정보는 그대로 살리되 문장 구조를 바꾸거나 비슷한 단어나 구를 사용하여 원래 문장을 간략하게 바꾸어 쓴 보기가 정답이다.

Perhaps the most overwhelming contributor to amphibian decline, however, is global climate change. The thinning of the ozone layer, a stratum of particles in the atmosphere that shields the Earth from the sun's rays, is particularly harmful to amphibians. Since amphibian eggs have a soft coating but no hard shell, they are vulnerable to ultraviolet rays and tend to hatch prematurely or result in offspring with poor immune systems.

Which of the sentences below best expresses the essential information in the highlighted sentence in the passage? *Incorrect* choices change the meaning in important ways or leave out essential information.

(A) Atmospheric ozone depletion is especially detrimental to amphibians.

(B) Amphibians are particularly harmed by direct exposure to sunlight.

(C) The ozone layer protects the Earth's organisms from the sun's rays.

(D) The ozone layer, which shields the Earth from the sun's rays, is thinning.

지문해석 p.291

1 음영 처리된 문장의 핵심 정보는 [1]The thinning of the ozone layer(오존층이 얇아지는 것)와 [2]is particularly harmful to amphibians(특히 양서류에게 유해하다)이다.

2 핵심 정보 [1]The thinning of the ozone layer를 Atmospheric ozone depletion(대기의 오존 고갈)으로, 핵심 정보 [2]is particularly harmful to amphibians를 is especially detrimental to amphibians(특히 양서류에게 유해하다)로 간략하게 바꾸어 쓴 보기 (A)가 정답이다.

TIP 음영 처리된 문장의 의미를 현저히 바꾸거나 핵심 정보를 빠뜨린 보기는 오답이다.

Hackers Practice

주어진 문장을 바르게 간략화한 문장을 고르시오.

01

> In 1662, even though he only had access to rudimentary technological equipment by today's standards, Irish physicist Robert Boyle discovered that if gases are kept under constant temperatures, the relationship between gas pressure and volume is inversely proportional.

(A) Experiments with gases conducted by Irish physicist Robert Boyle revealed the pressure of gas as being reciprocally proportionate to gas volume when under constant temperatures.

(B) Irish physicist Robert Boyle is famous because in 1662 he conducted gas experiments under constant temperatures even without the benefit of modern technological equipment.

02

> Pastoralists were nomadic tribes who focused almost exclusively on livestock agriculture by domesticating horses, sheep, and cattle, and who frequently moved around from place to place in search of water and suitable grazing pastures for their herds.

(A) Pastoralists were nomadic tribes who concentrated mainly on raising domesticated animals, and who often roamed the land in search of food and water for their livestock.

(B) Pastoralists were nomadic tribes who devoted most of their attention to livestock agriculture, and who traveled frequently in search of horses, sheep, and cattle to domesticate.

03

> Clyde Tombaugh, the astronomer credited for the discovery of Pluto, used a blink comparator, a device that detects shifts in positions of celestial bodies in images taken of a specific area of the sky, to confirm the existence of Pluto in 1930.

(A) Pluto was discovered by Clyde Tombaugh when it moved to a different part of the cosmos.

(B) In 1930, a machine that tracks changes in the location of objects in space was used by Clyde Tombaugh to establish the presence of Pluto.

---

01 **access**[ǽkses] 이용　**rudimentary**[rù:dəméntəri] 기초적인　**physicist**[fízəsist] 물리학자　**constant**[kánstənt] 일정한
inversely[invə́:rsli] 반비례하여　**proportional**[prəpɔ́:rʃənl] 비례하는　**reciprocally**[risíprəkəli] 역으로
proportionate[prəpɔ́:rʃənət] 비례하는

02 **pastoralists**[pǽstərəlists] 목축민　**nomadic**[noumǽdik] 유목의　**livestock**[láivstàk] 가축
domesticate[dəméstikèit] 길들이다　**herd**[hə:rd] 가축의 떼

03 **credit**[krédit] 공로를 인정하다, ~ 덕분으로 돌리다　**device**[diváis] 기기　**detect**[ditékt] 탐지하다　**shift**[ʃift] 변화
celestial[səléstʃəl] 천체의　**confirm**[kənfə́:rm] 확인하다

04

> The development of printing in China was made possible by the invention of paper, ink, and a technique for copying inscriptions from stone, but the innovation most significant to the technology was the stamp seal, an instrument used to imprint a signature.

(A) Some devices were useful to the advent of printing in China, although none were more important than the stamp seal.

(B) Several instruments and processes were invented around the time printing technology was developed in China.

05

> As the sun heats the earth and, in turn, the atmosphere, warm air rises and moves toward the poles from all directions, and this phenomenon creates paths for cool air from the poles to replace the warm air, a process resulting in wind.

(A) Air rises when heated by the sun, causing cool air to move from the poles, which creates wind.

(B) The sun heats the earth, giving rise to wind resulting from warm air mixing with cool air at the poles.

06

> In spite of their brilliant design and their capacity to attract people who established neighboring villages, Japanese castles have been given little recognition by much of the world because the term "castle" is most often associated with the fortress-like structures erected in Europe during the medieval period.

(A) Despite being well conceived and attractive to locals, Japanese castles have not received much attention globally due to a linguistic issue.

(B) Japanese castles were not as attractive and well known as the European castles constructed in the Middle Ages.

---

04 **printing**[príntiŋ] 인쇄술　**invention**[invénʃən] 발명　**inscription**[inskrípʃən] 새기기　**innovation**[ìnəvéiʃən] 혁신
stamp seal 봉랍 도장　**imprint**[imprínt] 찍다　**signature**[sígnətʃər] 서명

05 **atmosphere**[ǽtməsfìər] (지구를 둘러싼) 대기　**poles**[pouls] 양 극(남극과 북극)　**phenomenon**[finámənàn] 현상
replace[ripléis] 대신하다

06 **brilliant**[bríljənt] 훌륭한　**capacity**[kəpǽsəti] 능력　**attract**[ətrǽkt] 끌어당기다　**establish**[istǽbliʃ] 세우다
recognition[rèkəgníʃən] 인정, 인지　**term**[təːrm] 용어　**fortress**[fɔ́ːrtris] 요새　**erect**[irékt] 세우다
medieval[mìːdíːvəl] 중세의　**conceive**[kənsíːv] 계획하다, 생각하다

07

> Because highly specialized technical skills were needed to reproduce an art work faithfully and printing equipment was costly, the relationship between the artist and the printmaker became central to the production of perfectly-rendered copies.

(A) To ensure that an art work was dependably reproduced on paper, the artist assisted the master printmaker in all the technical processes involved.

(B) The relationship between an artist and a printmaker was more often a social rather than a professional one.

(C) Due to the skills and costs involved in making exact reproductions, the relationship between the artist and the printmaker became crucial.

(D) Artists sought only those printmakers who had the experience and facilities to reproduce art in a dependable and consistent manner.

08

> Most people suffer from physical discomfort when under the immediate influence of fever, but medical scholars and practitioners have long acknowledged the many positive roles of fever in the proper functioning of the body, especially how fever stimulates immunological resistance, facilitates the flow of blood, and combats harmful bacteria and viruses.

(A) Positive effects of fever acknowledged by the medical community include immunity and circulatory functions, as well as fever's ability to fight pathogens.

(B) Despite their understanding of the constructive functions of fever, medical scholars and practitioners know little about why it causes people to suffer.

(C) Although the effects of fever are usually unpleasant, people in the medical field understand the constructive role of fever in several bodily processes.

(D) The body's long-term ability to function properly can be harmed by the presence of fever, but medical professionals maintain a positive view of fever.

---

07 highly[háili] 매우　specialized[spéʃəlàizd] 전문적인　reproduce[rìːprədjúːs] 복제하다　faithfully[féiθfəli] 정확하게
printmaker[príntmèikər] 판화 제작자　rendered[réndərd] 묘사된　copy[kápi] 복제품

08 discomfort[diskʌ́mfərt] 불편　practitioner[præktíʃənər] 의사　immunological[ìmjunəládʒikəl] 면역의
resistance[rizístəns] 저항　facilitate[fəsílətèit] 용이하게 하다　combat[kəmbǽt] 싸우다

지문을 읽고 음영 처리된 문장을 바르게 간략화한 문장을 고르시오.

09

Only about a tenth of the surface of an iceberg in the ocean can be seen, but if this portion melted, part of the ice below the surface would rise. This illustrates Archimedes' principle of buoyancy, which applies to the Earth's crust. Crust floats on mantle, a viscous layer that flows. In some regions, the crust collects, forming a mass which slowly becomes a mountain. When a mountain erodes and decreases in height, because it floats on mantle like an iceberg floats in water, the new crust pushes upward.

(A) Only a tenth of an iceberg floating in an ocean is revealed at any given time.

(B) Icebergs remain on the surface of the ocean no matter how large they are.

(C) Buoyancy is best achieved when a large object such as an iceberg weighs less.

(D) An iceberg will partly ascend from the ocean if the visible section is removed.

10

In spite of the fact that the principle of using an arch to connect two supporting structures had been known to the Romans centuries earlier, it was not until the first century BC that they applied it systematically to their bridges, temples, and aqueducts. Semicircular arches, in particular, were popular among Roman masons, who constructed the curved structures using stone bricks. Bricks were arranged in a rounded arc with a central keystone and situated above two vertical columns, called imposts.

(A) Having known about the arch's application for centuries, mainly as a supporting structure, the Romans started to make comprehensive use of it in the first century BC.

(B) The Romans had invented the arch centuries earlier, but it was not until the first century BC that they started to use it systematically in their architecture.

(C) It was only after centuries of use that the Romans began to fully comprehend the application of the arch for constructing bridges, temples, and aqueducts.

(D) Though the Romans had understood its architectural application for centuries, they only began to use the arch systematically in buildings during the first century BC.

---

09 **iceberg**[áisbəːrg] 빙산 **portion**[pɔ́ːrʃən] 부분 **buoyancy**[bɔ́iənsi] 부력 **float**[flout] 뜨다 **viscous**[vískəs] 점성의
erode[iróud] 부식되다

10 **principle**[prínsəpl] 원리 **systematically**[sistəmǽtikəli] 계획적으로 **aqueduct**[ǽkwədʌkt] 수도
mason[méisn] 석공 **keystone**[kíːstòun] (아치 꼭대기의) 종석 **vertical**[vɔ́ːrtikəl] 세로의 **impost**[ímpoust] 아치굽

CH 1
CH 2
CH 3
CHAPTER 4
CH 5
CH 6
CH 7
CH 8
CH 9

Hackers TOEFL Reading Intermediate

11

During geographic speciation, a species is divided into two geographically distinct populations so that mixing of the gene pool stops. The division often occurs gradually due to phenomena such as geologic uplift or creation of previously nonexistent bodies of water. An example can be found in the uplifting of the Isthmus of Panama, which divided sea creatures between the Gulf of Mexico and the Pacific Ocean. Subjected to different habitats over time, aquatic animals in the Gulf developed dissimilar habits than their relatives in the Pacific in response to the new physical surroundings, and these adaptations resulted in complete reproductive incompatibility between members of previously unified species. For example, snapping shrimp off the eastern coast of Panama have become sexually distinct from those on the western coast and will not mate even if placed together in a tank.

(A) Previously compatible species developed reproductive responses that were inconsistent with the habits necessary for life in their new physical surroundings.

(B) Organisms that once made up a single species became disunited reproductively because of evolved behaviors developed under different environmental conditions.

(C) Aquatic animals once shared the same marine habitats, but changes in their reproductive habits resulted in their physical redistribution in the Gulf and the Pacific.

(D) Aquatic animals living and evolving in the Gulf developed different behaviors than similar species that were developing simultaneously in the Pacific.

12

The socioeconomic systems of Northern and Southern Europe in the later Middle Ages were wholly divergent, and as a result, development in these regions was unalike. Northern Europe's system was essentially based on ownership of land. A lord or landowner who put himself in the service of a sovereign such as a king was given complete authority over his land. Landlords entered into contractual relationships with the tenants residing on their property, giving them permission to establish small community farms in exchange for loyalty to the landlord and political allegiance to the king. The arrangement played an important role in maintaining the monarchy and in developing a large army that provided security to the land. Although the political system in Northern Europe was powerful, the socioeconomic system of the land guaranteed that the region would remain an agricultural one.

(A) In return for farming rights, tenants pledged their commitment to a landowner and king through contracts.

(B) A contract was necessary for a tenant to be permitted the use of land for farming.

(C) The king and landlord made arrangements with the tenants to grow crops as payment for their protection.

(D) Tenants of the land signed a deed that gave them the right to live on the property of a landowner.

---

11 speciation[spìːʃiéiʃən] 종분화 distinct[distíŋkt] 다른 gene pool 유전자 풀 geologic[dʒìːəládʒik] 지질의
uplift[ʌ́plift] 융기 subjected to ~의 영향을 받는 habitat[hǽbitæt] 서식지 incompatibility[inkəmpæ̀təbíləti] 불화합성

12 divergent[divə́ːrdʒənt] 다른 unlike[ʌ̀nəláik] 다른 sovereign[sávərən] 주권자 contractual[kəntrǽktʃuəl] 계약상의
tenant[ténənt] 소작인 allegiance[əlíːdʒəns] 충성 monarchy[mánərki] 군주제 guarantee[gæ̀rəntíː] 보증하다

13

[1]Concerning the sudden disappearance of organisms near the end of the Cretaceous period, paleontologists differ in their interpretation of the precise causes of the historical mass extinction, an event in which multitudes of species in virtually every taxonomic category were wiped out some 65 million years ago. One group of theorists focuses on evidence, such as cosmic dust found in the geologic record, of extraterrestrial objects impacting the Earth's surface. [2]If a meteorite were large enough, theorists argue, it could propel dust and noxious vapors high into the atmosphere, clouding out the sun and thereby lowering global surface temperatures, and leaving chemical compounds like sulfur dioxide in the stratosphere for years where they would mix with clouds to create toxic aerosols and produce acid rain. Another group emphasizes a terrestrial origin for the catastrophic decline of species. They cite massive volcanic eruptions as the cause, suggesting that the release of particulates and toxic gases into the atmosphere would have made conditions for life on land and in oceans unsuitable.

1. Which of the sentences below best expresses the essential information in the highlighted sentence in the passage? *Incorrect* choices change the meaning in important ways or leave out essential information.

   (A) Differing interpretations exist among paleontologists concerning the total number of taxonomic categories affected by the extinctions.

   (B) Paleontologists differ in their explanations of why so many species were unable to adapt to changing conditions around 65 million years ago.

   (C) There is no consensus among paleontologists regarding the exact causes of the mass extinctions at the end of the Cretaceous period.

   (D) Paleontologists disagree over precisely when the historical mass extinctions at the end of the Cretaceous period began and ended.

2. Which of the sentences below best expresses the essential information in the highlighted sentence in the passage? *Incorrect* choices change the meaning in important ways or leave out essential information.

   (A) Theorists contend that a large meteorite would send dust and toxic gases into the atmosphere, adversely affecting both surface temperatures and the atmosphere.

   (B) If a large meteorite were to hit the planet, dust and vapors propelled into the atmosphere would block the sun, leading to drastic changes in land temperatures.

   (C) Theorists argue that if a meteorite were large, it would cloud out the sun, leaving acid rain-causing chemicals in the stratosphere.

   (D) Falling land temperatures and acid rain offer evidence that toxic particles were propelled into the atmosphere by a large meteor striking the land.

---

13 cretaceous period 백악기 paleontologist[pèiliəntálədʒist] 고생물학자 interpretation[intə̀ːrprətéiʃən] 해석
multitude[mʌ́ltətjùːd] 수많음 taxonomic[tæ̀ksənámik] 분류의 cosmic dust 우주진
extraterrestrial[èkstrətəréstriəl] 외계의 impact[impǽkt] 충돌하다 meteorite[míːtiəràit] 운석
noxious[nákʃəs] 유독한 stratosphere[strǽtəsfìər] 성층권 terrestrial[təréstriəl] 지구상의

14

North American chipmunks, small squirrel-like rodents belonging to the family Sciuridae, are generally classified into Eastern and Western groupings. ¹Eastern chipmunks are confined to the deciduous forests of the Northeastern part of the United States, and consist of only a single species that dwells on the ground. In contrast, there are 21 Western chipmunk species, and their habitats are much more varied. ²Widely distributed in the Northwestern part of the United States, many Western species prefer to live in extensive burrows in the ground near bushes, fallen logs, or bedrock that serves as shelter. Thirteen species dwell in California, and the range of habitats in which these species reside tends to overlap: from undergrowth, scrubs, and bushes in forests to the middle and higher elevations of mountain slopes. The most common species, the Least Chipmunk, lives in a range where other larger species exist and so limits itself to sage and brush habitats. Other small species such as the Alpine and the Lodgepole are usually found at higher elevations, choosing to live in meadows at the timberline.

1. Which of the sentences below best expresses the essential information in the highlighted sentence in the passage? *Incorrect* choices change the meaning in important ways or leave out essential information.

   (A) Eastern chipmunks survive only in the forests of the Northeastern region of the United States.

   (B) The only chipmunk species known to live on the ground are the Eastern chipmunks of Northeastern United States.

   (C) The one Eastern chipmunk variety lives on the ground in the deciduous forests of Northeastern United States.

   (D) Eastern chipmunks prefer to live on the ground rather than in the trees of the Northeastern portion of the United States.

2. Which of the sentences below best expresses the essential information in the highlighted sentence in the passage? *Incorrect* choices change the meaning in important ways or leave out essential information.

   (A) Northwestern United States is home to many species of Western chipmunks.

   (B) Western chipmunks in the United States compete for shelter in undergrowth, trees, and rocks.

   (C) Chipmunks in the Northwestern section of the United States dig holes that function to protect them.

   (D) Western chipmunks subsist in extended tunnels in Northwestern United States.

---

14 chipmunk[tʃípmʌŋk] 얼룩다람쥐 rodent[róudnt] 설치류 family[fǽməli] 과 deciduous[disídʒuəs] 낙엽성의
dwell[dwel] 살다 burrow[bə́ːrou] 땅굴 bedrock[bédràk] 기반암 reside[rizáid] 살다 overlap[òuvərlǽp] 겹치다
undergrowth[ʌ́ndərgròuθ] 덤불 scrub[skrʌb] 덤불 range[réindʒ] 구역 sage[seidʒ] [식물] 샐비어
meadow[médou] 목초지 timberline[tìmbərláin] 수목한계선

15

In traditional theater, interactions between the audience and actors were limited, but experimental methods of actor-audience interaction have brought forth changes in acting methodology. One such method was developed in the twentieth century by noted arts director Viola Spolin, who founded the Young Actors Company, a Hollywood actor's school, in 1946. [1]Spolin believed that training should be expanded in scope to include theatrical games designed to stimulate creativity, explaining that actors on stage are more likely to inspire the audience through innovation rather than relying solely on memorization of lines and repetition of practice performances. Examples of games included assigning actors a particular animal or emotion to simulate spontaneously. [2]Spolin's ideas laid the foundation for an even more radical approach known as improvisation, a popular free performance style that developed in 1950s-era Chicago theaters, where actors asked the audience for inspiration in directing parts of the performance, thus departing entirely from the traditional model of actor as agent and audience as passive participant. Additionally, instead of carefully planning a staged act through studying lines, improvisational actors often performed spontaneously without a script.

1. Which of the sentences below best expresses the essential information in the highlighted sentence in the passage? *Incorrect* choices change the meaning in important ways or leave out essential information.

(A) Spolin felt that actors would give a more compelling performance if they innovated more on stage instead of just reproducing lines and rehearsing.

(B) Spolin came up with the idea that an audience, rather than actors or directors, should determine an actor's performance during rehearsal.

(C) Spolin required actors to rely on the reaction of the audience to determine what changes or improvisations to make during a theatrical performance.

(D) Spolin thought that an improvisational delivery of lines would be seen as more believable by an audience than a traditional on-stage performance.

2. Which of the sentences below best expresses the essential information in the highlighted sentence in the passage? *Incorrect* choices change the meaning in important ways or leave out essential information.

(A) Following the foundation laid by Spolin, actors in Chicago during the 1950s rejected traditional methods of acting, thus improvising on the traditional acting model.

(B) Chicago theaters in the 1950s included actors who sought direct audience participation, and their performances changed from those of the Spolin era.

(C) It was Spolin's groundwork that allowed the actors in 1950s-era Chicago theaters to move beyond the traditional actor-audience model that discouraged audience participation.

(D) Actors in 1950s-era Chicago theaters went beyond Spolin's work by including audience participation, which differed dramatically from the traditional acting model.

정답·해석·정답단서 p.291

---

15 interaction[ìntərǽkʃən] 상호작용 methodology[mèθədάlədʒi] 방법론 scope[skoup] 범위
stimulate[stímjulèit] 자극하다 inspire[inspáiər] 고무하다 solely[sóulli] 오로지 assign[əsáin] 지정하다
spontaneously[spɑntéiniəsli] 즉흥적으로 radical[rǽdikəl] 급진적인 improvisation[impràvəzéiʃən] 즉흥 연기
inspiration[ìnspəréiʃən] 영감 agent[éidʒənt] 행위자 passive[pǽsiv] 수동적인

Hackers Test

1 Pollen Analysis

1   Scientists analyze pollen in order to learn about past vegetation patterns and climate. Pollen analysis involves collecting, examining, and calculating pollen grains from multiple layers of rock or soil. Through analyzing the various pollen grains retained in the earth's sediment layers, we can estimate the number and types of plants that existed in a region and how they were distributed. Knowing the types of plants that were present also allows researchers to deduce historical climatic conditions.

2   [2]When flowering plants release pollen, much of it falls to the ground, and as sediment collects through glaciations and erosion, pollen grains are trapped within a layer of earth. Eventually, the soil compacts and becomes stratified. To obtain buried pollen, a core sample must be taken from the earth. This is accomplished by drilling a cylindrical hole into the soil and removing stratified layers of medium where pollen is likely to be trapped. The pollen core samples are then transported in a tube to a laboratory where they can be studied. Because sediments forming in anaerobic conditions best preserve the quality of pollen and keep it from decomposing, samples are often taken from bogs and dry lake beds.

3   Material from the lowermost layer of a pollen core sample is the oldest, and material from the uppermost layer is the newest; thus we can approximate the relative age of the pollen and when it was deposited. Today, the Great Lakes region of North America hosts a diverse array of flora in its wetlands and mixed forest ecosystems. However, pollen analysis reveals that the lush environments we see around the Great Lakes were once covered in snow and ice, with only a few scattered shrubs, and mostly consisted of lichens, mosses, sedges, and grasses. Using pollen from core samples as evidence, scientists can infer that the climate of the entire Great Lakes region was not always so temperate. In fact, as little as 11,000 years ago, the area shared more in common with today's Arctic tundra. It was a barren and very cold region that could not support the growth of large trees.

4   To be comprehensive, however, pollen analysis must be conducted in many different regions. [3]By understanding the plants that grew across broad sections of the Earth in the past, we can gather data about climate change and how climatic fluctuations have affected regional vegetative patterns. Pollen analysis therefore offers clues about how phenomena such as global warming are likely to influence the regional distribution of plants in the future.

1   The word "retained" in the passage is closest in meaning to

(A) preserved

(B) removed

(C) entrenched

(D) decomposed

2   Which of the sentences below best expresses the essential information in the highlighted sentence in the passage? *Incorrect* choices change the meaning in important ways or leave out essential information.

(A) Fallen pollen is carried away by sedimentation processes and collects on the Earth's surface.

(B) The process of sedimentation confines fallen plant pollen within soil layers.

(C) As flowering plants release pollen, some of it ends up falling to the ground.

(D) When pollen falls to the ground, it becomes trapped unless transported by glaciations and erosion.

3   Which of the sentences below best expresses the essential information in the highlighted sentence in the passage? *Incorrect* choices change the meaning in important ways or leave out essential information.

(A) We can collect information on climate change and its effect on plants through learning about past global plant distributions.

(B) Through understanding how fluctuations in plant populations have occurred in the past, we can learn about climate.

(C) By paying attention to the various growth patterns of plants, we can better comprehend their climatic requirements.

(D) We can only understand the broad distribution of the Earth's plants by comparing current and past climatic patterns.

4   According to the passage, what can be learned from pollen analysis?

(A) Clues about how plants evolved due to past climatic changes

(B) Ways in which vegetation is likely to influence climate patterns

(C) The types of soil conditions that different plants require

(D) The distribution of vegetation in past ecosystems

2 Ground Ice

Earth Science

1   Ground ice is frozen water on or in the soil. In some locations, ground ice remains throughout the year, such as in areas with permafrost. Examples include parts of Antarctica, the Arctic, and the world's high alpine regions. [1]Less extreme climates often have a seasonal frost-thaw cycle; therefore, in most temperate regions, ground ice formation is only a winter phenomenon.

2   Different freezing conditions result in different types of ground ice. Two common types of ground ice are pore ice and segregated ice. Ice that forms underground between grains of soil is termed pore ice. [2]In moisture-retentive soils, such as heavy clay, pore ice can be nearly invisible, particularly if the freezing results from a very rapid drop in temperature. In more permeable media, such as sand, larger ice formations occur in the spaces between sediments, making the ice crystals easily detectable to the naked eye. Pore ice conforms to the size and shape of the empty space it occupies and is distributed in varying densities throughout a soil layer.

3   ➡ Pore ice is associated with initial freezing, but often some unfrozen water remains in the ground. [4]If temperatures drop further, ground ice begins to accumulate at specific layers, either within the soil or at the soil surface. This layering is due to temperature gradients. As liquid water turns to ice along these gradients, molecular forces create suction, causing moisture to migrate. The process results in the separation of ice from the surrounding soil. Since little or no debris is contained within the ice, it is referred to as segregated ice. Segregated ice formations remain relatively clear of sediment and consist of mostly pure frozen water. Underground, the process forms thin, horizontal ice sheets called lenses. Segregated ice can also form at or very near the soil surface. Ice needles, thin slivers of ice named for their needle-like appearance, form under moist conditions where the soil subsurface temperature is greater than 0 degrees Celsius and the surface of the soil is at or below freezing.

4   Because ground ice often forms by depleting water from surrounding sediments, the soil becomes dry and brittle. Moreover, the freezing of water causes it to occupy more volume, and as ice grows and stretches, it shoves bits of soil aside, creating an uneven surface. This crumbly frozen ground is easily crushed under the weight of anything that moves over it. Once the ice thaws, what remains is weakly bonded soil particles, which can easily be swept away by rising rivers, wind, and rain. [7]The particle displacement from this process and subsequent distribution resulting from weathering are known as ice-induced erosion, a key element in the deterioration of stream banks. Formation of underground ice layers can also affect the surface. Continual formation (expansion) from freezing and retreat (contraction) from thawing can cause vertical displacement of soil. Known as frost heave, this event can destroy the roots of trees, damage the foundations of buildings, and create cracks in streets and sidewalks.

5   ➡ Even so, not all effects of ground ice formation are destructive. In places with warm climates like southern California where frosts are uncommon, farmers who anticipate

a frosty night can sometimes be seen spraying crops of strawberries and oranges with water. This creates a thick coating of ice on the plants and fruits. The practice may seem counterintuitive, but the farmers are actually safeguarding their crops against damage. One of the unique properties of water is that it releases warmth as it freezes, and this energy transfer tempers the cold temperatures by keeping plant tissues at, or even several degrees above, 0 degrees Celsius. Consequently, even if the temperatures dip below freezing, plant tissues won't freeze and rupture. A similar circumstance occurs beneath the surface: ground ice helps insulate subterranean crops like carrots and onions by enveloping the tubers in a natural heat blanket.

1   Which of the sentences below best expresses the essential information in the highlighted sentence in the passage? *Incorrect* choices change the meaning in important ways or leave out essential information.

   (A) Since freezing temperatures only occur in winter, temperate climates have little ground ice.

   (B) Due to changes in ground ice formation, temperate regions have extreme winter weather.

   (C) Because temperate climates have seasonal fluctuations, ground ice forms only in winter.

   (D) Due to seasonal thaws, frosts are less extreme in temperate regions during the winter period.

2   Which of the sentences below best expresses the essential information in the highlighted sentence in the passage? *Incorrect* choices change the meaning in important ways or leave out essential information.

   (A) Pore ice forms most quickly in moisture-retentive soils, such as in areas of heavy clay.

   (B) Quick drops in temperature can create virtually invisible pore ice in soils that readily retain water.

   (C) If temperatures are low, pore ice freezes rapidly because of the ability of soils to hold moisture.

   (D) When temperatures drop rapidly, ice forms in invisible pores in soils that are moisture retentive.

CH 1
CH 2
CH 3
CHAPTER 4
CH 5
CH 6
CH 7
CH 8
CH 9
Hackers TOEFL Reading Intermediate

3   The word "it" in the passage refers to

(A) ice

(B) size

(C) shape

(D) space

4   Which of the sentences below best expresses the essential information in the highlighted sentence in the passage? *Incorrect* choices change the meaning in important ways or leave out essential information.

(A) Formation of ground ice at certain layers results from additional drops in temperature.

(B) Further drops in temperature are contingent upon ground ice forming at distinct layers.

(C) Rapidly falling temperatures occur specifically at the water-ice juncture and soil surface.

(D) Accumulation of layered ice can occur at the surface and where ground temperatures are low.

5   All of the following are mentioned in paragraph 3 as characteristics of segregated ice EXCEPT:

(A) It forms along temperature gradients in the soil.

(B) It is composed primarily of pure frozen water.

(C) It is found in small spaces between soil particles.

(D) It occurs below ground and at the soil surface.

Paragraph 3 is marked with an arrow [➡].

6   The word "brittle" in the passage is closest in meaning to

(A) accessible

(B) breakable

(C) sturdy

(D) coarse

7   Which of the sentences below best expresses the essential information in the highlighted sentence in the passage? *Incorrect* choices change the meaning in important ways or leave out essential information.

(A) Water quality deterioration is one of the primary effects of ice-induced erosion.

(B) Particles from ice-induced erosion commonly end up in stream banks.

(C) Weathering around stream banks leads to the displacement of ice.

(D) Ice-induced erosion is a primary factor in the degradation of soil along streams.

8   According to paragraph 5, which of the following is true about the practice of spraying water on crops before a freeze?

(A) It can only be done in areas not prone to frequent frosts.

(B) It has a limited effect on underground plant parts.

(C) It stimulates plants to grow thicker stems and roots.

(D) It protects tender plant parts from falling temperatures.

Paragraph 5 is marked with an arrow [➡].

1   During the nineteenth century, the United States transformed from a comparatively minor, agricultural nation to a commercial and industrial power. Fast and inexpensive transportation networks developed, linking disparate areas and changing the face of the American city. ²People crowded into urban areas to take advantage of the new opportunities afforded by industrialization, a demographic trend that mobilized a new generation of academics who began to compile empirical data on growth in America's cities. In particular, scholars sought to explain the patterns of human migration to and within cities. The most influential body of work on the subject was conducted in Chicago; hence, it is known as the Chicago School of urban sociology.

2   ³The rapid industrialization and related population explosion in late nineteenth- and early twentieth-century Chicago made it a perfect object of sociological inquiry, and publication of *The City* in 1925 helped establish the study of urban sociology in academia. The book epitomizes the Chicago School and is known as one of the most important contributions to modern sociology. Edited by urban sociologist Ernest Burgess, the study set out a universal theory of urban development based on concentric circles. The basic premise of the Concentric Zone Model (CZM) is that when people gather to form cities, their settlement and land use occur in predictable patterns. According to the Chicago School, people initially congregate in the center, and as new migrants arrive and a city expands, additional rings of development with their own specialized businesses and infrastructures begin to emerge around the core. Each "loop" is representative of a different set of socio-economic variables related to status, access to resources, and overall quality of life.

3   ➡ In the CZM, the central zone serves as the primary business and manufacturing district. It is the political, economic, and cultural life center of the city and contains the city hall, the main transportation hubs, and museums. Immediately surrounding the core is a transition area which consists primarily of a blend of factories and low-rent housing occupied largely by immigrants. It is viewed as a place of deterioration by Burgess, with its slums, crime, and poverty. Yet he also considers it a place of regeneration and a source of radical ideas representative of its cosmopolitan residents, who are actively pursuing a new and better world.

4   ➡ Beyond the transition area is a residential zone comprising of two sections. ⁶The innermost section is composed of independent workers' homes (occupied by shop and factory workers), followed by an outer section with "better residences," which essentially functions as a second transition between the city and what lies beyond. In modern terms, the two parts of the residential zone correspond to the inner suburbs (lower-class residential zone) and outer suburbs (middle- to upper-class residential zone), respectively. Further still is the outermost zone in the CZM, a place reserved for those who have substantial financial resources or a desire to live in a more pleasant environment, far removed from the stresses of urban life. Many of the residents in the outermost zone have jobs in the city and spend a significant portion of each day traveling to and from work. It is thus referred to as the zone of commuters. Composed of single-family dwellings, the commuter zone offers spacious accommodations and convenient facilities without the pollution, crime, and other vices

associated with the inner city.

5　Burgess termed the migration of people to inner zones *invasion*, and referred to the dispersal of people away from the core as *succession*—both terms borrowed from the field of plant ecology. Succession in plants refers to changes in the composition of an ecosystem as plants adapt to and modify the environment. In humans, succession stems from housing pressures and competition for resources (e.g., land) in the inner city. People who can afford to relocate move outward, initiating a process whereby affluence continually moves toward the city's edge.

6　However, later sociologists highlighted the limitations of the Chicago School's demographic model. Although the CZM illuminated the early expansion of Chicago, it does not always work when applied to other cities. Some scholars have pointed out, for instance, that Los Angeles did not develop according to concentric circles. [8]Rather, LA expanded as a collection of loose, peripheral urban communities began to dominate the metropolitan area, leaving a comparatively abandoned inner city.

1　The word "linking" in the passage is closest in meaning to

(A) lengthening

(B) connecting

(C) fortifying

(D) supporting

2　Which of the sentences below best expresses the essential information in the highlighted sentence in the passage? *Incorrect* choices change the meaning in important ways or leave out essential information.

(A) Industrialization offered occasion for people to move to cities, inspiring new academic pursuits related to urban growth in America.

(B) By crowding into cities, people caused universities to encourage academics to collect information on America's new urban growth.

(C) Gathering statistical data on growth in America's cities was made possible by the academic opportunities in the crowded urban environments.

(D) Industrial development generated unforeseen consequences, provoking action on the part of academics to find empirical solutions for urban growth in America.

3 Which of the sentences below best expresses the essential information in the highlighted sentence in the passage? *Incorrect* choices change the meaning in important ways or leave out essential information.

(A) Chicago's rapid modernization at the turn of the nineteenth century helped the city's scholars gain academic prestige following the publication of *The City* in 1925.

(B) Urban sociology was made possible through the rapid industrialization of Chicago, which was the central object of study in the 1925 publication *The City*.

(C) Turn-of-the-century Chicago industrialized rapidly, and it became a central object of study for urban sociologists in academia after the publication of *The City* in 1925.

(D) The rapid modernization of Chicago at the turn of the nineteenth century made it ideal for study, and urban sociology emerged as a discipline after publication of *The City* in 1925.

4 The word "their" in the passage refers to

(A) cities

(B) patterns

(C) migrants

(D) rings

5 In paragraph 3, Burgess views the transition area as a place that

(A) offers a contrasting image of desperation and hope

(B) is overflowing with unemployed immigrants seeking jobs

(C) provides the city's main outlet for cultural interaction

(D) is an urban wasteland with no positive qualities

Paragraph 3 is marked with an arrow [➡].

6 Which of the sentences below best expresses the essential information in the highlighted sentence in the passage? *Incorrect* choices change the meaning in important ways or leave out essential information.

(A) Homes of shop and factory workers make up the section inside the "better residences."

(B) Beyond the independent workers' homes is a transitional section of "better residences."

(C) At the outskirts of the city are "better residences" occupied by independent workers.

(D) The independent workers' homes function as a transition between the city and suburbs.

7　According to paragraph 4, all of the following are true of people living in the outermost zone EXCEPT:

(A) They want to avoid problems associated with the inner city.

(B) They have the monetary means necessary to live at the city's edge.

(C) They enjoy the convenience of living near their places of employment.

(D) They designate a substantial amount of time for transportation.

Paragraph 4 is marked with an arrow [➡].

8　Which of the sentences below best expresses the essential information in the highlighted sentence in the passage? *Incorrect* choices change the meaning in important ways or leave out essential information.

(A) Alternatively, LA communities began to favor aspects of metropolitan life over the dominant urban interior.

(B) Instead, LA resulted from inner city expansion, which led to the formation of adjacent communities.

(C) Instead, LA grew into a group of perimeter communities surrounding a relatively vacant city interior.

(D) Alternatively, LA expanded to include communities on the city's edge, once abandoned for the inner city.

정답·해석·정답단서 p.293

CH 1
CH 2
CH 3
CHAPTER 4
CH 5
CH 6
CH 7
CH 8
CH 9
Hackers TOEFL Reading Intermediate

VOCABULARY LIST

Chapter 04에서 선별한 다음의 토플 필수 어휘를 단어암기 음성파일을 들으며 암기한 후 퀴즈로 확인해보세요.

*해커스 동영상강의 포털 해커스인강(HackersIngang.com)에서 단어암기 음성파일을 무료로 다운로드할 수 있습니다.

rudimentary [rùːdəméntəri] 기초적인 (=primitive)

constant [kánstənt] 일정한

inversely [invə́ːrsli] 반비례하여

proportional [prəpɔ́ːrʃənl] 비례하는

reciprocally [risíprəkəli] 역으로

domesticate [dəméstikèit] 길들이다

credit [krédit] ~ 덕분으로 돌리다

device [diváis] 기기

detect [ditékt] 탐지하다 (=recognize)

shift [ʃift] 변화 (=move)

celestial [səléstʃəl] 천체의 (=heavenly)

confirm [kənfə́ːrm] 확인하다

invention [invénʃən] 발명

innovation [ìnəvéiʃən] 혁신

phenomenon [finámənàn] 현상 (=occurrence)

replace [ripléis] 대신하다 (=substitute)

brilliant [bríljənt] 훌륭한

capacity [kəpǽsəti] 능력 (=ability)

attract [ətrǽkt] 끌어당기다 (=appeal)

establish [istǽbliʃ] 세우다 (=set up)

recognition [rèkəgníʃən] 인지, 인정

erect [irékt] 세우다 (=build)

highly [háili] 매우

specialized [spéʃəlàizd] 전문적인

reproduce [rìːprədjúːs] 복제하다 (=duplicate)

faithfully [féiθfəli] 정확하게

rendered [réndərd] 묘사된

copy [kápi] 복제품

discomfort [diskʌ́mfərt] 불편

resistance [rizístəns] 저항

facilitate [fəsílətèit] 용이하게 하다

combat [kəmbǽt] 싸우다

portion [pɔ́ːrʃən] 부분 (=part)

principle [prínsəpl] 원리 (=standard)

systematically [sìstəmǽtikəli] 계획적으로

vertical [və́ːrtikəl] 세로의

distinct [distíŋkt] 다른 (=separate)

subjected to ~의 영향을 받는

divergent [divə́ːrdʒənt] 다른

unalike [ʌ̀nəláik] 다른

sovereign [sávərən] 주권자

contractual [kəntrǽktʃuəl] 계약상의

allegiance [əlíːdʒəns] 충성

guarantee [gæ̀rəntíː] 보증하다 (=insure)

interpretation [intə̀ːrprətéiʃən] 해석

multitude [mʌ́ltətjùːd] 수많음

taxonomic [tæ̀ksənámik] 분류의

extraterrestrial [èkstrətəréstriəl] 외계의

impact [impǽkt] 충돌하다

noxious [nákʃəs] 유독한 (=harmful)

terrestrial [təréstriəl] 지구상의 (=earthly)

dwell [dwel] 살다

Quiz

각 단어의 알맞은 뜻을 찾아 연결하시오.

01 innovation	ⓐ 기기
02 specialized	ⓑ 혁신
03 multitude	ⓒ 묘사된
04 device	ⓓ 전문적인
05 faithfully	ⓔ 정확하게
	ⓕ 수많음

각 단어의 알맞은 동의어를 찾아 연결하시오.

06 rudimentary	ⓐ duplicate
07 phenomenon	ⓑ ability
08 reproduce	ⓒ primitive
09 portion	ⓓ substitute
10 capacity	ⓔ occurrence
	ⓕ part

ⓑ 01 ⓓ 02 ⓕ 03 ⓐ 04 ⓔ 05 ⓒ 06 ⓔ 07 ⓐ 08 ⓕ 09 ⓑ 10

overlap[òuvərlǽp] 겹치다

interaction[ìntərǽkʃən] 상호작용

scope[skoup] 범위

stimulate[stímjulèit] 자극하다 (=spur)

solely[sóulli] 오로지

assign[əsáin] 지정하다

spontaneously[spɑntéiniəsli] 즉흥적으로

radical[rǽdikəl] 급진적인 (=revolutionary)

vegetation[vèdʒətéiʃən] 식물

examine[igzǽmin] 조사하다 (=inspect)

calculate[kǽlkjulèit] 평가하다

retain[ritéin] 보존하다

estimate[éstəmèit] 추측하다

distribute[distríbju:t] 분포하다

deduce[didʒú:s] 추론하다

compact[kəmpǽkt] 굳다

stratify[strǽtəfài] 층을 형성시키다

core[kɔ:r] 중심의 (=center)

accomplish[əkámpliʃ] 이루다 (=achieve)

drill[dril] ~에 구멍을 뚫다

decompose[dì:kəmpóuz] 부패하다

approximate[əpráksəméit] 어림잡다

deposit[dipázit] 쌓이다

flora[flɔ́:rə] 식물

lush[lʌʃ] 무성한

comprehensive[kàmprihénsiv] 종합적인 (=complete)

conduct[kəndʌ́kt] 실행하다

fluctuation[flʌ̀ktʃuéiʃən] 변화 (=variation)

vegetative[védʒətèitiv] 식물의

retentive[riténtiv] 습기를 유지하는

permeable[pə́:rmiəbl] 투과성이 높은

detectable[ditéktəbl] 보이는

conform[kənfɔ́:rm] 합치하다 (=follow)

accumulate[əkjú:mjulèit] 축적되다 (=collect)

gradient[gréidiənt] 변화도

molecular[məlékjulər] 분자의

deplete[diplí:t] 고갈시키다 (=exhaust)

brittle[brítl] 잘 부서지는 (=breakable)

shove aside 밀어내다

crumbly[krʌ́mbli] 잘 바스러지는

deterioration[ditìəriəréiʃən] 침식

insulate[ínsəlèit] 단열하다

subterranean[sʌ̀btəréiniən] 지하의 (=underground)

disparate[díspərət] 나른

compile[kəmpáil] 수집하다

epitomize[ipítəmàiz] ~의 전형이다

congregate[káŋgrigèit] 모이다

regeneration[ridʒènəréiʃən] 개혁

cosmopolitan[kázməpálətn] 세계적인

dispersal[dispə́:rsəl] 흩어짐

affluence[ǽfluəns] 부

illuminate[ilú:mənèit] 해명하다 (=clarify)

Quiz

각 단어의 알맞은 뜻을 찾아 연결하시오.

01 deposit   ⓐ 변화도
02 affluence   ⓑ 오로지
03 deduce   ⓒ 쌓이다
04 disparate   ⓓ 부
05 solely   ⓔ 다른
    ⓕ 추론하다

각 단어의 알맞은 동의어를 찾아 연결하시오.

06 comprehensive   ⓐ revolutionary
07 deplete   ⓑ complete
08 illuminate   ⓒ follow
09 radical   ⓓ spur
10 stimulate   ⓔ exhaust
    ⓕ clarify

ⓓ 01 ⓔ 60 ⓕ 80 ⓔ 07 ⓐ 06 ⓑ 05 ⓔ 04 ⓕ 03 ⓓ 02 ⓒ 01

CHAPTER 05

Rhetorical Purpose

Rhetorical Purpose

Rhetorical Purpose 문제는 작가가 글에서 특정 표현을 언급한 의도, 또는 특정 단락의 기능을 가장 잘 나타내는 보기를 선택하는 유형이다. 여기서 rhetorical(수사적인)이란, 작가가 전달하고자 하는 바를 더욱 효과적이고 분명하게 나타내기 위하여 다양한 표현 방식을 사용하는 것을 뜻한다. Rhetorical Purpose 문제는 한 지문당 0~3개가 출제된다.

Rhetorical Purpose 문제를 풀기 위해서는 특정 표현의 쓰임에 목적이 있다는 것을 염두하며 글을 읽고, 작가가 왜 그 표현을 사용했는지 작가의 입장에서 생각하여 그 의도를 추측하는 연습을 해야 한다.

▶ 문제 살펴보기

Rhetorical Purpose 문제는 의도를 파악해야 하는 특정 단어나 구를 지문에 음영으로 표시한다. 음영으로 표시하지 않는 경우 특정 단락을 지정해 주며, 해당 단락은 화면에 화살표로 표시된다. 수사적 의도를 나타내는 4개의 구가 보기로 주어진다. 전형적인 질문 형태는 아래와 같다.

- Why does the author mention "▨▨▨▨▨" in the passage/paragraph #?
  왜 작가는 지문/단락 #에서 "▨▨▨▨"을 언급하는가?
- What is the purpose of paragraph # in the overall discussion?
  전체적인 맥락에서 단락 #의 기능은 무엇인가?

다음은 Rhetorical Purpose 문제의 공략법이다. 실전 고득점을 위해 이를 꼼꼼히 학습하고 Hackers Practice와 Hackers Test를 풀면서 반드시 적용해 본다.

1 문맥과 의도 파악하기

질문에서 묻고 있는 단어, 구 또는 절이 언급된 부분을 지문에서 찾아 전후 문맥을 살펴보고 이러한 표현이 지문에서 어떠한 의도로 쓰였는지 파악한다. 단락의 기능을 묻는 문제의 경우, 지문의 전체 흐름에 비추어 해당 단락이 하는 기능을 파악한다.

2 파악한 의도나 기능을 가진 보기를 찾아 내용 일치 확인하기

의도나 기능을 파악한 후에 정답으로 예상되는 보기를 찾고 그 내용이 지문과 일치하는지 확인한다. 의도나 기능, 내용이 모두 일치하는 보기가 정답이다.

수사적 의도나 기능을 나타내는 보기

설명	To explain, To describe	지지	To support
예시	To give an example of, To illustrate	반박	To contradict, To criticize
비교	To compare	부연	To further develop the idea
대조	To contrast	강조	To emphasize, To highlight

Native (bacteria and fungi can be transported) from place to place by bacteria, insects, and livestock. This is likely how chytrids, deadly infectious fungi known to attack amphibians, initially got into the water system and swept across six continents, killing off dozens of species to date. The spread of the disease is particularly rapid in cool forests and mountain regions, as the fungus performs poorly in hot temperatures.

Why does the author mention "birds, insects, and livestock"?

(A) To explain how bacteria and fungi can attack multiple organisms

(B) To provide examples of (vehicles for disease transmission)

(C) To highlight the biodiversity found in natural ecosystems

(D) To contrast the effects of disease on different species

지문해석 p.297

1 birds, insects, and livestock(새, 곤충, 가축)의 전후 문맥을 살펴보면, 한 지역 고유의 세균과 곰팡이는 새, 곤충, 가축에 의해 다른 지역으로 옮겨질 수 있다고 설명한다. 즉, birds, insects, and livestock은 질병 전파 매개체의 예를 들기 위하여 언급된 것임을 파악할 수 있다.

2 예시의 의도를 나타내는 보기는 To provide examples of라고 언급된 (B)이다. vehicles for disease transmission(질병 전파 매개체)이라는 내용이 지문의 bacteria and fungi can be transported(세균과 곰팡이는 옮겨질 수 있다)라는 내용과 일치하므로 정답은 (B)이다.

Hackers Practice

지문을 읽고 물음에 답하시오.

01

> The Black Death, or bubonic plague, is a disease that first appeared in Sicily in 1347. The illness was so infectious that people became ill simply by speaking to an ailing individual. It was called Black Death because plague victims manifested dark spots caused by damaged blood vessels. In a span of five years, 25 million people were dead, which made up one-third of Europe's population at the time. The disease was spread by infected people traveling on foot and horseback, but the starting point of the plague were the rodents that infested Europe.

Why does the author mention "one-third of Europe's population"?

(A) To emphasize the deadliness of the bubonic plague

(B) To compare the population size before and after the plague

(C) To give evidence of the largeness of the European population

02

> When a society develops on a technological level, families often need to make adjustments to their kinship systems to deal successfully with the change. In agrarian societies, extended families were the norm, as this type of family produced their own material requirements, such as food, clothing, and housing. This responsibility required the support of large families. However, the industrial revolution took away the extended family's function as producer. This, coupled with the geographic location of factories, made it necessary for families to restructure themselves into smaller units called "nuclear family," which consisted of a father, mother, and children.

Why does the author mention "father, mother, and children"?

(A) To list the members of a family

(B) To dispute the concept of nuclear family

(C) To explain the meaning of nuclear family

---

01 Black Death 흑사병 bubonic plague 선페스트 ail[eil] 병을 앓다 manifest[mǽnəfèst] 나타나다
blood vessel 혈관 span[spæn] 기간 infest[infést] 들끓다

02 kinship[kínʃip] 친족 관계 agrarian[əgrέəriən] 농업의 extended[iksténdid] 확대한 norm[nɔːrm] 표준
restructure[rìːstrʌ́ktʃər] 재구성하다 dispute[dispjúːt] 반론하다

03

> The soybean is a central part of the Asian diet. However, it was not widely consumed in the United States until the Food and Drug Administration (FDA) released its findings on the nutritional benefits of the plant in 1999. The agency stated that soybeans are a source of complete protein, meaning the vegetable contains all the essential amino acids needed to form the protein the body needs. The quality of soy protein is close to that of meat and eggs. For this reason, vegetarians consider the legume an excellent substitute for animal products.

Why does the author mention "meat and eggs"?

(A) To emphasize the high nutritional content of soybeans

(B) To give examples of protein of much higher quality than soy

(C) To list different types of vegetable and meat proteins

04

> Classical theater abounds with stories that are based on traditional Greek comedy. A famous case is Shakespeare's *A Midsummer Night's Dream*, whose comical characters gathered together at the end of the play in a festive marriage feast. In Greek, the merry singing and dancing at a wedding was called *komos*, the word from which "comedy" derived. Essentially, this sort of revelry was what made a theatrical comedy successful. The characters typically had major flaws, but in the end, their shortcomings were portrayed as ridiculous rather than serious.

Why does the author mention "Shakespeare's *A Midsummer Night's Dream*"?

(A) To compare the comic effectiveness of the play to those in ancient Greece

(B) To explain that comedy was not only used in ancient Greek theater

(C) To give an example of a literary work that is modeled on Greek comedy

---

03 **soybean**[sɔ́ibìːn] 콩 **nutritional**[njuːtríʃənəl] 영양상의 **essential**[isénʃəl] 필수의 **vegetarian**[vèdʒətɛ́əriən] 채식주의자
legume[légjuːm] 콩과 식물 **substitute**[sʌ́bstətʃùːt] 대체품

04 **abound**[əbáund] 가득하다 **derive**[diráiv] 유래하다 **revelry**[révəlri] 환락 **flaw**[flɔː] 결함 **shortcoming**[ʃɔ́ːrtkʌ̀miŋ] 결점
portray[pɔːrtréi] 묘사하다 **ridiculous**[ridíkjuləs] 우스꽝스러운

05

Jean Piaget began his career as a biologist, but became more interested in the thought processes involved in studying organisms than in the organisms themselves. His curiosity about how knowledge develops increased further when he noticed that children reason differently from adults. To acquire a deeper understanding, he observed children from infancy to adolescence and found that their intellectual development occurs in stages; they acquire new skills that form the basis for the next set of skills to be learned. From the age of one to three months, infants learn to put objects into their mouths. From three to seven months, they perceive that not all objects can be manipulated in the same way. A pacifier can be placed in the mouth, but a larger, round-shaped object such as a ball cannot.

Why does the author mention "A pacifier"?

(A) To illustrate how infants gradually acquire knowledge

(B) To identify objects that infants enjoy playing with

(C) To suggest that children quickly become bored with objects

(D) To describe a skill that all children learn early in life

06

Temperatures in mountain climates are significantly influenced by altitude. The general rule is that there is a 6.5°C decrease in temperature per kilometer of altitude. However, this is not always the case in areas where there are temperature inversions. In deep valleys, for instance, cold air sometimes descends down the mountain slopes and collects at the bottom, resulting in pockets of cold air beneath warmer air. Still, on the slopes and peaks of mountains, the altitude rule holds. Even the intense solar radiation that high mountain peaks receive has little effect on raising temperatures because there is less surface area at high elevations for the land to absorb heat. Therefore, there is less heat to transfer to the surrounding atmosphere.

Why does the author discuss "temperature inversions"?

(A) To illustrate how cold air sometimes descends down mountain slopes

(B) To point out an exception to the information previously stated

(C) To contrast the climatic significance of mountain slopes and valleys

(D) To offer a supporting example to the rule that was introduced

---

05 adolescence[ӕdəlésns] 청년기   perceive[pərsíːv] 인식하다   manipulate[mənípjulèit] 조작하다
pacifier[pӕsəfàiər] 고무젖꼭지

06 altitude[ӕltətjùːd] 고도   inversion[invə́ːrʒən] 전도   descend[disénd] 내려가다   beneath[biníːθ] 아래의
intense[inténs] 강한   elevation[èləvéiʃən] 고도

07

Wind erosion principally occurs in deserts and areas where the soil is dry and degraded. Wind is forceful enough to bring about significant changes to the land. These winds remove the top layer of the soil, which consists of materials, such as clay, organic matter, and silt, essential to the growth of crops. The loss of this layer has a devastating impact on agricultural systems, reducing crop yields, degrading seedlings and their potential for survival and growth, and depressing the marketability of crops that do survive. Agricultural productivity is affected in various parts of the world where Aeolian winds are common. One noteworthy case was the "Black Blizzard" of North America's Great Plains, which caused the destruction of nearly 100 million acres of land.

Why does the author mention "100 million acres of land"?

(A) To describe the extent of North America's Great Plains

(B) To give an example of an area prone to wind erosion

(C) To emphasize how destructive wind erosion can be

(D) To explain reduced crop yields during the Black Blizzard

08

A flowering plant's reproductive component is the flower, which includes the stamen, or male reproductive organ, and the stigma, the female reproductive organ. The stamen produces pollen—the fine, powdery material that contains male reproductive cells. To form seeds, the pollen must be transferred from the stamen to the stigma in a process called pollination. This process is facilitated by the stigma because it has a sticky surface that readily receives pollen grains. Sometimes, these grains are transferred straight from a flower's stamen to its stigma, a process known as self-pollination. More often, however, pollen is transferred by a pollinator from the stamen of one plant to the stigma of another. This is cross-pollination, and is a more effective system because it produces stronger plants. Hence, pollinators, of which bees are the most common, play a very important role in plant reproduction.

Why does the author mention "bees"?

(A) To provide an example of a pollinator

(B) To illustrate how cross-pollination takes place

(C) To compare two types of pollination

(D) To describe a species of pollinators

---

07 **erosion**[iróuʒən] 침식 **degrade**[digréid] 질을 떨어뜨리다 **silt**[silt] 미사 **seedling**[síːdliŋ] 식물, 묘목
potential[pəténʃəl] 가능성 **marketability**[màːrkitəbíləti] 시장성

08 **reproductive**[riːprədʌ́ktiv] 생식의 **stamen**[stéimən] 수술 **stigma**[stígmə] 암술 **pollen**[pálən] 꽃가루
pollination[pàlənéiʃən] 수분 **facilitate**[fəsílətèit] 촉진하다, 용이하게 하다

09

Can species of nonhuman animals feel the emotions of love, longing, jealousy, and grief? This is a question that scientists find difficult to answer because of the uncertainty of interpreting emotions in animals. Neuroscientists have the knowledge and technology to measure brain functions, but even if brain and chemical signals indicate that a dog feels pain when it is struck, these scientists will not conclude that, like a human being, it is aware that it is feeling pain. They are more inclined to believe that dogs are simply programmed to behave in a particular way when they are subjected to specific stimuli. For this reason, researchers agree that animals feel only primary emotions, that is, emotions that are instinctual: fear, anger, and the mental distress of physical pain. However, many people in society, particularly pet owners, are not as hesitant to represent animals as having human traits.

Why does the author start the passage with a question?

(A) To raise the issue of whether animals are capable of complex emotions

(B) To propose that scientists study the possibility that animals feel emotions

(C) To criticize the opinion that animals may feel human-like emotions

(D) To introduce the idea that animal emotions are difficult to understand

10

The Earth undergoes a natural cycle of warmer and colder climates. During these cycles, water is distributed and stored according to the prevailing climate. As such, climate change and ocean levels have a close connection. Throughout periods of freezing temperatures, which are called ice ages or glacial epochs, water evaporates from large water bodies, and instead of returning to the oceans as rain, it is stored as ice in glaciers, ice caps, and ice fields. As a result, sea water levels fall. In the last such epoch, the Last Glacial Maximum, which took place approximately 20,000 years ago, the sea level was known to be 125 meters lower than the present. Warming trends, on the other hand, cause ice to melt and ocean levels to rise. Scientists have recorded a steady rise in sea levels of about one millimeter per year.

Why does the author mention "the Last Glacial Maximum"?

(A) To support the notion that climate has an effect on sea levels

(B) To provide an example of a glacial epoch when temperatures dropped drastically

(C) To contrast a warming trend with a period of very cold temperatures

(D) To emphasize the effect that an ice age or glacial epoch can have on glaciers

---

09 **uncertainty** [ʌ̀nsə́ːrtnti] 불확실성 **interpret** [intə́ːrprit] 해석하다 **neuroscientist** [njùərousáiəntist] 신경과학자
instinctual [instíŋktʃuəl] 본능적인 **distress** [distrés] 고통 **hesitant** [hézətənt] 주저하는 **trait** [treit] 특징

10 **prevailing** [privéiliŋ] 지배적인 **connection** [kənékʃən] 관계 **glacial** [gléiʃəl] 빙하의 **epoch** [épək] 시대 **ice cap** 만년설
ice field 빙원 **steady** [stédi] 안정적인

지문을 읽고 물음에 답하시오.

11

Animals use camouflage to avoid detection by predators or to signal to others of their species that danger is present. The most basic form of camouflage is changing coloration to match the surroundings. Some organisms produce biochromes, or natural pigments, on the surface of their skin; these pigments allow the organism to take on appropriate coloration. Some pigments are produced at deeper-level cells called chromatophores. An animal that lives in a wooded area can thus acquire brown coloring to match its surroundings. In places where the seasons change, animals have physiological characteristics that allow them to adapt to changes in surroundings. It is similar to soldiers who wear camouflage uniforms suitable to the environment they do battle in, whether that be a jungle or a desert. Another type of coloration is countershading, a means used by animals with fur or feathers. Countershading is a coloration pattern that uses sunlight to cause visual disruption. Hues appear to blend together, producing a pattern that does not synchronize with the animal's shape. This makes it difficult to discern the animal's outline from the patterns in its surroundings. In broad daylight, for example, the coat of a spotted fawn sitting on the forest floor may appear more like patches of sunlight striking the leaves.

1. Why does the author mention "soldiers"?

   (A) To compare the surroundings of soldiers and animals

   (B) To explain animal coloration through a familiar concept

   (C) To suggest that animal camouflage is similar in color to soldiers' uniforms

   (D) To give a reason for coloration changes in animals

2. Why does the author mention "a spotted fawn"?

   (A) To support the idea that some forms of camouflage are more effective than others

   (B) To give an explanation for how some species are unable to detect other species

   (C) To demonstrate that darker-colored animals are able to hide themselves better

   (D) To provide an example of an animal that conceals itself by making use of light

---

11 **camouflage**[kǽməflɑ̀ːʒ] 위장 **detection**[ditékʃən] 발견 **pigment**[pígmənt] 안료 **chromatophore**[krəmǽtəfɔ̀ːr] 색소세포
countershading[káuntərʃèidiŋ] 대칭색 **disruption**[disrʌ́pʃən] 혼란 **hue**[hju:] 색조 **blend**[blend] 혼합하다
synchronize[síŋkrənàiz] 조화되다 **discern**[disə́ːrn] 구별하다 **fawn**[fɔːn] 새끼 사슴

12

The Polynesian Islands are one of three major subregions that compose a large group of islands called Oceania in the central and southern Pacific Ocean. Unlike the dark-skinned people of short stature in the other subregions, the people of Polynesia are lighter-skinned and taller. Although scientists today believe that Polynesia was colonized by cultures from South Asia, Europeans journeying through the Pacific in the late 1800s and early 1900s articulated a theory that the Egyptians had populated Polynesia. They believed the Egyptians settled the islands because they were the only civilization existing at the time Oceania was believed to have been populated. Researchers in the late 1970s pointed to the use of a layer of color applied to the eyes of some statues in Polynesia as evidence. Egyptians utilized the same technique in their sculptures to make them appear lifelike. In addition, Polynesia's birdman ceremony has as its parallel the traditional ritual quest for the egg of Egypt's sun god, Ra. However, vessel drift computer simulations based on ocean currents in the Pacific have proved that it was impossible for the Egyptians to have arrived at Polynesia even accidentally, and so they could not have populated the islands.

1. Why does the author mention "the eyes of some statues in Polynesia"?

   (A) To contrast the techniques used by Polynesians and Egyptians in statue-making

   (B) To give evidence that the Egyptians are ancestors of present-day Polynesians

   (C) To support an early view that Egyptians first occupied Polynesia

   (D) To criticize the Europeans for suggesting that Egypt discovered Polynesia

2. Why does the author mention "vessel drift computer simulations"?

   (A) To demonstrate that modern technology can record Pacific ocean currents

   (B) To give evidence that the European explorers' theory was wrong

   (C) To further develop the idea of parallels in Middle East and Pacific island traditions

   (D) To suggest that Polynesia was discovered at a later point in time

---

12 **subregion** [sʌ́briːdʒən] 소구역   **compose** [kəmpóuz] 구성하다   **stature** [stǽtʃər] 키   **colonize** [kɑ́lənàiz] 식민지화하다
articulate [ɑːrtíkjulèit] 분명하게 표현하다   **birdman** [bə́ːrdmæ̀n] 조인   **parallel** [pǽrəlèl] 유사점

13

The Everglades ecosystem is a vast expanse of freshwater marshes in the southern third of the US state of Florida. It is unique in the world because its waters are almost exclusively supplied by atmospheric precipitation, whereas most of the world's comparable wetlands are fed by periodically overflowing rivers. This huge "River of Grass," as it is popularly known, is so shallow that grasses can be seen gently swaying above the surface due to the slowly moving currents. Yet it is more than a habitat for grasses. In fact, it has a diverse ecology that boasts a large variety of marsh plants and an enormous number of wading birds.

In addition to its abundant wildlife, the Everglades region is valuable for its agricultural and hydrological resources. It supplies residents of the southeastern coast with high-quality water, and when water levels are controlled, crops such as sugar cane and rice thrive in the rich organic soil. Unfortunately, these benefits have been exploited too rapidly, changing the natural ecological balance of the wetlands. While draining parts of the Everglades has reduced its original size and displaced birds, high levels of phosphorous from agricultural runoff has altered its flora.

1. Why does the author discuss "atmospheric precipitation"?

(A) To highlight the natural process by which most wetlands are formed

(B) To suggest a similarity between the Everglades and comparable wetlands

(C) To give a reason for the uniqueness of the Everglades ecosystem

(D) To explain why some rivers periodically overflow and supply wetlands

2. Why does the author use the word "Unfortunately"?

(A) To emphasize that use of the region's resources has had negative effects

(B) To show that crops do not always succeed in the Everglades region

(C) To demonstrate that the size of the wetlands has been altered rapidly

(D) To argue that the region's resources are not as plentiful as people thought

정답·해석·정답단서 p.297

---

13 **precipitation**[prisìpətéiʃən] 강수 **comparable**[kámpərəbl] 필적할 만한 **sway**[swei] 흔들리다 **boast**[boust] 자랑하다
wading bird 섭금류 **abundant**[əbʌ́ndənt] 많은 **phosphorous**[fásfərəs] 인 **runoff**[rʌ́nɔ̀ːf] 유출수

Hackers Test

1 Hawaiian Island Biology

Biology

1 ➡ Many islands in the Pacific formed through volcanic processes. There was a time, in their early histories, when no life existed on the islands, but people who visit the island environments today find them teeming with life. The Hawaiian Islands are such an example. In Hawaii, thousands of species of plants and animals can be seen thriving side by side, but when the islands formed millions of years ago, the landscape was completely barren. How then did biological life forms originally come to colonize isolated patches of volcanic rock in the middle of the Pacific Ocean?

2 ➡ Because colonization took place intermittently over millions of years, it is hard to say exactly when particular organisms discovered the islands. What is clear, however, is that due to Hawaii's geographic isolation, new arrivals to the islands had to be good travelers. That is, they must have had some mechanism for long-distance dispersal. Seeds of plants like coconut palms floated on the water; seeds of other coastal evergreen trees were transported by wind. Among animals, migrating birds and bats simply flew to the islands, while most reptiles and amphibians probably swam or floated. Some organisms used a vehicle in order to make the transoceanic journey. Parasitic insects and barbed seeds "hitchhiked" on birds by attaching to their skin or feathers. Even small mammals occasionally found their way to the islands using floating organic matter, such as logs, as rafts.

3 ➡ Additionally, pioneer species had to be well-adapted or able to quickly evolve to meet the challenges of an unfamiliar environment. Plants that first arrived on the volcanic islands, such as simple ferns and grasses, must have been able to handle conditions characterized by little or no soil, and, because there was no shade, they had to initially endure intense solar radiation. Animals must have been able to locate food resources, and most importantly, reproduce. Species that failed to adapt and reproduce in the new island habitats simply would have died out. The combination of requirements, both long-distance travel and adaptive vigor, meant that successful colonization attempts were few and far between. Only several hundred insect species, for instance, are believed to have naturally found their way to the islands and survived—an average of merely one per 75,000 years. Natural colonization events prior to human activity were thus very rare.

1   Why does the author include a question at the end of paragraph 1?

(A) To summarize the ideas discussed in the introductory paragraph

(B) To explain why colonization of the Hawaiian Islands took millions of years

(C) To emphasize the diversity of plant life that exists in Hawaii

(D) To introduce a topic to be further analyzed in the passage

Paragraph 1 is marked with an arrow [➡].

2   The word "intermittently" in the passage is closest in meaning to

(A) involuntarily

(B) sporadically

(C) invariably

(D) steadily

3   According to paragraph 2, which of the following is true of the plant seeds that colonized the Hawaiian Islands?

(A) They mostly consisted of coconut palms and other trees.

(B) They were transported by water, wind, and birds.

(C) They were consumed and dispersed by migrating animals.

(D) They arrived earlier than most reptiles and amphibians.

Paragraph 2 is marked with an arrow [➡].

4   In paragraph 3, why does the author mention soil conditions of the volcanic islands?

(A) To offer a reason for why the first plant seeds to arrive did not survive

(B) To contrast their effect on pioneer species with that of solar radiation

(C) To give an example of difficulties that pioneer species would have faced

(D) To reject the notion that seeds were incapable of growing on exposed rock

Paragraph 3 is marked with an arrow [➡].

1   It would be no exaggeration to claim the Baroque (1600-1750) was a revolutionary stage in music history, and academic descriptions of the period are plentiful. A distinguishing feature of Baroque music was the principal role given to instruments, especially those of the violin family, in music ensembles. It was also a period of great creativity, which resulted in new musical genres.

2   ➡ One genre in which the bowed instruments were used prominently was the sonata. The term, as used in the context of the Baroque, refers to a mixed piece of music composed for one or two instruments (often violins), which were typically accompanied by a harpsichord and cello. Sonatas, which were meant to be played, may be viewed as distinct from cantatas, which were written to be sung. It is also notable that the words "cantata" and "sonata" did not exist prior to the sixteenth century, essentially because during earlier periods like the Renaissance, formal music was generally expected to be vocal. Thus, cantatas had existed for some time, whereas sonatas were a unique creation of the Baroque.

3   ➡ The sonatas of German composer and organist Johann Sebastian Bach (1685-1750), with their alternating fast and slow movements, are representative of the mature Baroque form. These instrumental works were characterized by a series of counterpoints sandwiched between a slowly developing introductory movement and a brisk finale. Counterpoints are musical lines written separately and with different rhythms, but which sound harmonious when played together. Music using this technique is known as contrapuntal. Contrapuntal music brought a sense of complexity to Baroque music. A single melody played alone was believed to express a single emotion, but combining more than one melody simultaneously allowed composers to convey complicated ideas, such as irony, with their music.

4   ➡ Another mixed form, the concerto, developed as the orchestra was beginning to take shape. The word "concerto" means "get together" and describes a genre implemented to blend two contrasting elements into one. Usually, the three-movement musical work involved a solo violinist and a larger instrumental ensemble. At the time, the orchestra mainly consisted of stringed instruments, but sometimes woodwinds or horns were added in ones and twos. Italian composer and violinist Antonio Vivaldi's *The Four Seasons*, a set of four independent concertos published in 1725, is among the most famous and beloved examples of Baroque music. It includes four pieces composed of a slow movement between two faster movements. Vivaldi composed the violin concerto to go along with four poems, which describe in detail the sights and sounds of spring, summer, autumn, and winter. Vivaldi's concerto is an early example of what has become known as program music, compositions written to depict imagery of the natural world. The final movement in the piece titled "Summer," for instance, musically represents the occurrence of a thunderstorm.

5   ➡ Opera, a dramatic performance combining dance, instruments, and voice, was also invented in the Baroque period. Opera began in Italy with the composer Jacopo Peri

and was soon adopted by composers in other countries. This new kind of musical performance allowed poetic scripts to be melodically vocalized in a narrative style. During an opera, the background music was frequently employed to evoke strong feelings by swaying the audience toward one emotion or another. Unlike concertos and sonatas, which were primarily performed in the chambers of private homes or churches, operas were public theatrical spectacles, open to a paying audience. As such, operas helped to introduce the public to complex musical compositions.

6 The new genres of the Baroque era were not accidental; the intellectual world in which the new musical forms arose was extremely creative. Like great philosophers, Baroque composers shared a belief in the rationality of the human mind, and some are still regarded as giants in the field of classical music. As a result, their works continue to be performed in symphony halls around the world centuries after their deaths. The persistent fame and influence of geniuses like Bach and Vivaldi are testaments to the importance of the Baroque period in the history of music.

Glossary

movement a distinct unit forming part of an extended musical composition having its own structure, rhythm, and key

1 Which of the sentences below best expresses the essential information in the highlighted sentence in the passage? *Incorrect* choices change the meaning in important ways or leave out essential information.

(A) The Baroque sonata was a musical piece written for one or two instruments played alongside a harpsichord and cello.

(B) The sonata of the Baroque period typically used a harpsichord and cello to amplify the sound of one or two instruments.

(C) One or two instruments, often violins, were frequently used alongside a harpsichord and cello in Baroque music.

(D) Accompanying the one or two instruments were a harpsichord and cello, which were standard in Baroque compositions.

2 In paragraph 2, why does the author include cantatas in the discussion of the development of Baroque musical styles?

(A) To provide an example of a genre on which sonatas were modeled

(B) To demonstrate a connection between instrumental and vocal music

(C) To contrast a conventional musical genre with an innovative form

(D) To explain the reason Baroque composers preferred instrumental music

Paragraph 2 is marked with an arrow [➡].

CH 1
CH 2
CH 3
CH 4
CHAPTER 5
CH 6
CH 7
CH 8
CH 9
Hackers TOEFL Reading Intermediate

3   What is the relationship between paragraphs 2 and 3 in the passage?

   (A) Paragraph 3 describes specific examples of a topic introduced in paragraph 2.

   (B) Paragraph 3 details the differences between the two ideas raised in paragraph 2.

   (C) Paragraph 2 gives the historical causes for what is discussed in paragraph 3.

   (D) Paragraph 2 raises some problematic issues that are resolved in paragraph 3.

   Paragraphs 2 and 3 are marked with arrows [➡].

4   All of the following statements about the concerto are supported by paragraph 4 EXCEPT:

   (A) The overall composition is structured into three parts.

   (B) Horns may be used in addition to stringed instruments.

   (C) Solo violinists are complemented by an orchestra.

   (D) Each piece has four movements developed around a unique theme.

   Paragraph 4 is marked with an arrow [➡].

5   Why does the author mention the final movement in Vivaldi's "Summer" in paragraph 4?

   (A) To introduce a piece that was influenced by traditional program music

   (B) To describe an instrumental piece that was inspired by contemporary poets

   (C) To give an example of a piece that symbolically portrayed natural events

   (D) To illustrate a piece that depicted the composer's attention to detail

6   The word "evoke" in the passage is closest in meaning to

   (A) dilute

   (B) arouse

   (C) preclude

   (D) violate

7   According to paragraph 5, which of the following was a feature that distinguished opera from other Baroque musical genres?

   (A) It was more successful in affecting the emotions of the audience.

   (B) It was more popular because it appealed to a wider audience.

   (C) It was performed in the private chambers of people's homes.

   (D) It was influential in pushing music into the public sphere.

   Paragraph 5 is marked with an arrow [➡].

8   The word "some" in the passage refers to

   (A) genres

   (B) musical forms

   (C) philosophers

   (D) Baroque composers

3 Earth's Core

1   Seismologists once believed that the Earth's core was entirely molten. They based their assumption on the fact that secondary(S) waves emanating from earthquakes could not be detected on the other side of the globe. This is because S-waves do not pass through liquids. On the other hand, primary(P) waves, which do travel through liquids, were detectable; so it was reasonable to assume the inner core was molten.

2   ➡ However, later research brought this hypothesis into question. Working with seismic waves in 1929, Danish seismologist Inge Lehmann noted that indirect signals of P-waves, or echoes, seemed to deflect off some sort of inner boundary. She attributed this to a discontinuity, or change in composition, within the core. In a 1936 paper known simply as "P Prime," she described the Earth's core as having solid and liquid layers. Since Lehmann was the first to demonstrate the existence of both an inner and outer core, the dividing line between them is known as Lehmann's discontinuity. Lehmann's hypothesis became widely accepted by the 1970s as more sensitive seismic instruments began to appear and more seismic data was compiled. Since Lehmann's time, scientists have learned much about the physical characteristics of the core.

3   ➡ The Earth's interior is layered like an onion. This is because gravity has sorted elements according to density. Deep within the Earth, 2,900 kilometers beneath the crust, is the core, which consists of an extremely dense solid inner section and a molten outer layer. The inner core has a radius of 1,255 kilometers and is made up of mostly iron and nickel, heavy elements which are under extreme pressure from the weight of the molten and solid rock above them. Temperatures in the inner core are similar to those on the Sun's surface, reaching somewhere between 4,500°C and 5,500°C. Pressure, temperature, and density of elemental material all drop by approximately half as you move away from the solid interior, and although heavy metals also constitute much of the outer core, there they exist in molten form. Small amounts of silicon and hydrogen are also present. These lighter elements move toward the upper limits of the outer core and may sometimes solidify beneath the mantle.

4   ➡ Such differences between the inner and outer core result in a dynamic relationship between the two, and the interaction of forces in the Earth's core has profound implications for the planet's surface. As the inner and outer core rotate, the liquid in the outer core circulates, generating temperature gradients within the hot, soup-like concoction. Some of the heat escapes into the upper layers, eventually finding its way to the surface via conduction or convection. This heat transfer, which is the principal cause of plate tectonics, moves continents, builds mountains, and causes earthquakes and the formation of volcanoes.

5   ➡ Additionally, since the inner core is isolated from the Earth's upper layers by the outer core, it rotates more rapidly than the rest of the planet. The differential between the spin of the inner and outer core creates electric currents, resulting in continual melting and solidification at the inner-outer core boundary. This activity generates a tremendous energy release and gives rise to the magnetic field of the Earth. It is the magnetic field that protects the Earth from solar wind, a stream of charged particles scattered from the Sun into space. It is also the force allowing compass navigation; because magnetism is stronger at the poles,

CH 1
CH 2
CH 3
CH 4
CHAPTER 5
CH 6
CH 7
CH 8
CH 9
Hackers TOEFL Reading Intermediate

it pulls the magnetized pointer of a compass toward a given pole.

6   Although the influence of the core on the Earth and space is continuous, it is nonetheless variable. Just as tectonic movement is stronger in some spots than others and does not occur in regular patterns or intervals, the Earth's magnetic field has varying intensities in different locations and changes over time. In fact, the direction of the magnetic field has reversed many times in the past. Such variations are direct consequences of changes occurring deep within the core.

1   What is the primary function of paragraph 2 in the overall passage?

(A) To introduce a theory about the Earth's core that contrasts with previous conceptions

(B) To argue that changes in the Earth's core caused seismologists to alter their thinking

(C) To criticize the methods Lehmann used to conduct her experiments

(D) To demonstrate how technological innovations altered the way research was conducted

Paragraph 2 is marked with an arrow [➡].

2   Why does the author mention "an onion" in paragraph 3?

(A) To emphasize that the Earth is not the only object with a layered interior

(B) To explain the Earth's inner structure with that of a familiar object

(C) To contrast the inner densities of two spherical objects

(D) To describe the similarities between the elemental composition of two objects

Paragraph 3 is marked with an arrow [➡].

3   According to paragraph 3, gravity is a factor in the layering of the Earth's interior because it can

(A) transform solids into molten material

(B) create differences in temperature

(C) exert pressure in varying intensities

(D) distribute matter based on denseness

4 Why does the author mention "plate tectonics" in paragraph 4?

(A) To show how energy moves back and forth within the core

(B) To make the point that temperature gradients exist in the core

(C) To give an example of an effect of the interaction between the cores

(D) To highlight the role of plate tectonics in geologic processes

Paragraph 4 is marked with an arrow [➡].

5 All of the following are mentioned in paragraph 5 as results of the differential rotation of the inner and outer core EXCEPT

(A) the flow of electric charges

(B) the generation of solar wind

(C) the magnetism of the Earth

(D) the liquefying and solidifying of material

Paragraph 5 is marked with an arrow [➡].

6 The word "it" in the passage refers to

(A) influence

(B) core

(C) Earth

(D) space

7 Which of the sentences below best expresses the essential information in the highlighted sentence in the passage? *Incorrect* choices change the meaning in important ways or leave out essential information.

(A) The tectonic movement on Earth is just as variable as the Earth's magnetic field.

(B) The Earth's magnetism and tectonic motion both vary according to time and place.

(C) The Earth's tectonic motion occurs in varying intensities, just like the Earth's magnetic field.

(D) The Earth's magnetic field and tectonic movement both change depending on the location.

8 The word "consequences" in the passage is closest in meaning to

(A) results

(B) episodes

(C) signs

(D) principles

정답·해석·정답단서 p.299

CH 1

CH 2

CH 3

CH 4

CHAPTER 5

CH 6

CH 7

CH 8

CH 9

Hackers TOEFL Reading Intermediate

VOCABULARY LIST

Chapter 05에서 선별한 다음의 토플 필수 어휘를 단어암기 음성파일을 들으며 암기한 후 퀴즈로 확인해보세요.

*해커스 동영상강의 포털 해커스인강(HackersIngang.com)에서 단어암기 음성파일을 무료로 다운로드할 수 있습니다.

ail[eil] 병을 앓다

manifest[mǽnəfèst] 나타나다 (=reveal)

kinship[kínʃip] 친척 관계

agrarian[əgrɛ́əriən] 농업의

extended[iksténdid] 확대한

norm[nɔːrm] 표준

restructure[rìːstrʌ́ktʃər] 재구성하다

nutritional[njuːtríʃənəl] 영양상의

essential[isénʃəl] 필수의 (=vital)

substitute[sʌ́bstətjùːt] 대체품 (=alternative)

abound[əbáund] 가득하다 (=teem)

derive[diráiv] 유래하다 (=originate)

revelry[révəlri] 환락

flaw[flɔː] 결함 (=fault)

shortcoming[ʃɔ́ːrtkʌ̀miŋ] 결점 (=disadvantage)

ridiculous[ridíkjuləs] 우스꽝스러운

adolescence[ædəlésns] 청년기

perceive[pərsíːv] 인식하다 (=discern)

manipulate[mənípjulèit] 조작하다 (=operate)

altitude[ǽltətjùːd] 고도 (=height)

descend[disénd] 내려가다

intense[inténs] 강한

elevation[èləvéiʃən] 고도

erosion[iróuʒən] 침식

degrade[digréid] 질을 떨어뜨리다

seedling[síːdliŋ] 식물

potential[pəténʃəl] 가능성

marketability[màːrkitəbíləti] 시장성

reproductive[rìːprədʌ́ktiv] 생식의

pollination[pàlənéiʃən] 수분

facilitate[fəsílətèit] 용이하게 하다

uncertainty[ʌnsə́ːrtnti] 불확실성

interpret[intə́ːrprit] 해석하다 (=explain)

instinctual[instíŋktʃuəl] 본능적인

distress[distrés] 고통 (=agony)

hesitant[hézətənt] 주저하는

trait[treit] 특징

prevailing[privéiliŋ] 지배적인

glacial[gléiʃəl] 빙하의

camouflage[kǽməflàːʒ] 위장

detection[ditékʃən] 발견

pigment[pígmənt] 안료

disruption[disrʌ́pʃən] 혼란

hue[hjuː] 색조 (=color)

blend[blend] 혼합하다 (=mingle)

synchronize[síŋkrənàiz] 조화되다

discern[disə́ːrn] 구별하다

subregion[sʌ́brìːdʒən] 소구역

compose[kəmpóuz] 구성하다

stature[stǽtʃər] 키

colonize[kálənàiz] 식민지화하다

articulate[ɑːrtíkjulèit] 분명하게 표현하다

Quiz

각 단어의 알맞은 뜻을 찾아 연결하시오.

01 reproductive   ⓐ 본능적인
02 instinctual   ⓑ 지배적인
03 hesitant   ⓒ 생식의
04 nutritional   ⓓ 우스꽝스러운
05 ridiculous   ⓔ 영양상의
    ⓕ 주저하는

각 단어의 알맞은 동의어를 찾아 연결하시오.

06 manifest   ⓐ teem
07 abound   ⓑ vital
08 altitude   ⓒ height
09 interpret   ⓓ explain
10 hue   ⓔ color
    ⓕ reveal

ⓔ 01 ⓐ 02 ⓕ 03 ⓔ 04 ⓓ 05 ⓕ 06 ⓐ 07 ⓒ 08 ⓓ 09 ⓔ 10

parallel[pǽrəlèl] 유사점

precipitation[prisìpətéiʃən] 강수

comparable[kámpərəbl] 필적할 만한 (=similar)

sway[swei] 흔들리다

boast[boust] 자랑하다 (=brag)

abundant[əbʌ́ndənt] 많은

runoff[rʌ́nɔ̀ːf] 유출수

volcanic[vɑlkǽnik] 화산의

teem[tiːm] 가득 차다

thrive[θrɑiv] 번성하다 (=flourish)

barren[bǽrən] 메마른 (=sterile)

intermittently[ìntərmítntli] 띄엄띄엄

coastal[kóustəl] 연안의

vehicle[víːikl] 매체

transoceanic[trænsouʃǽnik] 대양횡단의

parasitic[pærəsítik] 기생적인

pioneer[pàiəníər] 선구적인

adaptive[ədǽptiv] 적응성의

vigor[vígər] 힘

exaggeration[igzæ̀dʒeréiʃən] 과장

revolutionary[rèvəlúːʃəneri] 혁명적인

plentiful[pléntifəl] 풍부한 (=bountiful)

principal[prínsəpəl] 주된 (=central)

prominently[prámənəntli] 두드러지게

notable[nóutəbl] 주목할 만한 (=remarkable)

essentially[isénʃəli] 본래 (=basically)

alternate[ɔ́ːltərnèit] 교차하다 (=rotate)

sandwich[sǽndwitʃ] 사이에 끼우다

simultaneously[sáiməltéiniəsli] 동시에 (=concurrently)

depict[dipíkt] 묘사하다 (=portray)

imagery[ímidʒəri] 이미지

vocalize[vóukəlàiz] 노래하다

narrative[nǽrətiv] 이야기식의

employ[implɔ́i] 사용하다 (=utilize)

evoke[ivóuk] 떠올리다

accidental[æ̀ksədéntl] 우연적인

intellectual[ìntəléktʃuəl] 지적인

rationality[ræ̀ʃənǽləti] 합리성

persistent[pərsístənt] 끊임없는 (=continuous)

core[kɔːr] 핵 (=center)

emanate[émənèit] 방출하다

reasonable[ríːzənəbl] 논리적인

discontinuity[dìskɑntənjúːəti] 불연속성

compile[kəmpáil] 수집하다

sort[sɔːrt] 분류하다

crust[krʌst] 지각

radius[réidiəs] 반지름

constitute[kánstətjùːt] 구성하다 (=comprise)

dynamic[dainǽmik] 동적인

profound[prəfáund] 의미심장한

concoction[kɑnkákʃən] 조합물

intensity[inténsəti] 강도

Quiz

각 단어의 알맞은 뜻을 찾아 연결하시오.

01 precipitation   ⓐ 띄엄띄엄
02 intermittently   ⓑ 강수
03 alternate   ⓒ 선구적인
04 sway   ⓓ 우연적인
05 pioneer   ⓔ 흔들리다
     ⓕ 교차하다

각 단어의 알맞은 동의어를 찾아 연결하시오.

06 comparable   ⓐ brag
07 plentiful   ⓑ similar
08 boast   ⓒ utilize
09 persistent   ⓓ bountiful
10 constitute   ⓔ continuous
     ⓕ comprise

01 ⓑ 02 ⓐ 03 ⓕ 04 ⓔ 05 ⓒ 06 ⓑ 07 ⓓ 08 ⓐ 09 ⓔ 10 ⓕ

CHAPTER 06

Inference

Inference

Inference 문제는 지문을 바탕으로 추론할 수 있는 내용을 묻는 질문에 대해 가장 정확하게 답을 한 보기를 선택하는 유형이다. 추론이란, 지문에 직접 명확하게 언급되어 있지는 않지만, 지문에 제시되어 있는 사실 정보를 근거로 하여 함축되어 있는 생각을 알아내는 것을 말한다. Inference 문제는 한 지문당 0~2개가 출제된다.

Inference 문제를 풀기 위해서는 지문을 정확하게 이해하고 이를 근거로 추론하는 연습을 해야 한다.

문제 살펴보기

Inference 문제는 보통 특정 단락을 지정해 주며, 해당 단락은 화면에 화살표로 표시된다. 특정 단락을 지정하지 않는 경우 지문 전체 내용을 바탕으로 추론해야 한다. 4개의 단어, 구 또는 문장으로 된 보기가 주어진다. 전형적인 질문 형태는 아래와 같다.

- According to the passage/paragraph #, what can be inferred about _____?
  지문/단락 #에 의하면, _____에 관하여 무엇이 추론 가능한가?

- Which of the following can be inferred from the passage?
  다음 중 어느 것이 지문에서 추론 가능한가?

- It can be inferred from the passage/paragraph # that . . .
  지문/단락 #에서 …을 추론할 수 있다.

문제 공략하기

다음은 Inference 문제의 공략법이다. 실전 고득점을 위해 이를 꼼꼼히 학습하고 Hackers Practice와 Hackers Test를 풀면서 반드시 적용해 본다.

1 지문에서 질문의 키워드를 찾아 문맥 파악하기

질문의 핵심 내용인 키워드를 확인한 후 지문에서 키워드가 언급된 부분을 찾고 주변의 문맥을 파악한다.

2 찾은 정보를 바탕으로 바르게 추론한 보기 찾기

키워드 주변 내용을 바탕으로 보기와 비교하여 바르게 추론한 것을 찾는다. 정답은 지문의 몇 문장을 바탕으로 추론하거나 단락이나 지문 전체 내용을 종합적으로 이해하여 추론하기도 하므로, 키워드와 관련된 모든 지문 내용을 꼼꼼히 파악하고 이해하는 것이 중요하다. 주관적인 지식이나 상상이 아닌 지문의 정보를 바탕으로 하여 객관적으로 추론이 가능한 보기가 정답이다.

In the mid-1970s, scientists discovered (two species of stream-dwelling frogs, *Rheobatrachus silus* and *Rheobatrachus vitellinus*), in the rainforests of eastern Australia. These white or cream-colored frogs were found to have reproductive habits unknown among other amphibians. After fertilization, the female frogs swallow their eggs and hold them in their stomachs. Digestion completely shuts down during the incubation period, and no stomach acids are produced. After about a month, the female spits out the hatched tadpoles into areas of shallow water where they slowly grow and mature.

1 질문의 키워드 two Rheobatrachus species와 같은 의미인 two species of stream-dwelling frogs, Rheobatrachus silus and Rheobatrachus vitellinus(개울에 서식하는 개구리 두 종, Rheobatrachus silus 와 Rheobatrachus vitellinus)가 언급된 부분을 지문에서 찾는다. 키워드가 언급된 부분의 문맥을 살펴보면, 개구리들이 알을 뱃속에 넣고 부화시키며 그 기간 동안 소화가 완전히 중단되는 것을 파악할 수 있다.

Which of the following can be inferred about the (two *Rheobatrachus species*)?

(A) They are capable of self-fertilization.
(B) They have overlapping reproductive ranges.
(C) They stop eating during pregnancy.
(D) They feed their young after hatching.

2 지문에서 찾은 소화가 완전히 중단된다는 내용을 바탕으로 '임신 기간 동안 아무 것도 먹지 않는다'라는 것을 추론할 수 있으므로 정답은 (C)이다.

지문해석 p.303

TIP 지문의 내용과 상반되거나 지문에 언급되지 않은 보기, 비약해서 추론한 보기는 오답이다.

Hackers Practice

지문을 읽고 물음에 답하시오.

01

The Aztecs prized the beans of the cocoa tree more than gold or silver, and cocoa was used as a form of currency in the empire. However, the Aztecs could not grow cocoa because their climate was too cool and dry, so they had to acquire it from other areas. They achieved this by conquering other peoples and demanding tribute in the form of cocoa. People in the lowland provinces grew the plant, and it was sent to the Aztec capital along with other items like rubber and cotton.

Which of the following can be inferred about cocoa beans from the passage?

(A) They could be traded for other goods.

(B) They were the primary seeds cultivated by the Aztecs.

(C) They were grown along with cotton and rubber.

02

In the late 1960s, a study of the Mediterranean Sea floor, conducted as part of the University of California's Deep Sea Drilling Project, revealed physical features not commonly encountered on the ocean bottom. Scientists expected to find sand, gravel, and mud, as these sediments naturally settle on the ocean floor. Instead they uncovered evaporite deposits such as salt, gypsum, and oceanic basalt. These substances only form on land surfaces where water has completely evaporated. Drilling deeper, scientists found fossils of blue-green algae, a plant that survives only at ocean levels where sufficient light permits plant growth. This has led some scientists to suggest that the Mediterranean Sea may once have been a shallow body of water or even a dry desert at some point in time.

According to the passage, what can be inferred about evaporite deposits?

(A) They could only have come from another body of water.

(B) They are substances that are abundant in upper ocean levels.

(C) They are not normally found buried beneath the ocean floor.

---

01 prize[praiz] 높이 평가하다   currency[kə́:rənsi] 통화   tribute[trίbjuːt] 조공

02 conduct[kəndʌ́kt] 수행하다   reveal[rivíːl] 밝히다   encounter[inkáuntər] 마주치다   sediment[sédəmənt] 퇴적물
   uncover[ʌnkʌ́vər] 발견하다   evaporite deposit 증발광상(해수 증발에 의해 형성되는 광상)   gypsum[dʒípsəm] 석고
   basalt[bəsɔ́ːlt] 현무암   evaporate[ivǽpərèit] 증발하다   shallow[ʃǽlou] 얕은

03

In 1543, a Chinese ship veered off course and arrived on Japanese shores. Aboard the ship were three Portuguese merchants who had brought firearms called muskets. The Japanese were curious about these strange weapons and quickly summoned artisans and steelworkers to study them and learn their manufacture. Having a well-developed metallurgical industry already, Japan was able to copy the guns, and soon implemented them in warfare. The first to use the new weaponry successfully in a decisive battle was the warlord Nobunaga, who equipped three thousand infantrymen with muskets in the 1575 Battle of Nagashino, a battle that is widely regarded as the turning point in the history of Japanese warfare.

According to the passage, what can be inferred about muskets?

(A) They were purchased from Portuguese merchants.

(B) They were unknown to the Japanese prior to 1543.

(C) They were manufactured by the warlord Nobunaga.

04

The Coast Redwood (*Sequoia sempervirens*) occurs along the coast of northern California and is a member of the Cupressaceae, a family of coniferous trees. The Redwood is the tallest living tree on Earth, averaging 150 feet in height, although some have grown to heights of 350 feet or more. A single tree can weigh as much as 500 tons and attain a mean diameter of 14 feet. Redwoods live to a maximum of about 2,000 years and continue to grow until they die. As they reach the 100-year mark, however, their upward growth slows considerably because the process of lifting nutrients and water up the height of the trunk becomes more difficult. Much of the growth energy is instead directed toward radial expansion.

What can be inferred about Coast Redwood tree from the passage?

(A) It rarely reaches a height of more than 350 feet.

(B) Its capacity to grow vertically does not stop until it dies.

(C) Its radius experiences greater growth than its height.

---

03 **veer off course** 항로를 이탈하다 **firearm**[fáiərà:rm] 화기 **summon**[sʌ́mən] 소집하다 **artisan**[ɑ́:rtəzən] 장인
steelworker[stí:lwə̀:rkər] 제강소 직공 **manufacture**[mæ̀njufǽktʃər] 생산 과정 **metallurgical**[mètələ́:rdʒikəl] 야금의
warfare[wɔ́:rfɛ̀ər] 전쟁

04 **redwood**[rédwùd] 아메리카삼나무 **coniferous**[kouníferəs] 침엽수의 **diameter**[daiǽmətər] 지름 **radial**[réidiəl] 반지름의

지문을 읽고 물음에 답하시오.

05

Human bonding is commonly associated with the parent-child relationship. Mothers, for instance, generally form intense attachments with their children in the early stages of an infant's life. Maternal bonding begins during pregnancy and continues after birth during breastfeeding. The attachment has a physical basis: the mother actually experiences changes in her body chemistry during and after pregnancy, and these changes are believed to foster maternal behavior. Over time, emotional, or affectional, bonds develop. These arise due to close and consistent contact between mother and child and can lead to feelings of attraction whereby the mother misses the child when the two are apart. Strong affectional bonds also develop between father and child through activities such as cuddling, consoling, and playing. They continue to strengthen throughout the lives of the father and child and are closely related to feelings of security and comfort.

What does the author imply about paternal bonding in the passage?

(A) It is not as strong as maternal bonding.

(B) It is more physical than emotional.

(C) It begins later than maternal bonding.

(D) It stems from a desire to protect the child.

06

The Pangaea theory was first postulated by Alfred Lothar Wegener in his 1920 book *The Origin of Continents and Oceans*. Wegener stated that some 250 million years ago, the supercontinent Pangaea was formed from separate, large masses of land. He supported the idea with his theory of continental drift. Landmasses were able to move because they rested on the Earth's outer mantle, a layer consisting of the asthenosphere and the lithosphere. The lithosphere comprises several large plates of rock floating on the asthenosphere, a layer of hot mantle that flows very slowly like a river of thick, melted clay. The movement of the plates pushed the landmasses together to form Pangaea, which existed for some 100 million years during the Paleozoic and Mesozoic eras before separating into the continents that exist on Earth today. Pangaea first split into two huge landmasses called Laurasia, which roughly corresponds to today's Northern Hemisphere, and Gondwanaland, the mass that eventually formed the Southern Hemisphere. The two masses further split up into the Earth's seven continents.

What can be inferred about the separation of Pangaea into smaller landmasses?

(A) It was made possible by movement of the Earth's plates.

(B) It occurred subsequent to the formation of Gondwanaland.

(C) It took place because the lithosphere broke up into large pieces.

(D) It resulted from the collision of two large landmasses.

---

05 **associate**[əsóuʃièit] 관련시키다　**intense**[inténs] 강한　**attachment**[ətǽtʃmənt] 애착　**foster**[fɔ́ːstər] 촉진하다
consistent[kənsístənt] 한결같은　**cuddle**[kʌ́dl] 껴안다　**console**[kənsóul] 달래다

06 **postulate**[pástʃulèit] 주장하다　**rest**[rest] 위치하다　**asthenosphere**[æsθénəsfìər] 암류권　**lithosphere**[líθəsfìər] 암석권
plate[pleit] 판　**Paleozoic**[pèiliəzóuik] 고생대의　**Mesozoic**[mèzəzóuik] 중생대의

07

The earliest forms of dramatic theater in the Mediterranean world were ritualistic performances conducted for religious purposes. These performances were based on myths that people accepted as historical fact. Frequently, these myths had to do with a deity's creative powers, and ritualistic performances provided an avenue for people to reenact a myth through repeating what a particular deity did. Through ritually acting out a god's actions, participants could become like the god and enjoy a temporary magical power over the universe. A famous example occurred around 700 BC as the worship of the nature god Dionysus spread to ancient Greece. Devoted followers danced and sang songs in honor of the god, and these performances were always carried out in unison by the cult's members, who collectively made up a chorus. This style lasted until some point in the sixth century, when the Dionysian priest Thespis began stepping out of the chorus and acting out myths through dialogue rather than song. It was his innovation that created the dramatic role of the actor and ushered in the era of Greek playwrights.

Which of the following can be inferred from the passage about ritualistic performances?

(A) They spread to ancient Greece from abroad.

(B) They were performed in front of audiences.

(C) They were believed to reflect true events.

(D) They originated in the cult of Dionysus.

08

Comets move in an elliptical orbit around the Sun. The comets that are far away from the Sun have heads composed of a nucleus. The nucleus, usually less than ten kilometers in diameter, exists as a ball of frozen gases and dust when the comet is distant from the Sun. As it approaches the Sun, the nucleus begins to warm up and its volatile gases evaporate, forming a cloud of scattered material called a "coma". The coma becomes luminous as particles of dust reflect the Sun's electromagnetic radiation and gas molecules absorb ultraviolet radiation. Solar wind blows dust particles and gases from the nucleus and coma, causing a tail to stream out from the direction opposite the Sun. The comet's orbit brings it nearer to the Sun, making it difficult for the human eye to detect both head and tail. The comet's size and shape begin to change, sometimes splitting into two, as Comet Biela did in 1846. Comets lose material each time they approach the Sun. Eventually they break up into pieces and fall to Earth or float off into space.

What can be inferred about a comet that is visible from the Earth?

(A) Its coma has absorbed too much ultraviolet radiation.

(B) It has broken into pieces.

(C) It is not yet close enough to the Sun.

(D) It has an unusually large coma.

---

07 ritualistic[rìtʃuəlístik] 의식의   deity[díːəti] 신   reenact[rìːinǽkt] 재현하다   devoted[divóutid] 헌신적인
cult[kʌlt] 숭배자 집단   collectively[kəléktivli] 집단으로   usher in ~의 도래를 알리다

08 comet[kámit] 혜성   elliptical[ilíptikəl] 타원의   volatile[válətl] 휘발성의   luminous[lúːmənəs] 빛을 내는
electromagnetic radiation 전자기 방사선   ultraviolet radiation 자외선   detect[ditékt] 감지하다

지문을 읽고 물음에 답하시오.

09

Agricultural production was crucial for supporting the Mayan civilization's large population, which stretched from Mexico down to modern day Honduras. Cities were often located in areas that were not conducive to agricultural production, but the Maya developed advanced agricultural production methods to cope with the difficult conditions. They built dams and reservoirs for storing rainwater, and systems of canals for irrigating fields in arid regions. In marshy areas, they implemented techniques for draining and raising fields to protect the roots of plants from exposure to excess water. In densely forested areas, some people practiced slash and burn agriculture, while others moved around periodically in search of fertile grassland.

The Mayans' expert farming skills enabled them to grow a variety of crops in different regions to be traded and shared throughout the empire. The diet of the Maya consisted mostly of the staple foods of maize(corn), squash, beans and chili peppers, but fruits, cacao, sunflower seeds, and honey were also used in moderate quantities. These foods were occasionally supplemented by meat, which was obtained from hunting and fishing. To flavor their dishes, the Maya used a broad range of spices including onions, cinnamon, oregano, vanilla, and salt. In addition to consumable products, the Mayans also cultivated cotton for weaving cloth, and tapped rubber trees, whose latex was used for making balls and even rudimentary accessories or clothing.

1. What can be inferred from paragraph 1 about Mayan agriculture?

   (A) It developed specially adapted crops for marshy areas.

   (B) It was unproductive in arid ecosystems.

   (C) It was adaptable to different geographic conditions.

   (D) It utilized fertilizers for depleted soils.

2. Which of the following can be inferred from paragraph 2 about the Mayan diet?

   (A) It was mostly comprised of seafood in coastal communities.

   (B) It consisted primarily of foods derived from plants.

   (C) It included exotic spices imported from abroad.

   (D) It was unique according to each individual region.

---

09 conducive[kəndjúːsiv] 도움이 되는 reservoir[rézərvwὰːr] 저수지 canal[kənǽl] 수로 irrigate[írəgèit] 물을 대다
marshy[máːrʃi] 습지의 excess[ékses] 과다한 slash and burn 화전식의 periodically[pìəriάdikəli] 주기적으로
staple food 주식 maize[meiz] 옥수수 squash[skwɑʃ] 호박 supplement[sʌ́pləmənt] 보충하다
flavor[fléivər] 맛을 내다 cinnamon[sínəmən] 계피 oregano[ərégənòu] 오레가노(허브의 일종)
consumable[kənsúːməbl] 소모할 수 있는 cultivate[kʌ́ltəvèit] 재배하다 weave[wiːv] 천을 짜다
tap[tæp] (나무 따위에 칼자국을 내어) 액을 받다 rudimentary[rùːdəméntəri] 기초적인

10

The Pleistocene epoch was the most recent global ice age, and it was marked by several periods of glaciations, or expanding glaciers. The change in climate during this epoch had devastating consequences on many species of fauna and flora. As the glaciers advanced from the Earth's poles, particularly the North Pole, many larger mammalian species became extinct: mammoths, mastodons, saber-toothed tigers, giant ground sloths and beavers, musk oxen, and some camel and horse species. In North America alone, 32 genera of large mammals disappeared. Generally, smaller mammals survived the extinction process. Scientists have not been able to verify the reasons for this, although some biologists attribute their survival to the rapidness with which they mature and their ability to breed large numbers of offspring during a single mating season. In contrast, larger mammals take a longer period of time to reach sexual maturity and often produce only one or a few young at a time. Moreover, the bigger carnivores had great difficulty finding sustenance when certain species of prey died out. On the other hand, many smaller mammals were omnivorous or herbivorous. Surviving animals migrated not only to escape extremely cold temperatures but also to reach vegetation zones that had been displaced as ice sheets extended farther south. Soil studies suggest that spruce and pine forests that normally grow in northern regions extended even to the Mediterranean region in Europe and the northern part of Louisiana in North America.

1. According to the passage, what can be inferred about the faunal extinctions during the Pleistocene?

(A) They occurred more in large mammal species than in small mammal species.

(B) They were comparatively rare outside of North America.

(C) They were caused by reasons other than advancing glaciers.

(D) They consisted mostly of marine life in the Northern Hemisphere.

2. What does the author imply about spruce and pine forests during the Pleistocene in the passage?

(A) They had little chance of surviving in the more southern regions.

(B) They were displaced from their previous range by glaciers.

(C) They were the only type of forest that survived glacial advances.

(D) They sprang up from seeds that had been carried south.

---

10 Pleistocene[pláistəsìːn] 홍적세의 epoch[épək] 세(世), 시기 mark[maːrk] 특징짓다 glaciation[glèiʃiéiʃən] 빙결
glacier[gléiʃər] 빙하 devastating[dévəstèitin] 파괴하는 fauna[fɔ́ːnə] 동물 flora[flɔ́ːrə] 식물
mammalian[məméiliən] 포유류의 mastodon[mǽstədàn] 마스토돈(코끼리와 비슷한 고대의 대형 포유 동물)
saber-toothed tiger 검치 호랑이 sloth[slɔːθ] 나무늘보 genus[dʒíːnəs] 속 (pl. genera) verify[vérəfài] 입증하다
attribute[ətríbjuːt] ~의 결과로 보다, ~의 탓으로 돌리다 carnivore[káːrnəvɔ̀ːr] 육식 동물 sustenance[sʌ́stənəns] 생계 수단
omnivorous[ɑmnívərəs] 잡식성의 herbivorous[həːrbívərəs] 초식성의 displace[displéis] 옮기다

11

Ancient Egyptian statues, compared with the classical statues produced by the Greeks and the Romans, appear unnatural and distorted. Classical Greek statues display different human expressions and great freedom of movement, with human figures often posed as though they were in motion. Egyptian statues, on the other hand, have rigid postures; their heads and bodies never face any direction except straight ahead, and their arms are held close to their sides. Their faces are expressionless. Another feature of Egyptian statues is their peculiar proportions. The Egyptians were familiar with human anatomy, but only parts of the body were depicted in a realistic way. The body from the neck down was relatively faithful to the human form, but the head and at times the feet were disproportionately large.

Essentially, sculpture during ancient Egypt's Third Dynasty (around 2690 to 2575 BC) was created for specific purposes, which influenced to a large extent how humans were depicted. Statues were often used for rituals held at temples and tombs, and it was necessary for those representing kings and deities to face forward, a depiction called frontality. This allowed the statues to "witness" the Egyptians when they performed rites. Sculptures of elite male persons also faced forward to receive offerings during rituals. It was not until the Fourth Dynasty that representations of servants were added for decoration, and were portrayed busy at various tasks—grinding grain, washing clothes— to indicate their status in life.

1. According to paragraph 1, what can be inferred about the proportions of ancient Egyptian statues?

(A) They signified the importance of anatomy to the Egyptians.

(B) They were not meant to represent human beings.

(C) They did not always conform to the normal proportions of the human body.

(D) They reflected the Egyptians' lack of skills in sculpture making.

2. In paragraph 2, what can be inferred about the statues of kings, deities, and male elites?

(A) They did not have very much significance in ancient Egyptian rituals.

(B) They were more attractive than the statues made during the Fourth Dynasty.

(C) They were used in ceremonies involving the death of someone important.

(D) Their postures indicated how they were used during religious rites.

---

11 distorted[distɔ́ːrtid] 왜곡된 pose[pouz] 자세를 취하다 posture[pástʃər] 자세 peculiar[pikjúːljər] 특이한
proportion[prəpɔ́ːrʃən] 비례 anatomy[ənǽtəmi] 해부학 depict[dipíkt] 묘사하다
disproportionately[dìsprəpɔ́ːrʃənətli] 불균형적으로 frontality[frʌntǽləti] 정면성 offering[ɔ́ːfəriŋ] 제물
grind[graind] 빻다 conform[kənfɔ́ːrm] 따르다

12

Begun in 1725, the Salon was the official art exhibition of the Academy of Fine Arts in Paris. It soon became not only the most important art exhibition in France, but the greatest art event in the world. The primary focus of the Salon was to showcase the work of Academy graduates. It was held in the Louvre, and, at first, was open only to members of the Academy or the social elite. Not until 1737 did exhibitions become public events, which ran twice annually for several weeks. A jury of judges, who were all award-winning artists themselves, was introduced in 1748. Their main responsibility was to decide which works of art would be accepted for display.

The Salon held undisputed influence over the art world in France, and its immense power and influence later became unpopular. Because jurors were trained in conservative academic atmospheres, their perception of what constituted acceptable art was very narrow. They consistently turned down impressionistic works, angering artists who were interested in receiving recognition for their artistic experimentation. The number of artists rejected was particularly large in 1863, and complaints were printed in the mass media, causing a public uproar over the fairness of the selection system. In response, Emperor Napoleon III ordered that all rejected artists be allowed to exhibit their paintings in an annex to the Salon. This exhibition, the Salon des Refusés (Exhibition of Rejects), which opened on May 17 to large crowds, symbolized the birth of the avant-garde.

1. In paragraphs 1 and 2, the author suggests which of the following about the Salon between 1748 and 1863?

   (A) Its selections for display were mainly from artists who had won awards.

   (B) It limited its displays to works produced by graduates of the Academy.

   (C) Its methods for selecting artwork became increasingly unpopular.

   (D) It gradually increased the number of impressionistic works on display.

2. Which of the following can be inferred about the Salon des Refusés according to paragraph 2?

   (A) Journalists were influential in its creation.

   (B) Its paintings offended some of the attendees.

   (C) Artists with formal academic training were not invited.

   (D) Its opening drew larger crowds than the Salon's.

정답·해석·정답단서 p.303

---

12 exhibition[èksəbíʃən] 전시회 showcase[ʃóukèis] 소개하다 jury[dʒúəri] 심사원단 undisputed[ʌ̀ndispjú:tid] 명백한
immense[iméns] 막대한 juror[dʒúərər] 심사원 conservative[kənsɔ́:rvətiv] 보수적인 perception[pərsépʃən] 이해
impressionistic[imprèʃənístik] 인상주의의 uproar[ʌ́prɔ̀:r] 소동 annex[ənéks] 별관 symbolize[símbəlàiz] 상징하다

1 The Founding of Londinium

1   In the year AD 43, Roman soldiers seeking to expand the Roman Empire entered Britannia, the island currently known as Great Britain. Thereafter, around AD 47, the Romans established a town among the pristine rolling hills on the quiet banks of the river Thames. Built on the site of modern-day London, the city was known to the Romans by its Latin name, Londinium.

2   ➡ The precise positioning of Londinium was probably due to its favorable location. There, the river was broad and deep enough to support sea-going vessels, but narrow enough for bridge construction. Some scholars believe it was originally conceived as a military outpost, but very few early fortifications have been unearthed in archaeological excavations. In addition, there is evidence to suggest that it functioned primarily as a civilian city less than a century after its founding. The discoveries of looms for weaving clothing, an amphitheater, underground irrigation networks, and coins all attest to the commercial vivacity of the young city. Leatherworks, potteries, mills, and other factories sprang up sporadically around the city, and the square in the city's center held scores of shops.

3   ➡ Historical documents also support the notion of young Londinium as being mainly a civilian city. In AD 109, the Roman historian Tacitus described Londinium as "a busy commercial center for trade and traders." He also recorded that in AD 60, Boudica, queen of the Iceni tribe that had colonized the area northeast of Londinium, led a revolt against Roman towns in southeast Britannia, sacking Roman villages and burning entire communities, including Londinium, to the ground. Her success indicates that the city was probably not heavily fortified at the time of the invasion. Furthermore, historical records claim that the rebuilding of Londinium after Boudica's invasion was accomplished under the direct supervision of Gaius Alpinus Classicianus, the financial minister in Rome's province of Britannia. This fact indicates that civilian officials in Londinium were awarded the utmost level of power and responsibility.

4   ➡ Regardless of why the city was initially founded, Londinium soon attracted settlers who engaged in manufacturing and trade, and the city became an important commercial hub for exchange between Britannia and Roman colonies on the mainland. By the middle of the second century AD, Londinium had grown from a small provincial town to a city of close to fifty thousand. After that time, however, the city mysteriously declined, and little is known about Londinium during the Middle Ages.

1   According to paragraph 2, all of the following offer evidence of Londinium's civilian roots EXCEPT

(A) devices for making garments

(B) a place for public entertainment

(C) a storage facility for trade goods

(D) examples of currency

Paragraph 2 is marked with an arrow [➡].

2   The word "colonized" in the passage is closest in meaning to

(A) inhabited

(B) owned

(C) renounced

(D) surrendered

3   What can be inferred from paragraph 3 about Britannia at the time of Boudica's invasion?

(A) Its towns were not all set up for defense.

(B) It was commercially dependent on Rome.

(C) Its capital city was Londinium.

(D) It was no longer occupied by the Romans.

Paragraph 3 is marked with an arrow [➡].

4   According to paragraph 4, what can be inferred about Londinium?

(A) Its role in the Roman Empire changed in the Middle Ages.

(B) The Romans abandoned it because it was too difficult to defend.

(C) Its population peaked in the middle of the second century.

(D) The settlers eventually moved to colonies on the mainland.

Paragraph 4 is marked with an arrow [➡].

1   Much of the earth's solid matter is made up of minerals, which are defined as substances having a crystalline structure with atoms arranged in repeating patterns. The most exquisite minerals are almost perfectly symmetrical, and this characteristic, along with their sparkling colors, makes them highly valued. There are several distinguishing features that help mineralogists identify and understand minerals.

2   ➡ To the naked eye, different minerals often look the same. Quartz and diamond, for example, have a transparent form and can even be confused with non-minerals such as glass. Furthermore, impurities can affect the appearance of a mineral, including its color. Diamond has a crystalline structure that is very strong and exclusive, meaning very few elements can infiltrate its tightly-bonded carbon atoms. However, the few that can (nitrogen, hydrogen, and boron) cause the diamonds, which are normally colorless, to take on different hues. Because some minerals are the same color and the presence of impurities in a mineral can change its hue, mineral color alone is not a very effective means of differentiation.

3   ➡ A better way is to use a streak test. The color of a mineral in powder form is called its streak. Streak can be measured in two ways. Minerals can be dragged across a hard porcelain material called a streak plate or crushed into a powder. The former is the most common method for most minerals because it is easy and less destructive. The color of the mineral powder left on a streak plate is mostly unaffected by impurities because they do not strongly absorb, transmit, or reflect light in a fine grain of the mineral. As a result, the color of the streak is a more reliable identifier than the color of the mineral. Calcite, which can be many different colors, always has a streak that is white. The iron-based minerals hematite and magnetite often appear a similar dark gray and can sometimes be difficult to differentiate visually, but their streaks clearly differ. Magnetite produces a dark gray streak. The streak of hematite, on the other hand, is a dark, reddish brown.

4   ➡ The relative hardness of minerals is also a useful characteristic for recognizing them. The scale used to gauge hardness is known as the Mohs' scale, named after its creator Friedrich Mohs, a German mineralogist. The Mohs' scale uses ten examples representative of the hardness range of known minerals and ranks them from 1 to 10. At the bottom, with a hardness of 1, is talc, a soft mineral with the consistency of chalk, and at the top of the scale is diamond. Minerals and even other solid objects can thus be placed on the scale relative to one another. Hardness is easy to test, as an object with a lower number cannot leave a mark on an object with a higher number. A copper penny, which has a hardness of 3.5, can easily scratch talc, but it is not hard enough to leave a mark on quartz, which has a hardness of 7. Conversely, quartz is harder than a copper penny but will not scratch diamond.

5   ➡ Another distinguishing feature of minerals is their cleavage. Cleavage is a mineral's tendency to break along particular planes when subjected to stress. Because of their crystalline structure, many minerals make smooth, even surfaces when they break.

Minerals that break along a single plane are said to have perfect cleavage. Others break along multiple planes, leaving some smooth and some rough surfaces. If the smooth surface is greater than the rough surface, the mineral has good cleavage. On the other hand, if the rough surface is dominant, the mineral has poor cleavage. Some minerals even have no cleavage and splinter when broken, leaving behind jagged and rough surfaces that have no apparent plane.

6 ➡ Identifying properties of minerals is useful not only for mineralogists but also for jewelers and consumers. A trained eye and careful testing are essential for determining whether a particular mineral crystal is real or an imitation. Many fake gemstones are made of colored glass or plastic and appear identical to genuine emeralds or sapphires, for instance. It is the correct determination of the physical properties of a gemstone that guarantees its value.

1 Which of the sentences below best expresses the essential information in the highlighted sentence in the passage? *Incorrect* choices change the meaning in important ways or leave out essential information.

(A) The most exquisite minerals are prized for their symmetry and color.

(B) Some minerals are more highly prized than others.

(C) Symmetry is a highly valued characteristic in the most exquisite of minerals.

(D) Symmetry causes the colors of minerals to sparkle, making them very valuable.

2 According to paragraph 2, what is the reason that color is unreliable as an identifying feature of minerals?

(A) Colors are subject to change if minerals contain impurities.

(B) Some minerals appear colorful but are actually transparent.

(C) The crystalline structures take on different hues as they age.

(D) The color of a mineral appears differently at different angles.

Paragraph 2 is marked with an arrow [➡].

3 Which of the following can be inferred about the color of mineral streaks from paragraph 3?

(A) They cover the entire range of the color spectrum.

(B) They are only stable in minerals that do not require crushing.

(C) They lack the impurities found in large mineral chunks.

(D) They are sometimes the same color as the mineral.

Paragraph 3 is marked with an arrow [➡].

CH 1
CH 2
CH 3
CH 4
CH 5
CHAPTER 6
CH 7
CH 8
CH 9

Hackers TOEFL Reading Intermediate

4   Which of the following can be inferred from paragraph 4 about the hardness of minerals?

(A) Soft minerals break more easily than hard ones.

(B) Diamond is the hardest known mineral.

(C) A mineral's hardness is inverse to its size.

(D) Quartz will not scratch a copper penny.

Paragraph 4 is marked with an arrow [➡].

5   According to paragraph 5, all of the following are ways minerals react to stress EXCEPT

(A) breaking along a single plane

(B) disintegrating into jagged pieces

(C) splintering into pieces of equal size

(D) breaking along more than one plane

Paragraph 5 is marked with an arrow [➡].

6   The word "apparent" in the passage is closest in meaning to

(A) steady

(B) clear

(C) level

(D) obtuse

7   What is the relation of paragraph 6 to the passage as a whole?

(A) It explains the practical importance of the ideas in the passage.

(B) It introduces a new issue that requires further consideration.

(C) It restates a main idea that appeared earlier in the passage.

(D) It counters the opinions of the previous paragraphs.

Paragraph 6 is marked with an arrow [➡].

8   Which of the following can be inferred about imitation gemstones from paragraph 6?

(A) Laypeople are unable to distinguish them from genuine jewels.

(B) They are less valuable than true gems because they are readily available.

(C) Their true value can only be determined by professional mineralogists.

(D) Consumers prefer them to real jewels because of their affordability.

1   Around the seventh century, Japan's leaders embarked on a massive and deliberate cultural borrowing campaign. Numerous officials and scholars were sent to China to learn directly about its culture and institutions. They brought back with them knowledge of Chinese learning as well as patterns of bureaucratic administration and organization. These cultural elements were viewed as tools of civilization, even the marks of civilization itself, and were vigorously incorporated into Japanese life.

2   ➡ Governance in Japan had been traditionally divided among many kingdoms ruled by separate tribes and warlords. This changed in AD 645 after a coup d'état consolidated control under Emperor Kōtoku, who quickly enacted political reforms. Known as the Taika Reform Edicts, they established a centralized system of government based on the Chinese bureaucratic model. Accordingly, the emperor exercised supreme control over all provinces, and government officials were required to undergo a civil service examination modeled on that of China's Tang Dynasty (618-907). The capital of the newly unified Japan was established at Nara, and it was planned on a rectangular grid system to resemble the Chinese capital of Chang An, with an enclosed palace in the north, east-west avenues intersecting a wide central boulevard, and a main gate entrance in the south. The symbolic significance of this city planning strategy was to match the arrangement of the bureaucracy. Having the emperor's palace centered in the north signified his place above the people, as heaven is situated over the land. Large plots of land near the palace were reserved for residences of the nobility, and further out, plots were blocked into small sections, which were occupied by commoners.

3   ➡ Additional evidence of borrowing from the Asian mainland is reflected in art and architecture. The Japanese government formally embraced Buddhism as its state religion, and was keen on importing Buddhist art objects from Korea, China, and India. Locally, Chinese and Korean craftsmen created the vast majority of Buddhist sculptures and paintings in Japan prior to the eighth century, but as Japanese artisans gained more comprehensive knowledge, they commenced their own artistic endeavors in Chinese style. The Japanese court sponsored these activities and built large temples in the capital at great cost. The most impressive of these was Todaiji Temple, which was constructed on a gigantic scale in 752. Its celebrated work of art was a sixteen-meter statue of Vairocana Buddha. The statue was cast in bronze and was housed in the largest wooden structure in the world. Works by Japanese sculptors, such as renditions of famous Buddhist priests, were also displayed at the temple, along with painted works depicting prominent Buddhist figures.

4   In literature, the Chinese language factored strongly into the development of Japanese prose and verse. Since Japan had no script of its own, it borrowed Chinese characters for writing. This linguistic adoption gave the Japanese access to a vast amount of Chinese scholarship. In addition, it fostered intellectual creativity on the islands, as Japanese scholars soon began producing literary manuscripts themselves. The earliest extant texts of Japanese origin are dated to the start of the eighth century.

5   ➡ Much of the prose written in Chinese was tightly connected to Confucian classics and

the civil service exams: any Japanese man who sought to gain a government post had to study Chinese history and philosophy. However, Japanese writers also composed in their own language using Chinese characters. This application of the Chinese writing system to Japanese was difficult. Therefore, most poetry in Japan remained native, and Chinese characters were used merely to apply written signs to Japanese syllables, words, and endings. The oldest examples of Japanese poetry are found in the *Man'yōshū*, an anthology compiled in AD 759. Its poems are structurally formed with the Japanese language. These native poems, known as *waka*, seem to have had no class or gender limits and focused on popular topics like sorrow and love. These were distinct from poetry composed using Chinese word order and grammar, called *kanshi*, which was the scholarly verse of the upper class.

6   The influence of the mainland began long before the seventh century and continued long after Japan stopped sending official missions in 894, but for three centuries, Japan's embracement of Chinese culture was intentional and intensive. This is largely attributable to the concurrent stability and progress of Tang China, a civilization that held the utmost power and prestige in Asia.

1   The phrase "embarked on" in the passage is closest in meaning to

(A) talked about

(B) substituted for

(C) parted with

(D) started on

2   Paragraph 2 suggests which of the following about the government of Japan?

(A) It eliminated the provincial civil service exams.

(B) It had not been centralized prior to AD 645.

(C) It was influenced by reforms in China.

(D) It was renamed after Kōtoku came to power.

Paragraph 2 is marked with an arrow [➡].

3   According to paragraph 2, all of the following are aspects of Nara's city planning EXCEPT

(A) a rectangular layout

(B) a main gate in the south

(C) a perimeter wall

(D) a central boulevard

4   Why does the author mention "heaven" in paragraph 2?

(A) To explain the status of the emperor with an analogy

(B) To emphasize that there were large plots of land near the palace

(C) To show that the city design was very similar to that of Chang An

(D) To argue that the nobility were ranked below the emperor

5   Which of the following can be inferred from paragraph 3 about Japanese artisans?

(A) They exported their art to other East Asian countries.

(B) They were followers of the Buddhist religion.

(C) They drew inspiration from foreign art.

(D) They studied under Chinese and Korean immigrants.

Paragraph 3 is marked with an arrow [➡].

6   Which of the sentences below best expresses the essential information in the highlighted sentence in the passage? *Incorrect* choices change the meaning in important ways or leave out essential information.

(A) The temple also displayed sculptures by Japanese artists and paintings of notable Buddhists.

(B) The Japanese sculptures in the temple were displayed next to paintings of famous Buddhists.

(C) Buddhists were the prominent subjects of Japanese paintings and sculptures displayed in the temple.

(D) Buddhists were influential in attracting Japanese painters and sculptors to display their works in the temple.

7   In paragraph 5, what does the author imply about Chinese characters?

(A) They were only used for scholarly verse.

(B) They were only studied by members of the upper class.

(C) Their use was limited in native poems.

(D) Their use in the civil service exams was controversial.

Paragraph 5 is marked with an arrow [➡].

8   According to paragraph 5, which of the following is true of the *Man'yōshū*?

(A) Its poems were written in 759.

(B) It includes native and Chinese poems.

(C) It contains the earliest examples of Japanese verse.

(D) Its author was Japan's first native poet.

정답·해석·정답단서 p.306

VOCABULARY LIST

Chapter 06에서 선별한 다음의 토플 필수 어휘를 단어암기 음성파일을 들으며 암기한 후 퀴즈로 확인해보세요.

*해커스 동영상강의 포털 해커스인강(HackersIngang.com)에서 단어암기 음성파일을 무료로 다운로드할 수 있습니다.

prize [praiz] 높이 평가하다

currency [kə́:rənsi] 통화

tribute [tríbjuːt] 조공

reveal [rivíːl] 밝히다 (=expose)

encounter [inkáuntər] 마주치다 (=face)

uncover [ʌnkʌ́vər] 발견하다

evaporate [ivǽpərèit] 증발하다

shallow [ʃǽlou] 얕은 (=not deep)

summon [sʌ́mən] 소집하다 (=beckon)

artisan [áːrtəzən] 장인

associate [əsóuʃièit] 관련시키다 (=link)

intense [inténs] 강한

attachment [ətǽtʃmənt] 애착 (=affection)

foster [fɔ́:stər] 촉진하다

consistent [kənsístənt] 한결같은 (=coherent)

cuddle [kʌ́dl] 껴안다

console [kənsóul] 달래다

postulate [pástʃulèit] 주장하다 (=claim)

rest [rest] 위치하다

ritualistic [rìtʃuəlístik] 의식의

deity [díːəti] 신

reenact [rìːinǽkt] 재현하다

devoted [divóutid] 헌신적인

collectively [kəléktivli] 집단으로 (=unitedly)

volatile [válətl] 휘발성의

luminous [lúːmənəs] 빛을 내는 (=gleaming)

detect [ditékt] 감지하다

conducive [kəndjúːsiv] 도움이 되는

irrigate [írəgèit] 물을 대다

excess [ékses] 과다한

periodically [pìəridádikəli] 주기적으로

supplement [sʌ́pləmènt] 보충하다 (=add to)

flavor [fléivər] 맛을 내다

consumable [kənsúːməbl] 소모할 수 있는

cultivate [kʌ́ltəvèit] 재배하다

rudimentary [rùːdəméntəri] 기초적인 (=basic)

epoch [épək] 시기 (=era)

devastating [dévəstèitiŋ] 파괴하는

verify [vérəfài] 입증하다 (=confirm)

attribute [ətríbjuːt] ~의 탓으로 돌리다 (=ascribe)

sustenance [sʌ́stənəns] 생계 수단 (=food)

displace [displéis] 옮기다 (=supplant)

distorted [distɔ́:rtid] 왜곡된

pose [pouz] 자세를 취하다

posture [pástʃər] 자세

peculiar [pikjúːljər] 특이한 (=characteristic)

proportion [prəpɔ́:rʃən] 비례

depict [dipíkt] 묘사하다 (=picture)

grind [graind] 빻다

conform [kənfɔ́:rm] 따르다 (=observe)

exhibition [èksəbíʃən] 전시회 (=exposition)

showcase [ʃóukèis] 소개하다 (=display)

Quiz

각 단어의 알맞은 뜻을 찾아 연결하시오.

01	evaporate	ⓐ 특이한
02	supplement	ⓑ 입증하다
03	peculiar	ⓒ 보충하다
04	verify	ⓓ 생계 수단
05	sustenance	ⓔ 비례
		ⓕ 증발하다

각 단어의 알맞은 동의어를 찾아 연결하시오.

06	postulate	ⓐ gleaming
07	luminous	ⓑ claim
08	epoch	ⓒ basic
09	rudimentary	ⓓ observe
10	conform	ⓔ execute
		ⓕ era

ⓓ 01   ⓒ 02   ⓐ 03   ⓑ 04   ⓓ 05   ⓑ 06   ⓐ 07   ⓕ 08   ⓒ 09   ⓓ 10

undisputed[ʌ̀ndispjúːtid] 명백한

immense[iméns] 막대한 (=enormous)

conservative[kənsə́ːrvətiv] 보수적인

perception[pərsépʃən] 이해

uproar[ʌ́prɔ̀ːr] 소동

symbolize[símbəlàiz] 상징하다

pristine[prísti:n] 자연 그대로의 (=unspoiled)

favorable[féivərəbl] 좋은

conceive[kənsíːv] 여겨지다

unearth[ʌ̀nə́ːrθ] 발굴하다 (=excavate)

archaeological[àːrkiəládʒikəl] 고고학의

excavation[èkskəvéiʃən] 발굴

attest[ətést] 증명하다 (=support)

sporadically[spərǽdikəli] 산발적으로

revolt[rivóult] 반란

supervision[sùːpərvíʒən] 감독

utmost[ʌ́tmòust] 최고의 (=supreme)

hub[hʌb] 중심지 (=center)

exquisite[ikskwízit] 정교한 (=delicate)

symmetrical[simétrikəl] 대칭의 (=proportionally balanced)

transparent[trænspɛ́ərənt] 투명한 (=lucid)

impurity[impjúərəti] 불순물

infiltrate[ínfiltreit] 침투하다

drag[dræg] 끌다 (=draw)

destructive[distrʌ́ktiv] 파괴적인

scratch[skrætʃ] 긁다

tendency[téndənsi] 경향 (=nature)

subject[səbdʒékt] 겪게 하다

splinter[splíntər] 부서지다 (=pulverize)

embark[imbáːrk] 착수하다

deliberate[delíbərət] 계획적인 (=intentional)

borrowing[bárouiŋ] 차용

bureaucratic[bjùərəkrǽtik] 관료주의의

vigorously[vígərəsli] 활발하게

incorporate[inkɔ́ːrpərèit] 도입하다

consolidate[kənsáládèit] 통합하다 (=integrate)

enact[inǽkt] 제정하다 (=make into law)

reform[ri:fɔ́ːrm] 개혁

rectangular[rektǽŋgjulər] 직각의

significance[signífikəns] 의의 (=meaning)

signify[sígnəfài] 의미하다 (=denote)

nobility[noubíləti] 귀족

occupy[ákjupài] 차지하다

embrace[imbréis] 차용하다

commence[kəméns] 시작하다 (=inaugurate)

endeavor[indévər] 노력

prominent[prámənənt] 특출한

adoption[ədápʃən] 차용

extant[ékstənt] 현존하는 (=existing)

intensive[inténsiv] 집중적인

concurrent[kənkə́ːrənt] 동시대적인 (=concomitant)

prestige[prestíːʒ] 세력

Quiz

각 단어의 알맞은 뜻을 찾아 연결하시오.

01 symmetrical ⓐ 상징하다
02 incorporate ⓑ 착수하다
03 symbolize ⓒ 도입하다
04 embark ⓓ 대칭의
05 concurrent ⓔ 좋은
　　　　　　　　ⓕ 동시대적인

각 단어의 알맞은 동의어를 찾아 연결하시오.

06 extant ⓐ existing
07 consolidate ⓑ intentional
08 deliberate ⓒ pulverize
09 immense ⓓ integrate
10 splinter ⓔ lucid
　　　　　　　ⓕ enormous

ⓒ 01 ⓒ 02 ⓐ 03 ⓑ 04 ⓕ 05 ⓐ 06 ⓓ 07 ⓑ 08 ⓕ 09 ⓒ 10

CHAPTER **07**

Insertion

Insertion

Insertion 문제는 글의 흐름을 유기적이고 자연스럽게 연결할 수 있도록 질문에 제시된 삽입 문장을 지문의 적절한 위치에 삽입하는 유형이다. Insertion 문제는 한 지문당 1개씩 고정적으로 출제된다.

Insertion 문제를 풀기 위해서는 글의 흐름을 파악하고 문장과 문장이 어떻게 논리적으로 연결되어 있는지 파악하는 연습을 해야 한다.

문제 살펴보기

Insertion 문제는 지문에 네 개의 ■를 표시하여 삽입 문장이 들어갈 위치를 명시해 준다. 전형적인 질문 형태는 아래와 같다.

- Look at the four squares [■] that indicate where the following sentence could be added to the passage.

[삽입 문장]

Where would the sentence best fit?

Click on a square [■] to add the sentence to the passage.

다음 문장이 지문에 삽입될 수 있는 곳을 나타내는 4개의 네모박스[■]를 보아라.
어디가 가장 적절한가?
해당 네모박스[■]를 클릭하여 제시된 문장을 지문에 삽입하라.

CH 1
CH 2
CH 3
CH 4
CH 5
CH 6
CHAPTER 7
CH 8
CH 9

Hackers TOEFL Reading Intermediate

▶ 문제 공략하기

다음은 Insertion 문제의 공략법이다. 실전 고득점을 위해 이를 꼼꼼히 학습하고 Hackers Practice와 Hackers Test를 풀면서 반드시 적용해 본다.

1 삽입 문장의 단서로 위치 추려내기

삽입 문장 내의 단서를 이용하여 ■가 표시된 주변 문장을 읽으며 네 개의 ■ 중 삽입 문장이 들어갈 위치를 추려낸다. 삽입 문장의 단서가 가리키는 것이 무엇인지 확인하여 정답으로 예상되는 위치를 추려낼 수 있다. 단서를 이용할 수 없는 경우, 흐름으로 보아 삽입 문장 전후에 와야 할 내용이 무엇인지 추측해 본다. 단서가 될 수 있는 표현의 예는 아래와 같다.

삽입 문장에 종종 나오는 단서

관사	a, the
지시어	this, that, these, those, their, such
연결어	for example, however, therefore, accordingly, in addition, also, similarly

2 문맥에 맞는 위치 찾기

지문의 ■에 삽입 문장을 넣은 후 앞뒤 문장과 논리적으로 연결되는지 확인한다. 문맥이 자연스러운 위치의 ■가 정답이다.

Another factor in the decline is the spread of disease from one frog population to the next. ■ For decades, hobbyists have imported exotic breeds of amphibians for their aquariums, often transporting these pets across continents without undergoing (proper inspections). ■ Once in a tank, a sick frog can quickly infect others, and attempts to treat the foreign illness may prove ineffective. ■ More importantly, any pets that are released into the wild after exposure to a diseased frog go on to infect other amphibians. Because native amphibians have little or no resistance to foreign diseases, exposure can wipe out entire wild populations. ■

Look at the four squares [■] that indicate where the following sentence could be added to the passage.

(Such inspections) are usually required by law to ensure that diseases are not introduced from abroad.

Where would the sentence best fit?

지문해석 p.310

2 두 번째 ■에 삽입 문장을 넣어보면, 양서류가 적절한 검사를 거치지 않고 국내로 유입되는데, 외국으로부터 질병이 들어오지 않도록 검사가 필요하다는 내용이 되어 문맥이 논리적으로 연결된다. 따라서 정답은 두 번째 ■이다.

1 삽입 문장에서 Such inspections(이러한 검사)를 단서로 하여 ■ 주변 문장을 읽어보면, 두 번째 ■ 앞 문장의 proper inspections(적절한 검사)를 가리키고 있다는 것을 알 수 있다.

Hackers Practice

지문을 읽고 물음에 답하시오.

01

Erik Homburger Erikson, a Danish American developmental psychologist, formulated a theory of human development that covers several stages from birth to death. ■ Most developmental theories apply only to the childhood years, but Erikson believed that development continues into adulthood. ■ Each stage in Erikson's theory focuses on a particular conflict that usually appears in a specific period of a person's life. The individual must resolve the conflict in order for the phase to be successfully completed. ■

Choose the square where the sentence below could be added to the passage.

In the earliest stage, for example, a child in the first eighteen months of life struggles with the opposites of trust and mistrust.

02

Temperate and tropical rainforests around the world differ in some respects, such as seasonal temperatures, but they also share certain similarities. One distinguishing feature of all rainforests is the considerable precipitation that falls each year. ■ Temperate rainforest rainfall ranges from about 1,400 to 2,000 millimeters annually, while tropical forests range from 2,100 to 7,600 millimeters. ■ The large quantities of moisture ensure great diversity in plant and animal species in both types of rainforest. ■

Choose the square where the sentence below could be added to the passage.

These amounts include not only rain from clouds but also water from snow, mist and fog.

03

Native Americans were very resourceful and made clothing from the natural materials that were available to them. ■ After the arrival of colonists in the New World, European elements such as beads and embroidery were added to create a unique style of decoration on garments. ■ Women were responsible for making clothes and took their tasks quite seriously, fashioning items that were as beautiful as they were practical. ■

Choose the square where the sentence below could be added to the passage.

Animal skins, plant fibers, shells, and feathers were all used in creating clothing.

---

01 developmental[divèləpméntl] 발달의 formulate[fɔ́ːrmjulèit] 체계적으로 나타내다 apply[əplái] 적용되다
   conflict[kánflikt] 갈등 phase[feiz] 시기 opposite[ápəzit] 정반대의 것
02 precipitation[prisìpətéiʃən] 강수량 ensure[inʃúər] 보증하다
03 resourceful[riːsɔ́ːrsfəl] 수완이 비상한 colonist[kálənist] 식민지 개척자 bead[biːd] 구슬 embroidery[imbrɔ́idəri] 자수
   garment[gáːrmənt] 옷 fashion[fǽʃən] 만들다 practical[prǽktikəl] 실용적인

04

A coral reef is a mound composed of dead coral, living coral, and secretions from algae and other living organisms. ■ The living coral uses the secreted substances to bind itself to the coral skeletons that settle on the ocean floor. Growing at a rate of about 13 millimeters per year, coral structures usually reach an average length of approximately two to three meters. ■ A fully grown reef is a critical habitat for nearly 90 percent of marine species. ■

Choose the square where the sentence below could be added to the passage.

A particularly large one, the Great Barrier Reef just off the coast of northeastern Australia is about 2,000 kilometers in length.

05

Many ancient Egyptian paintings are found on the walls of tombs of royalty or the wealthy elite. Egyptian artists created funerary scenes that showed what would happen to the deceased in the afterlife. ■ Often, subjects were depicted with judges, who were present to make an accounting of the deeds the person performed while living. ■ These paintings demonstrated the continuity between life and death. ■

Choose the square where the sentence below could be added to the passage.

In addition, Egyptian artists sometimes portrayed more mundane activities, such as singing and dancing.

06

Animal organisms have an internal mechanism that responds rhythmically to an environmental cycle. The cycle may occur at twenty-four-hour intervals; it might conform to the average time between full moons. It could also be based on a seasonal pattern. The mechanism, called a biological clock, functions to make an animal aware of upcoming events. ■ For instance, a bear's clock perceives that the days are getting shorter, signaling that winter is near. ■ The bear responds to the signal by eating large quantities of food to store fat for hibernation. ■

Choose the square where the sentence below could be added to the passage.

Without that signal, the animal would not produce sufficient fat in time.

---

04 coral reef 산호초   secretion[sikríːʃən] 분비물   alga[ǽlgə] 조류   bind[baind] 묶다   ocean floor 대양저

05 royalty[rɔ́iəlti] 왕족   funerary[fjúːnərèri] 장례식의   deceased[disíːst] 사망한   afterlife[ǽftərlàif] 사후
   depict[dipíkt] 묘사하다   deed[diːd] 공적   continuity[kàntənjúːəti] 연속성   mundane[mʌndéin] 일상적인

06 internal[intə́ːrnl] 체내의   rhythmically[ríðmikəli] 주기적으로   cycle[sáikl] 주기   interval[íntərvəl] 간격
   conform[kənfɔ́ːrm] 따르다   perceive[pərsíːv] 지각하다   hibernation[hàibərnéiʃən] 동면

07

A defining characteristic of transcendentalists in nineteenth-century America was their contempt for the society around them. They viewed the American people as conformists who thoughtlessly followed prevailing political and social customs of the day, even when those conventions were morally corrupt. ■ Their convictions led them to speak out strongly against slavery, calling it a crime against humanity, and they actively encouraged others to get involved in social reform efforts like the women's rights movement. ■ They even went so far as to break laws as a form of civil disobedience in the name of justice. ■

Choose the square where the sentence below could be added to the passage.

Henry David Thoreau, for example, went to jail rather than pay taxes to an unjust government.

08

Electricity generation is sure to go through fundamental changes in the near future, as fossil fuel supplies begin to decrease. ■ Recently, concerns about global warming due to greenhouse gas emissions are forcing energy producers to rethink their energy policies and to seek cleaner sources of electricity. ■ Of the alternative energies, solar power is the most widely produced and creates no air pollution. ■ The sun is a valuable source of renewable energy for heating homes and powering commercial buildings, and does not have the costs of resource exploration and drilling. Innovations in solar panel technology have also made solar power production more economical and efficient.

Choose the square where the sentence below could be added to the passage.

No one knows exactly how long current stores of oil and gas will last, but it is clear that they will eventually be exhausted.

---

07 transcendentalist[trænsendéntlist] 초월론자 contempt[kəntémpt] 경멸 conformist[kənfɔ́ːrmist] 순응자
convention[kənvénʃən] 관습 morally[mɔ́ːrəli] 도덕적으로 corrupt[kərʌ́pt] 부패한 conviction[kənvíkʃən] 신념
humanity[hjuːmǽnəti] 인류 civil disobedience 시민 불복종

08 fundamental[fʌ̀ndəméntl] 근본적인 fossil fuel 화석 연료 greenhouse gas 온실가스 emission[imíʃən] 배출
solar panel 태양 전지판 exactly[igzǽktli] 정확하게 exhausted[igzɔ́ːstid] 고갈된

지문을 읽고 물음에 답하시오.

09

The culture of the ancient Romans was not entirely indigenous. Much of it was acquired through contact with other civilizations, most notably Greece, during the expansion of the Roman Empire. Following Rome's conquest of Greece in 146 BC, several elements were borrowed and incorporated into Roman life. ■ Chief among these was Greek religion. ■ Most Roman gods and goddesses were equated with a Greek deity, such as Zeus with Jupiter, Aphrodite with Venus, and Artemis with Diana. ■ Even the temples and other architectural structures built for religious purposes were modeled after the Greek style and simply modified over time to meet the Romans' urban requirements. ■

Choose the square where the sentence below could be added to the passage.

Accordingly, each of these deities was endowed with the attributes and myths of their Greek counterparts.

10

Biological taxonomy is a way of classifying living organisms. Modern classification is based on the system developed by Swedish scientist Carl Linnaeus. Linnaeus ranked living things in a hierarchy that moved from the general to the specific. Kingdom, the broadest level, was divided into plants and animals. ■ These wide divisions were then further compartmentalized into ever-smaller groups according to shared physical features. ■ He placed all animals with mammary glands, for instance, into the class Mammalia. ■ At the most specific level, he created a binomial nomenclature system so that each unique organism had a two-word Latin name that designated its genus and species. For humans, this binomial is *Homo Sapiens*. ■

Choose the square where the sentence below could be added to the passage.

Similarly, organisms with binocular vision and fingers for grasping were put in the order Primates.

---

09 indigenous[indídʒənəs] 고유의   notably[nóutəbli] 특히   equate[ikwéit] 동일시하다   deity[díːəti] 신
10 taxonomy[tæksánəmi] 분류법   rank[ræŋk] 분류하다   hierarchy[háiəràːrki] 계급제   kingdom[kíŋdəm] [생물] 계(界)
compartmentalize[kəmpɑːrtméntəlàiz] 구분하다   mammary gland 유선   class[klæs] [생물] 강(綱)
Mammalia[məméiliə] 포유류   binomial nomenclature 이명법   genus[dʒíːnəs] 속   species[spíːʃiːz] 종
binocular vision 쌍안시   order[ɔ́ːrdər] [생물] 목(目)   Primates[praiméitiːz] 영장류

11

Early astronomers used the naked eye to study the stars in the cosmos. The eye's small lens, however, gathers insufficient light and lacks the visual perception needed to spot fainter stars, measure distances, and gauge brightness. To overcome these weaknesses, astronomers developed new instruments to record, collect, and analyze images of stars. ■ The earliest, the refractor telescope, was invented in the Netherlands in 1608 and used a lens to form an image. Optical telescopes, most of which were produced in the early twentieth century, take in light from the electromagnetic spectrum, increasing the size and brilliance of distant objects. ■ The radio telescope, a 1931 invention, differed from optical telescopes in that it collected radio transmissions from astronomical objects via antenna to produce images of stars. ■ The Hubble telescope, launched in 1990, factors in the curvature of space, the constantly expanding universe, and phenomena in space that distort light to produce very accurate measurements. ■

Choose the square where the sentence below could be added to the passage.

Perhaps the most well-known and enduring of these is the telescope.

12

Deciduous trees respond to cold temperatures through the cessation of all growth and cellular activity. They achieve this by sending nutrients to their roots and dropping their leaves, only to resume active growth in spring. Evergreen trees, on the other hand, keep their leaves and continue to use sunlight to produce energy throughout winter. The needle-like leaves of conifers, such as cedars and spruces, have small surface areas and much smaller pores than the leaves of broadleaf trees. ■ This enables them to minimize water loss during winter when water is often unavailable. ■ The dark color of the leaves helps attract the warming rays of the sun. ■ Leaves are also densely packed and collect snow, which acts as a blanket that insulates the plants from extreme temperatures. ■ However, too much snow could overburden the plants and cause their branches to snap, so conifers have single, unbranched trunks and cone-shaped canopies to allow excess snow to fall to the ground.

Choose the square where the sentence below could be added to the passage.

Their coloration can lead to an increase of several degrees in temperature near the leaf surface.

---

11 astronomer[əstrάnəmər] 천문학자 naked eye 육안 cosmos[kάzməs] 우주 lens[lenz] 수정체
visual perception 시지각 gauge[ɡeidʒ] 측정하다 refractor[rifrǽktər] 굴절 렌즈 optical[ɑ́ptikəl] 광학의
electromagnetic[ilèktroumæɡnétik] 전기의 radio[réidiòu] 전파에 의한 transmission[trænsmíʃən] 송신
factor in ~을 고려하다, ~을 계산에 넣다 curvature[kə́ːrvətʃər] 만곡

12 deciduous[disídʒuəs] 낙엽성의 cessation[seséiʃən] 중지 resume[rizúːm] 재개하다 evergreen[évərgrìːn] 상록수
conifer[kóunəfər] 침엽수 cedar[síːdər] 히말라야삼목 spruce[spruːs] 가문비나무 pore[pɔːr] 기공
minimize[mínəmàiz] 최소화하다 ray[rei] 빛 insulate[ínsəlèit] 차단하다 extreme[ikstríːm] 극단적인
canopy[kǽnəpi] 초관(식물의 최상위 가지 및 잎의 형태) excess[ékses] 여분의

13

The term "cottage industries" refers to a range of small-scale enterprises, such as textile production, that are carried out in people's homes rather than in factories. Cottage industries were common in sixteenth-century England in rural areas and small towns. ■ They were characterized by low levels of organization and were often part-time and seasonal to permit adequate time for farming or other work. ■ Everyone in the family was involved in the process. ■ Children helped out with simple tasks, while mothers and fathers focused on more technical details. ■ In a cottage industry focused on clothing, children would prepare the yarn, making sure it was not tangled. Mothers and fathers then spun and weaved the yarn into finished products. In England, cottage industries were the precursors to the industrial factories that eventually replaced them, but they are still common throughout much of the developing world. Asian countries in particular still have thriving cottage industries, especially in rural areas.

Choose the square where the sentence below could be added to the passage.

They also occasionally sprang up in urban environments among the poor.

14

Etching is a method of creating a design or picture on metal that can be used to produce multiple, nearly identical, print copies of the composition. To achieve this, the artist first covers metal plates in wax. Then the artist "scratches" a design into the wax using a sharply pointed etching tool. After the design is completed, acid is poured over the plate. The acid eats away at the areas of metal that were exposed, creating grooves that correspond to the drawn lines. ■The wax is then removed and the plate is covered with ink, which is then wiped from the surface, leaving ink only in the depressed lines in the metal. ■ Finally, the metal plate is covered with paper and inserted into a high-pressure printing press. ■ The pressure imprints the ink onto the paper, and this process can be done many times to create multiple printed versions of a single etching. ■

Choose the square where the sentence below could be added to the passage.

However, between printings the ink is wiped clean and reapplied, so each reproduction is considered an original.

13 cottage industry 가내 공업　enterprise[éntərpràiz] 회사　textile[tékstail] 직물　rural[rúərəl] 농업의
seasonal[sí:zənl] 계절적인　adequate[ǽdikwət] 충분한　technical[téknikəl] 기술적인　yarn[jɑːrn] 실
tangle[tǽŋgl] 엉키게 하다　spin[spin] (실을) 잣다, 뽑다　weave[wiːv] 짜다　precursor[prikə́ːrsər] 전조
eventually[ivéntʃuəli] 결국　replace[ripléis] 대체하다　in particular 특히　thrive[θraiv] 성행하다　spring up 생겨나다

14 etching[étʃiŋ] 부식 동판술　multiple[mʌ́ltəpl] 다수의　identical[aidéntikəl] 똑같은　scratch[skrætʃ] 긁어 파다
pointed[pɔ́intid] 뾰족한　eat away 부식하다　expose[ikspóuz] 노출시키다　groove[gruːv] 가늘고 길게 패인 곳
correspond to 해당하다　depressed[diprést] 움푹 들어간　insert[insə́ːrt] 넣다　printing press 인쇄기
imprint[imprínt] 찍다

15

The Great Depression was the most severe economic downturn in US history. Economists disagree about the main cause of the economic depression, which is often associated with the collapse of the stock market in 1929, but one popular theory is that the event resulted from an imbalanced distribution of wealth. During the Roaring Twenties, America became a very prosperous nation because of greater worker productivity and lower costs of production. Overall, manufacturing production rose by one-third during the 1920s. ■[1]This boosted corporate profits by more than 60 percent, but worker salaries grew by only 8 percent. ■ Most of the profits from the production boom went to a few wealthy individuals. ■ A related phenomenon was the growing gap between supply and demand. ■ Overproduction made consumer goods widely available, but because the incomes of the masses were so low, the actual demand for these goods could not keep pace with supply.

A second explanation focuses on the policies of the Federal Reserve (Fed). ■[2]The recession made it difficult for businesses to pay their debts, and as a result, many of them defaulted on their loans, causing banks to fail. ■ Between 1929 and 1933, over half of US banks ceased operations. ■ This meant that there was a huge reduction in the money supply. The Fed could have solved this problem by purchasing bonds, but it did not. By refusing to act, the Fed caused interest rates to rise, making it even harder for people to get the credit they needed. ■

1. Choose the square where the sentence below could be added to the passage.

The entrepreneur Henry Ford, for example, had a yearly income of nearly twenty thousand times that of the average worker.

2. Choose the square where the sentence below could be added to the passage.

Economists who emphasize the role of the Fed claim that the Great Depression was entirely avoidable.

---

15 **Great Depression** 대공황 **downturn**[dáuntəːrn] 침체 **collapse**[kəlǽps] 붕괴 **stock market** 주식 시장
Roaring Twenties 광란의 20년대(미국의 1920년대) **prosperous**[práspərəs] 부유한 **overall**[óuvərɔ̀ːl] 전반적으로
corporate[kɔ́ːrpərət] 회사의 **boom**[buːm] 급격한 증가 **consumer good** 소비재 **the masses** 서민
Federal Reserve 연방준비은행 **recession**[riséʃən] 불경기 **default**[difɔ́ːlt] 채무를 이행하지 않다 **loan**[loun] 대부금
bond[bɑnd] 채권 **interest rate** 금리 **credit**[krédit] 융자, 신용

16

All predators play a role in ecosystems by controlling the populations of organisms at different levels of the food chain. ■[1]These predators affect the environment far more than their numbers would indicate, and their function is analogous to the keystone of an arch. ■ The keystone is the single piece in the center of an arch that bears the least amount of structural weight, but if the keystone is removed, the entire structure will crumble. ■ The same is true with keystone species. Though their numbers are small, without them, biodiversity in the ecosystem would collapse. ■

The keystone species concept was introduced by ecologist Robert Paine in 1969 and has become a standard term in biological literature. ■[2]Paine introduced the concept after an experiment with a small community of invertebrates along a stretch of Pacific Coast shoreline where he purposely removed a single species of starfish (*Pisaster ochraceus*). ■ He noticed that removal of the starfish caused some organisms to increase while others began to disappear. ■ This is because the starfish was the main predator of the mussel, *Mytilus californicus*. ■ In the absence of the starfish, the mussel colony grew and crowded out other creatures, such as urchins and anemones, on the rocky shores. Prior to the experiment, approximately fifteen species of invertebrates populated the area. That number was reduced to two by removal of the starfish.

1. Choose the square where the sentence below could be added to the passage.

   However, the presence or absence of certain predators can have dramatic effects.

2. Choose the square where the sentence below could be added to the passage.

   It can be found in virtually any textbook dealing with ecology and conservation.

정답·해석·정답단서 p.310

---

16 indicate[índikèit] 나타내다 be analogous to ~와 비슷하다 keystone[kíːstòun] 종석 arch[ɑːrtʃ] 아치
crumble[krʌ́mbl] 부스러지다 keystone species 핵심종 biodiversity[bàioudivə́ːrsəti] 생물 다양성
ecologist[ikálədʒist] 생태학자 literature[lítərətʃər] 논문 invertebrate[invə́ːrtəbrət] 무척추동물 starfish[stáːrfiʃ] 불가사리
mussel[mʌ́səl] 말조개 crowd out 밀어내다 urchin[ə́ːrtʃin] 성게 anemone[ənéməni] 말미잘
approximately[əpráksəmətli] 대략 populate[pápjulèit] 살다

1 Teotihuacan

1   The valley northeast of Mexico City contains the ruins of a majestic civilization. Much about the ancient society remains a mystery; we do not know exactly who built its main city, what it was called, or why it collapsed. ■²However, we do know that the civilization flourished from the second century BC to around AD 750. ■ Centuries later, when the Aztecs eventually discovered the central city, it had already been abandoned; yet they were awestruck by the grandeur of the ruins. ■ Because of the city's many religious monuments, the Aztecs named it Teotihuacan, which means "Place of the Gods." ■ Using the ruins and artifacts found on the vast site, archaeologists have been able to paint a picture of the ancient city.

2   ➡ Teotihuacan's position as a place of great importance in ancient Mesoamerica is reflected by its ceremonial structures, which were constructed on an immense scale. Situated in the city's center was a complex of buildings that includes the world's third largest known pyramid. Archaeologists refer to it as the Pyramid of the Sun and believe it was constructed to venerate a deity; however, the destruction of the temple atop the great structure prior to excavation made it difficult to determine the specific god to which the temple was dedicated. Vibrantly colored murals once plastered the interior walls of the pyramid, mostly reflecting natural symbols like jaguars, snakes, and astronomical bodies that the Teotihuacan people revered. Another pyramidal structure used as a key worship center was the Temple of Quetzalcoatl, so named for the Aztec word of an important dragon-like feathered serpent once exalted throughout Mesoamerica. Excavations of chambers near the temple uncovered human and animal skeletons, leading some archaeologists to interpret the findings as evidence of sacrificial rituals once performed in the sacred spaces.

3   Large mansions in proximity to the pyramids were probably homes for the families of priest-rulers, who had both spiritual and political duties. Other powerful families in the social hierarchy would have lived in stone structures lining the central avenue that runs through the city, whereas farmers occupied wooden homes spread out along the city's periphery. ■⁴Those in the agricultural class would have made daily treks to surrounding fields to tend crops for the large community of some 150,000 people, which, at the time, was one of the largest cities in the world. ■ There was also a class of potters and jewelers who resided in apartment buildings throughout the entire city. ■ Human figurines and arrowheads are among the common artifacts found at the sites, and the artisans frequently carved them out of obsidian collected from volcanic rock in the region. ■

1 The word "majestic" in the passage is closest in meaning to

(A) unusual

(B) magnificent

(C) perfect

(D) humble

2 Look at the four squares [■] that indicate where the following sentence could be added to the passage.

Nor do we comprehend how an ancient people could have built its impressive architecture.

Where would the sentence best fit?

Click on a square [■] to add the sentence to the passage.

3 According to paragraph 2, it is uncertain which deity the Pyramid of the Sun was dedicated to because

(A) the pyramid's once-vibrant murals have faded over time

(B) the pyramid's temple was destroyed before it was excavated

(C) the Teotihuacan people worshipped a variety of nature gods

(D) the Sun god was only known from other Mesoamerican cultures

Paragraph 2 is marked with an arrow [➡].

4 Look at the four squares [■] that indicate where the following sentence could be added to the passage.

Rooms within these community dwellings have yielded numerous handmade items fashioned for everyday use.

Where would the sentence best fit?

Click on a square [■] to add the sentence to the passage.

2 Drought Tolerance in Prairie Grasses

1   Prairie ecosystems are characterized by flat terrain or gently-sloped rolling hills, and by a predominance of herbaceous plant life. Trees, shrubs, and other woody plants are virtually absent in prairies, and there is very little shelter from the hot solar radiation and harsh gales. Prairies generally receive a moderate amount of yearly average precipitation, but summers are occasionally marked by severe drought. Consequently, for plants to thrive in the prairie ecosystem, they must endure seasonally dry conditions. Among the herbaceous plants suited for life in these ecosystems are prairie grasses, which have several adaptive mechanisms for survival.

2   ➡ Leaves of prairie grasses vary in width, but most are simply long, thin blades. ■²On the epidermal layer of the leaves are small holes, called stomata, which can be opened to let in carbon dioxide and release oxygen, or closed to retain moisture. ■ Because carbon dioxide is essential for plant photosynthesis and respiration, the stomata must remain wide for gas exchange; however, air spaces within the leaf are full of water vapor, which evaporates through transpiration unless the pores remain closed. ■This presents a challenge during dry conditions for plants because water is lost to the atmosphere. ■ To overcome the problem, prairie grasses have evolved to distinguish between day and night. In the daytime, when heat energy from the sun is most intense, the grasses keep their stomata shut to minimize moisture loss. The plants then expand the pores in the evening when the air is cooler for respiration. This allows them to get the carbon dioxide they need during dry periods without completely drying them out.

3   One group of prairie grasses has enlarged epidermal cells along and between the veins of their leaves. After a rain, the cells swell to their full capacity and are saturated with water, but during drought conditions the cells shrink. The shrinkage results in differences in volume between saturated tissues and unsaturated tissues, causing the leaves to coil and effectively envelop any water on the leaf's surface. This helps reduce evaporation from direct solar radiation by shading the surface of the leaves. ■⁵Another group of prairie grasses has pubescent leaves, meaning their foliage is covered in tiny bristles. ■ Pubescence decreases the surface temperature by filtering the sun's rays, and can increase humidity levels through the retention of water. ■ If the air has enough humidity, falling temperatures overnight will cause dew to form on plants. ■ Pubescent leaves are able to hold water droplets longer, as dew often simply runs off the smooth surface of glabrous(hairless) leaves.

4   ➡ Though prairie grasses have adaptations to help their leaves stay green and healthy, they can transition into foliar dormancy if conditions become too severe. Prairies may undergo weeks or months of rainless weather. In such circumstances, the leaves may die; but because many prairie grasses are perennials, the root systems continue to remain alive below ground. Root systems of prairie grasses can be quite extensive, and the deeper the roots, the longer a plant can go without rain. One plant, *Andropogon gerardii* (big bluestem), a large late-blooming North American

species, has particularly deep roots relative to its vegetative growth. In the first part of the growing season, the leaves emerge slowly, and most of the plant's resources are devoted to producing deep, substantial root systems. It accounts for the energy imbalance with slower above-ground growth and lower reproductive rates. By putting less energy into vegetative growth, the plant inevitably shortens its blooming season. On the other hand, its well-developed underground parts allow it to reach moisture deep in the soil and compete for nitrogen and other soil nutrients .

5   Prairie grasses have drawn the attention of people in the botanical community for their adaptive qualities. ■⁸Their toughness is extolled by environmentalists who advocate water conservation. ■ As a result, prairie grasses have recently become more common as candidates for lawns and gardens, particularly in regions where drought is a real concern. ■ By replacing moisture-dependent grasses with drought-tolerant prairie grasses, human communities can greatly reduce their dependence on water for horticultural uses. ■

1   The word "virtually" in the passage is closest in meaning to

(A) totally

(B) nearly

(C) strangely

(D) barely

2   Look at the four squares [■] that indicate where the following sentence could be added to the passage.

They attach to the stem near the plant's base, just above the root system.

Where would the sentence best fit?

Click on a square [■] to add the sentence to the passage.

3   Which of the following can be inferred about gas exchange in prairie grasses according to paragraph 2?

(A) It helps conserve moisture within the leaves of the plants.

(B) It is most efficient when carried out during the day.

(C) It ensures that oxygen and carbon dioxide are present in equal amounts.

(D) It is only possible when the stomata are open.

Paragraph 2 is marked with an arrow [➡].

4   Which of the sentences below best expresses the essential information in the highlighted sentence in the passage? *Incorrect* choices change the meaning in important ways or leave out essential information.

(A) Shrinkage from changes in water content causes differences in volume between adjacent tissues.

(B) Volume disparities due to tissue shrinkage cause leaves to coil, enclosing surface water.

(C) Leaves coil, saturating tissues with water by preserving any moisture on the leaf surface.

(D) In order to envelop water on the leaf surface, adjacent tissues must have different volumes.

5   Look at the four squares [■] that indicate where the following sentence could be added to the passage.

These may be sparsely or densely distributed on the leaves.

Where would the sentence best fit?

Click on a square [■] to add the sentence to the passage.

6   According to paragraph 4, what is true of *Andropogon gerardii*?

(A) It requires nutrient-rich soil for active growth.

(B) It sacrifices vegetative growth for root growth.

(C) It puts most of its energy into reproductive growth.

(D) Its roots have developed a quick method of water uptake.

Paragraph 4 is marked with an arrow [➡].

7   The word "emerge" in the passage is closest in meaning to

(A) enlarge

(B) descend

(C) mature

(D) appear

8   Look at the four squares [■] that indicate where the following sentence could be added to the passage.

In doing so, they can also save on their water bills.

Where would the sentence best fit?

Click on a square [■] to add the sentence to the passage.

3 The Port of Melaka

1 ■[1]Located in Malaysia on the narrowest point on the Strait of Melaka, the port of Melaka is situated on one of the world's busiest international waterways. ■ Melaka has a complex geopolitical history of more than half a millennium and was settled by a diversity of ethnic groups. ■ In addition, its location on one of the great arteries of global commerce gave it a strategic position for trade, particularly of spices, and made it subject to international political and economic forces. ■

2 The first to document and spread the word concerning the virtues of Melaka as an international hub for commerce was the famed naval admiral and maritime explorer Zheng He of China. Zheng He visited Melaka between 1405 and 1433 on five of his seven voyages throughout Southeast Asia, and sent news of the region's material wealth and natural resources to the Ming emperor, stimulating a vigorous demand for Southeast Asian products in fifteenth-century China.

3 ➡ Melaka during the fifteenth century was under the guidance of Sultan Mansur Shah. At the time, Zheng He's fleet included Muslim crew members who helped the Chinese develop intimate connections with the locals in Melaka. This relationship between Melaka and Ming China meant that spices produced in India could be easily shipped to China, with Melaka as a key stop-off point, rather than being transported overland through Central Asia. The sultan's tax policies reflected China's privileged position. Merchants from Arabia and India were taxed at a rate of 6 percent; those in the Malay region were taxed at only 3 percent; and Chinese traders were not taxed at all.

4 Muslim control of Melaka had a far-reaching effect in the West as well. ■[5]The spice trade provided the main impetus for Europeans to intervene in Southeast Asia. ■ Pepper and cinnamon, for example, were plentiful in the region and valued abroad for their exotic flavors. ■ Spices sent to Europe in the fifteenth century were first directed through the Turkish-controlled Persian Gulf, or via the Red Sea to Alexandria in Egypt. ■Therefore, Europeans had to go through Muslim merchants, who served as middlemen. Because the transfer of products through numerous hands made the price higher for the end buyer, European nations began to seek local control over the maritime spice trading routes. The fabled Spice Islands of the East thus became a competitive battleground for international powers. After 1500, the invasion of the Portuguese changed the power relations, and most of the products passing through the Strait of Melaka were shipped directly to Europe.

5 ➡ The Portuguese expelled the ruler of Melaka in 1511 and occupied the port city until 1641. During the early years of its occupation, the Portuguese state exercised a strict monopoly of the spice trade in Melaka, but by the 1530s, it began to extend trading rights to individual merchants. Soon, there were hundreds of Portuguese entrepreneurs buying and selling in Melaka, and transporting spices on their own private ships. Portugal was able to keep the trade routes secret during the sixteenth century, but the ascension of the Dutch as a naval power in the 1600s ended

Portuguese dominance. In 1641, the Dutch took control of Melaka from Portugal by force, and the port became a Dutch outpost.

6 → Of the local spices traded abroad in the Portuguese and Dutch periods, pepper was the dominant commodity. Production of the cash crop peaked with an annual trade of 8,500 tons in 1670 under the Dutch, after which time prices began to fall and farmers in the region began to grow other crops, such as cotton and sugarcane, instead. Melaka also became a major port for staples like textiles and rice, which were brought to Melaka's bustling market from smaller ports in the region.

7 In contrast to the brief transactions taking place in minor trading centers, Melaka's merchants set up markets for months. This practice gave rise to the presence of long-term residents. ■[8]Some traders from overseas made Melaka their home and intermarried with Malay women to establish local ties. ■ Among immigrants, the Chinese community came to dominate in absolute numbers, and ethnic Chinese are the largest minority population in Melaka even today. ■ The cosmopolitan history of Melaka is also evident in its buildings. ■ Local, Portuguese, and Dutch architecture remain in the historic center of Melaka City, offering a distinctive atmosphere still popular with tourists and commemorating its international roots.

1 Look at the four squares [■] that indicate where the following sentence could be added to the passage.

Approximately six hundred commercial vessels pass through its channels daily.

Where would the sentence best fit?

Click on a square [■] to add the sentence to the passage.

2 Which of the sentences below best expresses the essential information in the highlighted sentence in the passage? *Incorrect* choices change the meaning in important ways or leave out essential information.

(A) Demand for Southeast Asian goods in China resulted from the news Zheng He received from locals regarding the prosperity of the region around Melaka.

(B) Reports of the region's prosperity sent by Zheng He during his visits to Melaka incited demand for Southeast Asian goods in China.

(C) During Zheng He's seven voyages to Melaka, he sent news of the region's material wealth and natural resources to the Chinese emperor.

(D) The news sent by Zheng He about the wealth and resources of Southeast Asia was used by the Ming emperor to stimulate demand for the region's products.

3 The word "intimate" in the passage is closest in meaning to

(A) intrinsic

(B) complementary

(C) joint

(D) close

4   Why does the author discuss the sultan's tax policies in paragraph 3?

(A) To show that the sultan gave China a privileged trade status

(B) To argue that non-Chinese traders were taxed unjustly

(C) To emphasize the sultan's preference for Chinese goods

(D) To explain the trade incentives given to Muslim merchants

Paragraph 3 is marked with an arrow [➡].

5   Look at the four squares [■] that indicate where the following sentence could be added to the passage.

Various other local spices were also valued, and their rarity commanded high prices.

Where would the sentence best fit?

Click on a square [■] to add the sentence to the passage.

6   Which of the following can be inferred about the trade routes near Melaka from paragraph 5?

(A) They were the main avenues of trade for the Portuguese empire.

(B) They were unknown to the Dutch in the sixteenth century.

(C) They were used primarily by private merchants after the 1530s.

(D) They were the site of a prolonged war between the Portuguese and Dutch.

Paragraph 5 is marked with an arrow [➡].

7   According to paragraph 6, all of the following are true of pepper EXCEPT

(A) it was traded for staples like rice and textiles in Melaka's markets

(B) it was supplanted by other crops in the seventeenth century

(C) it was produced in the highest quantities during the Dutch period

(D) it was the primary local export under the Dutch and Portuguese

Paragraph 6 is marked with an arrow [➡].

8   Look at the four squares [■] that indicate where the following sentence could be added to the passage.

Other groups with significant numbers include those of Indian and Portuguese ancestry.

Where would the sentence best fit?

Click on a square [■] to add the sentence to the passage.

정답·해석·정답단서 p.313

VOCABULARY LIST

Chapter 07에서 선별한 다음의 토플 필수 어휘를 단어암기 음성파일을 들으며 암기한 후 퀴즈로 확인해보세요.

*해커스 동영상강의 포털 해커스인강(HackersIngang.com)에서 단어암기 음성파일을 무료로 다운로드할 수 있습니다.

apply[əplái] 적용되다 (=employ)

conflict[kánflikt] 갈등

phase[feiz] 시기 (=period)

opposite[ápəzit] 정반대의 것 (=contrast)

ensure[inʃúər] 보증하다

garment[gáːrmənt] 옷

bind[baind] 묶다

royalty[rɔ́iəlti] 왕족

funerary[fjúːnərèri] 장례식의

deceased[disíːst] 사망한

continuity[kàntənjúːəti] 연속성 (=flow)

rhythmically[ríðmikəli] 주기적으로

cycle[sáikl] 주기 (=sequence)

interval[íntərvəl] 간격 (=space)

conform[kənfɔ́ːrm] 따르다 (=comply)

hibernation[hàibərnéiʃən] 동면 (=sleep)

contempt[kəntémpt] 경멸

convention[kənvénʃən] 관습

conviction[kənvíkʃən] 신념 (=faith)

humanity[hjuːmǽnəti] 인류

emission[imíʃən] 배출

notably[nóutəbli] 특히

equate[ikwéit] 동일시하다

rank[ræŋk] 분류하다

compartmentalize[kəmpɑːrtméntəlàiz] 구분하다

naked eye 육안

cosmos[kázməs] 우주

gauge[geidʒ] 측정하다 (=measure)

factor in ~을 계산에 넣다

enterprise[éntərpràiz] 회사

rural[rúərəl] 농업의 (=country)

tangle[tǽŋgl] 엉키게 하다

precursor[prikɔ́ːrsər] 전조

identical[aidéntikəl] 똑같은 (=same)

eat away 부식하다

expose[ikspóuz] 노출시키다 (=reveal)

correspond to 해당하다

imprint[imprínt] 찍다

downturn[dáuntɔ̀ːrn] 침체

prosperous[práspərəs] 부유한 (=thriving)

overall[óuvərɔ̀ːl] 전반적으로

recession[riséʃən] 불경기

be analogous to ~와 비슷하다

crumble[krʌ́mbl] 부스러지다

crowd out 밀어내다

ruin[ruːin] 폐허

majestic[mədʒéstik] 웅장한

flourish[flɔ́ːriʃ] 번창하다 (=blossom)

abandon[əbǽndən] 버리다 (=desert)

awestruck[ɔ́ːstrʌ̀k] 충격받다

grandeur[grǽndʒər] 웅대함

ceremonial[sèrəmóuniəl] 의식의

Quiz

각 단어의 알맞은 뜻을 찾아 연결하시오.

01 funerary   ⓐ 우주
02 contempt   ⓑ 폐허
03 cosmos   ⓒ 장례식의
04 expose   ⓓ 보증하다
05 ruin   ⓔ 경멸
     ⓕ 노출시키다

각 단어의 알맞은 동의어를 찾아 연결하시오.

06 apply   ⓐ faith
07 continuity   ⓑ employ
08 conviction   ⓒ desert
09 gauge   ⓓ flow
10 prosperous   ⓔ thriving
     ⓕ measure

ⓔ 01 ⓕ 09 ⓔ 08 ⓓ 07 ⓑ 06 ⓑ 05 ⓐ 04 ⓕ 03 ⓔ 02 ⓒ 01

construct[kənstrʌ́kt] 건축하다

situate[sítʃuèit] 위치시키다 (=locate)

venerate[vénərèit] 숭배하다

atop[ətáp] 꼭대기의

excavation[èkskəvéiʃən] 발굴

dedicate[dédikèit] 바치다

revere[rivíər] 숭배하다

exalt[igzɔ́:lt] 찬양하다

hierarchy[háiərà:rki] 계급제

terrain[təréin] 지대 (=territory)

predominance[pridámənəns] 지배

moderate[mádərət] 적당한 (=reasonable)

adaptive[ədǽptiv] 적응의

retain[ritéin] 보유하다 (=preserve)

respiration[rèspəréiʃən] 호흡

pore[pɔ:r] 구멍

enlarge[inlá:rdʒ] 확장시키다

swell[swel] 부풀다 (=expand)

saturated[sǽtʃərèitid] 흠뻑 젖은

shrink[ʃriŋk] 오그라들다 (=shrivel)

envelop[invéləp] 감싸다

retention[riténʃən] 보유

dormancy[dɔ́:rmənsi] 휴면

extensive[iksténsiv] 광대한

imbalance[imbǽləns] 불균형

toughness[tʌ́fnis] 강인함

extol[ikstóul] 찬양하다 (=applaud)

advocate[ǽdvəkèit] 지지하다 (=support)

conservation[kànsərvéiʃən] 보존

artery[á:rtəri] 중추

spice[spais] 향신료

naval[néivəl] 해군의

maritime[mǽritàim] 해양의

voyage[vɔ́iidʒ] 항해

vigorous[vígərəs] 원기 왕성한 (=energetic)

overland[óuvərlænd] 육로로

privileged[prívəlidʒd] 특권이 주어진

far-reaching[fà:rí:tʃiŋ] 멀리까지 미치는 (=widespread)

value[vǽlju:] 높이 평가하다

flavor[fléivər] 풍미 (=savor)

abroad[əbrɔ́d] 해외에

middleman[mídlmæ̀n] 중개자

route[ru:t] 항로 (=course)

fabled[féibld] 전설적인

expel[ikspél] 내쫓다

monopoly[mənápəli] 독점

commodity[kəmádəti] 상품 (=goods)

peak[pi:k] 최고에 달하다

bustling[bʌ́sliŋ] 붐비는 (=busy)

absolute[ǽbsəlù:t] 절대적인

minority[minɔ́:rəti] 소수의

commemorate[kəmémərèit] 기념하다 (=celebrate)

Quiz

각 단어의 알맞은 뜻을 찾아 연결하시오.

01	envelop	ⓐ 해외에
02	naval	ⓑ 확장시키다
03	abroad	ⓒ 꼭대기의
04	bustling	ⓓ 감싸다
05	atop	ⓔ 붐비는
		ⓕ 해군의

각 단어의 알맞은 동의어를 찾아 연결하시오.

06	situate	ⓐ locate
07	moderate	ⓑ territory
08	extol	ⓒ goods
09	far-reaching	ⓓ reasonable
10	commodity	ⓔ widespread
		ⓕ applaud

ⓒ 01 ⓕ 02 ⓐ 03 ⓔ 04 ⓒ 05 ⓐ 06 ⓓ 07 ⓕ 08 ⓔ 09 ⓒ 10

CHAPTER 08

Summary

Summary

Summary 문제는 지문의 중심 내용(Major idea)을 가장 잘 담고 있는 보기 3개를 선택하여 전체 지문의 요약문을 완성하는 유형이다. Summary란, 글의 중심 내용을 추려내어 간략히 표현하는 것을 말한다. Summary 문제는 각 지문의 마지막 문제로 출제되며, 한 지문당 1개가 출제되기도 하고 간혹 출제되지 않기도 한다. Summary 문제가 출제되지 않을 경우에는 Category Chart 문제가 출제되지만, Summary 문제의 출제 빈도가 더 높다.

Summary 문제를 풀기 위해서는 글 전체와 각 단락의 주제를 파악하고, 각 보기가 글 전체에서 중심이 되는 내용인지 아니면 세부적이고 중요하지 않은 내용인지 파악하는 연습을 해야 한다.

📌 문제 살펴보기

Summary 문제는 디렉션, 도입 문장, 지문 요약을 위한 요약표와 6개의 보기를 준다. 6개의 보기 중 요약문을 완성시키기에 적절한 3개를 클릭하여 요약표에 끌어다 놓아야 한다. 전형적인 질문 형태는 아래와 같다.

• **Directions:** An introductory sentence for a brief summary of the passage is provided below. Complete the summary by selecting the THREE answer choices that express the most important ideas in the passage. Some sentences do not belong in the summary because they express ideas that are not presented in the passage or are minor ideas in the passage. **This question is worth 2 points**.

> Drag your answer choices to the spaces where they belong.
> To remove an answer choice, click on it. To review the passage, click on **View Text**.

[도입 문장]
-
-
-

Answer Choices

(A)   (D)
(B)   (E)
(C)   (F)

지시: 지문의 요약을 위한 도입 문장이 아래에 주어져 있다. 지문의 가장 중요한 내용을 나타내는 3개의 보기를 골라 지문 요약을 완성하라. 어떤 문장들은 지문에 언급되지 않은 내용이나 지문의 세부 내용을 나타내고 있으므로 지문 요약에 포함되지 않는다. 이 문제는 2점이다. 속하는 자리에 선택 항목을 끌어다 놓아라. 선택 항목을 삭제하려면 그 위에 클릭하라. 전체 지문을 다시 보려면 View Text 아이콘을 클릭하라.

다음은 Summary 문제의 공략법이다. 실전 고득점을 위해 이를 꼼꼼히 학습하고 Hackers Practice와 Hackers Test를 풀면서 반드시 적용해 본다.

1 도입 문장을 읽고 중심 내용 추려내기

도입 문장은 요약문의 도입 문장 또는 전체 지문의 주제 역할을 하므로 지문의 중심 내용을 고르는 데 큰 도움이 된다. 도입 문장을 큰 주제로 가정하고 하위 주제로 생각되는 보기 3개를 예상 정답으로 추려낸다.

2 중심 내용인지 확인하기

지문 전체의 흐름을 읽으며 정답으로 예상되는 보기가 지문의 내용과 일치하는지와 중심 내용인지를 확인한다.

According to recent studies, amphibian populations have declined globally during the last fifty years. Experts agree that (A)habitat destruction is partially to blame. The draining of marshes and damming of rivers have radically modified the water systems amphibians rely on for food and breeding, and devastation of forests has left many of these animals without adequate shelter. (C)Climate change has also been labeled as a likely culprit. Because their thin skin is permeable and their eggs lack shells, amphibians are extremely sensitive to changes in temperature and moisture. It has been hypothesized that global warming may interrupt breeding patterns and lead to physical ailments. A related issue is (F)the reduction of atmospheric ozone in recent decades. As cold-blooded animals, amphibians must bask in the sun to warm themselves. The higher UV levels have been linked to dwarfism and immunity problems in frogs.

> **Global amphibian populations are being threatened.**
> - (A) Loss of habitat has made it difficult for amphibians to live.
> - (C) Changes in climate have left amphibians vulnerable.
> - (F) Ozone depletion is harmful to the health of amphibians.

(B) Habitat loss is particularly destructive in rainforests.
(D) Global moisture levels became too high for amphibians.
(E) Ultraviolet light intensities are insufficient for frogs to stay warm.

지문해석 p.317

2 양서류 개체군이 감소한 원인을 설명하는 전체 흐름에서 보기 (A)는 habitat destruction is partially to blame(서식지 파괴가 부분적인 원인이다), 보기 (C)는 Climate change has also been labeled as a likely culprit(기후 변화 또한 가능성 있는 범인으로 분류되어 왔다), 보기 (F)는 the reduction of atmospheric ozone(대기 오존의 감소)과 일치함을 확인할 수 있다.

1 세계적으로 양서류 개체군이 위협을 받고 있다는 내용의 도입 문장을 큰 주제로 가정하면 서식지 감소, 기후 변화, 오존 고갈과 같은 위협의 원인을 언급한 보기 (A), (C), (F)를 예상 정답으로 추려낼 수 있다.

TIP 지문에 언급되지 않은 내용이나 사소한 정보를 나타내는 보기가 오답이다.

Hackers Practice

지문을 읽고 물음에 답하시오.

01

The Eighteenth Amendment to the United States Constitution, adopted by the House of Congress on December 18, 1917, was the only modification that took away a right of the people. Ratified in January, 1919, the law banned the sale, import, and export of intoxicating beverages. A subsequent law which validated the Amendment was passed on October 28, 1919 to define the alcoholic content of intoxicating beverages.

Social reform organizations backing the Progressive Movement and religious groups supporting the Temperance Movement had been calling for the closure of saloons. Known as Prohibition, the movement expressed alarm at public drinking behavior. The Progressive and Temperance groups had different reasons for supporting prohibition. The former was after a radical transformation of society into one where wealth was shared and people were given equal rights, while the latter wanted to advance principles of conservatism and moderation. Nevertheless, their union and the support of the American public resulted in the Eighteenth Amendment's ratification.

However, the result that the movement desired never actually materialized. The amendment did contribute to a thirty percent decline in alcohol consumption, but a younger generation of Americans eventually rejected the law and the quantity of alcohol consumed rose again until it reached pre-prohibition levels. Illicit liquor appeared on the black market and the bootlegging, or smuggling, of alcohol allowed criminal organizations to profit immensely. The government, however, could not tax the illegal production and sales of the beverage. Fourteen years after it was ratified, the amendment was repealed.

Complete the summary by selecting the TWO answer choices that express the most important ideas in the passage.

The Eighteenth Amendment to the US Constitution prohibited the sale and trade of alcoholic beverages.

-
-

(A) The Progressive and Temperance Movements promoted temperance for the same reasons.

(B) The Amendment indirectly caused an increase in illegal activities by organized crime.

(C) The Prohibition Movement contributed to the passage of the Eighteenth Amendment.

(D) The amendment was reversed because it did not solve the alcohol issue.

---

01 amendment[əméndmənt] (미국 헌법) 수정 조항, 개정   ratify[rǽtəfài] 승인하다   intoxicating[intάksikèitiŋ] 취하게 하는
subsequent[sʌ́bsikwənt] 이후의, 이어서 일어나는   validate[vǽlədèit] 정당성을 입증하다   Prohibition[pròuhəbíʃən] 금주법
conservatism[kənsə́ːrvətìzm] 보수주의   moderation[mὰdəréiʃən] 절제   materialize[mətíəriəlàiz] 실현되다
illicit[ilísit] 불법의   bootlegging[búːtlègiŋ] 밀매   smuggle[smʌ́gl] 밀수하다   repeal[ripíːl] 폐지하다

02

Advertising around the world is designed to appeal to consumers and induce them to purchase products and services. While adults are not always deceived by powerfully convincing messages in advertisements, children are easily misled. A 1991 study conducted by psychologists Kunkel and Roberts documented evidence that proves children lack the cognitive capacity to understand the persuasive intent of product promotion. Their work shows that advertisers exploit the appeal that cartoon characters and celebrities have for children, who often fail to discriminate between truths and falsehoods.

Advertisers are aware that children under six years of age cannot distinguish between reality and fantasy. A commercial for a brand of canned spinach might portray the cartoon character Popeye. Children know that, in the cartoon, Popeye becomes physically stronger after he eats spinach. They associate what they see in the cartoon with the advertising message in the commercial. Adults are aware that this is deceptive; children, however, will readily accept the message as truth. This is supported by a study conducted by the American Psychiatric Association (APA) on advertising and children, which concluded that the inability to perceive exaggeration makes children more susceptible to psychological pressure from advertising content.

The APA study also observed that compelling advertising can nurture a shift in values toward materialism. Advertisers encourage a preoccupation for material things by using children's favorite celebrities and cartoon characters in their advertisements. For example, the creators of Teenage Mutant Ninja Turtles have licensed hundreds of products, such as backpacks, lunch boxes, cereals, and toothbrushes. In 1989, sales of their products reached sixty-four billion dollars.

Complete the summary by selecting the TWO answer choices that express the most important ideas in the passage.

Young children are easily deceived by advertising because they are not aware of its influential content.

-
-

(A) The advertising industry can compel children to become obsessed with material things.

(B) Advertisers use Popeye and Teenage Mutant Ninja Turtles to generate billions of dollars in sales.

(C) Children are easily misled by the deceptive tactics of the advertising industry.

(D) The purpose of advertising to children is to encourage materialist values.

---

02 **induce**[indʤúːs] 야기하다 **mislead**[mislíːd] 속이다 **cognitive**[kágnətiv] 인식의 **promotion**[prəmóuʃən] 판촉
exploit[iksplɔ́it] 이용하다, 활용하다 **celebrity**[səlébrəti] 연예인 **discriminate**[diskrímənèit] 구별하다
falsehood[fɔ́ːlshùd] 거짓 **commercial**[kəmə́ːrʃəl] 광고 방송 **deceptive**[diséptiv] 믿을 수 없는
susceptible[səséptəbl] 영향 받기 쉬운 **compelling**[kəmpéliŋ] 저항할 수 없는 **materialism**[mətíəriəlìzm] 물질주의
preoccupation[priːɑkjupéiʃən] 선입견

03

Sociobiology is a field of study that seeks to explain the social behavior of animals within the parameters of the evolutionary advantage certain patterns might have. Behavior such as pack hunting and the hive society of social insects is often investigated. Organization is seen as an effort to preserve the population and involves a pattern of conduct related to reproduction and survival. Thus, in studying animal social behavior, researchers examine how animal species interact in a group context.

Some predatory species live in packs to ensure their survival. The wolf is one such species, forming familial groups of twelve to twenty wolves. Their organization enhances defense and thus helps protect the group while hunting and traveling. The alpha pair, the most dominant male and female wolves in the pack, and the beta pair, second to the alpha pair, are the principal members. The other wolves are lower in rank, but nonetheless contribute to the survival of the pack. By subordinating themselves to the leadership of the alpha pair, the lower-ranking members are unified in helping the pack's members survive.

Similarly, social insects such as bees have a highly-organized hive society that sustains the colony and helps it survive. A hive consists of 20,000 to 50,000 bees, with members divided according to function. The queen bee lays eggs, and the drones fertilize these eggs by mating with the queen. The worker bees maintain the hive and care for its members through a variety of tasks: comb construction, rearing the brood, providing the queen's needs, gathering nectar and pollen, and defending the hive. Organized as such, each bee ensures the survival of the colony.

Complete the summary by selecting the TWO answer choices that express the most important ideas in the passage.

Social behavior as it relates to the survival of the species is the focus of sociobiology.

●

●

(A) Bees in a hive society help a colony to survive by organizing themselves according to function.

(B) The most useful members of a hive are the queen, who lays the eggs, and the drones, who fertilize them.

(C) The alpha and beta pairs are the strongest and most influential wolves in a wolf pack.

(D) Wolves in a pack observe the classification of members to maintain unity and safeguard the pack.

---

03 parameter[pərǽmətər] (한정) 요소 hive[haiv] 벌집 conduct[kándʌkt] 행동 context[kántekst] (어떤 일의) 환경
    dominant[dámənənt] 지배적인 principal[prínsəpəl] 주요한 subordinate[səbɔ́ːrdənèit] 복종시키다 drone[droun] 수벌
    fertilize[fɔ́ːrtəlàiz] 수정시키다 comb[koum] 벌집 rear[riər] 기르다 brood[bruːd] 한배의 새끼 nectar[néktər] (꽃의) 꿀

04

The camel-like llama was once native to North America, but it disappeared from the continent during the last ice age. It survived in South America, where it was used by the native peoples of the Andes for various purposes. The Incas domesticated the llama as early as six thousand years ago and developed close ties with the animal.

Llamas provided the Incas with food and materials for textiles. A single adult male yielded one hundred kilograms of edible meat, which was often salted and dried for storage. Lightweight and nutritious, dried llama meat was a staple of Incan soldiers and travelers. The hides from the animals were transformed into quality leather for weather-resistant garments, such as ponchos or shoes. The soles of the Incan sandal, for instance, were made from skin taken from the neck, where it was thickest. Fiber from the fur was used to make cloth. Incans called it *aluascay*, and it was the standard material used for the clothes worn by common people.

By around 600 AD, the animals had also become important as beasts of burden. The Incas used them as pack animals for transporting goods and construction materials. A large male animal could carry approximately thirty kilograms of cargo up to twenty kilometers in a day. Though the pace of the animals was not great, their trainability made them well suited to the task. The llamas greatly alleviated the burden of carrying or hauling materials across significant distances by hand.

Complete the summary by selecting the TWO answer choices that express the most important ideas in the passage.

The Incas of South America domesticated the llama and used it to their advantage.

●

●

(A) Though useful as pack animals, llamas proved difficult to train.

(B) Different parts of the llamas were converted into food and textiles.

(C) Llamas were useful for transporting items from one place to another.

(D) Llamas were most often used in the construction of Incan cities.

---

04 **camel**[kǽməl] 낙타 **continent**[kántənənt] 북미 대륙 **yield**[ji:ld] 산출하다 **edible**[édəbl] 식용의 **salt**[sɔːlt] 소금에 절이다
staple[stéipl] 기본 식료품 **hide**[haid] 짐승의 가죽 **quality leather** 양질의 가죽 **poncho**[pántʃou] 판초(남미 원주민들의 외투)
sole[soul] 밑창 **fiber**[fáibər] 섬유 **cloth**[klɔːθ] 옷감 **standard**[stǽndərd] 일반적인 **beast of burden** 짐을 나르는 동물
pack animal 짐을 나르는 동물 **haul**[hɔːl] 운반하다

지문을 읽고 물음에 답하시오.

05   One attempt to explain the origin of the Moon is the capture hypothesis. According to this theory, the Moon formed somewhere else in the solar system, and as it traveled through space, it was "captured" by the gravitational field of the Earth and began orbiting our planet, as it does today. A strongpoint in this proposition is that the elemental differences between the Earth and the Moon can be explained by their formation in disparate regions of the solar system. However, many scientists are skeptical as to whether the speed of a passing body the size of the Moon would have been slow enough to be permanently influenced by the Earth's gravity.

Another possibility is that the Moon originated through fission. This theory proposes that the Moon was once part of the Earth, but later separated from it, just as a nuclear atom or biological cell can split into two. According to this model, the Earth may have been spinning so fast during its formative period that a bulge developed at its equatorial region. Eventually, as the spin continued, the bulky material broke off. A problem with this model is that the current orbit of the Moon is not aligned along the equator. However, some scientists who promote the fission theory claim that the Moon could have migrated away from the equator to follow a different orbit.

A third proposal is the giant impact theory, which claims that another planet of smaller size, and with a different elemental composition from that of the Earth, collided with the Earth after the solar system formed. Material from both objects broke off, joined, and later became the Moon. Such a scenario could clarify why the Moon is composed of rock rather than dense materials like iron and nickel that exist in the Earth's core: the collision would have displaced surface debris.

---

05 origin[ɔ́:rədʒin] 기원   gravitational field 중력장   orbit[ɔ́:rbit] 궤도를 그리며 돌다; 궤도   proposition[prɑ̀pəzíʃən] 주장
disparate[díspərət] 동떨어진   skeptical[sképtikəl] 회의적인   permanently[pə́:rmənəntli] 영구히
fission[fíʃən] 분열   split[split] 쪼개지다   bulge[bʌldʒ] 불룩한 부분   equatorial[ì:kwətɔ́:riəl] 적도의
align[əláin] 정렬시키다   promote[prəmóut] 지지하다   migrate[máigreit] 이동하다   composition[kàmpəzíʃən] 구성
clarify[klǽrəfài] 명백하게 설명하다   dense[dens] 고밀도의   displace[displéis] 옮겨 놓다   debris[dəbrí:] 파편

Complete the summary by selecting the THREE answer choices that express the most important ideas in the passage.

The origin of the Moon is poorly understood, but several theories have been proposed.

-
-
-

(A) The Moon may have formed from a distance before being pulled into its current orbit by the Earth's gravitational field.

(B) The giant impact theory could explain why the elemental composition of the Moon does not include heavy elements.

(C) Scientists disagree over whether the gravity of the Earth would have been sufficient to strongly affect the Moon.

(D) Earth could have collided with another planet, and the collision would explain the Moon's composition.

(E) The Moon may have originally broken off from the Earth near the equator due to the Earth's spin.

(F) Fission is generally accepted by scientists because it has fewer problems than other theories.

CH 1
CH 2
CH 3
CH 4
CH 5
CH 6
CH 7
CHAPTER 8
CH 9
Hackers TOEFL Reading Intermediate

06

The most widely accepted scientific theory for how life originated on Earth is *chemosynthesis*, which asserts that a gradual and progressive aggregation of chemicals on Earth and in its atmosphere facilitated the formation of organic compounds. It was these organic structures that became the building blocks for biological organisms. A very similar, but contradictory, proposition is that essentially the same process took place not on Earth but somewhere else in the universe, perhaps in space or on another planet. The molecular structures that held potential for life were not indigenous to Earth's formation, but rather were deposited by a foreign body, such as a meteorite or comet. This second argument is known as *panspermia*.

Regardless of where the process took place, scientists believe that the molecular compounds mandatory for life were created from a tiny fraction of known elements. How inorganic compounds could have synthesized to form organic compounds was demonstrated by Stanley Miller and Harold Urey in 1952. The two scientists mixed together the primitive gases ammonia, methane, hydrogen, and water vapor in a tube, and added an electrical spark. After a week, the container yielded organic compounds like amino acids, which are important for making proteins in living cells. The Miller-Urey experiment suggests that lightning and primitive gases could have mixed to create organic compounds.

Still, an organic compound alone is not life. Amino acids, for example, are created through chemical reactions, but additional steps are needed to generate life. So far, no experiment has proven exactly how this happens, but experts do believe the earliest life forms on Earth were prokaryotes(unicellular organisms). The first simple cells were heterotrophs that depended on the environment for their food. Some of these single cells evolved to produce their own food through photosynthesis. These are referred to as autotrophs. Over millions of years, DNA formed in the nucleus of some cells, and further evolution eventually led to complex multicellular life forms.

---

06 originate[ərídʒənèit] 생겨나다   chemosynthesis[kìːmousínθəsis] 화학 합성   assert[əsə́ːrt] 주장하다
progressive[prəgrésiv] 점진적인   aggregation[æ̀grigéiʃən] 집적   facilitate[fəsílətèit] 촉진하다
contradictory[kὰntrədíktəri] 모순된   indigenous[indídʒənəs] ~에 고유한   panspermia[pænspə́ːrmiə] 범종설
molecular[məlékjulər] 분자의   mandatory[mǽndətɔ̀ːri] 필수의   synthesize[sínθəsàiz] 합성하다
demonstrate[démənstrèit] 증명하다   primitive[prímətiv] 원시의   additional[ədíʃənl] 부가적인
generate[dʒénərèit] 일으키다   prokaryote[proukǽriòut] 원핵 생물   unicellular[jùːnəséljulər] 단세포의
heterotroph[hétərətrὰf] 종속 영양 생물   autotroph[ɔ́ːtətrὰf] 독립 영양 생물   nucleus[njúːkliəs] 핵
eventually[ivéntʃuəli] 결국

Complete the summary by selecting the THREE answer choices that express the most important ideas in the passage.

How life developed on Earth is one of the great mysteries in the natural sciences.

-
-
-

(A) Of the theories about how life on Earth originated, chemosynthesis is regarded as the most plausible by most scientists.

(B) Although scientists disagree on where the molecular structures responsible for life originated, they agree on the general process by which they were formed.

(C) The first simple cells, called heterotrophs, were unable to make their own food, but they later evolved into photosynthetic cells known as autotrophs.

(D) Miller and Urey demonstrated through experiment that lightning was inessential to the formation of life.

(E) An experiment by Miller and Urey helped explain how organic compounds could have resulted from inorganic sources.

(F) Scientists do not know how organic compounds generated life, but it is generally accepted that simple cells emerged first and evolved into more complex organisms.

CH 1
CH 2
CH 3
CH 4
CH 5
CH 6
CH 7
CHAPTER 8
CH 9

07

The ultimate influence of the mid-fifteenth century invention of the printing press in Europe on the history of print was significant, but its revolutionary impact was not immediately felt. This delay was due to a couple of factors. Even though the printing press made it possible to produce prints at unprecedented speeds, most people at the time were illiterate. Therefore, information found in books had to be read to those who were unable to read. In addition, the types of materials printed in those days were limited. Religious texts and reproductions of classics were common, but publication of new ideas was rare. These factors, in combination, resulted in a modest number of books being sold.

By the nineteenth century, a significantly greater range of publications was being printed. Nowhere was this more evident than in America. Faster printing presses and cheaper ink made producing large numbers of printed materials very efficient, and the invention of the telegraph in the 1830s allowed rapid communication over long distances. These developments fueled people's interest in the news, and newspapers were soon circulating throughout the country. By 1860, the state of Illinois had four hundred active newspapers, and its media capital, Chicago, had eleven dailies of its own.

Concurrently, public education had become widespread, vastly improving literacy rates. Newspaper companies took advantage of this by offering "all the news of the day at prices that everyone could afford." At only one cent each, penny newspapers promised fun and exciting articles at a fraction of the cost of conventional, more serious, periodicals. Moreover, their pages were filled with advertisements because the papers were funded by ads rather than annual or monthly subscriptions. Many companies utilized this new mass media option to reach working-class customers through advertising.

A similar development happened in the arena of fiction. Dime novels, so named because of their low prices, became a craze during the nineteenth century. These cheaply made popular books, with their sensational stories of adventure, became the most beloved stories in America and helped expand the fiction market to new types of consumers. The trend toward cheap publications could also be seen in Europe, but it was not nearly as pronounced. In places like Britain, people still preferred handmade books with elaborate bindings.

---

07 ultimate[ʌ́ltəmət] 궁극적인 printing press 인쇄기 revolutionary[rèvəlúːʃəneri] 혁명적인 impact[ímpækt] 효과
unprecedented[ʌnprésədèntid] 유례없는 illiterate[ilítərət] 글자를 모르는 modest[mɑ́dist] 별로 많지 않은
significantly[signífikəntli] 상당히 evident[évədənt] 분명히 나타난 circulate[sə́ːrkjulèit] 배부하다
concurrently[kənkə́ːrəntli] 동시에 arena[əríːnə] ~계(界) craze[kréiz] 대유행 sensational[senséiʃənl] 선정적인
beloved[bilʌ́vid] 가장 사랑하는 pronounced[prənáunst] 두드러진 elaborate[ilǽbərət] 정교한 binding[báindiŋ] 표지

Complete the summary by selecting the THREE answer choices that express the most important ideas in the passage.

After a long period of development, mass printing matured in the nineteenth century.

-
-
-

(A) The printing press had a profound impact on mass printing, but its eventual influence was stalled by illiteracy and limitations in the types of materials published.

(B) Technological innovations led to the widespread production of newspapers in nineteenth-century America.

(C) Because demand for handmade books remained in some European countries, cheaply produced works of fiction were only moderately popular.

(D) As literacy increased in the nineteenth century, inexpensive newspapers and novels gave advertisers an opportunity to reach new audiences.

(E) Despite the development of inexpensive and efficient methods of printing, the American public was slow to adopt newspapers as a form of mass media.

(F) The printing press had only a minor impact in Europe following its invention, due to the fact that many people could not read at the time.

정답·해석·정답단서 p.317

CH 1
CH 2
CH 3
CH 4
CH 5
CH 6
CH 7
CHAPTER 8
CH 9
Hackers TOEFL Reading Intermediate

Hackers Test

1 Assessing Auditory Perception in Infants

1   Infants enter the world with a severely limited comprehension of sounds due to their relative lack of life experience. However, their capacity to hear is only slightly less sensitive than that of adults, and auditory specialists agree that by six months of age, babies have fully developed auditory capabilities. Because hearing is important for childhood development, researchers have come up with a variety of methods to assess the auditory development of infants.

2   ➡ Unlike adults, infants are unable to follow verbal instructions during testing. This makes testing neonatal hearing a challenge. Fortunately though, infants, just like adults, give spontaneous physiological responses to certain sounds. These involuntary responses are most evident in the presence of loud and unexpected sounds. If infants are exposed to sudden noises, they immediately blink and show body reactions consistent with being startled. Ultrasound imagery has revealed that fetuses respond in a like manner while still in the womb. Another involuntary response is when infants hear something that generates interest. Infants with normal hearing will usually orient their heads in the direction of an interesting sound, such as a mother's voice, and this tendency also provides useful information to researchers about neonatal sound localization abilities.

3   ➡ Other tests centered on spontaneous responses include checking the effects of auditory signals on heart rates and brain waves. Heart rates, as with blinking frequency, often change involuntarily when a person is excited, and can be measured with a simple electronic monitor. Brain waves are measured by attaching electrodes to the scalp of infants and then studying brain wave charts at the intervals where an auditory signal was played. Known as Brainstem Evoked Auditory Response (BEAR), the test uses clicking noises to stimulate neurological activity between the ear and brain. The electrodes transmit wave data onto charts, which include peaks and dips if sound is detected by the infant. If the charts show no change in brain waves, it means the infant has hearing problems. The BEAR test is also useful for adult patients when the person being tested is unable to communicate: for example, an adult either in a coma or with a severe psychological disorder.

4   ➡ An additional strategy researchers employ is to test conditioned behavioral responses. Audiologists use an array of procedures designed to test an infant's capacity to distinguish between sounds by rewarding the infant for behavior associated with attentiveness to different sounds. One popular approach is to use a pacifier, lollipop, or other tool to generate a sucking behavior. Each time the infant is viewed sucking, researchers play a sound throughout the duration of the sucking. Gradually, the infant begins to associate sucking with that particular sound. Over time, however, the infant will tire of the sound and stop sucking. This loss of interest

is known as *habituation*. Once audiologists notice habituation in the infant, they will switch to a new sound and start the process again. The assumption is that if babies recognize the change in sound, they will perform the sucking behavior in order to hear the new sound.

5 Studies involving infants from birth to four months only offer clues about sound detection and localization abilities, but in older infants, useful information may be gained from studying eye movements in response to linguistic cues. Therefore, cognitive psychologists are keenly interested in the development of audio-visual linguistic perception as babies get older. An infant who can see and hear will use both senses(modes) to reinforce the other, and this is known as intermodal perception. ■ Eye movement experiments are widely used as bridges for connecting auditory discrimination studies with those testing early comprehension of language. ■ As such, speech sounds are among the central tools used to elicit infant eye movement responses. ■ For example, researchers may hold two picture cards, perhaps of a dog and a ball, in front of the infant and watch the eye movements of the infant when either word is spoken. ■

6 The objective of all methods for assessing auditory development in infants is to identify hearing problems at an early stage because early intervention can help prevent long-term negative effects. Numerous psychological studies have linked hearing deficiencies with lifelong problems in speech and language acquisition, poor academic performance, and related issues such as emotional strain stemming from difficulties in social interactions. Many of these issues can be avoided through early treatment and special education programs for hearing-impaired children.

1 The word "capacity" in the passage is closest in meaning to

(A) clarity

(B) ability

(C) efficacy

(D) vivacity

2   What can be inferred about loud and unexpected sounds from paragraph 2?

(A) Adults are less affected by them due to life experience.

(B) Infants automatically turn their eyes away from them.

(C) They evoke similar reactions in infants and adults.

(D) Their effects on fetuses still in the womb are unknown.

Paragraph 2 is marked with an arrow [➡].

3   According to paragraph 3, which of the following is true of the peaks and dips in brain wave charts?

(A) They represent neurological abnormalities in people's brains.

(B) They show that test subjects are capable of detecting sounds.

(C) They indicate the range of sounds infants can hear.

(D) They reflect the intensity of the various sound signals.

Paragraph 3 is marked with an arrow [➡].

4   According to paragraph 4, audiologists switch to a new sound during habituation studies because

(A) sometimes infants do not exhibit sucking behavior while the initial sound is played

(B) understanding an infant's hearing ability requires testing for multiple sounds

(C) infants eventually lose interest if the same sound is played indefinitely

(D) infants continue to respond to a single sound only if new rewards are given

Paragraph 4 is marked with an arrow [➡].

5   Which of the sentences below best expresses the essential information in the highlighted sentence in the passage? *Incorrect* choices change the meaning in important ways or leave out essential information.

(A) Sound detection and localization tests are useful in infants from birth to four months, but tests involving eye movements are informative only when conducted on older infants.

(B) Though younger infants are only suited for sound detection and localization studies, tests involving eye movements and language prompts in older infants offer helpful information.

(C) Studies that utilize sound detection and localization tests are useful not only for testing the hearing of older infants, but also for testing infants from birth to four months of age.

(D) Although the use of simple sound detection and localization tests is effective on infants from birth to four months, such tests are unfruitful when applied to older infants.

6 The word "objective" in the passage is closest in meaning to

(A) importance

(B) standard

(C) analysis

(D) purpose

7 Look at the four squares [■] that indicate where the following sentence could be added to the passage.

If the infant looks at the image corresponding to the spoken word, it is an indication of comprehension.

Where would the sentence best fit?

Click on a square [■] to add the sentence to the passage.

8 **Directions**: An introductory sentence for a brief summary of the passage is provided below. Complete the summary by selecting the THREE answer choices that express the most important ideas in the passage. Some sentences do not belong in the summary because they express ideas that are not presented in the passage or are minor ideas in the passage. **This question is worth 2 points.**

Drag your answer choices to the spaces where they belong.
To remove an answer choice, click on it. To review the passage, click on **View Text**.

Auditory perception in infants can be measured and analyzed in a number of ways.

- ●
- ●
- ●

Answer Choices

(A) In Brainstem Evoked Auditory Response tests, audiologists play clicking noises to evoke neurological responses of infants.

(B) Involuntary responses to sounds in infants allow researchers to accumulate data without requiring communication.

(C) Because young infants tend not to move in response to sound even when they are interested, their behavior must be conditioned.

(D) Tests involving more than one sense provide information on child hearing and the development of early language skills.

(E) Audiologists have created methods that enable infants who suffer from hearing loss to regain their hearing ability.

(F) Infants can be conditioned to perform specific behaviors in the presence of particular sounds.

1   When art historians and archaeologists explore ancient sites, they look for texts, works of art, and other physical remnants of civilizations long past. Of all historical artifacts, few are as important as pottery as enduring cultural symbols. Although ancient books and murals are rare finds, pottery is fairly common at archaeological sites due to its durability. ■ Pottery thus serves as a miniature window into the art and society of lost cultures. ■ The painted vases of ancient Greece, for example, provide us with a continuous history of Greek art. Unsurpassed in quality, these works have inspired countless artists and collectors. ■ These beautiful vases vary in style according to the time and place of production. ■

2   By the tenth century BC, geometric decoration universally ornamented Greek vases. The Greek obsession with math and logic is clearly evident in the pottery of the period up to 750 BC. Abstract shapes and bands were placed at prominent positions on the vases, most often on the shoulder and belly, and logical symmetry was consistent in the arcs, circles, and wavy lines arranged horizontally, often in repeated patterns. The curves later gave way to rectilinear and triangular shapes, and the wavy lines were largely replaced by sharper features like the herringbone pattern, a series of zigzag blocks connected at alternating forty-five-degree angles. Along with this technical refinement, objects began to be centered on the belly between the handles. These geometrical designs were applied in dark paint on a light reddish clay base, portraying a stark contrast between decor and background.

3   ➡ Moving into the end of the eighth century BC, figures began to appear on vases along with patterns. Believed to be the result of eastern influence from Egypt and Syria, the period is known as the "Orientalizing phase" of Greek pottery. The most influential potters during the Orientalizing period were in Corinth, which was a major trading center. Artisans in Corinth took advantage of foreign demand for pottery by manufacturing small, portable vases that were used to hold oil and perfume. They were fascinated by the imagery of the East and incorporated exotic animals, like lions, and idealized monsters, such as the phoenix, into their pottery. They painted figures in a naturalistic style using a black glaze and perfected a scratched-line technique to cut through the glaze into the lighter clay below. This expertise presented a means to display fine contrasting details, as in the feathers of birds or the intricate parts of flowers.

4   ➡ Evolution of Greek vase design peaked in Athens during the fifth century BC, a period of enhancement during which figure painting took on ever more natural qualities. A breakthrough that occurred around 500 BC was a transition from profiles to three-quarter frontal poses. To achieve this, Athenian artists used foreshortening. Foreshortening is an optical tactic through which the drawn object appears shorter than it really is due to its angled orientation in relation to the viewer. It created visual perspective so that three-dimensional scenes could be produced on two-dimensional space, such as on the surface of a vase. Perspective techniques were expanded to include overlapping figures to express a sense of spatial movement in the subjects.

5 ➡ A more naturalistic presentation of motion was useful because painted vases were often narrative rather than simply decorative. Artists depicted scenes of gods and heroes from stories handed down in Greek mythology. Innovations in perspective allowed the figures to be more expressive and convincing in conveying emotion, and a new style referred to as red-figure pottery further enhanced the potter's expressive options. Unlike the Corinthians, Athenian potters outlined their subjects with a black background, an innovation that meant they could apply final touches with brush instead of incision. The change made minute details even easier to portray and offered more flexibility in shading. Some red-figure vases even include inscriptions or the signature of the artist, although few of these examples have survived to the present day.

6 Evolving approaches to vase painting in ancient Greece suggest that similar explorations and innovations were occurring in other aspects of painting, but none of the ancient Greek murals have survived to the present day. Fortunately, however, many examples of pottery exist. The tens of thousands of vase shards and specimens that have survived are sought after by collectors and museums and often command high prices. They are valued not only for their tremendous beauty and for being an influential source of inspiration for modern figure painters, but also because of their importance in understanding the art of the ancient Greeks.

1 The word "remnants" in the passage is closest in meaning to

(A) assets
(B) locations
(C) remains
(D) piles

2 The word "ornamented" in the passage is closest in meaning to

(A) surrounded
(B) adorned
(C) furnished
(D) symbolized

3 Why does the author discuss "a scratched-line technique" in paragraph 3?

(A) To show an innovation that was necessary to accurately portray idealized figures
(B) To explain how Corinthian artists achieved naturalistic detail in their vases
(C) To provide an example of a technique Corinthian artists learned from the East
(D) To illustrate a method of etching that could only be accomplished using Corinthian clay

Paragraph 3 is marked with an arrow [➡].

4 According to paragraph 3, all of the following were true of pottery produced in Corinth EXCEPT:

(A) It was traded for goods from Egypt and Syria.

(B) It included exotic images from foreign lands.

(C) It was manufactured to hold liquid substances.

(D) It displayed figures and patterns together.

5 According to paragraph 4, Athenian artists were able to move beyond simple profiles in their figure painting by

(A) incorporating poses from a two-dimensional perspective

(B) angling objects to make them appear shorter

(C) applying techniques from wall paintings to their vases

(D) using optical shadowing tactics to convey a sense of motion

Paragraph 4 is marked with an arrow [➡].

6 Which of the following can be inferred from paragraph 5 about Athenian red-figure vases?

(A) They were more popular at the time than vases produced in Corinth.

(B) The minute details were incised on them rather than applied by brush.

(C) They were the first Greek vases to portray mythological themes.

(D) The identities of the artists for the majority of them are unknown.

Paragraph 5 is marked with an arrow [➡].

7 Which of the sentences below best expresses the essential information in the highlighted sentence in the passage? *Incorrect* choices change the meaning in important ways or leave out essential information.

(A) Changes in vase painting probably followed similar innovations in other areas of painting, even though comparatively few ancient Greek murals have survived.

(B) It is unclear, however, whether the innovative approaches being applied in vase painting were also being made in other areas of ancient Greek painting.

(C) Similar explorations have been conducted to uncover other aspects of ancient Greek painting, but no ancient Greek murals are known to exist in the present day.

(D) Despite the likelihood that changes in vase painting were also happening in other arenas of Greek art, no surviving examples of ancient Greek murals currently exist.

8 The word "tremendous" in the passage is closest in meaning to

(A) great

(B) timeless

(C) trivial

(D) undisputed

9 Look at the four squares [■] that indicate where the following sentence could be added to the passage.

Vases easily withstand fires, and pottery fragments last indefinitely, even when broken.

Where would the sentence best fit?

Click on a square [■] to add the sentence to the passage.

10 **Directions**: An introductory sentence for a brief summary of the passage is provided below. Complete the summary by selecting the THREE answer choices that express the most important ideas in the passage. Some sentences do not belong in the summary because they express ideas that are not presented in the passage or are minor ideas in the passage. **This question is worth 2 points.**

Drag your answer choices to the spaces where they belong.
To remove an answer choice, click on it. To review the passage, click on **View Text**.

Greek vases provide insights into the art of ancient Greece.

- ●
- ●
- ●

Answer Choices

(A) The most creative methods of ancient Greek pottery making developed in Corinth around the time it became a major trading center.

(B) Athenian potters revolutionized Greek pottery by implementing the red-figure technique, which made it easier to produce vases in greater numbers.

(C) The Orientalizing phase of Greek pottery occurred in Corinth and was characterized by an Eastern influence and new technical refinements.

(D) After the tenth century, Greek potters began to centrally position their geometrical designs on the area of the vase located between the handles.

(E) Early examples of Greek pottery were universally adorned with geometric designs in contrasting colors.

(F) Greek pottery reached its pinnacle in the hands of Athenian artists, who developed methods for creating depth and expressive detail.

Commedia Dell'arte

1   Commedia dell'arte was a stage performance that combined comic and dramatic elements. Literally, the term means "comedy of artists" and was first applied in the eighteenth century to a genre that was common in Britain and France. However, the genre actually originated in sixteenth-century Italy among groups of traveling theatrical performers who were influential in establishing stage acting as a profession. At the time, it was a very innovative approach to classical stage productions.

2   ➡ Many of the plot elements in commedia dell'arte can be traced back to ancient Roman and Greek theater and include topics such as love, money, pleasure, intergenerational conflict, and jealousy. ■ A common scenario would be a romantic conflict where something stands in the way of two lovers. ■ Usually, a pair of male and female characters falls in love, but an elder figure—typically the father of the female lover—disapproves of the relationship and attempts to impede its development. ■ During the course of the story, the amorous feelings of the female would temporarily subside, but the relentless suitor would continue to seek her love despite the elder's objections. ■

3   ➡ The suitor often used the help of a third party, such as a servant, to gain access to his beloved. But frequently another complication would develop, routinely in the form of a competing suitor to whom the father showed his favor. These additional figures resulted in a complex interaction of characters connected through either cooperation or antagonism. Tensions developed according to the various relationships involved, and these interpersonal relations were often constructed in a hierarchical manner: parent and child, master and slave, rich and poor. Nonetheless, the ending generally was a happy rather than tragic one, involving the marriage of the two destined lovers and forgiveness among all characters, a satisfactory conclusion that left the audience with a positive feeling.

4   ➡ Because the basic story lines of commedia dell'arte were modeled on traditional materials and characters, the plots were very familiar to audience members. The actors were essentially reproducing old stories, and large portions of the performances came from well-rehearsed speeches and dialogues. Actors were often committed to a particular role for a substantial amount of time and were experts in the nuances and details of a specific character. In addition, one of the foremost requirements of actors was a basic understanding of classical rhetoric, or the oral arts of persuasive speech. Consequently, members of a commedia dell'arte troupe often consulted literary works to study traditional techniques for memorizing speech, constructing arguments, and purposeful delivery of speech and gestures.

5   ➡ These fundamental skills were enhanced by interpretive freedoms on the part of dynamic actors. A character's true effectiveness depended on an actor's skill in taking wisdom received from written and oral traditions and strategically crafting it in improvisational ways. Scripts in commedia dell'arte were much reduced, and the performers were not responsible for memorizing detailed sequences of lines and

scenes; rather, in order to keep the attention of an informed audience, the actors made frequent use of improvisation. This introduced unexpected and comic material into their acting. The possibility of innovation allowed actors to respond to local tastes and conditions: for instance, by altering sequences to comically address local scandals or satirize current events.

6　➡ When on stage, actors wore costumes that conveyed their clearly defined characters to the audience, but changing masks and other costume disguises allowed them to take on other roles and add additional dynamic dimensions to their acting. The use of props was also central to their communication with the audience. An object known as the slapstick, which was a handheld baton or faux club, was used to carry out exaggerated violence during fights and arguments. The slapstick made a very loud noise when a character or object was struck, though it caused no harm to the individual. Due to its benign nature but excessive sound, the slapstick found its way into modern entertainment as a metaphor for any exaggerated physical action used to transmit a humorous message of absurdity—hence the phrase slapstick comedy.

7　Commedia dell'arte saw its heyday during the sixteenth to eighteenth centuries, and it was especially popular in Italy and France. Actors formed troupes of ten to twelve individuals who performed in public and often traveled together. Along the way, they set up stages that were used temporarily. Profits made from the performances were distributed among the group. In this sense, the troupes were self-supporting, and the members truly professional.

1　The word "impede" in the passage is closest in meaning to

(A) implant

(B) grow

(C) stabilize

(D) obstruct

2　All of the following are mentioned in paragraphs 2 and 3 as plot characteristics EXCEPT

(A) quarreling lovers

(B) hierarchical relationships

(C) competing characters

(D) intergenerational conflicts

Paragraphs 2 and 3 are marked with arrows [➡].

3   Which of the sentences below best expresses the essential information in the highlighted sentence in the passage? *Incorrect* choices change the meaning in important ways or leave out essential information.

(A) Still, despite a tragic beginning, the ending was generally considered acceptable by the audience.

(B) Even so, the ending provided a happy resolution, averting tragedy and leaving the audience feeling good.

(C) Nevertheless, the audience was left with a positive feeling after the marriage of the two destined lovers.

(D) The ending was nonetheless happy rather than tragic because competing characters forgave one another.

4   It can be inferred from paragraph 4 that commedia dell'arte actors

(A) were naturally gifted

(B) were literate

(C) attended academies

(D) listened to public speeches

Paragraph 4 is marked with an arrow [➡].

5   According to paragraph 5, performers improvised on stage in order to

(A) inject a comic dimension to their characters

(B) remember sequences of lines and scenes

(C) demonstrate their knowledge of written and oral traditions

(D) communicate plot details more clearly to the audience

Paragraph 5 is marked with an arrow [➡].

6   The word "it" in the passage refers to

(A) slapstick

(B) noise

(C) character

(D) object

7   In paragraph 6, why does the author mention "slapstick comedy"?

(A) To illustrate that violence in commedia dell'arte was merely comical

(B) To show how a commedia dell'arte prop developed a symbolic meaning

(C) To introduce a modern term that was used to describe commedia dell'arte

(D) To explain that costumes alone were not sufficient to entertain the audience

Paragraph 6 is marked with an arrow [➡].

8 The word "temporarily" in the passage is closest in meaning to

(A) in an isolated area

(B) for a limited time

(C) from beginning to end

(D) only when necessary

9 Look at the four squares [■] that indicate where the following sentence could be added to the passage.

The disapproval usually centered on the suitor's social standing or lack of wealth.

Where would the sentence best fit?

Click on a square [■] to add the sentence to the passage.

10 Directions: An introductory sentence for a brief summary of the passage is provided below. Complete the summary by selecting the THREE answer choices that express the most important ideas in the passage. Some sentences do not belong in the summary because they express ideas that are not presented in the passage or are minor ideas in the passage. **This question is worth 2 points.**

Drag your answer choices to the spaces where they belong.
To remove an answer choice, click on it. To review the passage, click on **View Text**.

Commedia dell'arte was a theatrical production that combined traditional and innovative elements.

- ●
- ●
- ●

Answer Choices

(A) Performers made use of costumes, masks, and props to diversify their characters and impress the audience.

(B) Actors in commedia dell'arte turned acting into a profession by forming companies and distributing profits among themselves.

(C) Conventional acting techniques were of little use to the actors of commedia dell'arte because their performances were fundamentally improvisational.

(D) Actors mastered their characters and developed conventional acting skills, but they also included improvisations in their performances.

(E) The plot of commedia dell'arte productions generally followed a predetermined sequence marked by conflict and eventual resolution.

(F) Props, such as the slapstick, used in commedia dell'arte are still important in modern comic performances that utilize improvisation.

정답·해석·정답단서 p.320

VOCABULARY LIST

Chapter 08에서 선별한 다음의 토플 필수 어휘를 단어암기 음성파일을 들으며 암기한 후 퀴즈로 확인해보세요.

*해커스 동영상강의 포털 해커스인강(HackersIngang.com)에서 단어암기 음성파일을 무료로 다운로드할 수 있습니다.

intoxicating[intάksikèitiŋ] 취하게 하는

subsequent[sʌ́bsikwənt] 이어서 일어나는

illicit[ilísit] 불법의 (=illegal)

repeal[ripíːl] 폐지하다

induce[indjúːs] 야기하다

mislead[mislíːd] 속이다

exploit[iksplɔ́it] 활용하다 (=use)

celebrity[səlébrəti] 연예인

discriminate[diskrímənèit] 구별하다 (=discern)

falsehood[fɔ́ːlshùd] 거짓

commercial[kəmə́ːrʃəl] 광고 방송

deceptive[diséptiv] 믿을 수 없는

susceptible[səséptəbl] 영향 받기 쉬운 (=prone)

compelling[kəmpéliŋ] 저항할 수 없는

preoccupation[priːɑkjupéiʃən] 선입견 (=absorption)

dominant[dάmənənt] 지배적인 (=prevailing)

subordinate[səbɔ́ːrdənèit] 복종시키다

rear[riər] 기르다 (=nurture)

yield[jiːld] 산출하다

edible[édəbl] 식용의

haul[hɔːl] 운반하다

origin[ɔ́ːridʒin] 기원 (=source)

disparate[díspərət] 동떨어진

skeptical[sképtikəl] 회의적인

permanently[pə́ːrmənəntli] 영구히

split[split] 쪼개지다

align[əláin] 정렬시키다

displace[displéis] 옮겨 놓다

assert[əsə́ːrt] 주장하다 (=declare)

contradictory[kὰntrədíktəri] 모순된 (=paradoxical)

mandatory[mǽndətɔ̀ːri] 필수의 (=compulsory)

synthesize[sínθəsàiz] 합성하다

demonstrate[démənstrèit] 증명하다

additional[ədíʃəl] 부가적인

generate[dʒénərèit] 일으키다 (=produce)

ultimate[ʌ́ltəmət] 궁극적인 (=supreme)

revolutionary[rèvəlúːʃəneri] 혁명적인

impact[ímpækt] 효과 (=influence)

unprecedented[ʌnprésədèntid] 유례없는

illiterate[ilítərət] 글자를 모르는

significantly[signífikəntli] 상당히

evident[évədənt] 분명히 나타난 (=obvious)

sensational[senséiʃənl] 선정적인 (=stimulating)

beloved[bilʌ́vid] 가장 사랑하는

elaborate[ilǽbərət] 정교한 (=detailed)

slightly[sláitli] 약간 (=somewhat)

auditory[ɔ́ːdətɔ̀ːri] 청각의

verbal[və́ːrbəl] 언어의

neonatal[nìːounéitl] 신생아의

involuntary[invάləntèri] 무의식적인

attach[ətǽtʃ] 부착하다 (=affix)

disorder[disɔ́ːrdər] 장애 (=chaos)

Quiz

각 단어의 알맞은 뜻을 찾아 연결하시오.

01 intoxicating   ⓐ 취하게 하는
02 illiterate   ⓑ 글자를 모르는
03 repeal   ⓒ 선정적인
04 disparate   ⓓ 동떨어진
05 synthesize   ⓔ 합성하다
           ⓕ 폐지하다

각 단어의 알맞은 동의어를 찾아 연결하시오.

06 exploit   ⓐ illegal
07 illicit   ⓑ discern
08 origin   ⓒ use
09 mandatory   ⓓ obvious
10 evident   ⓔ compulsory
           ⓕ source

ⓓ 01 ⓑ 02 ⓕ 03 ⓓ 04 ⓔ 05 ⓒ 06 ⓐ 07 ⓕ 08 ⓔ 09 ⓓ 10

reward[riwɔ́ːrd] 보상하다 (=recompense)

attentiveness[əténtivnis] 주의력

associate[əsóuʃièit] 연관 짓다

discrimination[diskrìmənéiʃən] 식별

intervention[ìntərvénʃən] 개입 (=interference)

deficiency[difíʃənsi] 결핍

lifelong[láiflɔ̀ːŋ] 일생의

acquisition[æ̀kwəzíʃən] 습득 (=acquirement)

avoid[əvɔ́id] 예방하다

remnant[rémnənt] 흔적 (=trace)

fairly[féərli] 상당히 (=moderately)

unsurpassed[ʌ̀nsərpǽst] 탁월한 (=superior)

inspire[inspáiər] 영감을 주다 (=motivate)

ornament[ɔ́ːrnəmənt] 장식하다 (=decorate)

obsession[əbséʃən] 몰두

refinement[ri:fáinmənt] 개선

stark[stɑːrk] 뚜렷한

portable[pɔ́ːrtəbl] 휴대용의

fascinate[fǽsənèit] 매혹하다

exotic[igzátik] 이국적인

intricate[íntrikət] 복잡한 (=complex)

enhancement[inhǽnsmənt] 향상

optical[áptikəl] 시각의

tactic[tǽktik] 기술 (=strategy)

perspective[pərspéktiv] 관점

innovation[ìnəvéiʃən] 혁신 (=novelty)

flexibility[flèksəbíləti] 탄력성

command[kəmǽnd] 팔리다

tremendous[triméndəs] 엄청난 (=gigantic)

literally[lítərəli] 문자 그대로 (=really)

apply[əplái] 응용하다 (=utilize)

originate[ərídʒənèit] 발생하다

profession[prəféʃən] 직업

innovative[ínəvèitiv] 혁신적인 (=inventive)

intergenerational[ìntərdʒènəréiʃənl] 세대 간

disapprove[dìsəprúːv] 반대하다

impede[impíːd] 방해하다 (=block)

amorous[ǽmərəs] 사랑의

subside[səbsáid] 가라앉다 (=abate)

relentless[riléntlis] 집요한

complication[kàmpləkéiʃən] 문제점

cooperation[kouàpəréiʃən] 협력

antagonism[æntǽgənìzm] 대립

foremost[fɔ́ːrmòust] 주요한 (=preeminent)

requirement[rikwáiərmənt] 요건 (=condition)

persuasive[pərswéisiv] 설득적인

memorize[méməràiz] 암기하다

satirize[sǽtəràiz] 풍자하다

disguise[disgáiz] 변장

exaggerated[igzǽdʒərèitid] 과장된

benign[bináin] 온화한

heyday[héidèi] 전성기

Quiz

각 단어의 알맞은 뜻을 찾아 연결하시오.

01	stark	ⓐ 대립
02	profession	ⓑ 휴대용의
03	antagonism	ⓒ 뚜렷한
04	avoid	ⓓ 응용하다
05	portable	ⓔ 예방하다
		ⓕ 직업

각 단어의 알맞은 동의어를 찾아 연결하시오.

06	tremendous	ⓐ acquirement
07	acquisition	ⓑ preeminent
08	intricate	ⓒ abate
09	innovative	ⓓ complex
10	foremost	ⓔ gigantic
		ⓕ inventive

ⓑ 01 ⓕ 60 ⓓ 80 ⓐ ʐ0 ⓔ 90 ⓑ 90 ⓔ ₽0 ⓐ 03 ⓕ ʐ0 ⓒ 10

CHAPTER 09

Category Chart

Category Chart

Category Chart 문제는 지문의 세부 정보들을 질문에 제시된 항목(Category)에 맞게 분류하여 표(Chart)를 완성하는 유형이다. Category Chart 문제는 각 지문의 마지막 문제로 출제되며, 한 지문당 1개가 출제되기도 하고 출제되지 않기도 한다. Category Chart 문제가 출제되지 않을 경우에는 Summary 문제가 출제된다.

Category Chart 문제를 풀기 위해서는 각 항목에 해당하는 세부 정보를 정확하게 파악하고 분류하여 정리하는 연습을 해야 한다.

문제 살펴보기

Category Chart 문제는 디렉션, 2개 또는 3개의 항목이 있는 분류표와 7개 또는 9개의 보기를 준다. 보기 중 2개는 항상 오답이므로 5개나 7개를 클릭하여 분류표에 끌어다 놓아야 한다. 보기가 7개일 때에는 3점, 9개일 때에는 4점이 만점이다. 전형적인 질문 형태는 아래와 같다.

- **Directions:** Select the appropriate phrases from the answer choices and match them to the type of to which they relate. TWO of the answer choices will NOT be used. **This question is worth 3 points.**

Drag your answer choices to the spaces where they belong.
To remove an answer choice, click on it. To review the passage, click on **View Text**.

Answer Choices	Category 1
(A)	●
(B)	●
(C)	●
(D)	
(E)	**Category 2**
(F)	●
(G)	●

지시: 보기에서 적절한 구를 골라서 관련된 항목에 알맞게 짝지어라. 두 개의 보기는 사용되지 않는다. 이 문제는 3점이다.
속하는 자리에 선택 항목을 끌어다 놓아라. 선택 항목을 삭제하려면 그 위에 클릭하라. 전체 지문을 다시 보려면 View Text 아이콘을 클릭하라.

문제 공략하기

다음은 Category Chart 문제의 공략법이다. 실전 고득점을 위해 이를 꼼꼼히 학습하고 Hackers Practice와 Hackers Test를 풀면서 반드시 적용해 본다.

1 질문과 지문에서 비교 항목 파악하기
   질문의 분류표에 제시된 비교 항목을 확인한 후 지문에서 각 항목이 설명되는 부분을 파악한다.

2 내용 일치 확인하기
   비교되는 항목의 세부 정보와 보기를 대조하여 보기가 지문의 내용을 바르게 바꾸어 썼는지, 어느 항목에 대해 설명하는지 확인한다.

(Ruminant) animals, such as water buffaloes, have a limited ability to process food and must rely on soft, leafy plant material from which nutrients are easy to extract. [F]The digestive organs of ruminant herbivores are very large. [B]Their digestion takes a long time, and their blood sugar levels rise gradually after a meal. Therefore, [D]they may appear sluggish and unresponsive when provoked. (Nonruminant) animals, such as rhinoceroses, are considerably more efficient at extracting nutrients and are thus not as dependent on highly nourishing foods. They [E]can survive on fibrous material like plant stems, which are [G]easily broken down in their highly acidic stomachs and by microbes in their intestines. Due to the stomach acids, sugars are released quickly into the bloodstream.

Answer Choices	(Ruminant)
(A) Rarely fight back when attacked (C) Stomach acids block sugars from entering the bloodstream	● (B) Slow to digest food ● (D) Are not easily aroused ● (F) Digestive systems make up a large portion of their bodies
	(Nonruminant)
	● (E) Can extract nutrients from fibrous plants ● (G) Have intestinal microorganisms that aid in digestion

지문해석 p.324

1 분류표에 제시된 두 개의 비교 항목 Ruminant(반추)와 Nonruminant(비반추)가 지문 전체에서 비교되고 있음을 파악한다.

2 보기 (B)는 지문의 Their digestion takes a long time(그들의 소화는 오랜 시간이 걸린다), 보기 (D)는 지문의 they may appear sluggish and unresponsive when provoked(자극했을 때 느리고 둔감한 모습을 보인다), 보기 (F)는 The digestive organs of ruminant herbivores are very large(반추 초식동물의 소화기관은 매우 크다)와 일치한다.
보기 (E)는 can survive on fibrous material(섬유질을 먹고 살 수 있다), 보기 (G)는 easily broken down ~ by microbes in their intestines(장 속의 미생물에 의해 쉽게 분해된다)와 일치한다.
따라서, 보기 (B), (D), (F)는 Ruminant, 보기 (E), (G)는 Nonruminant 항목에 각각 속함을 확인할 수 있다.

TIP 지문의 내용과 일치하지 않거나 지문에서 언급되지 않은 내용의 보기가 오답이다.

Hackers Practice

지문을 읽고 물음에 답하시오.

01

The outermost layer of the Earth is the lithosphere, a rock which consists of oceanic and continental crust and the uppermost mantle joined to the crust. Oceanic crust is 50 to 100 kilometers thick, while continental crust ranges from 40 to 200 kilometers in thickness. Although the crust and the upper mantle differ in their composition, they are referred to as the lithosphere because they advance as a single unit. Being at the Earth's surface, the lithosphere is the coolest layer, and as such, tends to solidify into a brittle and rigid rock over time. The brittleness causes the lithosphere to fragment into large plates which move independently of each other. Lying underneath the lithosphere is the asthenosphere, a layer that extends from 100 to 350 kilometers below the Earth's surface; in some areas, it has a depth of 700 kilometers. The difference between the lithosphere and the asthenosphere is how resistant these layers are to movement. The asthenosphere is a weaker and partially molten part of the mantle. Because of these characteristics, it does not crack as the lithosphere does, but behaves much like malleable clay. This allows the lithosphere to drift slowly or to slide along the asthenosphere, similar to ships on a slow-moving river.

Select the appropriate phrases from the answer choices and match them to the layer of the Earth to which they relate.

Answer Choices	Lithosphere
(A) Solidifies into hard rock with the passage of time	●
(B) Moves along in a stream due to its pliability	
(C) Breaks into large pieces due to its brittleness	●
(D) Resists movement the closer it is to the mantle	**Asthenosphere**
(E) Turns into clay as it cools down	●

---

01 **lithosphere**[líθəsfiər] 암석권 **oceanic**[òuʃiǽnik] 해양의 **continental**[kàntənéntl] 대륙의 **crust**[krʌst] 지각
composition[kàmpəzíʃən] 구성 **advance**[ædvǽns] 움직이다, 나아가다 **brittle**[brítl] 부서지기 쉬운 **rigid**[rídʒid] 단단한
fragment[frǽgmənt] 나뉘다 **plate**[pleit] 판 **asthenosphere**[æsθénəsfiər] 암류권 **resistant**[rizístənt] 저항하는
partially[páːrʃəli] 부분적으로 **malleable**[mǽliəbl] 부드러운 **clay**[klei] 찰흙 **drift**[drift] 떠다니다
pliability[plàiəbíləti] 유연성

02

Two of the most common descriptive studies for gathering data concerning population characteristics are cross-sectional and longitudinal. Cross-sectional studies aim to describe the relationship between variables as they exist in a given population at a specific point in time. As such, they are useful for unveiling the existence of a certain characteristic and possible associations, but they cannot clearly identify cause and effect. A cross-sectional study that seeks to ascertain the connection between smoking and lung disease in a country, for example, would measure exposure to smoke and the occurrence of the disease at the same time. If the majority of people surveyed with lung disease were smokers, the data would suggest a link between smoking and lung disease. If similar information is needed in the future, a new group of subjects is surveyed.

Longitudinal studies, on the other hand, attempt to correlate factors by observing them repeatedly over time. These studies can last decades and can therefore be very expensive to complete. Unlike single surveys, longitudinal studies track the same subjects throughout the duration of the project. This makes it possible to compare measurements taken at the beginning of the study with changes that occur at later periods. They are thus extremely valuable for establishing developmental associations. One example is behavior formation in children. Behavioral patterns in infants can be observed and documented and then analyzed based on their persistence or disappearance in childhood. A relationship can then be determined between the changes and an external variable, such as poverty or parental education.

Select the appropriate phrases from the answer choices and match them to the type of methodology to which they relate.

Answer Choices	Cross-sectional
(A) Information collected over a long period of time	●
(B) Causal relationships not definitively identified	
(C) A connection established between initial observations and subsequent changes	**Longitudinal**
(D) Comparisons made across similar populations of different ages	●
(E) Data applied in health studies	●

02 descriptive[diskríptiv] 기술적인 population[pàpjuléiʃən] [통계] 모집단 cross-sectional[krɔ́:ssékʃənl] 횡적의 longitudinal[làndʒətʃú:dənl] 종적의 variable[véəriəbl] 변수 unveil[ʌnvéil] 밝히다 ascertain[æsərtéin] 규명하다 measure[méʒər] 측정하다 exposure[ikspóuʒər] 노출 occurrence[əkɔ́:rəns] 발생 majority[mədʒɔ́:rəti] 대다수 survey[sə:rvéi] 조사하다 subject[sʌ́bdʒikt] 피실험자 correlate[kɔ́:rəlèit] 상호관련짓다 track[træk] 추적하다 establish[istǽbliʃ] 확립하다 persistence[pərsístəns] 지속성

03

In seventh century BC, Greece consisted of hundreds of small city-states that were self-governing. By the fifth century BC, two city-states had distinguished themselves. Athens established democratic rule to institute governmental forms and prevent tyrants from oppressing the people. Sparta was known for its oligarchical rule, which it installed and supported through a strong military.

When Athens established a democratic state around 508 BC, the city formed a council of 500 male citizen-delegates to decide on political matters. Women did not participate in government affairs, confining themselves to household duties. The city-state experienced a period of peace and prosperity after several other city-states attached themselves to the democracy. Athens used its powerful navy to provide protection to its affiliates, requiring a tribute from the smaller cities. As a democracy, Athens thrived culturally, becoming renowned for its architecture, literature, and art.

Sparta took an entirely different route: it relied on discipline to control the citizenry and brute force to conquer city-states. Sparta was a militaristic and totalitarian state requiring utter subjection from its citizens. It had no currency and refused to trade with its neighbors in order to prevent the people from seeking freedom. Starting at the age of seven, males were bred to become professional soldiers ready for military duty at any time; newborn males who were sickly and weak were abandoned to death. The women, although given the opportunity to become educated and own property, were single-minded in their devotion to raising their sons to be strong, dedicated soldiers. Sparta had the best military machine, but it was culturally and artistically backward.

Select the appropriate phrases from the answer choices and match them to the city-state to which they relate.

Answer Choices	Athens
(A) City-states democratized to show support	●
(B) Partner states obligated to give payment in exchange for security	
	Sparta
(C) Association with neighboring peoples forbidden in order to prevent conflicts	●
(D) Women dedicated to rearing their sons	
(E) Formation of dictatorial state and powerful army	●

---

03 **institute**[ínstətʃùːt] 조직하다　**tyrant**[táiərənt] 폭군　**oppress**[əprés] 억압하다　**oligarchical**[àləgáːrkikəl] 과두 정치의
install[instɔ́ːl] 설립하다　**council**[káunsəl] 의회　**delegate**[déligət] 대표　**matter**[mǽtər] 문제　**affair**[əféər] 문제
prosperity[praspérəti] 번영　**affiliate**[əfílièit] 동맹국　**tribute**[tríbjuːt] 공물　**entirely**[intáiərli] 전혀
discipline[dísəplin] 징벌　**brute**[bruːt] 난폭한　**totalitarian**[toutǽlətɛ́əriən] 전체주의　**utter**[ʌ́tər] 전적인
subjection[səbdʒékʃən] 복종　**single-minded**[sìŋglmáindid] 전념하는　**devotion**[divóuʃən] 헌신
dedicated[dédikèitid] 헌신적인　**backward**[bǽkwərd] 뒤떨어진

04

Intraspecific competition occurs when individuals of the same species compete for territory and resources. This type of competition is prevalent among birds of the same species because they have the same requirements, making competition for food and space particularly severe. One example is the tropical hummingbird, which will chase out its own kind to protect favored sites containing nectar-bearing flowers. When the population density of a species of birds becomes particularly high, limited resources have to be shared. This results in weaker individuals being forced to breed and nest in territories that are suboptimal. The Willow Warbler of Finland is a case in point. Its normal habitat is spruce birch forests, but in times of scant resources, less assertive ones are found in other habitats.

Interspecific competition is competition between individuals of two different species that occupy the same niche and utilize the same resources. If space and food are abundant, competition may be weak, and the two species may coexist, but if resources are scarce, or perceived to be scarce, intense competition is the norm. Generally, the species that is most efficient at harvesting the limited resource will be the victor. Intense and persistent competition can lead to extinction unless the weaker species finds a new niche or develops different dietary specifications. Interspecific competition not only affects the species directly involved but also can impact entire ecosystems because alterations in one population can have a ripple effect throughout a biological community.

Select the appropriate sentences from the answer choices and match them to the type of competition to which they relate.

Answer Choices	Intraspecific
(A) Breeding and nesting sites are shared, but there is competition for food. (B) The intensity of the competition can lead to extinction. (C) The rivalry is between members of the same species. (D) Stronger individuals offer protection to weaker members. (E) Competition may result in changes in the population dynamics of an ecosystem.	●
	Interspecific
	● ●

04 **intraspecific**[ìntrəspisífik] 동종의 **prevalent**[prévələnt] 널리 퍼진 **severe**[səvíər] 격렬한 **chase**[tʃeis] 쫓아내다
nectar[néktər] 꿀 **suboptimal**[sʌbáptəməl] 차선의 **spruce**[spruːs] 전나무 **birch**[bəːrtʃ] 자작나무
scant[skænt] 부족한 **assertive**[əsə́ːrtiv] 강한 **interspecific**[intərspisífik] 이종의 **niche**[nitʃ] 영역
abundant[əbʌ́ndənt] 풍족한 **coexist**[kòuigzíst] ~와 공존하다 **scarce**[skɛərs] 희소한 **norm**[nɔːrm] 전형
harvest[háːrvist] 채취하다 **victor**[víktər] 승리자 **extinction**[ikstíŋkʃən] 멸종 **alteration**[ɔ̀ːltəréiʃən] 변화
population[pàpjuléiʃən] 개체군 **ripple effect** 파급 효과

지문을 읽고 물음에 답하시오.

05

Insomnia is a symptom of a sleep disorder and manifests itself in the inability to obtain sufficient sleep. Some insomniacs fall asleep only in the early morning hours, while others fall asleep at an appropriate time but awake in the hours just after midnight. Researchers have identified two types of insomnia: acute and chronic. These types are based on the length of time an individual suffers from insomnia.

Acute sleep deprivation can last from a few days to three weeks. Stressors in the environment, insufficient sunlight during the winter season, extreme weather conditions, and jet lag can all produce sleeplessness. Stimuli such as coffee, alcohol, cigarettes, and medications can also trigger brief periods of insomnia. Once the stimulus that incited the insomnia is identified, the condition can be treated. Sleeping pills are usually prescribed for a limited time, or the individual is advised to change his habits at bedtime in order to remove the triggers that precipitated sleeplessness. More often, however, acute insomnia runs its course without treatment.

Chronic lack of sleep lasts more than three weeks. Its roots lie in the physiological and psychological condition of the person. Primary insomnia is usually related to the psychological state of the person. Major or traumatic events, including the loss of a job or a family member, and injury due to an accident or act of violence, can result in persistent lack of sleep. On the other hand, a condition with a physiological cause, such as an ongoing and persistent health problem, is called secondary insomnia. Physical discomfort and taking prescription medication with caffeine or a similar ingredient are some examples.

Chronic insomnia is much more serious than the acute variety because the hours of sleeplessness accumulate and, over time, have a devastating effect on the health of the individual. Advancements in medical technology have made it possible for researchers today to examine the effects of insufficient sleep on a physiological and neurological level. Sleep deprivation is now known to influence the secretion of hormones, the functioning of the immune system, and the fitness of the cardiovascular system. Hormones that affect growth, endocrine, and metabolic functions, as well as energy regulation, are secreted during sleep. The discharge of these fluids into the bloodstream is adversely affected when sleep is inadequate or delayed. Persons who are sleep-deprived have a lower immune response; they heal more slowly and their bodies are unable to fight infections and disease as effectually. Finally, increasing evidence indicates a link between sleep loss and cardiovascular health due to increased blood pressure levels.

---

05 insomnia[insάmniə] 불면증 disorder[disɔ́ːrdər] 장애 manifest[mǽnəfèst] 나타나다
insomniac[insάmniæ̀k] 불면증 환자 acute[əkjúːt] 급성의 chronic[kránik] 만성의 deprivation[dèprivéiʃən] 부족
stressor[strésər] 스트레스 유발 요인 jet lag 시차로 인한 피로 stimulus[stímjuləs] 흥분제 trigger[trígər] 유발하다; 요인
incite[insáit] 유발하다 prescribe[priskráib] 처방하다 precipitate[prisípətèit] 촉진시키다 run its course 자연히 사라지다
traumatic[trəmǽtik] 충격적인 persistent[pərsístənt] 지속적인 ingredient[ingríːdiənt] 성분
accumulate[əkjúːmjulèit] 축적되다 devastating[dévəstèitiŋ] 파괴적인 neurological[njùərəládʒikəl] 신경학상의
secretion[sikríːʃən] 분비 immune[imjúːn] 면역의 cardiovascular[kàːrdiouvǽskjulər] 심장혈관의
endocrine[éndəkrin] 내분비의 metabolic[mètəbálik] 신진대사의 discharge[distʃáːrdʒ] 분비
adversely[ædvə́ːrsli] 적대적으로 effectually[ifék tʃuəli] 효과적으로

Select the appropriate sentences from the answer choices and match them to the type of insomnia to which they relate.

Answer Choices	Acute
(A) A sufferer falls asleep at a proper time, but wakes in the very early hours of the morning.	●
(B) Usually, symptoms will go away on their own.	●
(C) The mental health of an individual is a contributory factor.	**Chronic**
(D) It typically lasts no more than a day or two.	●
(E) It can affect the overall state of the heart and blood vessels.	●
(F) Persons with this condition do not resist infection well because their immune system is weakened.	●
(G) Causal agents may include weather problems, seasonal variations, and environmental circumstances.	

CH 1
CH 2
CH 3
CH 4
CH 5
CH 6
CH 7
CH 8
CHAPTER 9
Hackers TOEFL Reading Intermediate

06

There are significant differences in the behavior of individuals when they are alone and when they are part of a crowd. Sociologists have noted that people in a crowd take less responsibility for their actions, even when the behavior is destructive, as seen in the violent acts of people at political demonstrations or sporting events. Some crowd behavior is not manifest, but has an influence, nevertheless. For example, people often follow market trends when making financial investments, unloading their stock during times of economic crisis and precipitating a stock market crash. Because the actions of a collective can have a powerful impact, it is essential for particular groups of people, such as economists, to understand crowd behavior. Several theories have been developed by sociologists to explain and predict this behavior, three of which are most prominent.

In his 1895 publication *The Crowd: A Study of the Popular Mind*, French sociologist Gustave Le Bon put forward the contagion theory, explaining that crowds have a captivating effect on individual members. Crowd members are riveted to something that is taking place. Instead of using their own thinking capacity to assess the situation, however, individuals submerge their identity, allowing their will and emotions to become secondary to those of the crowd's. Le Bon calls this group consciousness "crowd mind." Crowd mind is irrational because it forsakes cultural, moral, and personal learning and interests to the chaotic, instinctive, and primitive impulses of a crowd. Le Bon states that crowd members become barbarians, and the crowd as a whole, a mob.

Psychologist Gordon Allport's convergence theory holds that the crowd is not what causes people to act in a certain way but that people with certain tendencies are attracted to crowds. In other words, like-minded individuals tend to converge and form crowds, and the seemingly homogeneous behavior precedes the crowd formation rather than following from the experience of the crowd. A problem with the convergence theory is that it fails to explain why people of seemingly very diverse backgrounds and beliefs can come to form crowds.

The emergent norm theory of crowd behavior was an attempt to synthesize the contagion and convergence theories. In 1972, sociologists Ralph Turner and Lewis Killian posited that crowds are neither irrational nor driven by like-minded people but are composed of individuals who make spontaneous, rational decisions in response to the events they experience. Rather than being contagious, the behavior is rational because people think that if everyone else is doing something, the action cannot be wrong. Therefore, the crowd simply redefines the norm for acceptable behavior. The larger the crowd is, the more universal its position appears.

---

06 **significant**[signífikənt] 상당한 **destructive**[distrʌ́ktiv] 파괴적인 **manifest**[mǽnəfèst] 명백한
unload[ʌ̀nlóud] 처분하다 **precipitate**[prisípətèit] 촉진하다 **collective**[kəléktiv] 집단 **contagion**[kəntéidʒən] 감염
captivate[kǽptəvèit] 사로잡다 **rivet**[rívit] 집중하다 **assess**[əsés] 평가하다 **submerge**[səbmə́:rdʒ] 숨기다
consciousness[kánʃənis] 의식 **irrational**[irǽʃənl] 비이성적인 **barbarian**[bɑːrbɛ́əriən] 야만인 **mob**[mɑb] 폭도
convergence[kənvə́:rdʒəns] 수렴 **like-minded**[làikmáindid] 같은 생각의 **seemingly**[síːmiŋli] 겉으로 보기에
homogeneous[hòumədʒíːniəs] 동질의 **precede**[prisíːd] 먼저 일어나다 **synthesize**[sínθəsàiz] 종합하다
spontaneous[spantéiniəs] 자발적인 **acceptable**[ækséptəbl] 용인할 수 있는 **position**[pəzíʃən] 주장

Select the appropriate phrases from the answer choices and match them to the type of theory to which they relate.

Answer Choices	Contagion
(A) Considers the dictates of a crowd more powerful than the will of an individual	●
(B) Believes that people in a crowd rationally adjust their view of acceptable behavior	●
	Convergence
(C) Assumes that those who are inclined to join crowds are usually of a similar mindset	●
(D) Stresses the savage nature of the crowd as a whole	●
(E) Points to the refusal of the crowd to assume responsibility for any action	
	Emergent Norm
(F) Highlights the tendency of a crowd to destroy an economy	●
(G) Does not account for how people of different beliefs join crowds	

CH 1
CH 2
CH 3
CH 4
CH 5
CH 6
CH 7
CH 8

CHAPTER 9

Hackers TOEFL Reading Intermediate

07

The dominant theory on the formation of Jupiter is that the planet was created by a two-step process of core formation and gas accretion. Collisions between ice and rock in the solar nebula, a swirling disc of dust and gas, caused matter to collect and grow, eventually making a solid mass that became the core of the future planet. As additional solid material bombarded the surface of the protoplanet, its mass, pressure, and temperature all increased. These factors combined to radiate energy away from the core, and this energy initially prevented nebular gas from falling toward the young protoplanet. Core mass-building in Jupiter's protoplanet continued for a period of roughly half a million years until the solid clump reached a critical mass (i.e., the minimum mass threshold for gas accretion).

Once the critical mass was reached, a gradual migration of nebular gas toward the surface ensued, leading to the creation of a gaseous atmosphere that enveloped the core. After the mass of the gaseous component reached and surpassed the mass of the solid component, a rapid acceleration of gas accumulation began. This second phase of the core accretion model was responsible for the gigantic size of Jupiter. The rapid accretion is known as gas runaway, and the runaway continued as long as there was an abundant supply of gas in the vicinity of the protoplanet's orbit. In the case of Jupiter, there must have been plenty of gas available given its size. In other outer planets like Neptune and Uranus, the availability of nebular gas may have been less.

The primary alternative to core accretion is the disc instability model. According to some astrophysicists, disc instability could have created many planets rapidly, and a planet the size of Jupiter could have fully formed in just a few hundred years. In terms of space time, that is considered virtually spontaneous and would have only required a single step. The mechanism for this disc instability is assumed to be the nebula's own gravity. If gravitational forces were unstable, segments of gas and dust could have fragmented, forming gas planets with their own gravities. Disc instability was first proposed in the early 1950s, but it was largely discarded because the model seemed incompatible with the formation of a large core. Skeptics argued that dust and other solid debris would have disintegrated in the hot gas envelope before reaching the center of a massive gas planet. However, the theory has recently attracted attention due to some new proposals. In the late 1990s, scientists argued that Jupiter may have a very small core or no core at all. Yet such a proposition is at best tentative. Other similar simulations have suggested that Jupiter's core may be twice as large as previously thought.

---

07 **core**[kɔːr] 핵 **accretion**[əkríːʃən] 증대 **collision**[kəlíʒən] 충돌 **solar**[sóulər] 태양의 **nebula**[nébjulə] 성운
swirl[swəːrl] 소용돌이치다 **disc**[disk] 원반 **bombard**[bɑmbáːrd] 충격을 가하다
protoplanet[próutəplænit] 원시 행성 **radiate**[réidièit] 방출하다 **roughly**[rʌ́fli] 대략 **clump**[klʌmp] 덩어리
critical[krítikəl] 결정적인 **ensue**[insúː] 뒤이어 일어나다 **envelop**[invéləp] 싸다 **phase**[feiz] 단계
gigantic[dʒaigǽntik] 거대한 **runaway**[rʌ́nəwèi] 탈주 **abundant**[əbʌ́ndənt] 충분한 **vicinity**[visínəti] 근처
orbit[ɔ́ːrbit] 궤도 **instability**[ìnstəbíləti] 불안정 **astrophysicist**[æ̀stroufízisist] 천체 물리학자
spontaneous[spɑntéiniəs] 자연 발생적인 **segment**[ségmənt] 부분 **fragment**[frǽgmənt] 나뉘다
incompatible[ìnkəmpǽtəbl] 모순의 **skeptic**[sképtik] 회의론자 **debris**[dəbríː] 조각 **tentative**[téntətiv] 불확실한
previously[príːviəsli] 기존에

Select the appropriate phrases from the answer choices and match them to the type of model to which they relate.

Answer Choices	Core Accretion
(A) Near-instantaneous formation of a gaseous planet in a single step	●
(B) Gradual accumulation of solid material	●
(C) A rapid phase of massive gas collection	
(D) Fragmentation of gas and dust segments along gravitational gradients	●
(E) Indisputable proof that Jupiter's core is smaller than previously thought	**Disc Instability**
(F) A second sequence initiated by a greater gas-to-solid ratio	●
(G) A phase of gas collection resulting from increased mass, pressure, and temperature	●

정답·해석·정답단서 p.324

CH 1
CH 2
CH 3
CH 4
CH 5
CH 6
CH 7
CH 8
CHAPTER 9
Hackers TOEFL Reading Intermediate

1 Dinosaur Diets

1   The question of what dinosaurs actually ate has occupied paleobiologists for decades, and though no comprehensive consensus has emerged, informative traces of dinosaur feeding activities can be gathered from the fossil record. Methods for studying dinosaur diets fall into two general spheres: direct and indirect. Through studying fossilized remains of food inside dinosaurs and other physical evidence such as fossilized dung, scientists can gain firsthand knowledge about what kinds of things dinosaurs were eating prior to their extinction. Alternatively, scientists can study indirect clues and speculate about the feeding habits of these intriguing reptiles. ■

2   Indisputable proof of what foods particular dinosaurs consumed is hard to obtain because fossilized remains directly related to consumption are rare. ■ Occasionally, however, fortunate discoveries reveal information about all stages of the feeding process, from search and capture to consumption and defecation. ■ One such exceptional find occurred in the Gobi Desert in the form of two interlocked dinosaur species, a carnivorous Velociraptor and an herbivorous Protoceratops, with their entire skeletons intact. ■ The position of the Velociraptor, which had its claws tightly clutched on the jaw of the Protoceratops, indicates that it was feeding on the other dinosaur when it died, suggesting a predator-prey relationship between the two animals. Scientists, believing the arrangement could not have happened simply by chance, view the fossilized remains as clear evidence that the Velociraptor was a meat eater and that Protoceratops was part of its diet.

3   ➡ Even more convincing are well-preserved carcasses of dinosaurs that died soon after eating. Needles from conifers, seeds, and other plant materials have been found in the stomach cavities of some dinosaurs, clearly demonstrating an herbaceous diet. Similarly, lizards have been seen within the rib cages of fossilized dinosaurs, proving that some species fed on other reptiles. A more startling revelation was the position of immature Coelophysis specimens within the body cavity of a full-grown adult Coelophysis. One possibility was that the smaller dinosaurs had hatched from eggs inside the birth canal of a pregnant female, but scientists concluded that the smaller Coelophysis dinosaurs were too large for this theory to hold. Therefore, it seems that Coelophysis, in addition to being a carnivore, practiced cannibalistic behavior. The issue of whether the young were captured alive, however, is still a mystery. Direct clues can also come through fecal deposits. Coprolites, or fossilized feces, sometimes contain representations of food that had passed through the digestive systems of dinosaurs unchanged.

4   ➡ Complementing the sparse, straightforward clues provided by coprolites and food evidence are individual body parts, most notably teeth and jaws, which offer

indirect hints about consumption patterns. These sorts of fossilized remains are more common than the exceptional cases mentioned above, and the bone structure of some dinosaurs is well documented. Complete or near-complete jawbones with accompanying teeth have been reconstructed from theropod skeletons, for example. Their large teeth were elongated and curved, coming to a sharp point at the terminal end, and were finely serrated, making them ideal for cutting through flesh and crushing bones. In contrast, teeth of dinosaurs presumed to be herbivorous were often rectangular with blunt surfaces and coarse serrations, especially suited for grasping and chopping vegetation. Some sets of teeth, such as those of the gigantic sauropods, were widely spaced like the teeth of a rake. The spacing probably allowed the animals to grasp and pull off leafy material without breaking the harder, more fibrous plant stems and branches.

5 ➡ Paleontologists also look to dinosaur tracks for indications of how the animals may have moved around in search of food. Drawing conclusions from footprints requires a highly speculative approach, but feasible scenarios can be constructed. In Australia, for example, a densely packed collection of thousands of tracks was uncovered and studied. The site contained numerous footprints believed to have been deposited by hundreds of small dinosaurs and the tracks of a single large theropod. By measuring the distance between the tracks, the researchers determined that the small dinosaurs had suddenly scattered, running in various directions. It is reasonable to hypothesize that they were fleeing from a threatening presence, such as that of an approaching predator like the theropod. Although these tracks offer scientists no conclusive explanations, indirect clues are helpful for building a conceptual framework for piecing together information about the diets of dinosaurs.

1 The word "comprehensive" in the passage is closest in meaning to

(A) complete

(B) realistic

(C) permanent

(D) plausible

2   Which of the sentences below best expresses the essential information in the highlighted sentence in the passage? *Incorrect* choices change the meaning in important ways or leave out essential information.

(A) The two dinosaurs were apparently engaged in a struggle when they died, as is evident from the position of the Velociraptor's claws on the jaw of the Protoceratops.

(B) The position of the Velociraptor's claws around the jaw of the Proceratops seems to suggest that it was preying on the Protoceratops at the time of the dinosaurs' deaths.

(C) The position of the Velociraptor in relation to the other dinosaur indicates that it had its claws tightly clutched around the jaw of the Protoceratops when they died.

(D) The predator-prey relationship between the two dinosaurs was made more apparent because the Velociraptor's position indicates that it killed the Protoceratops with its claws.

3   Which of the following can be inferred from paragraph 3 about Coelophysis?

(A) It is unclear whether they were carnivores or herbivores.

(B) Their digestive systems were similar to those of other reptiles.

(C) Their young were hatched inside the mother's body.

(D) It is unknown whether they were predators or scavengers.

Paragraph 3 is marked with an arrow [➡].

4   Which of the following statements about the teeth of dinosaurs is supported by paragraph 4?

(A) Curved teeth were useful for grasping and holding prey.

(B) Sharp teeth were required for cutting through hard plant material.

(C) Rectangular teeth meant dinosaurs were herbivores.

(D) Coarsely serrated teeth meant dinosaurs were carnivores.

Paragraph 4 is marked with an arrow [➡].

5   The word "feasible" in the passage is closest in meaning to

(A) responsible

(B) dependable

(C) practicable

(D) eligible

6   In paragraph 5, what does the author say about the footprints found in Australia?

(A) They were probably left behind by a large group of theropods.

(B) They show that Australia was once densely populated by dinosaurs.

(C) They were made by dinosaurs converging from many different directions.

(D) They seem to have resulted from an encounter between predator and prey.

Paragraph 5 is marked with an arrow [➡].

7   Look at the four squares [■] that indicate where the following sentence could be added to the passage.

Most of the fossil record consists of bone fragments that offer no direct clues about diet.

Where would the sentence best fit?

Click on a square [■] to add the sentence to the passage.

8   **Directions**: Select the appropriate phrases from the answer choices and match them to the type of evidence to which they relate. TWO of the answer choices will NOT be used. **This question is worth 3 points.**

Drag your answer choices to the spaces where they belong.
To remove an answer choice, click on it. To review the passage, click on **View Text**.

Answer Choices	Direct
(A) Remains of egg shells inside the rib cages of dinosaurs	●
(B) Herbaceous material found within a dinosaur's stomach cavity	●
(C) The jawbones and teeth of dinosaur skeletons	●
(D) The complete skeletal remains of a predator engaged with its prey	
(E) Fossilized droppings of undigested food	**Indirect**
(F) The structural similarity between dinosaurs and other reptiles	●
(G) Sites containing preserved tracks of dinosaurs	●

CH 1
CH 2
CH 3
CH 4
CH 5
CH 6
CH 7
CH 8
CHAPTER 9
Hackers TOEFL Reading Intermediate

1   Architects typically used unprocessed raw materials during ancient times, and this trend continued until the nineteenth century. After 1800, manufactured materials began to play a more prominent role, and many modern buildings were constructed with processed materials. This transition was initiated by technological progress and changing perceptions about building materials.

2   ➡ The range of architectural materials used in ancient times was limited. Timber was used for some structural purposes in areas where it was available, particularly for beams and other parts of roofs. Later, wood was largely replaced by stone, except for relatively small items, such as doors and partitions. Indeed, by the medieval and early modern periods, virtually all European structures other than simple residences were formed using masonry.

3   ➡ Masonry construction was achieved by assembling and stacking stones or bricks. Sometimes, masons simply placed stones on top of one another. Other times, they squared the stones for better stacking or formed bricks from mud. Mortar was used occasionally to seal cracks or to temporarily bond stones together, but it had no great structural strength. Columns, beams, arches, and walls were all engineered in this way, and compaction through gravity gave the structures their stability.

4   ➡ Metals in preindustrial times were generally used only for superficial purposes, most often as minor decorative details, such as railings and windows. This limited application of metal stems in part from the fact that it was expensive to produce in large quantities. Though the technology for producing iron and steel existed, the means for cheap mass production was unavailable. Also, there was a strong preference for masonry as a building material among architects, and as a result, metal in structural architecture was mostly confined to bridges and greenhouses. Metal was considered inferior as a construction material for buildings because it was man-made and was viewed as having low aesthetic appeal.

5   ➡ Major changes occurred in the nineteenth century. For example, the economic concerns and aesthetic prejudices against using metal in building began to slowly erode. Some architects, like New York City's James Bogardus, openly advocated the use of cast iron for buildings. ■ In the 1850s, Bogardus used cast iron extensively in storefronts. ■ Because cast iron could be formed in almost any shape, it was easy to simulate the ornate exteriors that were usually meticulously carved into marble and stone. ■ Following the success of his buildings, Bogardus shifted his focus to structural materials and began to use metal to frame entire buildings. ■

6   ➡ For the purpose of supporting very heavy structures, cast iron proved to be inappropriate in the long term. Cast iron contains impurities like carbon. Though strong, its impurities make it brittle. It has a low tensile strength, so it is subject to breaking when exposed to high levels of stress. This property was discovered after several bridges collapsed during the 1800s, and the use of cast iron to support heavy

structures was phased out in the nineteenth century.

7 ➡ Wrought iron, which is iron with most of the impurities removed, provided a temporary solution. Unlike cast iron, wrought iron is ductile, meaning it can handle more stress without fracturing. However, its production is time-consuming and expensive. A more useful material is steel. Steel became easy and cheap to produce in the 1850s, and it combines the beneficial properties of cast iron and wrought iron. Like cast iron, it can be poured into a mold to form any shape, and like wrought iron, it can safely support heavy loads. By the end of the nineteenth century, steel had replaced all forms of iron as the primary metal for architectural purposes.

8 Almost simultaneously, architects and engineers began using concrete as an architectural material. At first, concrete was manufactured to appear like masonry because, like metal and other processed materials, it was generally frowned upon for use in sacred and municipal buildings. Only in the 1900s did manufactured materials adorn the venerated walls of churches and other architectural landmarks, and to a large extent, masonry continued to be the material of choice in the twentieth century. On the other hand, for industrial and commercial buildings, steel and concrete became standard, and they were used extensively in modern skyscrapers.

9 The technical prowess to produce metals cheaply, along with the gradual acceptance of manufactured materials like concrete by architects and builders, changed the architectural landscape. Urban environments, in particular, contain numerous examples of metal and concrete buildings constructed after the nineteenth century, including those that were crafted with both structural and aesthetic purposes in mind.

1 The word "initiated" in the passage is closest in meaning to

(A) terminated

(B) submitted

(C) tolerated

(D) started

2 According to paragraph 2, which of the following can be inferred about timber?

(A) Its scarcity led to a shift toward masonry in medieval and early modern Europe.

(B) Its use in constructing objects like doors and partitions remained unchanged.

(C) It was used when other materials, such as stone, were unavailable to the ancients.

(D) It was preferred to stone in ancient times because it was easy to work with.

Paragraph 2 is marked with an arrow [➡].

3   In paragraph 3, masons sometimes squared stones because

(A) it offered an alternative to making mud bricks

(B) it made the stones easier to stack on one another

(C) it helped the mortar to bond more easily with the stones

(D) it increased the stability of the structures

Paragraph 3 is marked with an arrow [➡].

4   All of the following were true of metals in preindustrial times according to paragraph 4 EXCEPT:

(A) They were not cheap to produce in large quantities.

(B) They were mainly utilized for minor decorative details.

(C) They were used with masonry in bridges and greenhouses.

(D) They were considered unattractive as a construction material.

Paragraph 4 is marked with an arrow [➡].

5   Why does the author discuss James Bogardus in paragraph 5?

(A) To demonstrate that knowledge among architects about cast iron was growing

(B) To show that tastes in the architectural community were beginning to change

(C) To argue that cast iron was used in architecture more than was once thought

(D) To criticize the aesthetic prejudices of previous generations of architects

Paragraph 5 is marked with an arrow [➡].

6   According to paragraphs 6 and 7, which of the following is true of cast iron and wrought iron?

(A) Cast iron is more expensive to produce than wrought iron.

(B) Wrought iron is better for supporting heavy structures than cast iron.

(C) They each have distinct structural advantages over steel.

(D) They are more difficult to mold into complex shapes than steel.

Paragraphs 6 and 7 are marked with arrows [➡].

7   Which of the sentences below best expresses the essential information in the highlighted sentence in the passage? *Incorrect* choices change the meaning in important ways or leave out essential information.

(A) Initially, concrete was processed like metals and other materials in order to make it appear like masonry.

(B) Because concrete was disapproved of for use in sacred and municipal buildings, it was initially made to look like masonry.

(C) At first, concrete was manufactured to look like masonry, but was not used in sacred and municipal buildings.

(D) Due to the fact that it was a processed material just like metal, concrete was initially frowned upon for use in sacred and municipal buildings.

8 The word "prowess" in the passage is closest in meaning to

(A) means

(B) expertise

(C) motivation

(D) imagination

9 Look at the four squares [■] that indicate where the following sentence could be added to the passage.

This meant storefronts could be erected without hiring expert masons and sculptors.

Where would the sentence best fit?

Click on a square [■] to add the sentence to the passage.

10 **Directions**: Select the appropriate sentences from the answer choices and match them to the time period to which they relate. TWO of the answer choices will NOT be used. **This question is worth 3 points.**

Drag your answer choices to the spaces where they belong.
To remove an answer choice, click on it. To review the passage, click on **View Text**.

Answer Choices	Before the Nineteenth Century
(A) Cast iron was replaced with stronger materials.	●
(B) Emphasis was placed on unprocessed architectural materials.	●
(C) Architects were more willing to use metal and concrete.	**After 1800**
(D) Masons shifted their focus from brick to stone and marble.	●
(E) Builders openly advocated the use of metal in bridge construction.	●
(F) Timber gave way to masonry as the dominant structural material.	●
(G) The production of architectural metals became less expensive.	●

CH 1
CH 2
CH 3
CH 4
CH 5
CH 6
CH 7
CH 8

CHAPTER 9

Hackers TOEFL Reading Intermediate

3 Nature, Nurture, and Human Emotion Psychology

1 Two main topics direct the study of human emotion: nature and nurture. Biological determinists believe emotion is determined by nature. They emphasize the intrinsic, natural causes of human emotion. Social determinists believe emotion is determined by nurture. They tend to highlight the role of the environment in emotional development.

2 ➡ Biological, or genetic, determinism is the theory that a person's genes represent the deciding factor on how a person behaves and changes over time. According to the genetic view, the brain is intrinsically wired to display a general range of emotions, and bodily factors can explain emotional differences at various stages of life. During puberty, for example, males and females undergo changes in the production of testosterone and estrogen, respectively. These are physiological changes, which can create mood swings that are purely biological.

3 ➡ Evidence for the biological approach can be found in the shared emotional qualities of people growing up in entirely different cultures. For their 1976 work *Unmasking the Face*, neuropsychologists Paul Ekman and Wallace Friesen undertook an extensive cross-cultural study of facial expressions. Ekman and Friesen interviewed isolated tribes in Papua New Guinea and showed them photographs of people from other parts of the world with whom the tribal people were completely unfamiliar. The psychologists discovered that the participants not only could clearly identify facial expressions with particular emotions but could also describe situations in which the expressions may arise. This led the authors to conclude that six basic human emotions (anger, disgust, fear, happiness, sadness, surprise), as well as physical expression of those emotions, are universal among people.

4 ➡ While biological determinists are impressed by the universality of human emotions, social determinists are interested in their diversity. Objections to the biological explanation emphasize that substantial differences can and do occur in the psychological and behavioral patterns of growing children, and that these changes can be explained by experiential factors. Social determinists point to variables such as parenting, poverty, education, and exposure to violence as primary influences on a child's emotional state. In addition, they view the genetic determinist position as dangerous because when taken to its logical conclusion, it seems to sever human responsibility from human action. The assumption that someone is born a certain way, they argue, offers an immediate defense for unwarranted behavior. A child who is easily angered, for example, may learn to excuse inappropriate actions by attributing them to his or her innate aggressive personality.

5 Thus, most adherents of the social determinism school are behaviorists who highlight the environment as a conditioning element. ■ According to the behaviorist view, a child experiencing the physical pain and emotional trauma of a dog attack will almost certainly develop a fear of dogs. ■ In contrast, a child who has only positive encounters with animals may perceive the barking of a dog as a pleasant sound and

feel no sense of anxiety when approaching them. ■ Therefore, emotional responses to stimuli are not a result of nature alone but also the experiences a growing child undergoes. ■

6 ➡ Cultural differences are also central to the nurture hypothesis. In some countries, the national anthem may not produce a strong emotional response, but in countries with robust patriotic traditions, people often respond to hearing the national anthem tearfully, demonstrating intense reactions based on feelings of patriotism. The fact that these emotional reactions appear spontaneous and are carried out unconsciously may seem to indicate that they are as natural as a yawn or a sneeze, but in reality they are the result of very detailed "cultural scripting," not simply bodily responses to a stimulus. This scripting occurs in all societies, and it is responsible for teaching people when and how to appropriately express their emotions. Similarly, some emotions themselves seem to be culturally determined. The Ifaluk people of Micronesia, for instance, have no direct term for "anger," but do have an emotion called *song*, which translates roughly as "justified anger." It has no connection to feelings of rage or aggression as found in the English word anger; rather, it conveys a sense of stern moral disapproval.

7 Because data supporting each perspective is so strong, most psychologists and biologists accept both genetic and environmental factors as contributing to human emotional development. As such, specialists now focus on the more relevant task of characterizing and understanding the complex interactions between nature and nurture in the formation of emotional temperaments.

1 According to paragraph 2, which of the following is true of puberty?

   (A) It can be treated with estrogen and testosterone.
   (B) It leads to the formation of new emotions.
   (C) It can produce dramatic shifts in mood.
   (D) It occurs at different ages in males and females.

   Paragraph 2 is marked with an arrow [➡].

2 What can be inferred from paragraph 3 about tribes in Papua New Guinea?

   (A) They were reluctant to be interviewed by outsiders.
   (B) They had never seen photographs prior to 1976.
   (C) They had little contact with foreigners before 1976.
   (D) Their facial expressions reflected only six basic emotions.

   Paragraph 3 is marked with an arrow [➡].

3 According to paragraph 4, which of the following is NOT a view of the social determinists?

(A) Psychological and behavioral changes are attributable to experiential factors.

(B) Excusing behavior as inborn can lead to unfavorable consequences.

(C) The aggressive personality of some children is due to innate tendencies.

(D) The diversity of human emotions is more notable than their universality.

Paragraph 4 is marked with an arrow [➡].

4 The word "sever" in the passage is closest in meaning to

(A) deviate

(B) divide

(C) prevent

(D) promote

5 Which of the sentences below best expresses the essential information in the highlighted sentence in the passage? *Incorrect* choices change the meaning in important ways or leave out essential information.

(A) In countries without robust patriotic traditions, the playing of the national anthem may not produce an intense emotional response.

(B) Hearing the national anthem may not always produce a strong emotional response, even among those in countries with strong patriotic traditions.

(C) In some countries, people are raised to feel strong emotions when the national anthem is played, whereas in other countries they are not.

(D) Hearing the national anthem often produces powerful emotional responses in countries with strong patriotic traditions, but not always in others.

6 In paragraph 6, what does the author say about "cultural scripting"?

(A) It is carried out as unconsciously as a yawn or a sneeze.

(B) It results in changes in the body's response to stimuli.

(C) It educates people on acceptable ways of emotional expression.

(D) It is more pronounced in some societies than in others.

Paragraph 6 is marked with an arrow [➡].

7 Why does the author include the discussion about the Ifaluk term *song* in paragraph 6?

(A) To demonstrate how linguistic differences affect how emotions are portrayed

(B) To provide an example of an emotion that is culturally determined

(C) To prove that not all cultures have a specific term for every emotion

(D) To describe how the Ifaluk teach people to appropriately express their emotions

8 The word "perspective" in the passage is closest in meaning to

(A) prospect

(B) viewpoint

(C) conclusion

(D) theorem

9 Look at the four squares [■] that indicate where the following sentence could be added to the passage.

Fearful tendencies can also result from hearing repeated warnings about the animals.

Where would the sentence best fit?

Click on a square [■] to add the sentence to the passage.

10 **Directions**: Select the appropriate sentences from the answer choices and match them to the theory to which they relate. TWO of the answer choices will NOT be used. **This question is worth 3 points.**

Drag your answer choices to the spaces where they belong.
To remove an answer choice, click on it. To review the passage, click on **View Text**.

Answer Choices	Biological Determinism
(A) Painful experiences can alter a child's emotions.	●
(B) Parenting and education affect behavioral development.	●
(C) Innate factors explain changes in human behavior.	●
(D) Genetic and environmental factors play an equal role in emotional development.	Social Determinism
(E) People in different cultures recognize the same basic emotions.	●
(F) Physiology affects mood more than learning.	●
(G) Some societies have no linguistic symbols for emotions.	

정답·해석·정답단서 p.327

VOCABULARY LIST

Chapter 09에서 선별한 다음의 토플 필수 어휘를 단어암기 음성파일을 들으며 암기한 후 퀴즈로 확인해보세요.

*해커스 동영상강의 포털 해커스인강(HackersIngang.com)에서 단어암기 음성파일을 무료로 다운로드할 수 있습니다.

composition[kàmpəzíʃən] 구성 (=formation)

advance[ædvǽns] 나아가다 (=proceed)

resistant[rizístənt] 저항하는

partially[páːrʃəli] 부분적으로 (=incompletely)

descriptive[diskríptiv] 기술적인

unveil[ʌ̀nvéil] 밝히다 (=disclose)

ascertain[æ̀sərtéin] 규명하다 (=discover)

measure[méʒər] 측정하다 (=gauge)

exposure[ikspóuʒər] 노출

subject[sʌ́bdʒikt] 피실험자

correlate[kɔ́ːrəlèit] 상호관련짓다

track[træk] 추적하다 (=chase)

establish[istǽbliʃ] 확립하다 (=constitute)

persistence[pərsístəns] 지속성

institute[ínstətjùːt] 조직하다 (=organize)

oppress[əprés] 억압하다 (=maltreat)

install[instɔ́ːl] 설립하다

prosperity[prɑspérəti] 번영

entirely[intáiərli] 전혀

utter[ʌ́tər] 전적인

devotion[divóuʃən] 헌신

dedicated[dédikèitid] 헌신적인

backward[bǽkwərd] 뒤떨어진

prevalent[prévələnt] 널리 퍼진 (=dominant)

assertive[əsə́ːrtiv] 강한

extinction[ikstíŋkʃən] 멸종

disorder[disɔ́ːrdər] 장애

acute[əkjúːt] 급성의

chronic[krɑ́nik] 만성의 (=persistent)

deprivation[dèprivéiʃən] 부족

trigger[trígər] 유발하다; 요인 (=cause)

incite[insáit] 유발하다 (=arouse)

prescribe[priskráib] 처방하다

precipitate[prisípətèit] 촉진시키다

traumatic[trəmǽtik] 충격적인

accumulate[əkjúːmjulèit] 축적되다 (=collect)

discharge[distʃɑ́ːrdʒ] 분비

adversely[ædvə́ːrsli] 적대적으로

effectually[iféktʃuəli] 효과적으로

destructive[distrʌ́ktiv] 파괴적인 (=ruinous)

manifest[mǽnəfèst] 명백한 (=evident)

unload[ʌ̀nlóud] 처분하다

collective[kəléktiv] 집단

contagion[kəntéidʒən] 감염

captivate[kǽptəvèit] 사로잡다 (=enthrall)

rivet[rívit] 집중하다

assess[əsés] 평가하다 (=evaluate)

submerge[səbmə́ːrdʒ] 숨기다

convergence[kənvə́ːrdʒəns] 수렴

precede[prisíːd] 먼저 일어나다

acceptable[ækséptəbl] 용인할 수 있는

radiate[réidièit] 방출하다 (=emit)

Quiz

각 단어의 알맞은 뜻을 찾아 연결하시오.

01 prosperity	ⓐ 유발하다
02 dedicated	ⓑ 명백한
03 trigger	ⓒ 번영
04 manifest	ⓓ 수렴
05 captivate	ⓔ 사로잡다
	ⓕ 헌신적인

각 단어의 알맞은 동의어를 찾아 연결하시오.

06 establish	ⓐ disclose
07 radiate	ⓑ persistent
08 unveil	ⓒ arouse
09 chronic	ⓓ constitute
10 incite	ⓔ emit
	ⓕ proceed

ⓒ 0ⓛ　ⓒ 60　ⓐ 80　ⓔ ㄣ0　ⓓ 90　ⓔ 90　ⓑ ㄣ0　ⓐ 80　ⓕ 70　ⓒ 10

roughly[rʌ́fli] 대략

critical[krítikəl] 결정적인 (=crucial)

ensue[insú:] 뒤이어 일어나다 (=succeed)

envelop[invéləp] 싸다

abundant[əbʌ́ndənt] 충분한

spontaneous[spɑntéiniəs] 자연 발생적인 (=uncompelled)

incompatible[ìnkəmpǽtəbl] 모순의

tentative[téntətiv] 불확실한

comprehensive[kàmprihénsiv] 종합적인 (=overall)

consensus[kənsénsəs] 합의 (=agreement)

firsthand[fə́:rsthǽnd] 직접적인

speculate[spékjulèit] 추측하다 (=hypothesize)

intriguing[intrí:giŋ] 흥미로운

exceptional[iksépʃənl] 특별한 (=abnormal)

interlock[ìntərlák] 맞물리다

intact[intǽkt] 온전한 (=undamaged)

arrangement[əréindʒmənt] 배치 (=configuration)

startling[stá:rtliŋ] 놀라운

revelation[rèvəléiʃən] 뜻밖의 사실 (=exposure)

immature[ìmətʃúər] 미숙한

complement[kámpləmənt] 보완하다

straightforward[strèitfɔ́:rwərd] 직접적인

elongate[ilɔ́:ŋgeit] 길어지다

terminal[tə́:rmənl] 끝의 (=final)

finely[fáinli] 미세하게

presume[prizú:m] 추정하다 (=assume)

indication[ìndikéiʃən] 단서 (=lead)

speculative[spékjulèitiv] 추론적인

conclusive[kənklú:siv] 결정적인 (=decisive)

conceptual[kənséptʃuəl] 개념적인

virtually[və́:rtʃuəli] 거의 (=nearly)

assemble[əsémbl] 모으다 (=collect)

stack[stæk] 쌓다 (=pile)

temporarily[tèmpəréráli] 일시적으로

compaction[kəmpǽkʃən] 압축

stability[stəbíləti] 안정성

superficial[sù:pərfíʃəl] 하찮은

preference[préfərəns] 선호

inferior[infíəriər] 열등한 (=shoddy)

prejudice[prédʒudis] 편견 (=bias)

erode[iróud] 사라지다 (=wear away)

advocate[ǽdvəkèit] 지지하다 (=assist)

extensively[iksténsivli] 광범하게

meticulously[mətíkjuləsli] 세밀하게 (=carefully)

expose[ikspóuz] 노출되다 (=exhibit)

temporary[témpərèri] 일시적인 (=transient)

venerate[vénərèit] 숭배하다 (=revere)

isolated[áisəlèitid] 고립된 (=solitary)

identify[aidéntəfài] 식별하다

experiential[ikspìəriénʃəl] 경험의

unwarranted[ʌnwɔ́:rəntid] 부당한

robust[roubʌ́st] 강한 (=sturdy)

CH 1
CH 2
CH 3
CH 4
CH 5
CH 6
CH 7
CH 8

CHAPTER 9

Hackers TOEFL Reading Intermediate

Quiz

각 단어의 알맞은 뜻을 찾아 연결하시오.

01	arrangement	ⓐ 배치
02	superficial	ⓑ 하찮은
03	meticulously	ⓒ 강한
04	robust	ⓓ 숭배하다
05	venerate	ⓔ 직접적인
		ⓕ 세밀하게

각 단어의 알맞은 동의어를 찾아 연결하시오.

06	exceptional	ⓐ solitary
07	terminal	ⓑ decisive
08	conclusive	ⓒ final
09	isolated	ⓓ overall
10	spontaneous	ⓔ abnormal
		ⓕ uncompelled

ⓕ 0L ⓔ 60 ⓐ 80 ⓒ L0 ⓔ 90 ⓑ 50 ⓒ 70 ⓕ 80 ⓑ 20 ⓐ L0

Hackers TOEFL
Reading
Intermediate

◇

Actual Test 1, 2

Actual Test 1

* 실전모의고사 프로그램을 통해, 실제 시험과 동일한 환경에서도 Actual Test를 풀어볼 수 있습니다.

1 Olmec Civilization in Mesoamerica

Anthropology

1 ➡ In Mesoamerica, which roughly corresponds to the location of modern-day Central America and southern Mexico, the first significant society in the Americas emerged around 1200 BCE and flourished for centuries before eventually declining a little more than half a millennium later. The Olmec culture was centered on San Lorenzo, the site of the modern city of Veracruz, and the new settlers established their homes in the tropical lowlands inland from the Gulf of Mexico. This is in sharp contrast to the ancient civilizations of Europe and Asia, which formed along major rivers. It is perhaps debatable whether the Olmecs originated from the north and accessed the San Lorenzo area via the Gulf as a few researchers have hypothesized or from the south, by way of land, which seems apparent from the archaeological record.

2 ➡ In either case, by around 900 BCE, the Olmec culture was thriving, and diffusion of Olmec traits occurred across a broad area. It is evident that the Olmec people enlarged their domain in the direction of the Pacific coast, and looking at surviving sculptures, it seems that they spread their culture by way of religion. Found objects include ritualistic masks made of jade and fashioned in the form of jaguar faces. It is believed that priests wore these masks in ceremonial performances to transform themselves into the sacred feline and to demonstrate their connection to divine forces. Evidence for this assertion comes from the discovery of the masks at fortified ceremonial centers with temples on raised earthen mounds. In addition, the Olmecs made small figures depicting gods of fire, rain, and corn as well as a feathered serpent deity, all of which became common theological symbols in the region.

3 ➡ Another important characteristic of the Olmec people was their skill in masonry and stonework, which is evident in the building of a pyramid that exceeds 30 meters in height as well as in the sculpting of gigantic heads, somewhat reminiscent of the great stone statues of Easter Island. Presumably, the rest of the body was ignored because of the widely held belief in Mesoamerica that only the head contained the true essence of a person. Seventeen of the heads have been discovered so far, and the largest approach 3 meters in height, 4.5 meters in circumference, and 8 tons in weight. They were sculpted from basalt boulders, which were mined from the mountains and transported up to 100 kilometers via huge rafts on water, log rollers on land, or a combination of both. And given that the Olmecs carved exclusively with stone tools, the amount of labor and time required to create these monuments must have been extraordinary. Therefore, the prevailing view is that the stone heads represented rulers or other revered individuals, such as athletes or warriors, in Olmec society. Although there is currently no verifiable proof that this was the case, archaeologists have found stone sculptures that were knocked over and buried, suggesting that some rivals either within or outside of Olmec culture intentionally destroyed the monuments.

4   In addition, it seems that the Olmec people were remarkably competent in their economic and agricultural activities. Commerce and exchange with the adjacent highlands was extensive, and trade extended at least south to Costa Rica. The Olmec people exchanged their pottery and rubber for jade and obsidian. ■ However, there is no obvious evidence that the Olmec people traded for food products as no traces of non-native foods have been discovered by archaeologists. What is clear is that they were successful agriculturalists who relied heavily on maize for subsistence. ■ They masterfully converted low-lying marshes into raised beds with a series of drainage canals so that their crop of choice could thrive in the well-drained conditions it requires for growth. ■ Once harvested, the grain was frequently ground and converted into a tortilla, a relatively imperishable form of flatbread that is easily portable. ■

5   ➡ Many elements of Olmec culture persisted in the region after the curious collapse of Olmec civilization, and thus it is reasonable to theorize that the Olmec people established the groundwork for the cultural achievements of the next millennium. The rise of the Mayan culture a few hundred years later in the south and the emergence of the great city of Teotihuacan in the north have both been attributed to a sort of rebirth of Olmec culture, which for whatever reasons lay dormant in the intervening periods other than a series of sparse villages here and there. While it is currently impossible to know the precise relationship between the Olmec people and these subsequent civilizations, their similarities in religion, architecture, and the shared obsession with astronomy and mathematics are too strong to ignore.

1 The word "flourished" in the passage is closest in meaning to

(A) survived

(B) replicated

(C) prospered

(D) dominated

2 In paragraph 1, what does the author imply about the settling of the Olmecs in the San Lorenzo area?

(A) There is no evidence to suggest that the Olmec people arrived by land.

(B) It is probable that the Olmecs colonized the area from the south.

(C) It is unlikely that the Olmecs were able to navigate the waters of the Gulf.

(D) There were already people in the vicinity when the Olmecs first arrived.

Paragraph 1 is marked with an arrow [➡].

3 According to paragraph 2, why is it believed that priests wore jaguar-shaped ritualistic masks during ceremonies?

(A) The priests used the masks to transform themselves into a supernatural being that people feared.

(B) Olmec records and oral histories provide clear evidence that the priests wore the masks.

(C) The masks were found in association with elevated temples and protected ceremonial centers.

(D) Small figurines depicting priests wearing the masks have been discovered at multiple ceremonial sites.

Paragraph 2 is marked with an arrow [➡].

4 All of the following are discussed in paragraph 3 in relation to the gigantic stone sculptures of the Olmec EXCEPT

(A) how the boulders were transported

(B) the upper limits of their size and weight

(C) what kind of implements were used to make them

(D) the monetary expense required to construct them

Paragraph 3 is marked with an arrow [➡].

5 The word "adjacent" in the passage is closest in meaning to

(A) inaccessible

(B) remote

(C) exotic

(D) nearby

6 The word "which" in the passage refers to

(A) the Mayan culture

(B) the great city of Teotihuacan

(C) a sort of rebirth

(D) Olmec culture

7 What is stated in paragraph 5 about the relationship between the Olmec civilization and others?

(A) It was violent at times, but they coexisted for the majority of the time.

(B) It cannot presently be confirmed, but they had some notable things in common.

(C) Its greatest moment occurred with the mutual collaboration to build a great regional city.

(D) Its similarities are hidden by the fact that they were culturally very different.

Paragraph 5 is marked with an arrow [➡].

8 What is the function of paragraph 5 in the passage as a whole?

(A) It concisely summarizes the main points that were introduced in the rest of the passage.

(B) It introduces a new topic that is fundamentally unrelated to the previous points and overall discussion.

(C) It discusses the ultimate ramifications of the things that were discussed earlier in the passage.

(D) It provides information that contrasts with that provided in the previous paragraphs.

9 Look at the four squares [■] that indicate where the following sentence could be added to the passage.

Experts know this because neither of these geological products were naturally occurring in the area.

Where would the sentence best fit?

Click on a square [■] to add the sentence to the passage.

10 Directions: An introductory sentence for a brief summary of the passage is provided below. Complete the summary by selecting the THREE answer choices that express the most important ideas in the passage. Some sentences do not belong in the summary because they express ideas that are not presented in the passage or are minor ideas in the passage. **This question is worth 2 points.**

Drag your answer choices to the spaces where they belong.
To remove an answer choice, click on it. To review the passage, click on **View Text**.

The first noteworthy civilization in the Americas was the Olmec culture, and it had an enduring impact even after its decline.

-
-
-

Answer Choices

(A) A prominent feature of Olmec life was agriculture, which relied on maize and required altering the land for optimum growth of the crop.

(B) Another important aspect of Olmec life was the tremendous amount of labor that was needed to create huge monumental statues.

(C) The Olmec people were experts in building and particularly their carving of rock, which is exemplified by the massive stone sculptures they left behind.

(D) Further evidence of their advanced level of cultural development comes from their economic and agricultural prowess.

(E) Although the civilization of the Olmec people was advanced for its time, its decline started only a few centuries after its founding.

(F) Apparently, the spread of Olmec culture was accomplished via their religion, and the discovery of relevant artifacts across a wide area attests to this.

2 Lightning

1   The atmosphere is filled with electric charges. During times when the sky is calm and clear, a neutral charge prevails because protons and electrons are dispersed somewhat evenly, but during a thunderstorm, positive and negative charges become segregated and concentrated. Sometimes the electric charges in the clouds move very rapidly, causing a tremendous release of energy. This violent energy expulsion is what we call lightning. Much of the scientific research about lightning focuses on the mechanisms behind its formation and methods for improving safety during thunderstorms.

2   ➡ A crucial mechanism for lightning formation is charge separation. It is characterized by the accumulation of negative charges (electrons) at the base of the cloud and positive charges (protons) at the top of the cloud. ■ This is made possible by updraft and temperature differences. ■ Updrafts are caused by rising air, which is why most thunderstorms occur during warm weather. ■ Rising air carries water droplets that cool as they increase in altitude, solidifying as they reach freezing point. ■ These cooled water droplets turn into ice crystals near the top of the cloud. As more water droplets and ice crystals ascend, they begin to collide, forming larger ice pellets. Once they are heavy enough, they fall, gathering more water and ice around them as they descend. As a result of these collisions, the lighter particles lose negative ions and become positive. In turn, the larger particles gain negative ions. This process results in an area of strong negative charge at the bottom of the cloud.

3   ➡ When charge separation is strong, it creates electron instability, but in order for lightning to strike, electrons must be released in massive quantities. Because like charges repel and opposite charges attract, the most plausible way for this to occur is for the concentrated area of electrons to be in opposition to a positively charged area. When a thundercloud hovers over the earth, for example, the electrons in the cloud "push" the electrons on land below the surface, leaving the land with a positive charge. Lightning is initiated when electrons leave the cloud in a "stepped leader." The stepped leader, sometimes no more than a few centimeters in diameter, is the pathway through which the electrons move at nearly half the speed of light, and is so named because lightning moves through the sky in distinct steps, which give it its jagged appearance.

4   ➡ The lightning that we see is actually a series of strokes that appears like a single flickering bolt. Electrons create a channel of air and continue to transfer between the cloud and the destination until the surplus of electrons at the source of the channel is exhausted. The area of positive charge is not always in the direction of the earth, so lightning can discharge in any direction. It can move within the cloud and from cloud to cloud. It can also extend vertically high above the cloud toward the ionosphere, a layer of charged particles in the atmosphere starting approximately fifty kilometers above sea level. Presumably, the thin air at that altitude allows fewer molecules to be heated, and

electric energy transmission creates luminous columns of red light. These "Red Sprites," which occur at altitudes between fifty and ninety kilometers, have been observed from aircraft.

5 ➡ Lightning is hardly a rare phenomenon in thunderstorms, as a large storm can produce as many as one hundred strikes per second. Viewed from afar, lightning storms seem splendid, but cloud-to-ground lightning can have particularly devastating consequences. Attraction points can be quite distant from the source of the electric energy, and lightning strikes of over one hundred kilometers in length are possible. This means that even objects located directly beneath a storm are not completely safe. Generally, the higher that an object projects above ground, the greater the chance it has of being struck. In areas prone to thunderstorms, lightning rods made of aluminum or copper are often erected to help prevent lightning from endangering people and structures. They are placed at the highest point, such as on a building's rooftop, where they attract the energy of lightning and conduct it safely to the ground.

6 ➡ Scientists are still learning about how lightning forms and how it can be diverted from hazardous paths. Lightning rods, though effective, are not perfect. Sometimes lightning strikes objects other than the rod, so new techniques are needed. As a result, promising research is now being conducted with ultraviolet lasers that, at least in the laboratory, create a planned channel for electron discharge.

11 The word "dispersed" in the passage is closest in meaning to

(A) united

(B) dismantled

(C) detached

(D) scattered

12 According to paragraph 2, which of the following occurs during charge separation?

(A) Temperatures rise within the cloud.

(B) Ice pellets become positively charged.

(C) Positive charges accumulate in thin layers.

(D) Electrons congregate at the base of the cloud.

Paragraph 2 is marked with an arrow [➡].

13 The word "ascend" in the passage is closest in meaning to

(A) stack

(B) retreat

(C) coalesce

(D) rise

14 According to paragraph 3, all of the following are true during a lightning strike EXCEPT:

(A) Electrons and protons are positioned in opposite locations.

(B) Electrons are attracted to the earth by negative charges.

(C) Electrons are depressed below the surface of the land.

(D) Electrons are discharged from the cloud in large numbers.

Paragraph 3 is marked with an arrow [➡].

15 Which of the sentences below best expresses the essential information in the highlighted sentence in the passage? *Incorrect* choices change the meaning in important ways or leave out essential information.

(A) The stepped leader, a narrow pathway through which electrons travel rapidly, is named for the way lightning moves through the sky in distinct steps.

(B) The stepped leader is the pathway through which electrons move at nearly half the speed of light, and its diameter is sometimes no more than a few centimeters.

(C) The stepped leader, named for the way lightning moves through the sky in distinct steps, is a pathway that is responsible for lightning's jagged appearance.

(D) The stepped leader is the jagged pathway through which electrons pass, and they are able to achieve rapid speeds due to its narrow diameter.

16 What can be inferred about "Red Sprites" from paragraph 4?

(A) They result from the abundance of molecules at high altitudes.

(B) They are unlikely to occur at or near the earth's surface.

(C) They have endangered passing aircraft in the past.

(D) They are visible from a distance of up to ninety kilometers.

Paragraph 4 is marked with an arrow [➡].

17 Why does the author discuss "Attraction points" in paragraph 5?

   (A) To give examples of the longest lightning strikes ever recorded
   (B) To show that the lightning can still be dangerous far from its source
   (C) To demonstrate that objects directly beneath storms are most at risk
   (D) To describe the frequency of lightning strikes in large thunderstorms

   Paragraph 5 is marked with an arrow [➡].

18 According to paragraphs 5 and 6, the dangers associated with lightning storms

   (A) have been eliminated by technological innovations
   (B) are greatest in the immediate vicinity of a lightning rod
   (C) have not been reduced despite the efforts of scientists
   (D) are necessitating new laboratory research involving lasers

   Paragraphs 5 and 6 are marked with arrows [➡].

19 Look at the four squares [■] that indicate where the following sentence could be added to the passage.

   It is also the reason that the majority of lightning strikes happen in summer.

   Where would the sentence best fit?

   Click on a square [■] to add the sentence to the passage.

20 **Directions**: An introductory sentence for a brief summary of the passage is provided below. Complete the summary by selecting the THREE answer choices that express the most important ideas in the passage. Some sentences do not belong in the summary because they express ideas that are not presented in the passage or are minor ideas in the passage. **This question is worth 2 points.**

Drag your answer choices to the spaces where they belong.
To remove an answer choice, click on it. To review the passage, click on **View Text**.

Lightning formation and its dangers are of interest to researchers.

-
-
-

Answer Choices

(A) Conditions conducive to lightning formation result from the separation of charged particles in clouds.

(B) Once charges are separated, electric charges pass quickly through channels, and this can occur in any direction.

(C) Lightning is dangerous, particularly for elevated objects, but because it is rare during storms, the threat is diminished.

(D) People have tried to control lightning because it can have severe repercussions when it descends from the sky.

(E) Because lightning is the leading cause of storm-related deaths, researchers have attempted to come up with innovative safety solutions.

(F) In order for lightning to form, there must be a strong updraft and significant temperature differences within a cloud.

정답·해석·정답단서 p.332

Actual Test 2

* 실전모의고사 프로그램을 통해, 실제 시험과 동일한 환경에서도 Actual Test를 풀어볼 수 있습니다.

1 Discovery of Pluto

Astronomy

1 ➡ Five of the planets in the solar system—Mercury, Venus, Mars, Jupiter, and Saturn—have been known since ancient times, but two of them, Uranus and Neptune, as well as the former planet, Pluto, are not visible to the naked eye; thus, advanced astronomical equipment had to be developed before these objects could be observed. Sir William Herschel, perhaps the greatest astronomer of the eighteenth century, discovered Uranus in 1781 after initially mistakenly identifying it as a comet, and Neptune was found in 1846 by British, German, and French astronomers after irregularities in Uranus's orbit led them to conclude that an unknown object was exerting gravitational forces on the planet.

2 ➡ The existence of Pluto, however, would not be revealed until the early twentieth century. The first seeming clue regarding Pluto's presence in the outer reaches of the solar system was produced by an analysis of periodic changes in Uranus's orbital patterns, which revealed that Neptune's gravity alone was not sufficient to account for the deviations. ■ Scientists immediately began their search for the object responsible for the discrepancy and tentatively named it Planet X. ■ One of them was Percival Lowell, a well-to-do amateur astronomer who had founded an observatory in Arizona in order to study Mars. ■ In the early 1900s, Lowell turned his attention to the search for Planet X, and after performing a complex series of calculations regarding Uranus's orbit, he identified an area of the sky within which he believed the unknown object could be found. ■

3 Lowell died in 1916 without having succeeded in his quest, but other astronomers at the observatory continued with the substantial task; one of them, twenty-three-year-old Clyde Tombaugh, systematically took successive photographs of various areas of the sky a few days apart and then analyzed them using a machine called a blink comparator, which rapidly alternated between the images in each pair. Essentially, it was a way for him to compare and find differences between two photographs, making it easier to notice and find objects that changed position in the sky. His work paid off in 1930, when he noticed a moving speck of light that matched the predicted location of Planet X. Telescopic analysis over the ensuing months identified the object's orbit and confirmed its presence, and it was subsequently named Pluto after the Greek god of the underworld.

4 ➡ There was only one problem: Pluto was much fainter, and thus was believed to have a much smaller mass than Lowell's calculations had predicted. In fact, the newly discovered object was not nearly large enough to cause the irregularities in Uranus's orbit. Consequently, Pluto, while still an enormously significant and valuable scientific discovery, was not the object Lowell and Tombaugh had been searching for. Convinced that Planet X was still out there waiting to be discovered, Tombaugh continued the

arduous work of photograph comparison, spending thousands of hours over the next fourteen years analyzing many hundreds of images. Ironically, decades later it was learned that the calculations used to predict the existence and location of Pluto had been based on an incorrect estimation of Neptune's mass. After more accurate measurements were made by Voyager 2's flyby mission in 1989, it was concluded that the gravitational pull of Neptune was, in fact, entirely sufficient to explain deviations in Uranus's orbit. This meant that Planet X had been an illusion, and it was mere coincidence that Pluto had been discovered at the same location where Lowell's calculations—based on erroneous assumptions—had anticipated a planet would be found.

5 ➡ Pluto lost its status as a planet because human understanding of the solar system expanded. In the 2000s, astronomers began to observe and catalogue a number of large objects in the Kuiper Belt, a distant, doughnut-shaped region of the solar system that lies beyond Neptune and was first identified in 1992. Many of these bodies have masses that are similar to or greater than that of Pluto. Thus, experts were left with the choice of either acknowledging that the solar system contains dozens or even hundreds of small, undiscovered planets, or refining and restricting the definition of the word. They chose the latter, and in 2006, the International Astronomical Union declared that full-fledged planets are limited to spherical objects that orbit the sun and have cleared the neighborhood of their orbit; in other words, they do not share their orbital region with any objects of comparable size. As the new definition excluded Pluto and other bodies found in the Kuiper Belt, a new terminology—dwarf planet—was created specifically for them.

1 What can be inferred about Sir William Herschel from paragraph 1?

(A) He was unaware of the distinction between comets and planets.

(B) He had access to modern astronomical tools.

(C) He made precise measurements of Uranus's orbit.

(D) He observed Neptune but did not identify it as a planet.

Paragraph 1 is marked with an arrow [➡].

2 The phrase "account for" in the passage is closest in meaning to

   (A) explain
   (B) detail
   (C) identify
   (D) notice

3 According to paragraph 2, which of the following is true of Percival Lowell?

   (A) He built a special observatory in order to locate Planet X.
   (B) He became rich as a result of his successes in astronomy.
   (C) He predicted Planet X's location based on the orbit of Uranus.
   (D) He performed an analysis of Neptune's path around the sun.

   Paragraph 2 is marked with an arrow [➡].

4 The word "substantial" in the passage is closest in meaning to

   (A) pointless
   (B) fruitful
   (C) impossible
   (D) considerable

5 The author mentions a "blink comparator" in order to

   (A) identify a piece of equipment that enabled the discovery of Pluto
   (B) emphasize the laborious nature of astronomical work in the early twentieth century
   (C) illustrate the manner in which astronomical photographs were taken
   (D) demonstrate the advanced state of the technology available to Clyde Tombaugh

6 According to paragraph 4, why was it concluded that Pluto was not Planet X?

   (A) Pluto's mass was insufficient to modify Uranus's orbit.
   (B) Planet X had already been discovered by Percival Lowell.
   (C) Pluto was found at a location different from that predicted for Planet X.
   (D) Planet X was believed to be less bright than Pluto.

   Paragraph 4 is marked with an arrow [➡].

7 Which of the sentences below best expresses the essential information in the highlighted sentence in the passage? *Incorrect* choices change the meaning in important ways or leave out essential information.

(A) Therefore, experts changed the meaning of the word "planet" in order to restrict the number of recognized planets.

(B) As a result, experts had to accept the possibility of many more planets or redefine the concept.

(C) Since the solar system was now thought to contain up to hundreds of planets, experts were forced to redefine the term.

(D) Consequently, experts concluded that small, unknown bodies within the solar system should not be considered planets.

8 According to paragraph 5, which of the following is NOT true of the Kuiper Belt?

(A) It is located in the outer solar system.

(B) It contains a number of dwarf planets.

(C) Its position is between Pluto and Neptune.

(D) Its shape is similar to that of a doughnut.

Paragraph 5 is marked with an arrow [➡].

9 Look at the four squares [■] that indicate where the following sentence could be added to the passage.

Thus, it was inferred that another body must be bringing forces to bear on the planet.

Where would the sentence best fit?

Click on a square [■] to add the sentence to the passage.

10 **Directions**: An introductory sentence for a brief summary of the passage is provided below. Complete the summary by selecting the THREE answer choices that express the most important ideas in the passage. Some sentences do not belong in the summary because they express ideas that are not presented in the passage or are minor ideas in the passage. **This question is worth 2 points.**

Drag your answer choices to the spaces where they belong.
To remove an answer choice, click on it. To review the passage, click on **View Text**.

The search for Planet X began when an analysis of Uranus's orbit suggested the presence of a previously unknown planet.

-
-
-

Answer Choices

(A) A planet, later named Pluto, was identified by a young researcher who compared pairs of successive photographs.

(B) Based on his calculations of Pluto's orbit, Clyde Tombaugh determined that Planet X was merely an illusion.

(C) Pluto's classification was revised after new discoveries regarding the Kuiper Belt were made in the early twenty-first century.

(D) Unfortunately Percival Lowell passed away before the work he began at the observatory was completed.

(E) It was concluded that Pluto was not Planet X because its mass was too small, and it was later learned that Planet X did not even exist.

(F) Early in the twenty-first century, a number of previously unknown dwarf planets were discovered in the far reaches of the solar system.

2 Memphis as the Capital of Ancient Egypt

History

1 ➡ One of the oldest civilizations in the world, Egypt was established more than 5,000 years ago along the banks of the mighty Nile River. The period of Egyptian history from around 5500 BC to 3100 BC is referred to as the predynastic period because at that time ancient Egypt was divided into two regions. The southern portion was called Upper Egypt due to its proximity to the upper reaches of the Nile River, and the northern, downriver area, where the Nile River fans out in a delta and meets the Mediterranean Sea, was referred to as Lower Egypt. These lands were ruled by separate kings until approximately 3100 BC, when the country was united for the first time. Traditionally, this act is credited to a pharaoh of Upper Egypt named Menes, who, upon assimilating Lower Egypt, established his capital at Memphis, a new city he founded on the Nile River.

2 Some Egyptologists question this legendary account, arguing that an ancient decorative carving of a ruler named Narmer bearing the royal symbols of both Upper and Lower Egypt demonstrates that it was actually he who ruled as the first pharaoh of a united Egypt. Other scholars regard Menes and Narmer as the same person. Regardless of the founding monarch's precise identity, it is beyond doubt that during eight consecutive royal dynasties that spanned most of the next thousand years, Memphis was to serve as the political, cultural, religious, and economic capital of Egypt, and based on the huge size of the cemeteries found nearby, some historians believe that it may have been the largest city in the world at the time, with a population as high as 100,000 at its peak. The longevity of Memphis as the leading Egyptian city can be ascribed to a number of important advantages it offered.

3 ➡ Convenience of administration may have been the primary motivation behind establishing the capital at Memphis. In fact, the new capital is believed to have initially served mainly as a headquarters for royal administrators, and it was later during the Third Dynasty of the Old Kingdom that Memphis became home to the royal residences as well. One reason that Memphis was well situated for governance was the ease with which it could communicate with the rest of the kingdom. The Nile River was an important artery for communication in Egypt, with ships constantly traversing its length to carry messages up and down the country. Memphis's location on the Nile facilitated the sending of royal messages to outlying areas in a timely fashion. The notices included everything from orders in regard to unlawful acts and their punishments to changes in laws prompted by complaints and grievances by concerned members of the population.

4 ➡ There is also evidence to suggest that the location was chosen in hopes of better responding to the seasonal droughts and floods in the region. The Nile River had yearly floods because of seasonal rains in the highland region upriver. Egyptians relied heavily on these floods to irrigate their crops. However, too little water led to drought and famine

as crops could not grow, and surplus water resulted in floods that destroyed villages. Situated thirty or so kilometers south of the delta's edge, Memphis was close enough to benefit from the rich alluvial soil and far enough upstream to naturally avoid some of the flooding. Moreover, according to oral history handed down by priests, Menes specifically segregated Memphis from the Nile with a dam and drained the land with a series of canals, which would have offered further refuge and allowed residents to occupy the city with the comfort of knowing they were safe from floods.

5　➡ Finally, Memphis was enriched by its strategic location with respect to international trade, allowing rulers to steadily gain access to materials for practical everyday affairs as well as luxury goods for their pleasure. Archaeologists have discovered large doors and support beams made of cedar, which must have been imported from Lebanon, more than 300 kilometers to the northeast. ■ Gold was acquired from Nubia in central Africa, and wine was brought in from Asia Minor. ■ In addition to its proximity to the Mediterranean and the Nile, which made trade by boat easy, Memphis benefited from the dry river bed in the desert to the east that served as a major overland trade route connecting the city with its trading partners in Phoenicia and Mesopotamia. ■ Moreover, the presence of jade at some archaeological sites shows that Memphis participated in indirect trade with cultures as far away as East Asia. ■

11　According to paragraph 1, which of the following is true of Egypt's predynastic period?

(A) It officially began when Menes established the capital at Memphis.

(B) It was during that time that Egypt's first pharaoh came to power.

(C) It was marked by a continuous rivalry between Upper and Lower Egypt.

(D) It ultimately ended with the unification of Upper and Lower Egypt.

Paragraph 1 is marked with an arrow [➡].

12 Why does the author mention "a ruler named Narmer"?

(A) To challenge the traditional narrative regarding the unification of Egypt

(B) To give an example of a powerful early Egyptian pharaoh

(C) To show that Egyptian rulers often had multiple names

(D) To indicate that Menes did not have exclusive control over Egypt

13 According to paragraph 3, the proximity of Memphis to the Nile River allowed for

(A) rapid transmission of cultural values throughout the kingdom

(B) effective communication between the pharaoh and his ships

(C) easy relocation of administrative headquarters

(D) prompt dissemination of the ruler's instructions

Paragraph 3 is marked with an arrow [➡].

14 The word "outlying" in the passage is closest in meaning to

(A) far from center

(B) similarly remote

(C) centrally located

(D) in between

15 What can be inferred about Menes from paragraph 4?

(A) He made an effort to improve the soil around Memphis.

(B) Issues with seasonal water fluctuations were alleviated by his efforts.

(C) Droughts and floods caused him to leave his native village.

(D) His attempt to drain the land was largely unsuccessful.

Paragraph 4 is marked with an arrow [➡].

16 The word "segregated" in the passage is closest in meaning to

(A) protected

(B) separated

(C) removed

(D) withdrew

17 The word "that" in the passage refers to

(A) the Mediterranean

(B) the Nile

(C) the dry river bed

(D) the desert to the east

18 Which of the following was NOT mentioned in paragraph 5 as an imported good?

(A) a precious metal

(B) an alcoholic beverage

(C) a type of boat

(D) an ornamental rock

Paragraph 5 is marked with an arrow [➡].

19 Look at the four squares [■] that indicate where the following sentence could be added to the passage.

These objects have survived due to the fairly arid climate and this particular wood's natural resistance to decay.

Where would the sentence best fit?

Click on a square [■] to add the sentence to the passage.

20 Directions: An introductory sentence for a brief summary of the passage is provided below. Complete the summary by selecting the THREE answer choices that express the most important ideas in the passage. Some sentences do not belong in the summary because they express ideas that are not presented in the passage or are minor ideas in the passage. **This question is worth 2 points.**

Drag your answer choices to the spaces where they belong.
To remove an answer choice, click on it. To review the passage, click on **View Text**.

Memphis had a number of important advantages as the capital city of ancient Egypt.

- ●
- ●
- ●

Answer Choices

(A) A reason for the chosen location could have been the area's fertile soil as well as the need to manage water levels.

(B) Memphis was an ideal location for the establishment of agriculture and the successful production of crops.

(C) The city had extensive trade networks, which made it possible for leaders to acquire various products from international sources.

(D) Pharaohs built their palaces in the city because it was located in a region with a favorable climate.

(E) Menes established the city between Upper and Lower Egypt to make the capital easily defensible against foreign invasion.

(F) The city was built on the Nile River, making it well suited to sending directives throughout the kingdom.

정답·해석·정답단서 p.335

이로써 교재 학습이 모두 끝났습니다.
Actual Test 1, 2는 실전모의고사 프로그램으로도 제공되니, 실전 환경에서 최종 마무리 연습을 해보시기 바랍니다.

＊ 해커스인강(HackersIngang.com)에서 이용하실 수 있습니다.

MEMO

중급 학습자를 위한 토플 독해서

HACKERS TOEFL
READING Intermediate

개정 5판 3쇄 발행 2025년 1월 6일
개정 5판 1쇄 발행 2023년 6월 30일

지은이	David Cho ︱ 언어학 박사, 前 UCLA 교수
펴낸곳	(주)해커스 어학연구소
펴낸이	해커스 어학연구소 출판팀

주소	서울특별시 서초구 강남대로61길 23 (주)해커스 어학연구소
고객센터	02-537-5000
교재 관련 문의	publishing@hackers.com
동영상강의	HackersIngang.com

ISBN	978-89-6542-610-3 (13740)
Serial Number	05-03-01

외국어인강 1위,
해커스인강(HackersIngang.com)

해커스인강

- 실전 감각을 극대화하는 **iBT 리딩 실전모의고사**
- 토플 시험에 나올 어휘를 정리한 **단어암기 MP3**
- 토플 리딩/리스닝 실력을 한 번에 높이는 **지문녹음 MP3**
- 해커스 토플 스타강사의 **본 교재 인강**

전세계 유학정보의 중심,
고우해커스(goHackers.com)

고우해커스

- **토플 보카 외우기, 토플 스피킹/라이팅 첨삭 게시판** 등 무료 학습 콘텐츠
- 고득점을 위한 **토플 공부전략 강의**
- **국가별 대학 및 전공별 정보, 유학 Q&A 게시판** 등 다양한 유학정보

[외국어인강 1위] 헤럴드 선정 2018 대학생 선호브랜드 대상 '대학생이 선정한 외국어인강' 부문 1위

전세계 유학정보의 중심
고우해커스

goHackers.com

HACKERS

TOEFL
READING
Intermediate

David Cho

정답 · 해석 · 정답단서

해커스 어학연구소

HACKERS

TOEFL
READING
Intermediate

정답 · 해석 · 정답단서

해커스 어학연구소

*각 문제에 대한 정답단서는 지문에 초록색으로 표시되어 있습니다.

1. (B) Vocabulary
2. (B) Sentence Simplification
3. (A) Fact
4. (B) Inference
5. (B) Fact
6. (A) Vocabulary
7. (D) Negative Fact
8. (B) Rhetorical Purpose
9. 4th ■ Insertion
10. (A)-2~3단락, (D)-4단락, (E)-5~6단락 Summary

11. (D) Sentence Simplification
12. (A) Fact
13. (C) Negative Fact
14. (A) Fact
15. (B) Vocabulary
16. (A) Inference
17. (B) Rhetorical Purpose
18. (C) Vocabulary
19. 4th ■ Insertion
20. (D)-2단락, (E)-5~6단락, (F)-3~4단락 Summary

1 Bird Dialects 새의 방언

1 새들은 어릴 때부터 부모와 환경으로부터 소리 정보를 배운다. 새의 발성 중 가장 복잡한 형태는 새 노래로, 주로 번식기에 내는 보통 선율이 있는 일련의 의사소통 소리이다. 개체군에 지리적인 경계가 있는 경우에는 노래에 차이가 나타날 수 있는데, 만약 이 지리적인 경계가 확실하면 한 개체군 내에 공유되는 노래 유형을 방언이라고 한다. 조류학자들은 이 방언이 어떻게 형성되는지, 유전적인 요소들이 어느 정도까지 방언의 다양성에 영향을 주는지에 많은 관심을 가지고 있다. 이러한 관점에서 가장 많이 연구되는 명금 중 하나가 흰관참새, 즉 'Zonotrichia leucophrys'로 몇 가지 아종과 많은 방언을 가지고 있는 종이다.

2 'Zonotrichia leucophrys'는 수컷이 가장 다양한 방언을 보인다. 따라서, 수컷 새를 연구하는 것은 방언의 형성을 이해하는 데 가장 좋은 기회를 제공한다. [3]새의 노래를 해석하기 위해, 과학자들은 노래를 더 작은 단위로 나눈다. 예를 들면 한 악구는 노래 단위 아래에서 큰 범주이고, 휘파람, 박자, 윙윙거리는 소리 같은 특정한 소리 유형이 한 악구의 독립적인 소리 부분, 즉 음절을 나타낸다. 구체적인 부분들이 따로 분석되고 다른 개체마다 비교될 수 있도록 악구는 노래 안의 위치에 따라 정리된다.

3 일부 악구는 다른 악구보다 더 큰 변화성을 보이고, 일단 과학자들이 특정한 범주에서 변화성을 발견하면 그들은 이후의 연구에서 노래의 그 부분에 집중할 수 있다. 다시 말해, 마지막 구에 변화가 가장 많으면 비교를 위해 녹음을 편집하여 그 부분만 골라낼 수 있다. 대부분의 흰관참새 노래는 하나 또는 두 가지 휘파람으로 비슷하게 시작한다. 따라서, 첫 순서가 하위 집단에서 일반적으로 가장 일관적인 구성 요소이다. 또한, 수컷 흰관참새의 편리한 특징은 각 성체가 일반적으로 하나의 노래를 부르기 때문에, 일상적으로 여러 노래를 배우는 노래참새('Melospiza melodia')와 같은 다른 조류 종에 비해 집단 간 분석이 상대적으로 쉬운 과제가 된다. **이 종의 성숙한 수컷 한 마리는 열한 곡의 다른 노래를 부르는 것으로 기록되었다.**

4 집단 사이에 존재하는 변화는 일부 과학자들로 하여금 방언의 고유성에 유전적인 근거가 있을지도 모른다고 고민하게 했다. 어쩌면 일부 개체군의 진화 과정에서의 고립을 통해 (예를 들면, 암컷이 자신과 같은 방언을 가진 수컷을 선호하는 것) 노래의 차이가 다양한 유전자 구성의 표현형을 반영할 정도까지 유전자풀의 분산이 느려진 것일 수도 있다. 비록 유전자설이 더 그럴 듯해 보이지만, 연구실 실험은 특정 방언 집단의 흰관참새 새끼들이 자신들과 같은 아종의 다른 집단의 노래는 물론이고 다른 아종의 방언까지 배울 수 있다는 것을 발견했다. [4]성체의 녹음된 소리를 사용하여, 과학자들은 어린 새가 다수의 방언을 만들어내도록 훈련시킬 수 있었지만, 약 일곱 곡이 최대이다. 게다가, 혈액 표본 DNA에서 얻은 유전자를 비교했을 때 약한 차이를 보였다. 어떤 경우에는, 하나의 방언 집단 내 개체 간의 유전적 차이가 아종과 같은 더 상위

집단 간의 유전적 차이보다 큰 것으로 나타났다.

5 만일 유전적 차이가 문화적 차이에 비해 중요하지 않다면, 영역이 겹치는 참새들은 왜 같은 들판에서 하나의 노래만 부를까? Nuttall 참새라고 알려진 텃새의 아종과 같은 일부 새는 다른 방언 집단과 실제로 마주친다. 이주하는 아종인 Gambell 참새는 Nuttall 참새가 서식하는 캘리포니아 해안 지역에서 겨울을 난다. 흥미롭게도, 10월과 3월 사이 Gambell 참새와의 접촉에도 불구하고 Nuttall 참새 수컷은 일반적으로 그들만의 고유한 노래를 부른다. [5]이것은 두 아종 사이의 만남이 조류의 생애 첫 두 달 동안인 1차 노래 결정화 시기가 아닐 때 일어나기 때문이다.

6 상세한 현장 연구는 종의 일부 예외적인 구성원이 다수의 노래에 통달하긴 하지만 지식 습득은 다른 집단과 두 가지 방법 중 하나로 접촉한다는 조건 하에 이루어진다는 발견으로 이어졌다. [7A/B]하나는 어린 새들이 언어 습득 형성기에 이주하는 아종과 접촉하는 것이고 다른 하나는 방언 경계선에서 사는 것이다. [7C]제철 초기나 말기에 부화하는 Nuttall 참새는 Gambell 참새에게 노출될 가능성이 더 크지만, 3월 후나 10월 전에 부화하는 새끼들은 거의 같은 종의 다른 구성원들과 만 접촉할 것이다. 마찬가지로, 방언 영역 주변 근처에 살고 있는 개체는 정기적으로 인접 집단의 노래를 듣고 다중 언어 능력을 발달시킬 수 있다.

7 이러한 발견을 고려했을 때, 대부분의 과학자들은 지리적인 차이가 유전자 확산을 다소 제한할 수 있지만, 확실한 언어 장 벽을 만들기에는 유전자 고립이 충분히 강하지 못했다는 결론을 내렸다. [8]따라서 새의 방언 다양성은 주로 문화적인 현상 으로 볼 수 있다.

어휘
acoustic[əkúːstik] 소리의 population[pὰpjuléiʃən] 개체군 extent[ikstént] 정도 subspecies[sʌ́bspìːsiːz] 아종, 변종
syllable[síləbl] 음절 order[ɔ́ːrdər] 정리하다 variability[vὲəriəbíləti] 변화성 dispersal[dispə́ːrsəl] 분산
plausible[plɔ́ːzəbl] 그럴듯한 fledgling[fléɡliŋ] 어린 새 unsubstantial[ʌ̀nsəbstǽnʃəl] 약한
insignificant[insiɡnífikənt] 무의미한 overlap[òuvərlǽp] 겹치다 sedentary[sédntèri] 텃새
overwinter[òuvərwíntər] 겨울을 나다 crystallization[krìstəlizéiʃən] 결정화 contingent[kəntíndʒənt] ~라는 조건 하에
margin[máːrdʒin] 끝 brood[bruːd] 새끼 mildly[máildli] 다소 restrict[ristríkt] 제한하다

2 Definition of Art 예술의 정의

1 예술이 정의되는 방식은 역사적으로 변화해 왔고, 넓은 범위의 때때로 모순적인 의미에까지 이르렀다. 고대 사회에서, 이 용어는 엄격히 시각 예술만 가리키는 것이 아닌 넓은 의미로 사용되었다. 오로지 회화, 조각, 인쇄물 형태의 작품에 대해서 만 '예술'이라는 단어를 적용하는 것은 르네상스에 이르러서야 발생했으며 이후 18세기에 이 용어의 사용은 음악과 시를 포함하도록 확장되었다. 그 후 현대에 새로운 의미가 유행하기 시작했고 예술인 것과 예술이 아닌 것 간의 차이를 애매하 게 하였다.

2 고대 사회에서는, 예술과 기술 사이에 명백한 차이가 없었다. 그리스어와 라틴어에서, 'techne'와 'ars'라는 용어는 둘 다 '예술'이라고 번역되었고, 규칙이 있고 전문 기술이 요구되는 모든 활동을 뜻했다. 따라서 그것은 의학과 법학에서부터 대 장장이 일까지 넓은 범위의 분야와 관련하여 사용되었다. 예술 생산에 관여하는 사람들은 기술자로 간주되었으며, 이는 예술가보다는 육체 노동자에 더 가까웠다. 고대인들에게 예술은 규칙에 따라 학습되지만 독특한 영감이 필요하지는 않다 고 여겨지는 기술을 요구하는 일이었다. 회화와 조각은 고등 교육에서 특별한 위치를 갖지는 않았는데, 오로지 음악과 시 만 학문으로 가르쳐졌기 때문이다. [12]시각 예술은 단순히 육체적 기술로 여겨졌고, 고대인들이 육체 노동을 경시했기 때문 에 장인은 사회 계층의 밑바닥을 차지했다.

3 중세 시대는 예술에 대한 이러한 관점을 물려받았지만, 르네상스 시대에 상황이 변하기 시작했다. 이러한 변화의 선두에 는 화가, 조각가, 건축가의 신분 상승이 있었다. 르네상스 예술가들은 점차 과학적인 방법을 사용하기 시작했고, 수학은 그들의 일에 있어서 중요해졌다. 그들의 작품은 단순히 기계적인 것이 아니라 지적이기까지 했기 때문에, 예술가들은 자 신들이 단순한 기술자보다 우월하다고 주장했고, 그들의 존경에 대한 요구는 여론을 좌우하기 시작했다. 예술가들은 서서 히 창조적인 천재로서 인정을 받았고, 그들의 평판은 시인의 평판과 동등할 정도로 좋아졌다. [13A/B]회화, 조각, 건축은 학

교에서 고유한 위치를 부여받았고 예술은 '고전 예술'과 동의어가 되었다. 1700년대에 예술(fine art)의 개념이 생겨나면서 정의가 약간 확장되었다. [13D]집합적으로, 고전 예술은 음악과 시와 함께 예술을 뜻하게 되었다.

4   '장인'이라는 용어가 처음 등장한 것도 르네상스 시대였다. 이 단어는 예술과 기술을 명확히 구분하기 위하여 사용되었다. 예술은 학문적 훈련을 필요로 하였고, 그것의 목표는 미의 확립된 원리를 따른 완벽하고 이상화된 현실 묘사를 창조하는 것이었다. 이것은 대부분 일상 생활 용도로 만들어진 구슬 세공이나 바구니 만들기 같은 기술과 대비된다. **기술의 다른 예는 도예품과 금속세공품을 포함했다.** [14]그렇게 실용적이거나 단지 장식적이기만 한 물건들을 생산하는 기술자는 장인이라고 불렸다. 그들은 종종 스승 기술자로부터 일에 대해 배웠지만, 학교에서 예술을 공부하지는 않았다. 예술과 기술의 명백한 구분은 18세기에 정점에 달했다.

5   19세기에, 근대주의자들은 '예술을 위한 예술'이라는 개념을 장려하려고 했고 전통적인 정의를 거부하였다. 예술가들은 고전주의 전통에 의해 방해 받는다는 것을 느꼈고 양식적인 표현을 지지하는 형식을 무시하기 시작하였다. 동시에, 그들은 일부 동시대 예술가들의 신념을 거부하였는데, [16]그들은 예술이 기본적으로 실용적이고 사회에 유용해야 한다고 주장하였다. 근대주의자들은 도덕적이든 정치적이든 목적은 예술이 가치를 가지기 위한 중요한 기준이라는 것을 부정하였다. 따라서, 그들은 모든 예술이 그 자체의 고유한 가치를 가지고 있다고 믿었다. 또한 예술가들은 새로운 기법과 주제를 가지고 실험하였다. 그들은 학습된 기법보다 실험적인 기법을 강조하며 인상주의적이고 추상적인 디자인을 더 많이 포함하기 시작하였다.

6   [17]예술을 목적 그 자체로 보는 이 새로운 인식은 마침내 예술가와 장인의 구분을 없앴다. 고전주의 전통에 대한 전적인 조롱으로서 예술의 개념은 사람이 창조하는 모든 것을 포함하도록 확장되었다. 따라서, 기술과 소위 예술의 구분을 효과적으로 없앴다. 바구니를 만드는 사람과 고전주의 양식으로 유화를 그리는 사람은 다르지 않았다. 그들은 모두 무엇인가를 창조하기 위해 기술을 사용하고 있었다. 이것은 어떤 창조적인 작품이든지 참되고 훌륭한 것으로 여겨질 수 있다는 것을 의미했다. 더 나아가, 예술은 생산적인 창조의 범위를 넘어섰다. 일부 예술가는 일상 생활의 물건을 무작위로 모아 전혀 손을 대지 않은 채 그것들을 '창조적인 조각'으로 전시하였다.

7   예술의 개념은 현저하게 변화하였고 많은 혼란을 낳았다. 오늘날 이 용어의 의미에 대한 합의는 없으며, 그것은 매우 주관적으로 적용된다. 증거는 원시 유물부터 비디오 작품과 광고 그래픽까지 모든 것을 다루는 박물관과 미술관에서 볼 수 있다. 확실히, 무엇이 예술을 구성하는가에 대한 질문은 크게 주관적이 되었다.

어휘
come into fashion 유행하기 시작하다   obscure[əbskjúər] 애매하게 하다   manual laborer 육체 노동자
pursuit[pərsúːt] 일   employ[implɔ́i] 사용하다   call[kɔːl] 요구   sway[swei] 좌우하다   be on par with ~와 동등하다
synonymous[sinánəməs] 동의어의   merely[míərli] 단지   conviction[kənvíkʃən] 신념
contemporary[kəntémpərèri] 동시대 사람   intrinsic[intrínsik] 고유한   end[end] 목적   fragmentation[fræ̀gməntéiʃən] 구분, 분열
randomly[rǽndəmli] 무작위로, 되는 대로   consensus[kənsénsəs] 합의

CHAPTER 01 Fact & Negative Fact

문제 공략하기 p.35

양서류는 전 세계적으로 아주 중요하다. 이러한 상대적으로 크기가 작은 동물들은 먹이 사슬에서 중요한 구성원이고, 그들의 생존은 전반적인 생태계 건강에 필수적이다. 그들의 왕성한 식욕은 곤충 개체수를 통제하며 그들은 수 많은 커다란 포식자에게 먹이가 된다. 결과적으로, 개구리와 도롱뇽 같은 양서류의 감소는 전 지구적 생물 다양성에 결정적인 위협으로 인식된다. 게다가, 그들의 팔다리를 재생산하는 능력은 세포 기능과 유전학 연구에 큰 흥미를 불러 일으킨다.

HACKERS PRACTICE p.36

01 (C)   02 (B)   03 (C)   04 (B)   05 (B)   06 (B), (C)   07 (D)   08 (B)   09 1. (C) 2. (B)   10 1. (B) 2. (B)
11 1. (B) 2. (A)   12 1. (B), (D) 2. (D)

01 몽골 근처의 러시아 공화국인 투바에는 화성으로 노래 부르는 데 상당한 실력을 보이는 터키족 사람들이 살고 있다. 특유의 음악 재능으로 유명한 투바 가수들은 동시에 하나 이상의 음으로 노래하는 기술을 터득했다. 그들은 목구멍을 수축시키고 후두(목소리 상자)를 통해 공기가 지나갈 때 발성 조직의 특정 부위를 조심스럽게 조절해서 그것을 해낸다. 이 기술은 발성 기관에 대한 강력한 물리적 제어를 포함한다. 예를 들어, 숙련된 전문가들은 성대 안과 성대 주위의 특정 부위를 조작하여 후두 입구의 섬유 조직 사이에 위치한 가성대로 알려진 얇은 막을 진동시킬 수 있다.

02 자연 발생론, 즉 생명이 무생물에서 생겨나는 능력이 있다는 주장은 19세기까지 많은 지식인에게 받아들여졌다. 그리스 철학자 아리스토텔레스는 생명이 무생물체에서 나타날 수 있다고 주장했을 때 그 생각에 대한 일반적인 동의를 조성한 최초의 사람들 중 한 명이다. 그는 그것이 유성생식과 무성생식 말고도 생명이 생겨날 수 있는 가능한 방법이라고 단언했다. 아리스토텔레스의 증거는 식물액을 먹고 사는 부드러운 몸을 가진 곤충인 진디가 명백한 외부적인 원인 없이 식물의 이슬에서 생겨나는 현상을 근거로 했다. 그가 언급한 다른 증거는 둘 다 마치 마법처럼, 부패하는 물질에서 나오는 구더기와 오래된 건초 더미에서 출현하는 쥐였다.

03 자동차 윤활유로 팔리는 석유는 석유의 점도, 즉 흐름에 대한 석유의 저항에 따라 분류된다. 석유의 점도는 정해진 양의 석유가 틈을 지나는 데 얼마나 걸리는지로 측정된다. 자연히 묽은 석유는 진한 석유에 비해 틈 사이를 빨리 지나갈 것이다. 즉, 묽은 석유는 점도가 낮다. 그러나 석유 점도는 석유 온도와 반비례하기 때문에, 모든 점도 등급은 온도 정보를 포함해야 한다. 이러한 이유 때문에, 상업용 석유 등급을 매기는 전문 조직인 미국 자동차 기술자 협회(SAE)는 이중분류법을 사용한다. 예를 들면 10W-40 표시에서 첫 번째 숫자는 석유의 차가울 때(겨울) 점도이고 두 번째 숫자는 뜨거운 엔진에서의 운전 점도이다.

04 정신 분열증은 세계 인구의 1~1.5퍼센트 정도에게 영향을 주는 뇌 질환이며 병에 걸린 개인이 현실을 인식하지 못하는 것으로 특징지어진다. 증상은 가벼운 것에서 매우 심한 것까지 있는데, 어떤 경우에는 정신 분열을 암시하는 모든 범위의 행동을 나타내기도 한다. 사회적인 고립이나 원래 참여했던 활동에서 빠지는 것은 물론 이상한 말도 덜 분명한 증상으로 간주되는 반면에, 환각, 망상, 그리고 왜곡된 감각 인식은 심각한 장애를 암시한다. 일부 정신 분열증 환자들은 환청을 듣고, 다른 환자들은 보이지 않는 사람들에게 학대당하고 있다고 믿는다. 병에 대한 연구가 이루어지고 있지만, 아직도 어떤 사람들이 왜 정신분열증에 걸리는지 확실하지 않다. 가장 유력한 설은 유전적인 경향과 환경적인 스트레스에 일찍 노출되는 것을 원인으로 지목한다.

05 세균성 미생물은 때때로 최적의 성장에 부적절한 조건에 처한다. 만일 기온이 너무 극단적이거나 영양, 산소, 그리고 습도의 정도가 불충분하면, 이 미생물들은 단단한 세포벽을 만들어 '미생물 포낭'이라는 단계에 들어감으로써 적응한다. 단단해지는 과정은 미생물 세포의 신진대사 활동을 방해하여 휴면 상태로 보내고, 성장을 위한 적절한 조건이 회복되면 다시 활성화된다. 휴면기에 미생물은 먹지도 움직이지도 않으며 영양소 섭취 필요량을 줄인다. 그동안, 단단한 외막은 휴면 중인 유기체를 황폐한 환경으로부터 보호한다. 오랜 건조기의 종결과 같이 알맞은 조건이 회복되면 외막의 파괴가 개시된다. 미생물이 휴면 상태로 남아있는 한 그것은 보호되지만, 일단 활동기에 들어서면 바로 취약해진다. 이것은 항생 약품이 병원성 세균이 활동할 때만 효과가 있는 이유를 설명해준다.

06 중력은 질량이 있는 두 물체 간의 당기는 힘이다. 약한 힘이긴 하지만, 우주의 모든 물질에 영향력을 행사한다. 중력의 광범위함이 그것을 우주에서 가장 지배적인 힘이 되게 한다. 두 물체에 대한 중력의 크기는 물체 사이의 거리와 각각의 질량에 의해 좌우된다. 두 물체가 서로 더 멀리 있을수록 더 약한 힘이 물체에 작용한다. 또한, 물체의 질량이 클수록 물체가 발휘하는 중력도 커진다. 질량은 물체 내 물질의 양으로, 물체가 어디에 위치하든 똑같이 유지된다. 그러나 물체의 무게는 물체에 중력이 작용하는 정도를 측정한 것이므로 그 물체는 장소에 따라 무게가 달라질 것이다. 예를 들어, 사람의 무게는 달보다 지구에서 더 큰데, 이는 지구가 달보다 더 질량이 크고 더 큰 중력을 행사하기 때문이다.

07 자연선택과 관련 지어볼 때 적응도의 생물학적 개념은 단순히 자원을 위해 경쟁하는 능력이 아니다. 이는 같은 종의 다른 일원들과 비교하여 유전자 구성 또는 유전자형을 다음 세대에 전달하는 개체의 능력이다. 그러므로, 적응도는 번식의 성공과 밀접하게 연결되어 있다. 확실히, 개체의 생존 능력은 자손을 낳을 가능성에 영향을 끼친다. 빨리 성숙하고 오래 사는 개체가 젊어서 죽는 생물보다 유전 정보를 넘겨 줄 기회가 더 많다. 한편, 불임인 개체는 수명과 상관 없이 상대적으로 적응도 수준이 낮을 것이다. 비교를 위해, 비둘기 세 마리를 생각해보자. 하나는 보라색, 하나는 하얀색, 그리고 하나는 불임이다. 보라색 비둘기의 적응도 등급을 1이라고 지정하자. 흰 비둘기가 보라색 비둘기의 반만큼 자식을 낳으면 0.5의 상대적 적응도 등급을 받을 것이다. 불임 비둘기는 자손을 절대 갖지 못할 것이라고 가정하면 적응도 등급이 0이다.

08 1930년대와 1940년대에, 미국과 유럽 정권은 정치적인 목표를 지지하고 시민들에게 애국심을 주입시키기 위해 다큐멘터리 영화의 사용을 확대하였다. 다큐멘터리 선전으로 알려져 있는 이 영화들은 현실 사건들의 실제 영상을 사용하면서 시청자들에게 원하는 반응을 불러내기 위해 내용을 왜곡했다. 미국 역사상 가장 유명한 예는 총합하여 'Why We Fight'라는 제목의 일곱 편의 영화 시리즈로 미국인 감독 프랭크 카프라가 제작하였다. 미국 정부에게 주문을 받은 카프라는 제2차 세계대전 동안의 군사 활동과 작전을 기록했다. 그의 영화는 군사 집회와 애니메이션 지도, 그리고 가끔 통계와 짧은 메시지를 보여주는 글이 중간중간 배치된, 군사 지도자들의 짧은 연설 영상을 포함했다. 전쟁에 대한 병사들의 지지를 활성화하고 신병을 모집하기 위해 이용된 첫 에피소드는 믿을 수 없을 정도로 성공적이었다. 프랭클린 D. 루스벨트 대통령은 너무나 감동받아서 이를 대중이 볼 수 있도록 하라고 요청했고, 1945년에는 5천만 이상의 미국인들이 이 다큐멘터리를 보았다.

09 연극 공연은 흔히 '블로킹'을 포함하는데, 이것은 무대 위 배우들의 배치와 움직임을 설명하는 데 사용되는 용어다. 이 개념은 원래 19세기 연극에서 감독들이 문자 그대로 모형 무대의 구역을 나눈 것을 가리켰다. 그러나 오늘날, 블로킹이라는 개념은 등장인물이 하는 어떤 활동이나 동작, 특히 이런 행동과 물리적인 무대 장치의 관련성도 포함하게 되었다. 무대 동작은 종종 명확한 지시가 필요한데, 실생활에서 사용되는 자연스러운 움직임이 반영되지 않을 수도 있기 때문이다. 그러므로, 배우와 감독 간에 친밀한 협동과 관객에 대한 일관된 지각이 블로킹의 필수 요소이다. 예를 들어 간단한 블로킹 규칙은 절대로 관중에게 등을 보이지 말라는 것이다. 반면, 블로킹 지침의 엄격한 고수는 지나치게 인위적인 공연을 낳을 수도 있다. 따라서, 블로킹의 기초에 통달한, 경험이 많은 연극 배우에게는 극의 장에서 계획되지 않은 행동을 포함할 수 있는 자유가 주어질 수도 있는데, 심지어 그 행동이 정해진 블로킹 기준에 모순될지라도 그럴 수 있다. 이 자유는 뛰어난 배우들이 무대 공연 연출에 창조적인 참여자가 되도록 해준다.

10 1920년대에는 녹음을 활동사진과 일치시키는 기술이 아직 발달하지 않았기 때문에 영화는 무성이었다. 이야기를 구성하는 생각은 어떤 것이든 배우의 표정이나 동작을 통해 관객에게 전달되었지만, 일부 언어 정보 또한 삽입자막의 형태

로 전달되었다. 삽입자막은 인쇄된 텍스트 카드의 이미지로, 영화의 다양한 지점에서 화면에 나타났다. 그것은 등장인물을 구별하거나 날짜나 위치를 제공하여 전후관계를 성립시키기 위해 가장 흔히 사용되었다. 어떤 경우에는 대사가 글로 보여졌지만, 배우가 연기 중에 말하는 모든 것을 포함하는 오늘날의 자막과 달리, 삽입자막은 중요한 주제, 특히 배역상의 동작만으로는 관객에게 전달하기 어려운 것만 보여주었다. 이는 각 대화의 끝이나 각 배우가 대사를 끝냈을 때 텍스트 카드를 삽입하는 것은 너무 많은 시간이 걸렸고 영화의 속도를 상당히 늦췄을 것이기 때문이었다. 어떤 관객에게는 쓸모 있었지만, 삽입자막은 글을 읽을 수 있는 사람들에게만 도움이 된다는 단점이 있었다. 1930년대에는 유성영화, 또는 발성영화가 영화 제작자들이 더 효과적으로, 더 많은 관중들과 의사소통 하도록 도와주었다.

11 이른 봄에, 개구리는 동면에서 깨어나고 수생 번식지로 나아간다. 수컷이 먼저 도착하고 그들의 존재를 알리기 위해 큰 짝짓기 울음소리를 내면서 암컷을 유혹한다. 성공한 수컷은 암컷과 포접이라고 알려진 짝짓기를 하고, 일단 얕고 흐르지 않는 물 속에 암컷이 알을 낳으면 그 알을 수정시킨다. 수천 개가 될 수 있는 이러한 알들은 약한 배아를 보호하기 위해 물속에서 부푸는 젤리와 같은 물질에 의해 쌓였다. 알과 젤리의 집합적 덩어리를 개구리 알이라고 한다. 배아가 자라면서 올챙이가 되고, 부드러운 알에서 나온다. 그들은 조류를 먹기 시작하기 전까지 처음 며칠 동안은 개구리 알을 먹는다. 올챙이는 물속에서 숨을 쉴 수 있게 하는 아가미가 있고, 수영을 할 수 있게 하는 꼬리가 있다. 몇 주 뒤에, 올챙이는 변태를 겪기 시작한다. 물고기와 같은 아가미는 사라지고, 그 자리에 폐가 자란다. 비슷한 시기에, 다리가 생기고 자라나는 몸에 꼬리가 흡수된다. 그들은 이제 작은 성체를 닮게 되고 물을 떠날 수 있다.

12 아타카마 사막은 칠레의 열대 남아메리키의 서부에 위치한 해안시막이다. 높은 고원에는 강수량이 거의 없고, 두 가지 지리적 현상이 결합하여 아타카마를 지구에서 가장 메마른 곳으로 만든다. 극에서 온 한류가 대륙의 서해안을 지나면서 위의 공기를 차갑게 하기 때문에, 공기가 떠올라 비구름을 형성하는 것을 억제한다. 이 과정이 안개와 습한 공기를 해안 가장자리에 머무르게 하는데, 그들이 서부 칠레 해안산맥을 올라서 넘어가지 못하기 때문이다. 또한 사막의 동쪽 끝에는 비그늘 현상이 일어난다. 높은 안데스 산맥이 동쪽에서 오는 따뜻하고 습한 공기를 막고, 동쪽의 따뜻한 공기가 올라가서 차가워지면 수분이 응결하여 동쪽 사면과 열대 우림에 비로 내린다. 공기가 안데스 산맥의 서쪽 면에 접근할 때쯤에는, 사실상 모든 수분을 떨어뜨린 상태이며 강수를 만들어내지 못한다. 극단적인 지형 때문에, 건조한 환경에서의 삶에 적응한 동물군만 아타카마에 살며, 야생 생물의 다양성이 매우 낮다. 복원력으로 유명한 세균과 같은 유기체조차도 드물다.

HACKERS TEST

*각 문제에 대한 정답단서는 지문에 초록색으로 표시되어 있습니다.

1 Venetian Salt Trade 베니스의 소금 무역   p.44

1. (C)	2. (B)	3. (B)	4. (D)

1 소금은 베니스인들에게 중요한 수익원이었다. 베니스는 적어도 기원후 6세기에는 소금 생산을 시작했고 첫 몇 세기 동안은 자신의 석호 내 제염소를 사용하는 데 만족하는 듯 했다. 그러나 후에 베니스는 이웃으로 눈을 돌렸고 그 지역의 소금 시장에 대한 지배권을 주장하기 시작했다.

2 처음에 베니스는 소금 생산 지방으로 세워졌지만, 후에 생산에 영향을 끼치는 문제들이 부상했다. 인접 지역은 석호가 종종 폭풍에 노출되는 지리적 배치였기 때문에 석호가 자주 거친 물결에 노출되었다. 사나운 물결은 제염소 건축을 힘들게 했고 일시적으로 생산을 멈추게 할 수 있었다. 더 중요한 것은, [1]포 강과 피아베 강을 통해서 석호로 들어오는 지속적인 담수가 석호 지역 일부의 염도를 서서히 감소시켰다. 13세기에 이르러서는 석호의 북쪽과 중앙 쪽에 있는 많은 제염소가 소금 생산을 완전히 멈추어버렸다. 대부분의 베니스 소금 생산은 키오자의 남쪽 항구에 국한되었고, 이 도시의 생산량은 베니스 내륙 고객들의 수요를 충족시키기에는 불충분했다. 이러한 생산력 문제는 베니스에게 경쟁 공급자들로부터 이익을 빼앗기는 것을 방지하기 위하여 소금 거래에 대해 계속적으로 증가하는 지배력을 추구할 동기를 주었다.

3 베니스는 생산 대신 북이탈리아를 가로지르는 아드리아 해의 하구에서 시작되는 배수 유역인 포 강 골짜기 마을의 소금 거래를 통제하는 일에 집중하기 시작했다. 베니스는 남쪽의 경쟁 상대인 라벤나와의 전쟁을 통해 지역에 대한 권리를 마침내 얻었고, 베니스를 먼저 거치지 않고는 라벤나의 소금을 북쪽으로 수송하는 것을 법적으로 금지하였다. 1238년에는, 라벤나가 베니스에만 소금을 수출하는 것에 동의하였다. 따라서, 베니스에서 생산된 소금이나 베니스를 거친 소금만이 북이탈리아에서 거래될 수 있었고, 베니스는 가격을 80퍼센트까지만큼이나 올릴 수 있었다. 거래를 독점하는 것이 생산하는 것보다 더 이득이 된다는 것을 깨닫자, 베니스 정부는 소금 수송에 대한 지배를 아드리아 해 전체로 늘리기로 했고, 이를 훌륭하게 해냈다. [4]거래에서 나온 이익은 군사 작전에 투자되었고 베니스가 지역의 소금 수송에 대해 종종 무자비한 지배력을 행사할 수 있게끔 하는 상호 강화 협정을 탄생시켰다. 14세기 중반에는 베니스의 선박이 아니면 어떤 선박도 아드리아 해에서 소금을 운송할 수 없었다. 절정일 때에, 베니스는 일년에 3만 톤 이상의 소금을 운반했을 거라고 추측된다.

어휘
revenue[révənjùː] 수익 **saltworks**[sɔ́ːltwə̀ːrks] 제염소 **lagoon**[ləgúːn] 석호 **assert**[əsə́ːrt] 주장하다
surface[sə́ːrfis] 부상하다 **immediate**[imíːdiət] 인접한 **expose**[ikspóuz] 노출시키다 **rough**[rʌf] 거친
temporarily[tèmpərérəli] 일시적으로 **halt**[hɔːlt] 멈추게 하다 **constant**[kánstənt] 지속적인 **salinity**[səlínəti] 염도
cease[siːs] 멈추다 **impetus**[ímpətəs] 동기 **drainage basin** 배수 유역 **monopolize**[mənápəlàiz] 독점하다
mutually[mjúːtʃuəli] 상호간에 **reinforce**[rìːinfɔ́ːrs] 강화하다 **ruthless**[rúːθlis] 무자비한 **estimate**[éstəmèit] 추측하다

2 Popular Poetry 대중 시

1. (C) 2. (B) 3. (D) 4. (D) 5. (D) 6. (D) 7. (B) 8. (A)

1 시가 매일 라디오에서 방송되거나 사실상 모든 잡지와 신문에 발행된다고 상상해보자. 이것은 바로 19세기에서 20세기 중반까지 현대 대중 매체의 도래로 일어난 미국의 상황이었다. 대학교, 문예지나 지식인 집단 간의 사적인 대화에 국한되어 있기 보다는, 시는 주류 문화의 일부였다. [1]대중 매체는 포부를 가진 시인들의 배출구와 그들이 이름을 알리고 작품을 대중화시킬 수 있는 무대를 제공하였다. 어떤 경우에는 출판이 상대적으로 알려지지 않은 시인들을 스타의 위치로 올려주었다.

2 에드거 앨런 포의 경우가 그 예인데, 그는 그의 1845년 시 '갈까마귀'를 'New York Evening Mirror'에 제출했다. 그 시는 출판이 허락되었고 전국적으로 수많은 정기 간행물에 증쇄되었다. 포의 작문 경력 중 가장 중요한 사건이자 가장 유명한 작품인 '갈까마귀'는 미국에서 교육받은 사람이라면 누구에게나 친숙한 시이다. [2]서정적으로 이야기하는 것 같은 형식으로 서술된 이 시는 문학과 신화에서 사용되는 활기차고 재미있는 언어를 활용하여 헌신, 상실, 그리고 슬픈 회상에 대한 이야기를 한다. 시의 감성적인 내용은 많은 독자의 감수성을 자극하고, 말하는 갈까마귀의 캐릭터가 종종 음울한 어조 및 소재와 희극적인 균형을 이룬다.

3 그러나 포의 형식은 지식인들을 외면하지 않았고, 시의 구조는 굉장한 정성을 들여, 복잡하게, 그리고 세부 사항까지 주의하여 구성되었다. 포는 더 세련된 취향을 가진 이들의 흥미를 끌기 위해 행간운 기법과 우의적 표현을 결합하였다. [5]시의 여섯 행으로 된 열여덟 연은 문학 학자들도 적절하다고 생각할 길이라고 포는 믿었다. 포의 생각이 옳다는 것이 드러났는데, 1845년에 시가 출판되었을 때 많은 평론가들 사이에서 높은 평가를 받았기 때문이다. 대중적인 독자와 비평적인 독자의 취향을 모두 충족시키는 작품을 만들겠다는 포의 목표는 성공적이었다.

4 '갈까마귀'에 대한 찬사는 포의 시대를 넘었고, 심지어 문학 영역 자체보다도 멀리 나아갔는데, 이것은 한 시인이 어떻게 역사의 흐름을 바꿀 수 있는지를 보여주는 증거이다. [7D]많은 후대 시인들이 포를 모방하였지만, 그의 영향은 영화와 같은 문화의 다른 분야에서도 느껴졌다. 알프레드 히치콕이 연출한 1963년의 할리우드 스릴러 '새'는 갈까마귀들이 황량한 배경 앞에 앉아있는 비슷한 이미지를 그려내 관객들에게 등골이 오싹한 장면을 선사한다. 히치콕은 심지어 공포 영화를 만드는 데 최초의 관심을 가지게 한 것이 포였다고 인정하기도 했다. [7A]포는 그의 작품이 영화 제작에 갖는 가능성을 알아본 제작자와 감독들의 큰 존경을 받았다. [7C]150편을 훨씬 넘는 텔레비전과 영화 작품이 그의 작품을 각색한 것이었다. '갈까

276 토플 인강·단어암기 MP3 HackersIngang.com

마귀'는 또한 미국 문학 역사상 가장 많이 패러디된 작품 중 하나이다.

5   20세기 중반 이후, 하나의 양식으로서 시의 인기는 급감했다. [8C]비록 아직도 시인들이 작품을 제출할 수 있는 전문 정기 간행물들이 몇 가지 있지만, 이런 간행물은 매우 제한적인 판매 부수와 독자층을 갖는다. 미국의 대중 시의 감소는 복합적인 여러 요소에서 비롯되었지만, 가장 중요했던 것은 대중 매체에서 다른 형태의 대중 오락이 시를 대체한 것이다. 대중 음악, 소설, 그리고 텔레비전 프로그램은 모두 1950년 이후 엄청난 인기를 얻었다. [8B]21세기의 미국에서 대중 미술, 음악, 그리고 춤은 아직도 있지만, 시를 위한 전통적인 매체 배출구는 굉장히 적다. 라디오, 방송국, 잡지, 그리고 신문은 거의 1960년대 이후로 시를 외면했다. 긍정적으로 본다면, [8D]인터넷의 존재는 최근에 대중적이고 전통적인 시의 방대한 집합체에 대해 전에 없던 접촉이 생겨나게 했고, 이 기술적인 발달은 미래에 대한 밝은 가능성을 제시한다.

Glossary

연: 일련의 행으로 이루어진 시의 단위

어휘

virtually[vớːrtʃuəli] 사실상 **precisely**[prisáisli] 바로 **advent**[ǽdvent] 도래 **verse**[vəːrs] 시
mainstream[méinstrìːm] 주류 **outlet**[áutlèt] 배출구 **aspiring**[əspáiəriŋ] 포부가 있는 **submit**[səbmít] 제출하다
periodical[pìəriádikəl] 정기 간행물 **lyrical**[lírikəl] 서정적인 **folklore**[fóuklɔ̀ːr] 신화 **devotion**[divóuʃən] 헌신
dreary[dríəri] 음울한 **abandon**[əbǽndən] 외면하다, 버리다 **allegorical**[æ̀ligɔ́(ː)rikəl] 우의적인
urbane[əːrbéin] 세련된 **adequate**[ǽdikwət] 적절한 **testament**[téstəmənt] 증기 **alter**[ɔ́ːltər] 바꾸다
scores[skɔːrs] 많은 **imitate**[ímətèit] 모방하다 **conjure**[kándʒər] 그리다 **perch**[pəːrtʃ] (새가) 앉다 **stark**[staːrk] 황량한
backdrop[bǽkdràp] 배경 **eerie**[íəri] 오싹한 **tremendous**[triméndəs] 엄청난 **unprecedented**[ʌnprésədèntid] 전에 없던

③ Natural Gas 천연가스   p.49

1. (D)	2. (A)	3. (A)	4. (A)	5. (B)	6. (C)	7. (B)	8. (C)

1   천연가스는 화석 연료인데, 이는 천연가스가 일정량만 존재하고 빠르게 다시 채워지지 않는다는 것을 뜻한다. 석유와 같은 다른 광물 연료처럼 천연가스는 유기 물질이 퇴적 작용을 통해 갇히고 수천 년 넘게 열과 압력의 영향을 받으면서 불침투성의 바위 층에 생긴다. 가장 흔한 가스 덩어리 중 일부는 지구의 지각에 있는 이판암과 사암 층에서 생성된다. 사람들이 천연가스를 사용하기 위해서는, 그것을 반드시 지표면으로 가져와야 한다.

2   가스는 보통 시추 작업으로 추출된다. [2]가스 덩어리의 위치와 깊이에 따라 어떤 종류의 시추 과정과 장비가 필요한지 결정된다. 지표면 바로 밑에 위치한 매장물은 시추 장치를 장소 바로 위에 놓아 지상 우물을 만듦으로써 접근할 수 있지만, 해안에서 떨어진 바다 밑의 매장물은 부유 작업대 건설을 필요로 하는데, 이것은 대양의 해류를 감안해서 정박되고 고정되어야 한다. [3D]얕은 천연가스 저장소에 닿기 위해, 기술자들은 케이블 또는 충격식 시추라는 기술을 사용한다. 케이블 시추는 케이블에 부착된 무거운 쇠 비트를 바위를 뚫기 위해 반복해서 떨어뜨려 비트가 떨어질 때마다 점점 더 깊게 바위를 파면서 작동한다. [3C]더 깊은 저장소의 경우, 보통 사용되는 방법은 회전식 시추를 사용하는 것인데, 이것은 날카로운 금속 비트를 돌려서 땅속 깊이 박는다. 거대한 회전식 시추는 지각 안 깊숙이 우물을 팔 수 있고, 수천 피트의 깊이에 닿을 수 있다. 일단 저장소에 닿으면, [3B]가스를 지표면 쪽으로 뽑아내기 위해 강력한 펌프가 사용된다. 저장소가 생산적인 것으로 밝혀지면, 투자자가 다수의 드릴을 현장에 건설하여 추출을 최대화하려고 할 수도 있다.

3   그 후 가스는 현장에서 가공 시설로, 그리고 마침내 의도된 소비자 시장으로 운송된다. 대부분의 경우에, 가스는 최후의 사용 지점까지 엄청난 거리로 운반된다. 첫 단계는 가공하지 않은 가스를 추출 현장에서 기술자들이 가스의 불순물을 제거하는 근처 가공시설로 퍼 올리는 것이다. 비록 통칭은 하나의 가스를 나타내지만, 가공되지 않은 천연가스는 사실 몇 개의 탄화수소로 만들어져 있는데, 원유, 메탄, 프로판, 에탄, 그리고 부탄을 포함한다. 또한 수증기, 헬륨, 질소, 그리고 이산화탄소와 섞인 채로 발견될 수도 있다. 천연가스의 거의 90퍼센트를 이루는 무색무취의 메탄은 사람들의 집과 자동차에 사용되는 천연가스의 주요 성분이다. 따라서, [5]다른 성분들은 일반적으로 제거된다. 각종 성분의 제거는 분리되는 물질의 화

학 구성에 따라 다수의 과정을 수반한다. 메탄을 분리하고 다른 요소를 처리하는 과정은 천연가스를 생산하는 데 드는 비용에 추가된다. 그러나 [5]어떤 부산물은 비용을 상쇄하기 위해 판매될 수도 있다. [6]예를 들어 프로판, 원유, 그리고 부탄은 모두 연료로서 가치가 있다.

4 가스는 가공된 후, 단단한 탄소강으로 만들어진 주 수송관을 따라 운송되고 종종 주, 지방, 아니면 국제 경계선까지도 가로질러야 한다. 광대하고 비싼 유통망은 정제된 가스를 효율적으로 공급하는 데 필수적이다. 가장 흔한 방법은 여러 작은 연결 수송관이 있는 주 수송관을 건설하여 가스를 한 곳에서 다른 곳으로 보내는 것이다. [7]계량소가 수송관 길이를 따라 건설되어, 회사가 가스의 흐름을 꼼꼼하게 감시하고 측정할 수 있도록 한다. 큰 밸브 또한 약 10킬로미터마다 놓여진다. 이 밸브는 수송관을 통해 가스의 흐름을 조절하기 위해 열거나 잠글 수 있다. 정비가 필요한 상황이 생길 때에는, 밸브를 잠가 정비팀이 관 내부로 들어갈 때 안전하게 접근할 수 있도록 한다. 마지막으로 가스는 공급관으로 방향을 바꿔, 지역 공급자들에게 전해져 그 곳에서 난방, 전기, 그리고 자동차 동력원으로 사용된다.

Glossary
비트: 드릴링 부품

어휘
fossil fuel 화석 연료   replenish[ripléniʃ] 다시 채우다   impermeable[impə́ːrmiəbl] 불침투성의
sedimentation[sèdəməntéiʃən] 퇴적 작용   shale[ʃeil] 이판암   sandstone[sǽndstòun] 사암   extract[ikstrǽkt] 추출하다
drilling[dríliŋ] 시추   drilling rig 시추 장치   anchor[ǽŋkər] 정박하다   secure[sikjúər] 고정하다   account for 감안하다
reservoir[rézərvwàːr] 저장소   percussion[pərkʌ́ʃən] 충격   rotary[róutəri] 회전식의   spin[spin] 돌리다
intend[inténd] 의도하다   eventual[ivéntʃuəl] 최후의   operator[ápərèitər] 기술자   impurity[impjúərəti] 불순물
indicate[índikèit] 나타내다   hydrocarbon[hàidrəkáːrbən] 탄화수소   odorless[óudərlis] 무취의
principal[prínsəpəl] 주요한   constituent[kənstítʃuənt] 성분   dispose[dispóuz] 처리하다
by-product[báipràdʌkt] 부산물   offset[ɔ́ːfsèt] 상쇄하다   pipeline[pàipláin] 수송관   provincial[prəvínʃəl] 지방의
meter[míːtər] 계량하다   meticulously[mətíkjuləsli] 꼼꼼하게   deflect[diflékt] 방향을 바꾸다

문제 공략하기
p.57

미국, 중남미, 호주에서는 개울에 사는 개구리 수십 종이 최근 갑작스런 개체수의 감소를 겪거나 완전히 사라졌다. 이 현상을 관찰한 사람들은 여러 가능한 원인을 제안하는데, 기록에 의해 충분히 입증된, 인간 활동으로 야기된 서식지 소실 문제를 포함한다.

HACKERS PRACTICE
p.58

01 (C) 02 (C) 03 (A) 04 (B) 05 (A) 06 (C) 07 (B) 08 (B) 09 1. (D) 2. (B) 10 1. (A) 2. (C)
11 1. (B) 2. (C) 12 1. (A) 2. (D) 13 1. (C) 2. (D) 3. (D) 14 1. (D) 2. (A) 3. (A) 15 1. (A) 2. (D) 3. (A)
16 1. (A) 2. (C) 3. (D)

01 대부분의 교육 전문가들은 아이들이 다른 속도로 배운다는 생각을 받아들이지만, 대체적으로 공통적인 기한과 유인이 전반적인 학생의 성과를 높일 수 있다는 것에는 동의한다.

02 원시인이 만든 도자기의 가장 초기 형태는 똘똘 말은 점토를 바탕 점토에 둘러 세운 다음 땅 화덕이나 구덩이 화로에서 구워서 만들어졌다.

03 유대류는 갓 태어난 새끼가 바깥의 자연 환경 자원에서 살아남을 능력을 갖추기 오래 전에 새끼를 낳는다. 이것에 대한 해결책으로, 성숙한 암컷은 새로 태어난 새끼에게 충분한 거처가 되어주는 주머니를 가진다.

04 인간과의 접촉에서 차단되어 자랐기 때문에 야생 아동은 심리학자들에게 큰 관심거리인데, 왜냐하면 그들이 어떤 행동이 본능적인지와 어떤 것이 환경에서 습득된 것인지에 관련된 초기 인간 발달에 대한 정보를 제공하기 때문이다.

05 성격 검사는 사람들이 세상을 어떻게 지각하고 그들이 어떻게 결정을 내리는지를 밝히기 위해 질문지를 이용한다. 어떤 검사는 성격의 전반적인 개관을 설명하려고 하는 반면, 다른 것은 피험자 심리의 구체적인 특징에 집중한다.

06 사막의 건조함과 극한 온도는 그곳에 거주하는 동식물의 생활 조건을 어렵게 만든다. 사막에 적응하지 못하거나 거기에서 벗어나지 못하는 생물들은 죽는다.

07 다른 구석기 시대의 동굴 벽화에서처럼, 프랑스의 쇼베 동굴은 동굴 벽에 묘사된 말과 순록 같은 흔한 동물의 모습을 포함하지만, 이 유적지는 사자와 하이에나 같은 육식성 동물을 포함한다는 것이 독특하며, 이것은 다른 모든 알려진 빙하기 시대의 벽화에는 거의 없다.

08 초식 동물은 초목이 늘 풍부하기 때문에 보통 먹이를 찾아 다닐 필요가 없다. 초식 동물과 달리, 육식 동물은 사냥감이나 동물의 유해를 획득하기 위해 전략을 사용해야 한다. 그것은 식물만큼 많지 않고, 자주 사냥하고 잡아야 하며, 다른 포식 동물과 공유해야 할 수도 있다.

09   수력 발전소는 터빈과 발전기를 사용하여 흐르는 물의 에너지를 전기로 전환한다. 발전소 건설은 보통 상당한 투자인 수억 달러가 들지만, 이 비용은 발전소의 상대적으로 낮은 운영비용과 풍부하고, 공짜이며, 재생 가능한 에너지원의 사용으로 상쇄된다. 석탄이나 석유가 생산에 필요하지 않기 때문에 터빈은 탄소를 배출하지 않는다. 그러나 단점은 물리적인 환경과 그 속에 있는 생물에게 주는 해로운 효과와 그 지역의 주민을 이주시켜야 할 필요성을 포함한다. 수력 발전소는 넓은 공간을 차지하고, 그것이 건축된 곳의 동물 서식지가 파괴되는 결과를 낳는다.

10   북미 토착민들은 약 11,000년 전에 대륙에 출현하자마자 시각적 작품들을 만들기 시작했다. 여기에는 옷, 구슬세공, 이불과 깔개, 도자기, 바구니, 작은 입상, 가면 그리고 토템 폴이 포함되었다. 박물관과 미술관으로부터 진가를 인정받았음에도 불구하고, 이 물건들은 본래 예술적인 목적보다는 기능적이고 상징적인 목적을 위해 만들어졌다. 예를 들어, 나선형 무늬는 자연과 우주의 모양을 의미하는 반면, 토템 폴은 종종 신성한 신화나 문화적 신념을 나타내기 위해 조각되었다. 이 물건들은 또한 영혼의 세계에 소원을 빌기 위해 수행되었던 제사와 의식에서 요구되었다. 예를 들어, 가면은 단지 예술품이 아니라 부족의 종교 생활에 없어서는 안 될 영적 부분으로 간주되었다.

11   바위, 흙, 또는 퇴적물의 온도가 2년 이상의 기간 동안 0℃ 또는 영하의 상태로 머무른다면, 그 물질은 영구 동토층이라고 부른다. 땅의 온도가 유일하게 영구 동토층 형성에 관련 있는 요소다. 기온, 흙의 습도, 눈 덮임은 중요하지 않다. 영구 동토층은 지구의 순 열평형이 수년 동안 마이너스일 때 생긴다. 이것은 들어오는 태양열이 지표면이 방출하는 열보다 적다는 뜻이다.

12   과학자들은 지구 온도의 점진적인 상승을 인간 활동이 발생시킨 대기 오염의 탓으로 돌린다. 제조, 건축, 전기제품과 생산품의 사용은 화석 연료를 태우고 대기에 오염 물질을 늘리는 활동 중 일부이다. 한 오염 물질인 이산화탄소는 지구 온도 증가에 중요한 역할을 한다. 화석 연료의 연소에서 나오는 이산화탄소는 대기에 쌓이면서, 밀도가 높아지고 태양 열을 가둔다. 이는 공기가 따뜻해지게 한다. 중국은 2006년에 62억 톤이나 발생시키며 21세기 가장 큰 이산화탄소 오염원으로 드러났다.

13   많은 유기체들은 위장을 하여 주변의 자연 환경에 조화되는데, 이는 그들의 생존을 돕는 숨는 방식이다. 상어와 돌고래 같은 포식 동물은 그들이 서식하는 바다 환경의 색과 비슷한 회청색 피부를 가지고 있다. 그들의 착색법은 눈에 띄지 않은 채로 잠재적인 먹이에게 다가갈 수 있도록 해준다. 비슷하게, 도다리처럼 바닥에 사는 물고기는 해저와 유사한 무늬를 가지고 있다. 그들의 몸이 배경 환경과 구분하기 어렵다는 점은 이 물고기들이 포식자의 눈에 띄는 것을 쉽게 피할 수 있도록 도와준다. 어떤 동물은 심지어 색을 바꿀 수도 있다. 예를 들면, 북극 여우는 겨울에는 눈이 쌓인 풍경에 맞는 흰색 가죽이지만, 여름에는 외피가 흙색이 된다.

14   고대 아즈텍인들은 청동이나 철로 된 도구를 소유하지 않았고 손잡이에 부착된 돌이나 구리 날을 주된 절단 도구로 사용했다. 이렇게 복잡한 도구가 없었음에도 불구하고, 아즈텍인들은 융통성 있는 장인이었고 매우 다양한 종류의 신전, 피라미드, 도시 건축물, 그리고 호화로운 궁전을 지을 수 있었다. 대부분의 아즈텍 건물은 종교적인 목적을 가지고 있었고 사람들에 의해 신성한 중심지로 여겨졌다. 피라미드 위에는 신전이 있었는데, 그곳에서는 인신 공양과 다른 종교 의식이 수행되었다. 아즈텍인들은 신에 가까워지려는 직접적인 시도로 이 매우 높은 건축물을 만들었다.

15   아틀란티스 도시는 일반적으로 플라톤이 창조한 신화라고 여겨진다. 플라톤은 자연 재해에 의해 하나의 낮과 밤이라는 기간 동안 바다로 삼켜진 진보된 이상 사회에 관해 서술했다. 그러나 어떤 학자들은 플라톤이 그의 이야기를 실제 사건에 근거했을 수도 있다고 주장한다. 더 많이 논해지는 생각 중 하나는 아틀란티스가 산토리니 섬에 위치했던 도시라는 것이다. 섬의 화산 폭발이 플라톤이 언급한 손상을 가했을 수도 있었을 것이고, 섬 자체가 아틀란티스의 특징 및 묘사와 맞아 떨어진다. 섬에서 발견된 고고학적인 증거 역시 그곳의 거주자들인 미노아 사람들이 복잡한 토목 기술 체계를 개발하였고, 거기에는 다층 빌딩, 수도관 체제, 지진에 강한 벽과 같이 기술적으로 그들의 시간보다 훨씬 앞선 것들이 포함되었다는 것을 보여 준다.

16   과학자들은 뱀의 갈래 진 혀가 후각과 관련된 서골비기관(VNO)과 함께 사용된다는 것을 알고 있다. 혀의 갈래 진 구조

는 포식을 용이하게 해 주는 것으로 믿어지지만, 혀의 정확한 기능은 명확하지 않다. 1994년 가설은 갈래 진 혀가 각 뽀족한 끝을 사용해 화학 정보를 따로따로 수집하여 외측 가장자리를 따라 냄새(의 방향)를 탐지하는 데 사용된다고 시사하였다. 이 이론에 따르면, 하나의 뽀족한 끝은 냄새에 머무르고 다른 뽀족한 끝은 냄새의 흔적을 떠나 감각 정보를 서골비기관으로 보낸다. 이후의 연구에서, 과학자들은 방울뱀의 서골비 신경 중 하나만을 절단하고 포식 면에서 이 동물을 관찰함으로써 이 주장을 실험했다. 그들은 흔적을 쫓는 행동에서 차이점을 발견하지 못 했고 일면적인 절단은 먹이의 위치를 성공적으로 파악하는 데 영향을 주지 않는다고 결론 지었다. 따라서, 갈래 진 구조는 단순히 뱀이 혀를 날름거릴 때 화학 표본을 추출하는 범위를 넓히고 공중의 화학 물질을 휘저어 놓는 역할일 것이다.

HACKERS TEST

* 각 문제에 대한 정답단서는 지문에 초록색으로 표시되어 있습니다.

1 Mapping the Ocean Floor 해저 지도 제작하기 p.66

1. (D)　　2. (B)　　3. (D)　　4. (B)

1 지상 지질학자들과 달리, 해양 지질학자들은 그들의 실험 대상을 직접 연구하는 일이 드물다. 해저 산맥, 골짜기, 그리고 분지는 굉장한 양의 물 아래 있다. 보통 깊이가 너무 깊어서 자연광이 통과하지 못하고, 압력이 막대해서 스쿠버 장치를 가지고 잠수하는 것이 불가능하다. 그러나 다행히도, 다른 기술이 지질학자들의 해저 연구를 가능하게 해준다.

2 잠수함은 과학자들이 정보를 수집하는 데 사용할 수 있는 효과적인 도구이다. 압력의 영향을 받지 않는 절연된 잠수함을 타고 움직이면서, 과학자들은 심해 속을 이동할 수 있고, 전자광의 도움으로 바위와 해저 표면의 특징을 직접 관찰할 수 있다. 유인 해저 탐험의 문제는 많은 시간 투자를 필요로 한다는 것이다. 지금까지 실행되었던 것 중에 가장 깊이 들어간 것은 1961년 스위스가 설계한 '트리에스테호'에서였다. 잠수함이 내려가고 올라가는 데 거의 8시간이 걸렸지만, 전지로 움직였던 선박은 해저에서 30분 밖에 머무르지 못했다. 이론적으로 어떤 원자력 잠수함은 연료를 보급하지 않고도 몇십 년간 잠수할 수 있지만, ³수중에 오랫동안 있는 것은 선원들에게 불편할 수 있다. 따라서, 유인 잠수함은 때때로 로봇 잠수함으로 대체된다. 카메라와 기계 팔이 장착된 로봇 잠수함은 나중의 연구를 위한 흙과 바위 표본을 모으면서 해저 사진을 찍을 수 있다.

3 수중 운송수단과 로봇은 해저 표면의 모습을 살짝 보여주지만, 해저 모양에 대한 철저한 이해를 하기 위해서는 엄청난 양의 지역을 다루어야 한다. 수중 음파 탐지기(Sound Navigation and Ranging의 두문자어)는 깊이를 측정하기 위해 음파를 사용하는 원격 탐지 기술로, 이를 성취하는 한 가지 방법이다. 음파는 물 속에서 빨리 움직이므로 (초당 1,500미터) 표면 위를 움직이는 선박은 금방 소리 신호를 보내고 받을 수 있는데, 이 신호는 해저를 튕기고 돌아온다. 그 후 그 '메아리'의 왕복 시간을 측정하고, 수학적인 계산으로 이동한 거리를 알아낸다. ⁴잠수함을 내보내는 것 보다는 덜 비싸지만, 수중 음파 탐지기로 지도를 제작하는 것은 이미지를 포함하지 않고 거대한 자료를 축적하고 해석해야 한다. 수중 음파 탐지 측량법만을 사용한다면 해저 전체의 정확한 지도를 만들기 위해서는 백 년 이상 일을 해야 할 것이라고 예상된다.

4 그 외에, 컴퓨터와 위성 기술이 과학자들이 해저를 굉장히 자세하게 관찰할 수 있게 해준다. 과학자들은 몇십 년 전만 해도 몇 년간 집중적인 연구를 해야 볼 수 있었을 것을 이제는 즉시 볼 수 있다. 위성 지도는 해저 표면의 명확한 이미지를 보여줄 뿐만 아니라, 퇴적, 지질 구조, 온도의 작용에 따라 해저가 어떻게 바뀌는지에 대한 암시도 해준다.

어휘
terrestrial[təréstriəl] 지상의　geologist[dʒiálədʒist] 지질학자　range[reindʒ] 산맥　basin[béisn] 분지
beneath[biní:θ] 아래의　vast[væst] 굉장한　penetrate[pénitrèit] 통과하다　immense[iméns] 막대한
submarine[sʌ̀bməríːn] 잠수함　maneuver[mənúːvər] 이동하다　aid[eid] 도움　observe[əbzə́ːrv] 관찰하다
investment[invéstmənt] 투자　descent[disént] 내려감　ascent[əsént] 오름　theoretically[θìːərétikəli] 이론적으로
submerge[səbmə́ːrdʒ] 잠수하다　seabed[síːbèd] 해저　roundtrip[ráundtríp] 왕복　calculation[kæ̀lkjuléiʃən] 계산
determine[ditə́ːrmin] 알아내다　accumulate[əkjúːmjulèit] 축적하다　entire[intáiər] 전체의　satellite[sǽtəlàit] 위성
examine[igzǽmin] 관찰하다　extraordinary[ikstrɔ́ːrdənèri] 굉장한　in an instant 즉시　indication[ìndikéiʃən] 암시, 징조

❷ The Auditory System of Fish 물고기의 청각기관

> 1. **(C)**   2. **(C)**   3. **(D)**   4. **(A)**   5. **(B)**   6. **(D)**   7. **(D)**   8. **(A)**

1 얼핏 보기에, 물고기는 별로 발달되지 않은 청각을 가진 것으로 보인다. 외이의 부재와 청각 기관과 바깥 세상을 연결해주는 고막이나 관의 결핍이 물고기가 물 속을 이동하는 소리의 진동을 감지하기에는 부실한 귀를 가지고 있음을 나타내는 것으로 보일 것이다. 그러나 생물학자들은 물고기의 청각 기관이 매우 민감함을 알아냈다.

2 포유류와 같은 다수의 고등 척추동물들은 외이와 중이가 있지만, 물고기들은 없다. 물고기들은 내이만 있다. 물고기 귀는 위쪽과 아래쪽 부분으로 나뉜다. 위쪽, 또는 등 부분은 'pars superior'인데, 세 개의 반고리관으로 다시 나뉜다. 액체와 감각모로 가득 차있는 이 관들은 중력을 감지하고 또한 물고기에게 균형 감각을 준다. pars superior가 없으면, 물고기들이 물 속에서 수직적인 위치를 판단하는 방법은 표면에서 오는 빛을 기준으로 하는 방법으로 제한된다. 그러나 어류학자들은 귀의 윗부분이 소리를 감지하는 데 사소한 역할만 한다고 믿는다. ^{2B}청각 신호를 받을 때 없어서는 안 될 도구는 아랫부분, 'pars inferior'이다. pars inferior에 닿는 음파는 '이석', 또는 '귀돌'이라고 불리는 단단한 수용 기관을 관통하는데, 이것은 이석을 감각모 세포와 연결하는 조직과 나란히 정렬되어 있다. ^{2A/D}음파는 이석을 진동시켜 감각모 세포를 자극하고 청신경의 감각 뉴런을 활성화 한다. 물고기들은 청신경을 통해 전달되는 신호가 뇌에 닿으면 그 신호를 '청각'으로 해석한다.

3 모든 알려진 어류들은 귓속 소리 입자의 움직임을 감지할 수 있지만, 일부는 청각 능력을 높여주는 주변 조직을 발달시켰다. 이러한 조직이 있는 물고기들은 청각 전문가라고 불리고, 이러한 조직이 없는 물고기들은 청각 일반인이라고 불린다. 대부분의 청각 일반인은 소리를 30헤르츠 이하에서부터 1,000헤르츠 정도까지의 저주파 범위에서 감지한다. 전문가는 훨씬 더 넓은 범위의 소리를 감지할 수 있다. 예를 들어, 미국 청어는 180,000헤르츠까지 되는 주파수의 초음파도 감지할 수 있다. 이것은 20,000헤르츠가 대략 평균 성인이 들을 수 있는 자연음의 상한선인 인간의 청각보다 훨씬 민감한 것이다.

4 청각 조직의 유명한 예는 귀 가까이에 부레가 있는 물고기이다. 부레는 물고기의 부력을 조절하기 위해 사용되는 조직으로, 몸이나 주위의 물보다 훨씬 낮은 밀도를 가지고 있다. 미국 청어는 부레를 귀에 바로 연결해주는 기체 관이 있다. 메기와 잉어는 부레가 변형된 척추골에 의해 간접적으로 귀와 연결되어 있다. ⁶밀도 차 때문에 음압파는 부레 안의 기체를 쉽게 압축할 수 있어서, 부레가 주기적으로 팽창하고 수축하게 한다. 그 후 이러한 파동은 귀로 보내질 수 있다. 그래서 부레는 많은 물고기에서 소리 수신에 중요한 역할을 담당하는 것으로 믿어진다. 대서양 대구에 관한 연구는 부레의 존재가 특히 고주파에서 소리에 더 민감하게 만든다는 것을 확실하게 보여 주었다. 부레에서 공기를 빼기 위해 피하 주사를 사용하고, 결과를 표로 만들기 위해 오디오그램을 사용하여, 과학자들은 부레가 비었을 때 음압에 대한 대구의 민감도가 떨어지고 들리는 주파수의 범위가 한정된다는 것을 확인할 수 있었다.

5 이전에 생각했던 것보다 물고기들이 더 민감한 청각 기관을 가지고 있다는 것을 이해하게 되면서, 해양과학자들은 바다에 증가한 소음의 잠재적인 영향을 논의하기 시작했다. 1970년대 이래, 지구의 바다의 소음 수준이 10퍼센트 이상 증가했다. ⁷배, 유람선, 그리고 석유 채굴은 모두 음파를 물 속으로 삽입하고, 최근의 연구는 이러한 소음이 물고기 귀에 손상을 가할 수 있음을 나타냈다. 이러한 발견에 대한 대응으로, 과학자들은 사람들이 해양 환경에서 소리를 낼 때 조심하기를 촉구하기 시작했다.

어휘
at first glance 얼핏 보기에 **absence**[ǽbsəns] 부재 **external**[ikstə́ːrnl] 외부의 **lack**[læk] 결핍
eardrum[íərdrÀm] 고막 **auditory**[ɔ́ːdətɔ̀ːri] 청각의 **indicate**[índikèit] 나타내다 **detect**[ditékt] 감지하다
vibration[vaibréiʃən] 진동 **remarkably**[rimáːrkəbli] 매우 **vertebrate**[və́ːrtəbrət] 척추동물 **dorsal**[dɔ́ːrsəl] 등의
canal[kənǽl] 관 **sensory**[sénsəri] 감각의 **vertical**[və́ːrtikəl] 수직의 **ichthyologist**[ìkθiɑ́lədʒist] 어류학자

serve[sə:rv] 역할을 하다 integral[íntigrəl] 없어서는 안 될 receptive[riséptiv] 수용의 tissue[tíʃuː] 세포
excite[iksáit] 자극하다 interpret[intə́:rprit] 해석하다 peripheral[pərífərəl] 주변적인 enhance[inhǽns] 높이다
ultrasonic[ʌ̀ltrəsánik] 초음파의 approximate[əpráksəmət] 대략의 notable[nóutəbl] 유명한 gas bladder 부레
adjacent[ədʒéisnt] 가까운, 인접한 buoyancy[bɔ́iənsi] 부력 variance[vέəriəns] 차이 compress[kəmprés] 압축하다
rhythmically[ríðmikəli] 주기적으로 expand[ikspǽnd] 팽창하다 contract[kəntrǽkt] 수축하다
pulsation[pʌlséiʃən] 파동 presence[prézns] 존재 hypodermic[hàipədə́:rmik] 피하 deflate[difléit] 공기를 빼다
previously[prí:viəsli] 이전에 barge[bɑ:rdʒ] 유람선 urge[ə:rdʒ] 촉구하다 cautious[kɔ́:ʃəs] 조심하는

◳ Attribution Theory 귀인 이론

1. (A)   2. (A)   3. (D)   4. (D)   5. (D)   6. (A)   7. (C)   8. (B)

1   심리학자들은 사람들이 어떻게 자신의 행동을 설명하고, 그에 대한 핑계를 대고, 정당화하는지에 대한 학설을 만들었다. 그것은 귀인 이론이라고 알려져 있는데, 사람들이 사건의 정황에 따라 자신 또는 다른 사람의 행동을 내적 또는 외적인 원인으로 돌리고 싶어한다고 주장한다. 이러한 관점에 따르면, 인과관계에 대한 지각은 한 사람이 성공과 실패의 정도를 해석하는 방법에 영향을 줄 수 있다.

2   귀인 이론은 오스트리아의 심리학자 프리츠 하이더의 1958년 '대인관계의 심리학'이라는 책에서 처음 수상된 것으로, 모든 인간의 행동이 내부 또는 외부 요소에 의해 동기가 부여된다고 추정한다. 따라서, 인과관계에 대한 인간의 판단은 이러한 내외부 패러다임을 반영하고 개인과 세상 사이에 지각된 이분법의 결과가 생길 것이다. 한 사람이 정황이 그의 재량권 밖에 있다고 느끼면 책임감을 덜 느낄 것이다. 예를 들어, 전형적으로 시간을 잘 지키는 사원이 임의의 교통 정체로 회사에 늦게 나타나면, 인과의 책임을 밖으로 돌리는 경향이 있다. 이렇게 원인을 외부로 돌리는 것을 '상황적 귀인'이라고 한다. 반대로, ²ᶜ만일 한 사람이 자신이 어떤 사건의 결과에 직접적인 영향을 끼쳤다고 느낀다면 그 사람은 책임감을 느낄 가능성이 크다. 시험을 위해 열심히 공부하는 것, 축구 시합을 위해 부지런히 훈련하는 것, 좋은 부모가 되기 위해 최선을 다하는 것은 모두 한 사람의 내적 특성에서 비롯한다고 볼 수 있다. 이런 경우에, ²ᴮ⁄ᴰ사람들은 자신의 노력과 성격을 자신의 행동의 원인으로 설명할 것이다. 심리학자들은 이 설명을 '기질적 귀인'이라고 부른다.

3   예상하지 못한 사건을 외부 세력에 돌리는 것은 쉽지만, 상황적 귀인과 기질적 귀인 사이의 경계는 종종 확실하지 않을 때가 있다. 한 사람이 열띤 언쟁에 참여하고 있는 것이 보이는 상황을 상상해보자. 그 사람, 또는 행위자가 큰 소리로 말을 하고 있거나 공격적인 자세를 취하고 있다면, ⁴보통 관찰자는 행위자가 쉽게 화를 낸다거나, 천성적으로 비이성적이거나 나쁜 심성을 가지고 있다고까지 생각할 수 있다. 보통 이런 귀인은 다툼이 일어난 전체적인 틀에 대한 고려 없이 즉시 일어난다. 관찰자는 관찰된 행동이 행위자의 성격에서 나온 단독적인 결과라고 추측한다. 이렇게 행동에 대한 상황적 원인과 반대로 기질적 원인을 강조하는 관찰자들의 경향은 '대응 편향'으로 알려져 있다. 이제 1인칭 시점에서 같은 시나리오를 상상해보자. 행위자는 어떤 엄청난 불평등의 피해자가 된 것처럼 느낄 것이며 자신의 태도는 자기방어를 하려는 정당한 반응이라고 느낄 것이다. 사람들이 자신의 태도와 다른 사람의 태도를 해석하는 데 있어서의 모순을 '행위자-관찰자 편향'이라고 부른다.

4   '자기 고양적 편향'이라고 불리는 비슷한 경향은 사람들이 자신의 긍정적, 부정적 경험에 대해 가지는 다른 반응에서 볼 수 있다. 개인이 긍정적인 경험을 할 때, 예를 들면, 승진을 하거나, 책을 출판하거나, 목표를 이루었을 때, 사람들은 자신을 행위자로 보고 성공을 자신의 노력과 연관시키는 경향이 있다. 반대로, ⁶사람들이 부정적인 경험을 할 때는 편향이 전도되고, 성공적이지 못한 결과를 정황적 요소의 탓으로 돌리고 싶어한다. 사람들은 실패를 성격의 결함, 능력의 부족, 또는 불충분한 노력 탓으로 돌리기 보다는 자신의 재량권 밖에 있는 요소를 확대한다. 정신적으로 책임을 밖으로 돌림으로써, 사람들은 자신들의 불행에 대해 정황 또는 다른 사람을 원망할 수 있고 자신들을 정황의 희생자로 볼 수 있다.

5   비록 심리학자들이 여전히 귀인을 단편적으로 이해하고 있기는 하지만, 그들은 귀인이 사람들에게 낙천적인 생각이 스며들게 함으로써 기분이 좋아지도록 도와준다고 믿는다. ⁸행동에 대한 내부적, 그리고 외부적 원인을 제공하는 것은 우리가 우리의 긍정적인 면을 강조할 수 있도록 해주고, 이는 자부심을 돋우고 호의적인 감정이 생겨나게 하면서 우리의 부정적

인 특성을 정당화하여 낙심과 같은 느낌을 피하게 해준다.

어휘

excuse[ikskjú:s] 핑계 justify[dʒʌ́stəfài] 정당화하다 attribution[æ̀trəbjú:ʃən] 귀인 postulate[pɑ́stʃulèit] 주장하다
presume[prizú:m] 추정하다 judgment[dʒʌ́dʒmənt] 판단 causality[kɔːzǽləti] 인과관계 reflect[riflékt] 반영하다
perceive[pərsíːv] 지각하다 diminished[dimíniʃt] 감소된 punctual[pʌ́ŋktʃuəl] 시간을 잘 지키는
tendency[téndənsi] 경향 diligently[dílidʒəntli] 부지런히 stem[stem] 비롯하다 engage[ingéidʒ] 참여하다
aggressive[əgrésiv] 공격적인 posture[pɑ́stʃər] 자세 prone[proun] ~하기 쉬운 irrational[irǽʃənl] 비이성적인
mean-spirited[míːnspíritid] 나쁜 심성을 지닌 instantaneously[ìnstəntéiniəsli] 즉시에 emphasize[émfəsàiz] 강조하다
perspective[pərspéktiv] 시점 victim[víktim] 피해자 injustice[indʒʌ́stis] 불평등 self-defense[sèlfdiféns] 자기방어
discrepancy[diskrépənsi] 모순 promotion[prəmóuʃən] 승진 agent[éidʒənt] 행위자
incline[inkláin] ~하는 경향이 있다 associate[əsóuʃièit] 연관시키다 invert[invə́ːrt] 전도하다 ascribe[əskrɔ́ib] 탓하다
insufficient[ìnsəfíʃənt] 불충분한 magnify[mǽgnəfài] 확대하다 blame[bleim] 원망하다 instill[instíl] 스며들다
boost[buːst] 돋우다 favorable[féivərəbl] 호의적인 avoid[əvɔ́id] 피하다 discouragement[diskɔ́ːridʒmənt] 낙심

문제 공략하기 p.79

양서류 알은 부드러운 껍질을 갖고 있지만 단단한 외피가 없기 때문에, 자외선에 취약하여 이르게 부화하거나 약한 면역 체계를 가진 새끼가 나오는 경향이 있다. 게다가, 개구리는 변온동물로서 체온을 조절하기 위해 햇빛을 사용해야 하기 때문에 얇아지는 오존층의 영향을 받는다.

HACKERS PRACTICE p.80

01 (C) 02 (A) 03 (A) 04 (A) 05 (B) 06 (C) 07 (B) 08 (D) 09 (B) 10 (D) 11 1. (C) 2. (D)
12 1. (B) 2. (B) 13 1. (D) 2. (D) 14 1. (B) 2. (A)

01 기원전 7세기까지 그리스인들은 이집트인들로부터 돌 조각 기술을 배웠고 대리석으로 쿠로이라고 알려진 조각상을 만들고 있었다. 이 실물 크기의 조각상은 옆구리에 주먹을 쥐고 왼발을 앞으로 내민 나체의 젊은 남성들을 묘사하였다.

02 송어는 연어과에 속하는 유명한 먹거리이자 낚싯고기이다. 비록 대부분이 전적으로 민물과 시냇물에서 사는 것으로 알려져 있지만, 바다송어로 알려진 몇 가지 종은 약 한 살이 되었을 때 바다에 가서 약 2~5년 후에 원래의 민물 서식지에서 산란하기 위하여 상류로 돌아온다.

03 원석 같은 희귀 광물은 아름다움과 한정된 공급량 때문에 굉장한 상업적 가치를 지닌다. 원석에 대한 수요가 높지만 이용가능성이 제한되어 있기 때문에 탐사 기업은 경쟁자 이전에 새로운 매장물을 발견하기 위해 부지런히 일해야 한다. 그들 중 가장 성공적인 기업은 탐사를 원조하기 위해 광범위한 일련의 정밀 기술을 이용한다.

04 토네이도는 다른 어떤 나라보다도 미국에서 가장 자주 발생하는 격렬하고 파괴적인 폭풍이다. 텍사스에서 노스다코타에 걸친 땅인 Tornado Alley에서 가장 많이 일어나는 토네이도는 자동차를 공중으로 내던지고 건물을 무너뜨릴 만큼 강력하다. 그것들은 지름이 평균 약 60미터이지만 폭 1.6킬로미터까지 확장할 수 있다.

05 박쥐 기생충은 주로 박쥐의 피를 먹고 사는 생물이지만, 보통의 숙주를 이용할 수 없으면 인간, 새, 설치류도 문다. 가장 창궐 가능성이 높은 장소는 박쥐의 보금자리이다. 일부는 다락방, 사용하지 않는 굴뚝, 벽의 텅 빈 공간에 위치해 있다. 만약 이러한 장소가 파괴되면 기생충은 다른 먹이 공급처를 찾을 것이다.

06 처음으로 전기를 이용한 의사소통 형태는 전보였는데, 이것은 1828년에 Harrison Dyar가 발명한 간단한 기계로, 전기 스파크를 전선을 통해 보내 화학 처리된 종이 위에 일련의 점과 선을 태워 나타냈다. 이러한 점과 선은 메시지로 해석될 수 있는 기본적인 부호였다. 이후, 1837년에 Samuel F. B. Morse가 흔한 전기보다는 전자기를 이용한 새로운 전보를 발명하고 특허를 얻었다.

07 자유시장경제는 사람들이 정부의 간섭 없이 물건이나 서비스를 교환하는 곳에서 항상 실존해 왔는데, 18세기에 처음으로 자유시장 이데올로기가 정치 이론의 일부가 되었다. '~하는 것을 허락하다'라는 의미의 프랑스어 슬로건 'laissez-faire'에 충실히 기반한 자유시장 이데올로기는 정부가 시장을 통제하려 하지 않고 구매자와 판매자가 자유롭게 가격을 결정하도록 허락해야 한다는 믿음에 중점을 두고 있다.

08 지구에서 가장 총명한 동물 중 하나로 여겨지는 돌고래는 그들의 지적 능력의 본질을 알아내기 위해 연구된다. 연구원들은 이 바다 포유동물에 흥미를 갖는데 왜냐하면 돌고래는 명확한 목적이 없는 것으로 보이는 행동, 예를 들어 수면 위로 곡예 회전을 하면서 뛰어오르는 행동을 하기 때문이다. 과학자들은 이 행동이 기능적인 것인지 아니면 오락적인 재미로 하는 것인지 모른다. 또 다른 별난 행동은 다른 생물에게 사회적으로 행동하려는 돌고래의 성향이다. 그들은 종종 바다나 수영장에서 헤엄치는 사람들과 장난치듯이 상호작용한다.

09 유아는 엄마의 목소리와 다른 사람의 목소리를 영리하게 구별한다. 이는 발달심리학자 DeCasper와 Fifer가 실시한 1980년 연구에서 밝혀졌는데, 그들은 친숙하거나 친숙하지 않은 목소리에 대한 유아의 반응이 사실상 태어나기도 전에 학습된다는 사실을 관찰하였다. 캐나다의 간호학 교수인 Barbara Kisilevsky 박사는 태아가 시를 읽어주는 친엄마의 음성 녹음 테이프와 같은 시를 읽어주는 낯선 여자의 또 다른 음성 녹음 테이프에 어떻게 반응하는지 실험한 후 2003년에 이 결론에 도달했다. 태아의 심장 박동은 엄마의 목소리를 들었을 때 빠르게 가속하였고, 이는 그 둘을 구분하는 능력을 암시한다.

10 북극 툰드라는 북극을 둘러싸고 북쪽 상부 위도의 침엽수림으로 뻗어가는 반면에, 고산 툰드라는 전세계의 높은 고도 지역에서 발견될 수 있다. 둘 다 황폐한 환경으로 특징지어지는데, 북극 툰드라는 춥고 사막 같으며 고산 툰드라는 건조하고 바람이 분다. 놀랍게도, 다양한 동물이 두 종류의 툰드라에서 살아갈 수 있으며, 그렇게 하기 위해서 지방층을 더 발달시킨다. 수백 종의 식물 또한 툰드라에서 잘 자라지만 모두 높이가 몇 피트 밖에 안 된다.

11 당 왕조는 극동 지역, 특히 일본, 한국, 베트남에 중국 문화를 퍼뜨리는 데 영향이 컸다. 제국의 부와 힘에 고취된 이웃 국가들은 문화 요소를 그들 자신의 이익에 따라 사용하길 바라는 마음에서 연구하고 차용하기 시작했다. 예를 들어, 중국 문자와 글은 세 나라에서 모두 최상류층 사람들이 사용하는 정부의 언어가 되었다. 종교적인 면에서는, 인도의 원본에 기반을 두고 도교를 포함한 중국 고유 철학과 섞인 불교 신앙과 관습 또한 수입되었다. 게다가, 공자의 이론과 가치가 이 지역에서 지배적인 사회정치적 세력이 되었다.

12 최초의 그림은 벽화였다. 벽화는 떼어낼 수 없었지만 이후에 패널에 그림을 그리는 기법이 발달하였다. 패널화는 하나의 목판이나 얇고 가느다란 나무조각들을 함께 붙인 것 위에 그려졌다. 이러한 작품들은 들고 다닐 수 있었고 따라서 쉽게 옮겨질 수 있었다. 14세기에 화가들은 캔버스를 사용하기 시작했다. 천으로 만든 캔버스는 가벼워서 작업하고 운반하기 쉬웠다. 캔버스의 표면은 나무보다 물감을 훨씬 잘 흡수하였고 잘 휘거나 금이 가지 않았다. 그러나 짜여진 천은 르네상스 화가들이 싫어하는 방식으로 그림의 질감에 영향을 끼쳤다. 그래서 그들은 그림의 표면을 매끄럽게 하는 데에 모든 노력을 다해서 그림이 마치 사진의 표면처럼 윤이 났다.

13 수목한계선은 산에서 나무가 자랄 수 없는 선 혹은 고도이다. 멀리서 이러한 수목한계선은 쉽게 구분되는 것으로 보일지도 모르지만, 가까이서 보면 관찰자들은 변화가 사실상 점진적이라는 것을 명확히 알아볼 수 있다. 선에 가까운 나무들은 작거나 왜소하기까지 하며 선에 가장 가까운 나무들은 관목 덤불처럼 보인다. 온도, 일조량, 풍향, 기압, 수분 결핍 같은 환경 조건은 상하위 수목한계선의 위치를 결정한다. 그러나 어떤 산은 똑같은 조건에 동일하게 영향 받지 않는다. 산의 한쪽은 햇빛에 더 많이 노출되어 더 높은 수목한계선을 가지며, 그늘진 곳의 수목한계선은 더 낮을 것이다.

14 1808년에 미국 재무부 장관 앨버트 갤러틴은 국가를 가로지르는 도로와 다른 교통 체제 건설을 위한 자금을 정부가 제공해야 한다고 제안했지만, 그 제안은 의회에서 충분한 표를 얻지 못했다. 1812년 영국과의 전쟁 때에야 당국자들은 국가에 도로가 절실히 필요하다는 것을 깨달았다. 서부에 배치되어 있던 군대가 최전선에 필요했지만, 충분한 교통 망의 부족 때문에 군사 지도자들은 그들을 이동시키는 것이 매우 느릴 것이라는 걸 깨달았다. 해결책은 유료 고속도로라고 불리는 개인적으로 건설된 도로 부지의 형태로 나타났는데, 이것은 그것들의 사용에 대한 요금을 부과함으로써 큰 이익을 얻길 바라는 민영 회사들에 의해 유지되었다. 보통 역마차 길을 따라 건설된 이러한 초기의 유료 도로는 현대 고속도로와 주간 고속도로의 전형이었으며, 결국 대부분 20세기에 주립 고속도로 부서에 이양되었다.

HACKERS TEST

* 각 문제에 대한 정답단서는 지문에 초록색으로 표시되어 있습니다.

1 Avian Navigation 조류의 비행　　　　　　　　　　　　　　　　　　　　　　　p.88

1. (A)　2. (C)　3. (C)　4. (D)

1 　어떤 새들은 텃새들로 겨울 서식지에서 살아남는 것에 적응했거나 적도 근처와 같이 온도가 상대적으로 고정되어 있는 곳에 서식한다. 그럼에도 불구하고 계절적으로 황폐한 환경에 사는 많은 조류 종은 철새들이다. 겨울은 보통 새들이 음식, 피난처, 물과 같은 필수적인 요소들을 접하기에 가장 어려운 시기이므로, 많은 새들은 가을에 낮이 점점 짧아지고 기온이 떨어짐에 따라 더 적절한 서식지로 이동하여 그런 조건으로부터 벗어난다. 흥미롭게도, 철새들은 보통 매년 똑같은 둥지 짓는 지역으로 돌아가며 비슷한 비행로를 따라 겨울 거주지로 향한다.

2 　과학자들은 이러한 비행이 어떻게 이루어지는지에 대해 밀접히 관련된 두 가설을 제안했다. 첫 번째는 새에게 내재된 별 나침반이 있다는 설이다. 이 설에 의하면, 새는 방향을 결정하기 위해 별들의 위치와 간격뿐만 아니라 이들의 규칙적인 움직임을 이용한다. 미국 조류학자 스티븐 엠렌은 1970년대에 유리멧새로 실험을 하면서 밤 하늘을 흉내내기 위해 천문관을 이용했다. 엠렌은 새들을 깔때기 모양의 새장에 넣어 위 방향만 보이도록 하였다. 새장 밑에는 축축한 잉크 판을 놓고 벽은 종이로 덮었다. 이후에 종이를 떼내어 연구함으로써, 엠렌은 가둔 곳 내부에서 새들의 움직임을 추적할 수 있었고 멧 새들이 별의 움직임에 따라 끊임없이 방향을 바꾼다는 것을 확인할 수 있었다.

3 　그러나 이 설을 복잡하게 만드는 것은 새들이 구름 아래에서 별들이 제대로 보이지 않을 때에도 밤에 효율적으로 계속해서 비행한다는 사실이다. 자기 나침반 설은 새들이 자기장을 이용하여 자신의 위치를 결정한다는 것으로, 새들이 시각적인 단서 없이 어떻게 계속 비행할 수 있는지 설명하려는 시도이다. [3]최근 연구는 새들이 미세한 양의 산화철을 머리와 부리에 가지고 있다는 것을 보여준다. 이런 자기 결정체가 나침반의 바늘처럼 새의 방위 변화에 상관 없이 북쪽으로 정렬되어 새들에게 뇌로 지속적으로 흐르는 방향 정보를 보낸다.

4 　새들이 어떻게 비행하는지에 대해 연구하면서, 과학자들은 또한 우연히 새들의 이동하려고 하는 경향에 대한 단서를 알게 되었다. 야행성 철새들은 밤에 새장에 갇혀 있으면 불안한 태도를 보였는데, 마치 평상시의 이동 방향으로 무의식적으로 끌려가는 것 같았다. 조류학자들은 이러한 새들의 이동 자극을 '이망증'이라고 부르는데, 이것은 이동과 불안을 뜻하는 독일 어원에서 파생된 용어이다. 새들은 이동을 하려는 선천적인 충동을 가지고 있는데, 이것은 철새가 아닌 개체들에서는 훨씬 완화되었지만 새 종 사이에서는 공통적인 것이라고 여겨진다.

어휘

permanent resident 텃새　adapt[ədǽpt] 적응하다　habitat[hǽbitæt] 서식지　relatively[rélətivli] 상대적으로
stable[stéibl] 고정적인　equator[ikwéitər] 적도　seasonally[síːzənli] 계절적으로　inhospitable[inháspitəbl] 황폐한
indispensable[indispénsəbl] 필수적인　shelter[ʃéltər] 피난처　escape[iskéip] 벗어나다　migrate[máigreit] 이동하다
suitable[súːtəbl] 적절한　navigational[næ̀vəgéiʃənəl] 비행의　propose[prəpóuz] 제안하다
interrelated[ìntərriléitid] 관련된　hypothesis[haipáθəsis] 가설　spacing[spéisiŋ] 간격
ornithologist[ɔ̀ːrnəθálədʒist] 조류학자　planetarium[plæ̀nətɛ́əriəm] 천문관　simulate[símjulèit] 흉내내다, 만들다
funnel-shaped[fʌ́nlʃèipt] 깔때기 모양의　visible[vízəbl] 보이는　enclosure[inklóuʒər] 가두기　confirm[kənfə́ːrm] 확인하다
alter[ɔ́ːltər] 변경하다　consistently[kənsístəntli] 끊임없이　complicate[kámpləkèit] 복잡하게 하다
assert[əsə́ːrt] 주장하다　magnetic[mægnétik] 자석의　iron oxide 산화철　align[əláin] 정렬시키다
orientation[ɔ̀ːriəntéiʃən] 방위　unwittingly[ʌ̀nwítiŋli] 우연히　inclination[ìnklənéiʃən] 경향
nocturnal[naktə́ːrnl] 야행성의　involuntarily[inváləntèrili] 무의식적으로　stimulus[stímjuləs] 자극　term[təːrm] 용어
derive[diráiv] 파생하다　innate[inéit] 선천적인　impulse[ímpʌls] 충동　subdued[səbdjúːd] 완화된

1. (C)   2. (B)   3. (A)   4. (C)   5. (C)   6. (A)   7. (D)   8. (B)

1 초기 근대에 걸쳐 유럽은 인구 순환기를 거쳤는데, 이는 유리한 정치, 경제적인 환경에 의해 촉진된 인구 증가와 흉작, 질병, 전쟁에 의해 시작된 사망 위기를 포함했다. 이러한 사망률의 단기 변동은 유럽 거주자들 사이에 큰 공황을 일으켰다. 이탈리아 작가 보카치오는 흑사병에 관한 중세 작품인 '데카메론'의 도입부에서 혼돈스러운 광경을 묘사하였는데, 여기에서 피렌체의 시민들은 세계의 종말이 가까워졌다고 생각했다. [1]모두가 곧 죽을 것이며 전염병과 관련된 죽음은 신성한 것이라는 믿음으로 사람들은 법률, 심지어는 애도의 의식조차도 신경 쓰지 않았고, 매일이 마지막 날인 것처럼 살아가기 시작했다.

2 이러한 음울한 장면은 14세기 유럽 문학에 걸쳐 발견되는데, 당시는 전염병과 극심한 인구 감소로 황폐해졌던 시기였다. 비슷한 상황이 17세기에 다시 나타났다. 유럽에는 전염병이 계속 부활했고, 광범위한 전쟁이 생명을 유린하고 농업을 파괴했으며 교통망을 차단했다. 가장 극심한 일부 전쟁은 수십 년간 지속되었다. 이러한 어려움의 결과로, 유럽 인구는 1300~1800년대 동안 서서히 증가하는 것에 그쳤다. 극심한 변동이 있었던, 이러한 순환적인 인구통계학상 패턴과 인구의 생존 위기에 대한 관련된 두려움은 19세기에 이르러 끝이 났다. 1800년과 1914년 사이에, 유럽은 1억8천8백만에서 4억5천8백만으로의 극적인 인구 증가를 목도하였다.

3 역사가들은 이 시기를 '거대한 전환'이라고 부르는데, 이 기간에는 이전의 인구망이 꾸준한 출산률과 합쳐진 평균 사망률의 감소로 특징지어지는 현대적인 형태로 전환되었다. 수백 년 동안 유럽인의 평균 수명은 40년 이하였으나, [4A]이 수치는 농업 생산의 주요한 개선이 이행되면서 증가하기 시작하였다. 더 좋은 도구, 기계의 광범한 사용과 생산적인 종자의 선별은 모두 농부들에게 더 많은 수확량을 주는 데 기여하였고, 이는 기근을 상쇄하도록 분배될 수 있었다. 이러한 발전은 미국으로부터의 새로운 작물 도입과 함께 유럽 식단의 다양화와 더 균형 있는 영양을 가져왔다. 게다가, [4B/D]19세기 말 무렵 향상된 의학 지식은 수명을 연장하고 유아사망을 줄이는 요인으로 작용하였다. 생물학적 연구는 매개체와 전염병의 관계(예를 들어, 이는 발진티푸스, 모기는 말라리아, 사람은 결핵의 매개체이다) 뿐만 아니라 전염과 감염된 사람을 격리시킬 필요에 대해 더 깊은 이해를 보여주었다.

4 전반적으로, 대부분의 유럽 국가들은 19세기 동안 15~20년의 수명 증가를 경험하였다. 대조적으로 이 시기에 출산률은 감소하였는데, 일부분은 믿기 어려운 원인 때문이었다. 영국인 인구 통계학자 토마스 맬더스는 피임에 대한 그의 반대에도 불구하고, 1798년 논문 '인구론'을 통해 간접적으로 산아제한 움직임을 유발했다. 논문에서 맬더스는 세계 자원을 위협하는 것이 인구과잉 때문이라고 하였는데, 이는 인구과잉이 아닌 인구 '부족'으로 인한 대참사 광경을 그린 보카치오와 같은 이전 작가들의 관점과는 완전히 반대되는 것이다. 이후에 산아제한의 지지자들은 자발적인 피임을 장려하기위해 맬더스의 가설에 의존하였는데, 자발적 피임은 전통적으로 고립된 공동체나 개개의 가정에서만 시행되던 관습이었다. 그들의 노력은 결국 성과를 거두었다. 1870년과 1910년 사이에, 사람들은 언제 아이를 가질지와 아이를 가질지 말지에 대해 점차 개인적인 선택을 하기 시작하였고, 결과적으로 몇십 년 만에 여성의 평균 출산률이 30퍼센트 감소하였다.

5 연장된 수명과 적은 출생의 결합은 현대의 산업화된 유럽의 표준이 되었다. 두 세계 대전을 포함하는 시기를 제외하면, 20세기의 유럽은 계속적인 의학 발전, 향상된 영양, 계속 줄어드는 출생률을 경험했다. [8]21세기의 첫 10년에, 유럽의 인구는 현대에 처음으로 자연적인 마이너스 성장을 경험했다. 대륙의 상대적인 평화와 안정의 시기에, 출산률은 사실상 사망률 밑으로 내려갔다. 당시 널리 낙태를 허가한 것을 포함하는 법적인 변화 또한 인구 변동에 기여했다. 자연적인 마이너스 성장은 무기한으로 계속될 것으로 예측된다. 유럽의 인구는 2005년에 7억2천8백만 정도였으며, UN 인구분과위원회는 이 수치가 2050년까지는 6억6천5백만 이하로 내려갈 것으로 추정한다.

어휘
demographic[dì:məgrǽfik] 인구의 upswing[ʌ́pswìŋ] 증가 foster[fɔ́:stər] 촉진하다 mortality[mɔːrtǽləti] 사망
plague[pleig] 전염병 divine[diváin] 신성의 rite[rait] 의식 mourn[mɔːrn] 애도하다 dismal[dízməl] 음울한
ravage[rǽvidʒ] 황폐하다 resurgence[risə́:rdʒəns] 부활 devastate[dévəstèit] 유린하다 endure[indjúər] 지속되다
subsistence[səbsístəns] 생존 mark[mɑːrk] 특징지어지다 fertility rate 출생률 life expectancy 수명

implement[ímpləmənt] 이행하다 offset[ɔ́:fsèt] 상쇄하다 famine[fǽmin] 기근 diversification[divə̀:rsəfikéiʃən] 다양화
contagious[kəntéidʒəs] 전염성의 lice[lais] 이 typhus[táifəs] 발진티푸스 tuberculosis[tjubə̀:rkjulóusis] 결핵
contagion[kəntéidʒən] 전염 isolate[áisəlèit] 격리하다 infected[inféktid] 감염된 unlikely[ʌ̀nláikli] 믿기 어려운
objection[əbdʒékʃən] 반대 contraception[kàntrəsépʃən] 피임 indirectly[ìndəréktli] 간접적으로
give rise to 유발하다, 발생하게 하다 reversal[rivə́:rsəl] 반대 catastrophe[kətǽstrəfi] 대참사 advocate[ǽdvəkèit] 지지자
draw on ~에 의존하다 promote[prəmóut] 장려하다 voluntary[váləntèri] 자발적인 exception[iksépʃən] 예외
stability[stəbíləti] 안정 dip[dip] 내려가다 legal[líːgəl] 법적인 abortion[əbɔ́:rʃən] 낙태 indefinitely[indéfənitli] 무기한으로

3 Brazilian Independence 브라질의 독립   p.93

1. (D) 2. (D) 3. (D) 4. (A) 5. (A) 6. (D) 7. (B) 8. (C)

1 1500년에 포르투갈 탐험가 페드루 알바레스 카브랄은 브라질에 도착하여 그 지역을 포르투갈 왕국의 일부라고 주장했다. 다음 몇백 년 동안, 포르투갈 사람들은 새로운 식민지로 이동하여 토착민과 아프리카 노예의 노동력을 이용하여 정착지를 수립했다. 1800년대 초반에, 브라질 원주민은 전체 인구의 5퍼센트 정도뿐이었다. 따라서, 브라질에서 독립적인 국가 정체성을 창조하는 데, 그리고 결국 새로운 국가를 창조하는 데 주 역할을 한 것은 포르투갈 식민지 개척자 자신들이었다.

2 실제로, 브라질의 첫 황제 돔 페드루 1세는 포르투갈에서 태어났다. 군사 훈련 중 말 위에서 기병대에게 전한 그의 1822년 독립연설 'O Grito do Iparanga'는 상대적으로 적은 유혈로 성공한 브라질 독립 운동의 상징이 되었다. 일부 작은 전투들이 일어나긴 했지만, 브라질의 독립은 대부분 경제적이고 정치적인 통로를 통해 찾아왔다. 브라질 독립의 많은 경제적, 정치적 토대는 돔 페드루의 아버지 돔 조앙이 놓은 것인데, 그는 왕자이자 포르투갈 왕좌의 후계자였다.

3 브라질 독립을 처음으로 두드러지게 촉진시킨 것은 1808년 프랑스가 나폴레옹의 지휘 하에 스페인을 거쳐 침략하여 포르투갈 왕실 전체가 왕국에서 도망쳐야 했을 때였다. 정부는 남미 식민지로 재배치되고 포르투갈의 수도를 포르투갈의 리스본에서 브라질의 리우데자네이루로 이전했다. 포르투갈 당국자들이 도착했을 때, 그들은 엄청난 천연자원이 있지만 기초적인 경제적, 산업적 기반을 가진 한 식민지를 발견했다. 식민지의 초라한 상황을 목격하자 돔 조앙 밑의 새로운 정부는 브라질에서 야심찬 개발 사업에 착수했다.

4 그 후 13년 동안, 포르투갈인들은 기반시설의 많은 발달을 일으켰다. ^{5B/D}도로를 건축하고 항구를 넓혔으며 은행을 설립했는데, 이것들은 상업 활동을 활성화시키는 데 필수적인 개발이었다. 다른 추가된 것에는 식물원, 국립 도서관, 해군 사관학교, 국립 박물관이 포함되는데, 모두 리우데자네이루에 위치한다. ^{5C}그림과 조각을 완비한 정교한 식민지 건축물도 지어졌다. 이러한 기반시설의 발전은 미국 대륙은 물론이고 포르투갈 왕국에서도 브라질의 권력과 위신에 상당히 기여했다. 그들은 브라질에 사는 식민지 개척자들 사이에 브라질 국민성을 창조하는 데 매우 영향력이 컸다.

5 그러나 유럽에서 나폴레옹이 패배한 후, 포르투갈의 최상류층으로부터 권력의 토대를 다시 리스본으로 옮기라는 압력이 증가하였고, 이것은 브라질 독립 운동을 더욱 촉진시킨 일련의 사건들로 이어졌다. 나폴레옹의 패배와 같은 해인 1815년, 돔 조앙은 브라질의 지위를 왕국으로 올려 포르투갈과 정치적으로 동등하게 만들었다. 그 후 1816년에 그는 포르투갈의 지도자로 임명되었지만, 브라질에 남는 것을 선택했다. 돔 조앙의 결정은 일부 포르투갈인들의 반대에 부딪혔다. ⁶브라질의 인구는 원주민, 아프리카계 미국인과 유럽의 후손이 섞여 있었기 때문에 포르투갈에 사는 사람들은 브라질을 여전히 식민지에 불과한, 즉 왕국의 이득을 위해 착취당해야 할 열등한 인간들로 보았다. 이런 태도는 브라질에 사는 많은 사람들의 감정을 상하게 했고, 지역의 정치적인 지식인 지도자들 사이에서 혁명적인 생각들이 생겨났다. 1821년에, 리스본에 충성했던 애국자들은 돔 조앙을 대면하여 왕으로 남고 싶으면 포르투갈로 이동할 것을 요구했다. 왕위를 포기하기 싫었던 돔 조앙은 승낙했고 리스본으로 이전했다. 그는 아들 돔 페드루를 남겨 브라질의 통치자를 하도록 하였다.

6 돔 조앙의 귀환 뒤, 리우데자네이루가 포르투갈 왕국을 1808년부터 지배했음에도 불구하고 리스본은 브라질의 식민지로서의 지위를 회복시키려고 적극적인 노력을 쏟았다. 포르투갈의 의회 'Cortes Gerais'는 브라질 교역에 대해 독점적인 지배력을 복구하기 위한 법안을 통과시켰다. 의회는 브라질에 대한 리스본의 직접적인 권한을 공식적으로 회복시키고 확대

CHAPTER 3

Hackers TOEFL Reading Intermediate

Chapter 03 Reference **289**

되는 독립 운동의 토대를 무너뜨리고 싶어 했다. 계획의 일부로, 의회는 돔 페드루가 포르투갈로 귀환할 것을 명령했다. 그러나 독립을 지지하는 민족주의자들이 리스본의 요구에 저항하라고 격려해주었고, 1822년 1월 9일, 돔 페드루는 브라질에 머물겠다는 그의 계획을 공식적으로 발표했다. [8]같은 해 9월, 리스본이 돔 페드루에게 권리를 박탈하는 명령을 보냈을 때, 돔 페드루는 브라질의 독립을 선언하고 자신에게 황제의 지위를 부여하였다. 짧은 부정의 기간 후 1825년에 포르투갈은 브라질의 독립을 인정했다.

어휘

indigenous[indídʒənəs] 토착의 native[néitiv] 원주민 primary[práimeri] 주요한 ultimately[ʌ́ltəmətli] 결국
indeed[indíːd] 실제로 independence[ìndipéndəns] 독립 cavalry[kǽvəlri] 기병의 symbolic[simbálik] 상징적인
comparatively[kəmpǽrətivli] 상대적으로 bloodshed[blʌ́dʃèd] 유혈 heir[ɛər] 후계자 throne[θroun] 왕위
invade[invéid] 침입하다 entire[intáiər] 전체의 flee[fliː] 도망하다 relocate[rìːloukéit] 재배치하다
rudimentary[rùːdəméntəri] 초보의 infrastructure[ínfrəstrʌ̀ktʃər] 기반시설 witness[wítnis] 목격하다
embark[imbáːrk] 착수하다, 시작하다 ambitious[æmbíʃəs] 야심적인 initiate[iníʃièit] 일으키다, 시작하다 botanical garden 식물원
contribute[kəntríbjuːt] 기여하다 influential[ìnfluénʃəl] 영향력 있는 defeat[difíːt] 패배시키다 mount[maunt] 증가하다
catalyze[kǽtəlàiz] 촉진시키다 elevate[éləvèit] 승격시키다 disapproval[dìsəprúːvəl] 반대 offend[əfénd] 감정을 상하게 하다
regent[ríːdʒənt] 통치자 restore[ristɔ́ːr] 복원하다 parliamentary[pàːrləméntəri] 의회의 reestablish[rìːistǽbliʃ] 복구하다
resist[rizíst] 저항하다 declare[diklɛ́ər] 공표하다 denial[dináiəl] 부정, 부인

문제 공략하기

p.101

그러나 아마도 양서류 감소에 가장 압도적인 요인은 지구의 기후 변화일 것이다. 태양 광선으로부터 지구를 보호하는 대기 입자 층인 오존층이 옅어지는 것은 특히 양서류에게 유해하다. 양서류 알은 단단한 외피 없이 부드러운 껍질을 갖고 있기 때문에 자외선에 취약하여 알이 너무 이르게 부화하거나 취약한 면역 체계를 가진 새끼가 나오는 결과를 낳는다.

HACKERS PRACTICE

p.102

01 (A) 02 (A) 03 (B) 04 (A) 05 (A) 06 (A) 07 (C) 08 (C) 09 (D) 10 (D) 11 (B) 12 (A)
13 1. (C) 2. (A) 14 1. (C) 2. (D) 15 1. (A) 2. (D)

01 1662년에, 아일랜드 물리학자 로버트 보일은 오늘날의 기준으로는 기초적인 기술 장비 밖에 이용할 수 없었음에도 불구하고, 기체가 일정한 온도로 유지되면 기체의 압력과 부피의 관계가 반비례 한다는 것을 발견했다.

02 목축민은 유목 민족으로, 그들은 말, 양과 소를 길들임으로써 거의 오로지 가축을 이용한 농업에만 집중하였고, 가축 떼를 위한 물과 적절한 방목지를 찾아 이곳 저곳 자주 옮겨 다녔다.

03 명왕성 발견의 공로를 인정받은 천문학자 클라이드 톰보는 1930년에 명왕성의 존재를 확인하기 위해, 하늘의 특정 지역을 찍은 사진으로 천체의 위치 변화를 탐지하는 기기인 깜빡이 비교기를 이용했다.

04 중국의 인쇄술 발달은 종이, 잉크, 그리고 탁본하는 기술의 발명 덕분에 가능했지만, 그 기술에서 가장 중요한 혁신은 서명을 찍기 위한 도구인 봉랍 도장이었다.

05 태양이 지구를, 그리고 차례로 대기를 가열하면서 따뜻한 공기가 떠올라 모든 방향에서 양 극 쪽으로 움직이는데, 이 현상은 양 극으로부터 오는 차가운 공기가 따뜻한 공기를 대신할 통로를 만들며, 이 과정의 결과가 바람이다.

06 훌륭한 디자인과 인근 마을을 세운 사람들을 끌어당기는 능력에도 불구하고, 일본 성은 대부분의 세상 사람들에게 거의 인정받지 못했는데, 이는 '성'이라는 용어가 보통 중세시대 동안 유럽에 세워진 요새와 같은 건축물을 연상시키기 때문이다.

07 예술 작품을 정확하게 복제하기 위해서는 매우 전문적인 기술이 필요했으며 인쇄 도구가 비쌌기 때문에, 예술가와 판화 제작자 간의 관계는 완벽히 묘사된 복제품을 생산하는 데 중요해졌다.

08 대부분의 사람들은 열의 직접적인 영향을 받을 때 육체적인 불편에 시달리지만, 의학자와 의사들은 신체가 적절하게 기능하는 데 있어 열의 많은 긍정적인 측면, 특히 열이 면역적인 저항을 촉진하고, 혈액순환을 용이하게 하며, 해로운 세균 및 바이러스와 싸우는 것과 같은 면을 오랫동안 인정해왔다.

09 바다에 있는 빙산의 표면은 10분의 1 정도만 보이지만, 이 부분이 녹으면 표면 아래 얼음의 일부가 떠오른다. 이것은 지구의 지각에 응용되는 아르키메데스의 부력의 원리를 예증해준다. 지각은 흐르는 점성의 층인 맨틀 위에 떠있다. 어떤

지역에서는 지각이 모여, 서서히 산이 되는 큰 덩어리를 형성한다. 산이 부식되어 높이가 줄어들면, 빙산이 물 위에 떠 있듯이 산도 맨틀 위에 떠있기 때문에 새로운 지각이 밀고 올라온다.

10 두 지지물을 연결하기 위해 아치를 사용하는 원리가 로마인들에게 수 세기 전에 알려져 있었다는 사실에도 불구하고, 기원전 1세기에서야 그들은 다리와 사원, 수도에 계획적으로 그것을 적용하였다. 특히 반원형의 아치는 로마 석공들에게 인기가 많았는데, 그들은 바위 벽돌을 이용하여 곡선 모양의 건축물을 지었다. 벽돌은 중심의 종석과 함께 둥그런 호 모양으로 놓였고 아치굽이라고 불리는 두 개의 세로 기둥 위에 배치되었다.

11 지리적 종분화 기간 동안, 한 종은 두 개의 지리적으로 다른 집단으로 분리되어 유전자 풀의 혼합이 정지된다. 이러한 분리는 종종 지질의 융기나 전에는 존재하지 않았던 수역이 생기는 등의 현상으로 인해 서서히 이루어진다. 파나마 지협의 융기에서 한 예를 찾을 수 있는데, 이 융기로 인해 멕시코 만과 태평양 사이의 해양 생물들이 분리되었다. 오랜 시간에 걸쳐 다른 서식지의 영향을 받으면서, 멕시코 만의 해양 생물들은 새로운 물리적 환경에 대응하여 태평양의 친척들과 다른 습성을 발달시키게 되었으며, 이러한 적응 형태는 과거에는 하나였던 종 일원들 간의 완전한 생식적 불화합성이라는 결과를 낳았다. 예를 들어, 파나마 동해안의 딱총새우는 서해안에 있는 것들과 성적으로 달라졌으며 수조에 같이 놓여있다고 해도 짝짓기를 하지 않을 것이다.

12 중세 후기 시대의 북유럽과 남유럽의 사회경제 체제는 완전히 달랐으며, 결과적으로 이 지역들의 발달은 달랐다. 북유럽 체제는 본질적으로 땅의 소유권에 기초를 두었다. 왕과 같은 주권자 밑으로 들어간 영주나 지주는 자신의 땅에 대한 완전한 권력을 얻었다. 영주들은 그들의 땅에 거주하는 소작인들과 계약 관계를 맺어 영주에 대한 충성과 왕에 대한 정치적 충성을 요구하는 대신 그들에게 작은 농촌을 수립할 허가를 주었다. 이 협정은 군주제를 유지하고 지역의 안전을 제공하는 큰 군대를 만드는 데 중요한 역할을 하였다. 북유럽의 정치 체제는 강력했지만, 그 땅의 사회경제 체제는 그 지역이 농업 지역으로 남아 있도록 보증하였다.

13 백악기 말기 즈음에 생물이 갑작스럽게 사라진 것에 관하여, 고생물학자들은 역사적인 대량 멸종, 즉 실질적으로 모든 분류 항목에 있는 수많은 종들이 약 6,500만 년 전에 전멸했던 사건의 정확한 원인에 대한 해석을 달리한다. 한 이론가 집단은 지질학적 기록에서 발견된 우주진과 같은 증거, 즉 외계 물체들이 지구 표면에 충돌했다는 증거에 주목한다. 운석이 충분히 크다면 먼지와 유독한 증기를 대기권 높이 올려 보내 태양을 가릴 수 있고, 그것이 지구 표면 온도를 낮추고 아황산 가스와 같은 화합물을 성층권에 수년간 남겨 두어 그곳에서 구름과 섞이면서 독성 에어로졸을 만들고 산성비를 생성할 수 있다고 이론가들은 주장한다. 다른 집단은 비극적인 종 감소에는 지구상의 원인이 있음을 강조한다. 그들은 원인을 거대한 화산 폭발이라고 언급하며 대기권으로의 미립자와 독성가스의 방출이 육지와 바다에서의 생활 조건을 부적합하게 만들었을 거라고 말한다.

14 청솔모과에 속하는 작은 다람쥐 같은 설치류인 북미산 얼룩다람쥐는 일반적으로 동쪽과 서쪽 집단으로 분류된다. 동쪽 얼룩다람쥐들은 미국 북동쪽의 낙엽성 숲 내에 머물며, 땅에 사는 단 한가지 종으로만 구성된다. 반면, 서쪽 얼룩다람쥐는 21종이 있고, 서식지도 훨씬 다양하다. 미국 북서쪽에 널리 퍼져 있는 많은 서쪽 얼룩다람쥐는 피난처 역할을 하는 관목, 쓰러진 통나무 또는 기반암 근처의 넓은 땅굴에 사는 것을 선호한다. 13종이 캘리포니아에 살고, 이 종들이 사는 서식지의 범위는 숲 속의 풀, 덤불, 관목에서부터 중간과 더 높은 고도의 산비탈까지 겹치는 경향이 있다. 가장 흔한 종인 Least Chipmunk는 다른 더 큰 종들이 존재하는 구역에 살기 때문에 샐비어와 관목이 자라는 서식지에 한정하여 산다. Alpine과 Lodgepole 같은 다른 작은 종은 수목한계선에 있는 목초지에서 사는 것을 선택하여 더 높은 고도에서 주로 발견된다.

15 전통 연극에서는 관객과 배우 사이의 상호작용이 제한되었지만, 실험적인 배우-관객 상호작용 방법이 연기 방법론에 변화를 가져왔다. 이러한 방법 중 하나는 20세기에 유명한 미술감독 비올라 스폴린에 의해 만들어졌는데, 그녀는 Young Actors Company라는 할리우드 배우 학교를 1946년에 설립했다. 스폴린은 창의성을 자극하기 위해 고안된 연극 게임을 포함할 수 있도록 훈련의 범위가 확장되어야 한다고 믿었으며, 무대 위에 선 배우들이 대사 암기와 연습 공연의 반복에만 의존하기 보다는 새로운 시도를 통해 관중을 고무시킬 가능성이 더 크다고 설명했다. 게임의 예로는 배

우들에게 특정 동물이나 감정을 지정해주고 즉흥적으로 흉내내도록 한 것이 있다. 스폴린의 아이디어들은 즉흥 연기로 알려진 훨씬 더 급진적인 방법의 기초가 되었는데, 이는 1950년대 시카고 극장에서 생겨난 인기 있고 자유로운 연기 방식이며, 배우들은 관객에게 공연의 일부를 이끌어가기 위한 영감을 요구하였고, 따라서 행위자로서의 배우와 수동적인 참여자로서의 관객이라는 전통적인 모델에서 완전히 벗어났다. 게다가, 즉흥 배우들은 대사를 연구하여 연출된 연극을 신중히 계획하는 대신, 종종 대본 없이 즉흥적으로 연기하곤 했다.

HACKERS TEST

* 각 문제에 대한 정답단서는 지문에 초록색으로 표시되어 있습니다.

1 Pollen Analysis 꽃가루 분석

p.110

1. (A) 2. (B) 3. (A) 4. (D)

1 과학자들은 과거의 식생 패턴과 기후에 대해 알기 위해 꽃가루를 분석한다. 꽃가루 분석은 암석이나 토양의 여러 층에서 꽃가루 알갱이를 수집, 조사, 평가하는 일을 포함한다. [4]지구의 퇴적층에 보존된 다양한 꽃가루 알갱이를 분석함으로써, 우리는 어떤 지역에 존재했던 식물의 수와 종류, 그리고 그들이 어떻게 분포되어 있었는지를 추측할 수 있다. 존재했던 식물의 종류를 아는 것은 또한 연구자들이 역사적인 기후 상황을 추론해낼 수 있도록 한다.

2 종자식물이 꽃가루를 방출할 때 대부분은 땅에 떨어지고, 빙하 작용과 풍식 작용을 통해 퇴적물이 모이면서 꽃가루 알갱이는 땅의 층 안에 갇힌다. 마침내, 흙이 굳으며 층이 형성된다. 묻힌 꽃가루를 얻기 위해서는, 땅에서 중심 표본을 채취해야 한다. 이것은 원통 모양의 구멍을 땅에 뚫고 꽃가루가 갇혀있을 가능성이 높은 중간 토양층을 파냄으로써 이루어진다. 그 후 꽃가루 중심 표본은 관에 넣어진 상태로, 연구될 수 있는 실험실로 운송된다. 산소가 없는 상태에서 형성된 퇴적물이 꽃가루의 질을 가장 잘 보존하고 부패를 막기 때문에, 표본은 종종 습지와 마른 호수 바닥에서 채취된다.

3 꽃가루 중심 표본의 최저층 물질은 가장 오래된 것이고, 최고층 물질은 가장 새로운 것이다. 따라서 우리는 꽃가루의 상대적 나이와 언제 그것이 퇴적되었는지를 어림잡을 수 있다. 오늘날, 북미 오대호 지역의 습지대와 복합적인 숲 생태계에는 다양한 식물이 살고 있다. 그러나 꽃가루 분석은 오대호 주위에서 볼 수 있는 무성한 환경이 한때 소수의 흩어져 있는 관목과 함께 눈과 얼음으로 덮여 있었고, 대부분 지의류, 이끼, 사초, 그리고 잡초로 이루어져 있었음을 밝혀냈다. 중심 표본에서 나온 꽃가루를 증거 삼아, 과학자들은 오대호 지역 전체의 기후가 항상 그렇게 온화하지는 않았음을 추론할 수 있다. 사실상 겨우 11,000년 전에, 이 지역은 오늘날의 북극 툰드라와 더 많은 공통점이 있었다. 이곳은 큰 나무들의 성장을 지탱할 수 없는 메마르고 굉장히 추운 지역이었다.

4 그러나 종합적인 결과를 내리려면, 꽃가루 분석은 수많은 다양한 지역에서 실행되어야 한다. 과거에 지구의 광대한 영역에 걸쳐 자란 식물을 이해함으로써, 우리는 기후 변화와 기후 변화가 지역의 식생 패턴에 어떤 영향을 끼쳤는지에 대한 자료를 모을 수 있다. 그러므로 꽃가루 분석은 지구 온난화와 같은 현상이 미래에 식물의 지역적 분포에 어떤 영향을 끼칠지에 대한 단서를 제공한다.

어휘

pollen[pálən] 꽃가루 vegetation[vèdʒətéiʃən] 식물 examine[igzǽmin] 조사하다 calculate[kǽlkjulèit] 평가하다
grain[grein] 알갱이 layer[léiər] 층 retain[ritéin] 보존하다 sediment[sédəmənt] 퇴적물 estimate[éstəmèit] 추측하다
distribute[distríbju:t] 분포하다 deduce[didjúːs] 추론하다 flowering plant 종자식물 glaciation[glèiʃiéiʃən] 빙하 작용
erosion[iróuʒən] 풍식 작용 compact[kəmpǽkt] 굳다 stratify[strǽtəfài] 층을 형성시키다 core[kɔːr] 중심의
accomplish[əkámpliʃ] 이루다 drill[dril] ~에 구멍을 뚫다 cylindrical[silíndrikəl] 원통의 anaerobic[ǽnəròubik] 산소가 없는
decompose[dìːkəmpóuz] 부패하다 bog[bɑg] 습지 bed[bed] 바닥 approximate[əpráksəmèit] 어림잡다
deposit[dipázit] 쌓이다 flora[flɔ́ːrə] 식물 wetland[wétlænd] 습지대 lush[lʌʃ] 무성한 shrub[ʃrʌb] 관목 lichen[láikən] 지의류
moss[mɔːs] 이끼 sedge[sedʒ] 사초 comprehensive[kàmprihénsiv] 종합적인 conduct[kəndʌ́kt] 실행하다
fluctuation[flʌ̀ktʃuéiʃən] 변화 vegetative[védʒətèitiv] 식물의

1. (C)   2. (B)   3. (A)   4. (A)   5. (C)   6. (B)   7. (D)   8. (D)

1 저빙은 땅 위 또는 속에 있는 얼은 물이다. 영구 동토층 지역 같은 일부 지역에서는 저빙이 일년 내내 유지된다. 예로는 남극의 일부, 북극, 그리고 세계의 높은 고산 지역들이 포함된다. 덜 극심한 기후에서는 종종 계절적인 동결 융해 주기가 있으므로 대부분의 온대 지역에서 저빙 생성은 겨울에만 일어나는 현상이다.

2 결빙 환경이 다르면 저빙의 종류도 달라진다. 저빙의 두 가지 흔한 종류는 pore ice와 segregated ice이다. 지하의 흙 알갱이 사이에서 생기는 얼음을 pore ice라고 부른다. 무거운 진흙처럼 습기를 유지하는 토양에서는, 특히 아주 급속한 기온 저하의 결과로 얼은 것이라면, pore ice는 거의 보이지 않을 수도 있다. 모래처럼 투과성이 더 높은 환경에서는, 퇴적물 사이 공간에서 더 큰 얼음이 만들어져 빙정이 육안으로 쉽게 보이게 된다. pore ice는 그것이 차지하는 빈 공간의 크기 및 모양과 합치하고, 토양층에 걸쳐 다양한 밀도로 분포된다.

3 pore ice는 최초 결빙과 관련이 있지만, 종종 약간의 얼지 않은 물이 땅에 남는다. 만일 온도가 더 내려가면, 저빙은 토양 내부나 토양 표면의 특정 층에서 축적되기 시작한다. 이러한 층 형성은 온도 변화도 때문이다. ⁵ᴬ이 변화도에 따라 물이 얼음으로 바뀌면서, 분자력이 흡인력을 발생시켜 습기가 이동하도록 한다. 이 과정은 주위의 토양으로부터 얼음의 분리를 일으킨다. 얼음 안에 부스러기가 적거나 아예 없기 때문에, 이를 segregated ice라고 부른다. ⁵ᴮsegregated ice 생성물은 상대적으로 퇴적물이 없고 거의 순수한 얼은 물로 이루어져 있다. 지하에서는 이 과정이 lense라고 불리는 얇은 수평의 얼음판을 만든다. ⁵ᴰ또한 segregated ice는 토양 표면에서 또는 토양 표면 매우 가까이에서 만들어질 수 있다. 바늘처럼 생긴 모양에서 이름이 붙은 얇고 가느다란 얼음 조각인 얼음바늘은 토양 표면 밑의 온도가 0℃보다 높고 토양 표면은 0℃ 또는 그 이하인 습한 조건에서 생성된다.

4 저빙은 보통 주변 퇴적물의 물을 고갈시키면서 생성되기 때문에, 토양이 건조하고 잘 부서지게 된다. 게다가, 물이 얼면 더 많은 부피를 차지하게 되고, 얼음이 발달하고 늘어나면서 일부 토양을 밀어내며 울퉁불퉁한 표면을 만들어낸다. 이러한 잘 바스러지는 얼은 땅은 그 위로 지나가는 모든 것의 무게에 쉽게 부서진다. 얼음이 녹으면 남는 것은 느슨하게 결합된 토양 입자이고, 이는 차오르는 강물, 바람, 그리고 비에 의해 쉽게 쓸려 나갈 수 있다. 이 과정으로 인한 토양 입자 이동과 풍화 작용의 결과로 뒤따라 일어나는 토양 분포는 얼음으로 유발된 침식으로 알려져 있는데, 이는 시냇가 침식의 핵심 요소이다. 지하의 얼음층 생성도 표면에 영향을 줄 수 있다. 결빙으로 인한 지속적인 생성(팽창)과 해빙으로 인한 후퇴(수축)는 토양의 수직적인 이동을 일으킬 수 있다. 동상현상으로 알려진 이 현상은 나무의 뿌리를 파괴하고, 건물의 토대를 손상시키고, 길과 보도에 금을 낼 수 있다.

5 그렇다 하더라도, 저빙 생성의 모든 영향이 파괴적인 것은 아니다. 서리가 흔하지 않은 남부 캘리포니아처럼 따뜻한 기후에서는, 서리가 내릴 듯이 추운 밤을 미리 걱정하는 농부들이 딸기와 오렌지 작물에 물을 뿌리는 것을 간혹 볼 수 있을 것이다. 이것은 식물과 과일 위에 두꺼운 얼음 막을 만들어낸다. 이 행위는 반직관적으로 보일 수도 있지만, 사실은 농부들이 작물이 손상되지 않도록 보호하는 것이다. ⁸물의 고유한 특징 중 하나는 얼면서 온기를 내는 것인데, 이 에너지 이동은 식물 조직을 0℃ 또는 영상 몇 ℃ 위로 유지함으로써 차가운 기온을 완화시킨다. 결과적으로, 기온이 빙점 밑으로 떨어지더라도 식물 조직은 얼어서 터지지 않을 것이다. 지표면 밑에서도 비슷한 상황이 일어난다. 저빙은 덩이줄기 작물을 자연적인 열 이불로 감싸서 당근과 양파 같은 지하 작물이 단열되도록 도와준다.

어휘
ground ice 저빙 **permafrost**[pə́ːrməfrɔ̀ːst] 영구 동토층 **thaw**[θɔː] 융해, 해빙; 녹다 **retentive**[riténtiv] 습기를 유지하는
clay[klei] 진흙 **invisible**[invízəbl] 보이지 않는 **permeable**[pə́ːrmiəbl] 투과성이 높은 **detectable**[ditéktəbl] 보이는
conform[kənfɔ́ːrm] 합치하다 **accumulate**[əkjúːmjulèit] 축적되다 **gradient**[gréidiənt] 변화도 **molecular**[məlékjulər] 분자의
suction[sʌ́kʃən] 흡인력 **horizontal**[hɔ̀ːrəzántl] 수평의 **sliver**[slívər] 가느다란 조각 **deplete**[diplíːt] 고갈시키다
brittle[brítl] 잘 부서지는 **shove aside** 밀어내다 **crumbly**[krʌ́mbli] 잘 바스러지는 **deterioration**[ditìəriəréiʃən] 침식
retreat[ritríːt] 후퇴 **vertical**[və́ːrtikəl] 수직의 **frost heave** 동상현상 **sidewalk**[sáidwɔ̀ːk] 보도
counterintuitive[kàuntərintjúːətiv] 반직관적인 **rupture**[rʌ́ptʃər] 터뜨리다 **insulate**[ínsəlèit] 단열하다

3 Urban Sociology 도시 사회학   p.116

1. (B)	2. (A)	3. (D)	4. (D)	5. (A)	6. (B)	7. (C)	8. (C)

1 19세기 동안 미국은 상대적으로 중요하지 않은 농업 국가에서 상업적이고 산업적인 강국으로 바뀌었다. 빠르고 저렴한 교통망이 발달하여 다른 지역들을 잇고 미국 도시의 외관을 바꾸어 놓았다. 사람들은 산업화로 제공된 새로운 기회를 이용하기 위해 도시 지역으로 몰렸고, 이는 미국 도시들의 성장에 대한 경험적인 자료를 수집하기 시작한 새로운 세대의 학자들을 동원시킨 인구학적 동향이었다. 특히, 학자들은 도시로의, 그리고 도시 내 인간의 이동 패턴을 설명하려고 했다. 그 주제에 대한 연구의 가장 영향력 있는 부분이 시카고에서 이루어졌다. 따라서 그것은 도시 사회학의 시카고 학파라고 알려져 있다.

2 19세기 후반과 20세기 초반 시카고의 급속한 산업화와 그와 관련된 인구 폭발은 시카고를 사회학 연구의 완벽한 대상으로 만들었고, 1925년 'The City'의 출판은 학계에 도시 사회학 학문을 수립하는 데 기여했다. 그 책은 시카고 학파를 전형적으로 보여주며 현대 사회학에 대한 가장 중요한 공헌 중 하나로 알려져 있다. 도시 사회학자 어니스트 버제스에 의해 편집된 그 연구는 동심원에 기초한 노시 발달에 관한 보편적인 이론을 구축하였다. 동심원지대이론(CZM)의 기본 전제는 사람들이 도시를 이루기 위해 모일 때, 그들의 정착과 땅의 이용이 예측 가능한 패턴으로 일어난다는 것이다. 시카고 학파에 의하면, 사람들은 처음에는 중심에 모이고, 새로운 이주자들이 도착해서 도시가 확장될수록 전문 사업과 기반 시설이 포함된 고리 모양의 추가 개발 지역이 중심 주위에 생기기 시작한다. 각 '고리'는 지위, 자원 접근성, 전체적인 삶의 질과 관련된 사회경제 변수들의 다양한 집합을 대표한다.

3 CZM에서는 중심지대가 주요 상공업 지역의 역할을 한다. 그곳은 도시의 정치, 경제, 문화 생활의 중심지이며 시청, 주요 교통 중심지, 그리고 박물관을 포함한다. 중심을 바로 둘러싸고 있는 것은 점이지대로, 공장과 주로 이민자들이 살고 있는 저렴한 주택지의 혼합으로 대부분 이루어져 있다. ⁵버제스에 의하면 빈민가, 범죄, 그리고 가난이 있는 이 지역은 퇴보된 곳으로 간주된다. 하지만 그는 또한 그곳을 개혁의 장소, 그리고 새롭고 더 좋은 세상을 적극적으로 찾고 있는 세계적인 거주자들을 대표하는 급진적인 사상의 원천으로 보기도 한다.

4 점이지대 너머로 두 구역으로 이루어진 주거지역이 있다. 내부 구역은 가게 및 공장 노동자들이 살고 있는 자립근로자 거주지역이며, '더 좋은 거주지역'이 있는 외부 구역이 그 뒤를 따르는데, 이곳은 주로 도시와 그 외부 사이의 두 번째 점이지대로 기능한다. 현대 용어로, 주거지역의 두 구역은 각각 내부 교외(하층 거주지역)와 외부 교외(중상층 거주지역)에 해당한다. ⁷ᴮ더 멀리 나가면 CZM의 가장 외곽 지역이 있는데, 이곳은 상당한 재정 자산을 가지고 있거나 도시 생활의 스트레스로부터 멀리 떨어진 더 쾌적한 환경에서 살고 싶어하는 사람들을 위한 곳이다. ⁷ᴰ가장 외곽 지역의 거주자 중 다수는 도시에 직장이 있고 매일 상당한 시간을 출퇴근하는 데 소비한다. 따라서 이곳은 통근자 지역이라고 불린다. ⁷ᴬ단독 주택들로 이루어진 통근자 지역은 내부 도시에 존재하는 오염, 범죄, 그리고 다른 결함이 없는 넓은 생활 공간과 편의 시설을 제공한다.

5 버제스는 사람들이 내부지대로 이동하는 것을 '침입'이라고 불렀고, 중심으로부터 사람들이 흩어지는 것을 '천이'라고 불렀다. 두 용어 모두 식물 생태학 분야에서 차용한 것이다. 식물의 천이는 식물이 환경에 적응하고 환경을 개조하면서 생태계 구성에 일어나는 변화를 뜻한다. 인간에 있어서, 천이는 내부 도시의 주거지에 대한 부담과 땅과 같은 자원에 대한 경쟁으로부터 비롯된다. 이주할 여유가 있는 사람들은 외부로 이동하여 부가 계속 도시 외곽으로 옮겨가는 현상을 일으킨다.

6 그러나 훗날 사회학자들은 시카고 학파의 인구학적 모형의 한계점을 강조하였다. 비록 CZM이 시카고의 이른 확장을 설명해주긴 했지만, 다른 도시에 적용시켰을 때 항상 맞는 것은 아니다. 예를 들어 어떤 학자들은 로스앤젤레스가 동심원에 따라 발달하지 않았다는 사실을 지적하였다. 오히려, LA는 산재한 주변의 도시 사회 집단이 수도권을 지배하기 시작하면서 확장하였고, 내부 도시는 상대적으로 버려졌다.

어휘

disparate[díspərət] 다른　demographic[dìːməgrǽfik] 인구학의　mobilize[móubəlàiz] 동원하다

compile[kəmpáil] 수집하다　empirical[impírikəl] 경험적인　inquiry[inkwáiəri] 연구　epitomize[ipítəmàiz] 전형적으로 보여주다

concentric circle 동심원　premise[prémis] 전제　predictable[pridíktəbl] 예측 가능한　congregate[kɑ́ŋgrigèit] 모이다

infrastructure[ínfrəstrʌ̀ktʃər] 기본 시설　emerge[imə́ːrdʒ] 생기다　loop[luːp] 고리　variable[vɛ́əriəbl] 변수

status[stéitəs] 지위　deterioration[ditìəriəréiʃən] 퇴보　regeneration[ridʒènəréiʃən] 개혁　radical[rǽdikəl] 급진적인

cosmopolitan[kɑ̀zməpɑ́lətn] 세계적인　pursue[pərsúː] 찾다　suburb[sʌ́bəːrb] 교외　substantial[səbstǽnʃəl] 상당한

commuter[kəmjúːtər] 통근자　vice[vais] 결함　dispersal[dispə́ːrsəl] 흩어짐　succession[səkséʃən] 천이

affluence[ǽfluəns] 부　illuminate[ilúːmənèit] 설명하다, 해명하다　peripheral[pərífərəl] 주변의

CHAPTER 05 | Rhetorical Purpose

문제 공략하기 p.125

한 지역 고유의 세균과 곰팡이는 새, 곤충, 가축에 의해 다른 지역으로 옮겨질 수 있다. 이것이 양서류를 공격하는 것으로 알려져 있는 치명적인 전염성 곰팡이인 키트리드균이 최초로 수계에 들어가 여섯 대륙을 휩쓸며 현재까지 많은 종을 멸종시킨 방식으로 보인다. 곰팡이는 높은 온도에서 제대로 활동하지 못하므로, 질병의 전파는 시원한 숲과 산 지역에서 특히 빠르다.

HACKERS PRACTICE p.126

01 (A)   02 (C)   03 (A)   04 (C)   05 (A)   06 (B)   07 (C)   08 (A)   09 (A)   10 (A)   11 1. (B) 2. (D)
12 1. (C) 2. (B)   13 1. (C) 2. (A)

01 흑사병 혹은 선페스트는 시칠리아에서 1347년에 처음 등장한 병이다. 그 병은 너무나 전염성이 강해서 병든 사람과 이야기하는 것만으로 병에 걸렸다. 전염병의 희생자들에게는 혈관이 파괴되어 생긴 검은 반점이 나타났기 때문에 흑사병이라고 불렸다. 5년이라는 기간 동안 2천5백만 명의 사람들이 죽었는데, 이는 당시 유럽 인구의 3분의 1이었다. 병은 걷거나 말을 타고 이동하는 감염된 사람들에 의해 확산되었지만, 전염병의 시작은 유럽에 들끓었던 쥐들이었다.

02 사회가 기술적인 수준에서 발달하면, 가족은 변화에 효과적으로 대처하기 위해 종종 친족 관계를 조정할 필요가 있다. 농업 사회에서는 확대 가족이 표준이었는데, 이러한 형태의 가족은 음식, 옷, 집과 같은 필요물을 스스로 생산했기 때문이다. 이런 책무는 큰 가족의 지원을 필요로 했다. 그러나 산업 혁명은 생산자로서 확대 가족의 기능을 빼앗았다. 이는 공장의 지리적 위치와 더불어 가족이 아버지, 어머니, 그리고 아이들로 구성되는 '핵가족'이라는 더 작은 단위로 재구성되는 것을 필요하게 하였다.

03 콩은 아시아 음식의 주요 부분이다. 하지만 미국에서는 1999년에 식품의약국(FDA)에서 콩의 영양상 이점에 대한 연구결과를 발표하기 전까지 널리 소비되지 않았다. 이 기관은 콩이 완벽한 단백질 공급원이라고 했는데, 이는 몸에서 필요한 단백질을 형성하는 데 필요한 필수 아미노산을 이 채소가 모두 가지고 있다는 것을 의미한다. 콩 단백질의 질은 고기와 달걀의 것과 비슷하다. 이러한 이유 때문에, 채식주의자들은 콩과 식물을 동물성 제품의 훌륭한 대체품이라고 생각한다.

04 고전 연극은 전통적인 그리스 희극에 바탕을 둔 이야기로 가득하다. 유명한 예는 셰익스피어의 '한여름 밤의 꿈'으로, 희극적인 등장인물들이 극의 마지막에 즐거운 결혼잔치에 한데 모인다. 그리스에서 결혼식의 즐거운 노래와 춤을 'komos'라고 불렀는데, 이 단어에서 'comedy'가 유래했다. 본질적으로, 이러한 종류의 환락이 희극을 성공적으로 이끈 요소이다. 등장인물은 전형적으로 큰 결함이 있지만, 마지막에는 그들의 결점이 심각하기 보다는 우스꽝스럽게 묘사되었다.

05 장 피아제는 생물학자로 일을 시작했지만, 유기체 자체보다는 유기체를 연구하는 데 관련된 사고과정에 더 관심을 가지게 되었다. 지식이 어떻게 발달하는지에 대한 그의 호기심은 아이들이 어른들과 다르게 사고한다는 것을 알아차리면서 더욱 커졌다. 더 깊이 있는 이해를 얻기 위해, 그는 아이들을 유년기에서 청년기까지 관찰했고 그들의 지적 발달이 단계적으로 일어난다는 것을 발견하였다. 그들은 다음으로 배워야 하는 기술의 기본이 되는 새로운 기술을 배운다. 1개월에서 3개월까지, 유아는 물건을 입에 넣는 것을 배운다. 3개월에서 7개월까지는, 모든 물건들이 같은 방식으로 조작될 수

있는 것이 아니라는 것을 인식한다. 고무젖꼭지는 입에 넣을 수 있지만, 공과 같이 더 큰 동그란 모양의 물건은 넣을 수 없다.

---

06 고산 기후의 온도는 고도의 영향을 크게 받는다. 일반적인 법칙은 고도 1킬로미터당 온도가 6.5℃ 감소한다는 것이다. 그러나 기온역전이 일어나는 지역의 경우 이 법칙이 항상 성립하는 것은 아니다. 예를 들어, 깊은 골짜기에서 차가운 공기가 때때로 산을 타고 내려와서 아래에 쌓여, 더 따뜻한 공기 아래 차가운 공기 주머니가 생긴다. 그래도 비탈과 산 정상에서는 고도 법칙이 성립한다. 심지어 높은 산의 정상이 받는 강한 태양복사열도 온도를 높이는 데 큰 영향을 미치지 못하는데, 이는 높은 고도에서는 땅이 열을 흡수하기 위한 표면적이 적기 때문이다. 따라서, 주변 대기로 전달할 열이 적다.

---

07 풍화작용은 대개 사막과 흙이 마르고 질이 낮아진 지역에서 일어난다. 바람은 땅에 큰 변화를 가져올 정도로 강하다. 이 바람은 모래의 위층을 제거하는데, 이는 작물의 성장에 필수적인 흙, 유기물, 미사와 같은 물질로 구성되어 있다. 이 층의 손실은 농업 체제에 파괴적인 영향을 미치는데, 작물 수확량을 줄이고 식물과 식물의 생존 및 성장의 가능성을 퇴화시키고 살아남은 작물의 시장성을 저하시킨다. 농업 생산력은 Aeolian 바람이 흔한 세계의 다양한 지역들에서 영향을 받는다. 한 가지 주목할 만한 경우는 북미 대초원 지대의 '검은 폭풍'인데, 이것은 거의 1억 에이커 땅의 파괴를 야기했다.

---

08 종자식물의 생식 구성요소는 꽃인데, 이는 남성 생식 기관인 수술과 여성 생식 기관인 암술을 포함한다. 수술은 남성 생식 세포를 담고 있는 고운 가루 같은 물질인 꽃가루를 생성한다. 씨를 만들기 위해, 꽃가루는 수분이라는 과정을 통해 수술에서 암술로 운송되어야 한다. 이 과정은 암술에 의해 촉진되는데, 그것은 꽃가루를 즉시 받아들이는 끈적한 표면이 있기 때문이다. 이 가루는 때때로 꽃의 수술에서 암술로 바로 운송되는데, 이는 자가수분으로 알려져 있는 과정이다. 그러나 대개 꽃가루는 매개자에 의해 한 식물의 수술에서 다른 식물의 암술로 운송된다. 이것은 타화수분이며 더 건강한 식물을 생산하기 때문에 더 효율적인 방식이다. 그러므로 매개자는 식물 생식에 매우 중요한 역할을 하며, 가장 흔한 것은 벌이다.

---

09 인간이 아닌 동물 종들이 사랑, 갈망, 질투 그리고 비탄의 감정을 느낄 수 있을까? 이것은 동물 감정 해석의 불확실성 때문에 과학자들이 대답하기 힘들어하는 질문이다. 신경과학자들은 뇌의 기능을 측정하는 지식과 기술이 있지만, 뇌와 화학 신호가 개가 맞았을 때 고통을 느낀다는 것을 보여준다 해도, 이 과학자들은 개가 인간처럼 고통을 느끼는 것을 인식한다고 결론짓지 않을 것이다. 그들은 개가 특정 자극을 받았을 때 특정 방식으로 행동하도록 단순히 프로그램이 되어있다고 믿는 경향이 있다. 이 때문에, 연구원들은 동물이 기초적인 감정, 즉 두려움, 분노, 그리고 물리적인 고통으로 인한 정신적인 고통과 같은 본능적인 감정만 느낀다는 것에 동의한다. 그러나 사회의 많은 사람들, 특히 애완동물 주인들은 동물에게 인간적인 특징이 있다고 말하는 데 그렇게까지 주저하지 않는다.

---

10 지구는 따뜻한 기후와 추운 기후의 자연스러운 주기를 겪는다. 이런 주기 동안에, 물은 지배적인 기후에 따라 분포되고 저장된다. 이처럼, 기후 변화와 해수면은 밀접한 관련을 갖는다. 빙하기 또는 빙하시대라고 불리는 기온이 영하였던 시기에 물은 큰 수역에서 증발하여 비로 바다에 돌아가는 대신, 빙하, 만년설, 빙원에 얼음으로 저장된다. 결과적으로, 해수면의 높이는 낮아진다. 마지막으로 이랬던 시대는 약 2만년 전에 있었던 마지막 최대 빙하기로, 해수면은 현재보다 125미터가 낮았던 것으로 알려져 있다. 반대로, 따뜻해지는 경향이 있으면 얼음이 녹고 해수면이 올라간다. 과학자들은 매년 1밀리미터 정도의 안정적인 해수면 상승을 기록하고 있다.

---

11 동물들은 포식 동물에게 발견되는 것을 피하거나 같은 종의 다른 이들에게 위험하다는 것을 알리기 위해 위장을 사용한다. 가장 기본적인 위장의 형태는 주변에 맞게 착색하는 것이다. 어떤 유기체는 생물색소 또는 천연 안료를 피부 표면에 생산하는데, 이 안료는 유기체가 적절한 색을 갖도록 해준다. 어떤 안료는 더 깊은 곳에 있는 세포인 색소세포라는 곳에서 생산된다. 즉, 숲이 울창한 곳에 사는 동물은 주변의 색에 맞게 갈색을 얻을 수 있다. 계절이 바뀌는 장소에서는 동물이 주변의 변화에 적응할 수 있도록 해주는 신체적인 특징이 있다. 이것은 정글이든 사막이든 자신들이 전쟁하는 환경에 맞는 위장 군복을 입는 군인들과 비슷하다. 다른 종류의 착색은 대칭색으로, 털이나 깃털이 있는 동물이 이용하는 방법이다. 대칭색은 햇빛을 이용해 시각적인 혼란을 일으키는 착색 방법이다. 색조들이 서로 혼합되는 것처럼 보이

고, 동물의 모양과 조화되지 않는 무늬를 만든다. 이것은 동물의 윤곽을 주변의 무늬로부터 구별하는 것을 힘들게 한다. 예를 들면, 대낮에 숲 바닥에 앉아있는 점박이 새끼 사슴의 가죽은 햇빛이 나뭇잎에 군데군데 비치는 것과 더 흡사하게 보일 수 있다.

12 폴리네시아 섬들은 태평양 중심과 남부에 오세아니아라고 불리는 큰 섬의 집합을 구성하는 가장 큰 세 소구역 중 하나이다. 다른 소구역에 사는 작은 키의 피부가 검은 사람들과 달리 폴리네시아 사람들은 피부색이 더 옅고 키도 더 크다. 비록 오늘날의 과학자들은 폴리네시아가 남아시아의 문화에 식민지화되었다고 믿기도 하지만, 1800년대 후반과 1900년대 초반에 태평양을 여행한 유럽인들은 이집트인들이 폴리네시아에 살았다는 가설을 분명하게 표현했다. 그들은 오세아니아에 사람이 살았다고 믿어졌던 시기에 존재했던 문화가 이집트뿐이었기 때문에 이집트인들이 이 섬에 정착했다고 믿었다. 1970년대 후반에 연구원들은 폴리네시아의 일부 조각상의 눈에 색을 한 겹 칠한 것을 증거로 지적했다. 이집트인들은 그들의 조각상에 같은 기술을 사용하여 더 살아있는 것처럼 보이게 했다. 또한, 폴리네시아의 조인 의식은 이집트의 태양신 Ra의 알을 찾는 전통적인 의식 과제와 유사점을 갖고 있다. 그러나 태평양의 해류를 근거로 한 선박 표류 컴퓨터 시뮬레이션은 이집트인들이 폴리네시아에 우연히라도 도착하는 것이 불가능하므로 그들이 섬에 거주했을 리 없다는 것을 증명했다.

13 에버글레이즈 생태계는 미국 플로리다 남부의 3분의 1에 해당하는 커다란 담수 습지대이다. 에버글레이즈는 전세계에서 유일한데, 세계의 다른 필적할 만한 습지는 대부분 주기적인 강의 범람으로 채워지는 반면 이곳의 물은 거의 전적으로 대기의 강수로 공급되기 때문이다. 잘 알려진 것처럼 이 거대한 '풀의 강'은 매우 얕아서, 천천히 흐르는 물 때문에 풀이 표면 위에서 잔잔하게 흔들리는 것을 볼 수 있다. 그러나 이곳은 풀의 서식지 이상의 기능을 한다. 사실상, 다양한 습지 식물과 어마어마한 수의 섭금류를 자랑하는 다양한 생태를 가진다.

많은 야생 생물에 더하여, 에버글레이즈 지역은 농업적, 수문학적 자원으로 가치가 있다. 남동 연안의 거주자들에게 양질의 물을 공급하고, 수위가 조절되면 유기질이 풍부한 토양에서 사탕수수와 쌀과 같은 작물이 번성한다. 불행하게도, 이러한 혜택은 너무 빠르게 착취되어, 습지의 자연적인 생태균형을 변화시켰다. 에버글레이즈의 배수 지역은 기존의 크기가 줄었고, 새들을 떠나게 했으며, 농업 유출수에서 오는 높은 농도의 인은 식물을 바꾸어 놓았다.

HACKERS TEST

• 각 문제에 대한 정답단서는 지문에 초록색으로 표시되어 있습니다.

1 Hawaiian Island Biology 하와이 섬의 생태   p.134

1. (D)   2. (B)   3. (B)   4. (C)

1 태평양에 있는 많은 섬은 화산 활동을 통해 형성되었다. 초기 역사에서는 생명체가 섬에 존재하지 않았을 때가 있었지만, 오늘날 섬을 방문하는 사람들은 그곳에 생명체가 가득 차 있다는 것을 발견한다. 하와이의 섬이 그러한 예이다. 하와이에서는 수천 종의 식물과 동물이 나란히 번성하는 것을 볼 수 있지만 수백만 년 전에 섬이 생겼을 때는 풍경이 완전히 메말라 있었다. [1]그러면 애초에 어떻게 태평양 중간에 있는 고립된 화산암 지역을 생물들이 개척하게 되었을까?

2 개척이 수백만 년 동안 띄엄띄엄 일어났기 때문에, 정확히 언제 특정 생명체가 섬을 발견했다고 말하기 어렵다. 그러나 확실한 것은 하와이의 지리학적인 고립 때문에 섬에 처음 도달한 이들은 유능한 여행자들이었을 것이다. 즉, 분명히 장거리 분산을 위한 어떤 장치가 있었을 것이다. [3]코코넛 야자나무와 같은 식물의 씨는 물 위에 떠서 갔다. 다른 연안의 상록수 씨는 바람으로 운송되었다. 동물 중에서는 철새와 박쥐가 섬으로 쉽게 날아갔고, 대부분의 파충류와 양서류는 아마도 수영하거나 떠갔을 것이다. 어떤 유기체들은 대양횡단을 하기 위해 매체를 이용했다. [3]기생 곤충들과 가시 돋친 씨들은 새의 피부나 깃털에 달라붙어서 새에 '히치하이크'를 하였다. 작은 포유류들도 때때로 통나무 같이 떠다니는 물질을 뗏목으로 사용해 섬을 찾아왔다.

3 [4]덧붙이자면, 선구 종들은 낯선 환경의 도전에 맞서기 위해 잘 적응하거나 빨리 진화할 수 있어야 했다. 간단한 양치류와

잔디 같이 처음으로 화산 섬에 도착한 식물들은 흙이 적거나 없다는 특징을 가진 조건에 대처할 수 있어야 했을 것이고, 그늘이 없었기 때문에 강력한 태양복사열을 처음으로 견뎌야 했다. 동물들은 식량 자원을 찾아야 했을 것이고 가장 중요하게는 번식을 해야 했을 것이다. 새로운 섬 서식지에서 적응하고 번식하는 데 실패한 종들은 아주 사라졌을 것이다. 장거리 이동과 적응력이라는 조건의 조합은 성공적인 개척 시도가 극히 드물었음을 뜻했다. 예를 들면, 오직 몇백 개의 곤충 종들이 섬으로 자연적으로 찾아와서 생존했다고 믿어지는데, 평균적으로 75,000년에 겨우 하나 정도이다. 즉, 인간 활동 이전에 자연적인 개척 사건은 매우 드물었다.

어휘

volcanic[vɑlkǽnik] 화산의 teem[tiːm] 가득 차다 thrive[θraiv] 번성하다 barren[bǽrən] 메마른
intermittently[intərmítntli] 띄엄띄엄 coastal[kóustəl] 연안의 amphibian[æmfíbiən] 양서류 vehicle[víːikl] 매체
transoceanic[trænsouʃiǽnik] 대양횡단의 parasitic[pæ̀rəsítik] 기생적인 log[lɔːg] 통나무 raft[ræft] 뗏목
pioneer[pàiəníər] 선구적인 fern[fəːrn] 양치류 shade[ʃeid] 그늘 adaptive[ədǽptiv] 적응성의 vigor[vígər] 힘

2 Music of the Baroque Period 바로크 시대 음악

1. (A) 2. (C) 3. (A) 4. (D) 5. (C) 6. (B) 7. (D) 8. (D)

1 바로크 시대(1600~1750)가 음악사에서 혁명적인 시기였다고 주장하는 것은 과장이 아닐 것이며 그 시대에 대한 학문적인 설명도 풍부하다. 바로크 음악의 구별되는 특징은 합주곡에서 악기, 특히 바이올린군에 주어진 주된 역할이다. 바로크는 새로운 음악 장르를 낳은, 굉장한 창의성의 시대이기도 했다.

2 활을 사용하는 악기가 두드러지게 사용된 한 장르는 소나타였다. 이 용어는 바로크 양식과 관련하여 사용되었을 때 하나 또는 두 개의 악기(흔히 바이올린)를 위해 작곡된 혼합된 음악을 일컫는데, 전형적으로 하프시코드와 첼로가 곁들여졌다. [2]연주 목적으로 만들어진 소나타는 노래하기 위해 작곡된 칸타타와 대비되는 것으로 볼 수 있다. '칸타타'와 '소나타'라는 단어가 16세기 전에는 존재하지 않았다는 것도 주목할 만한데, 본래 르네상스 같이 더 이전의 시대에는 격식을 차린 음악은 대체적으로 노래를 하는 것으로 여겨졌기 때문이다. 즉, 칸타타는 꽤 오랫동안 존재해온 반면, 소나타는 바로크 시대만의 유일한 창조물이었다.

3 [3]요한 세바스찬 바흐 독일 작곡가이자 오르간 연주자(1685~1750)의 소나타는 교차하는 빠르고 느린 악장들로 성숙한 바로크 양식을 대표한다. 이 기악 작품들은 천천히 전개되는 서장과 활기찬 종악장 사이에 끼워진 일련의 대위선율이 특징이다. 대위선율은 개별적으로 다른 리듬으로 작곡되었지만 함께 연주되면 조화롭게 들리는 음악 선율이다. 이 기법을 사용한 음악을 대위법 음악이라고 한다. 대위법 음악은 바로크 음악에 복잡성을 가져다 주었다. 홀로 연주되는 단일 멜로디는 하나의 감정을 표현하는 것으로 생각되었는데, 하나 이상의 멜로디를 동시에 혼합하면서 작곡가들은 반어와 같은 복잡한 생각을 음악으로 전달할 수 있게 되었다.

4 콘체르토라는 다른 혼합된 형식은 오케스트라가 모습을 갖추기 시작하면서 생겨났다. '콘체르토'라는 단어는 '모이다'라는 뜻이고 두 가지 상반되는 요소들을 하나로 혼합하는 데 사용된 장르를 말한다. [4A/C]보통, 이 3악장의 음악작품은 바이올린 독주자와 더 큰 악기의 합주곡을 포함했다. [4B]당시 오케스트라는 주로 현악기로 구성되었지만, 때때로 목관 악기나 호른이 하나 둘씩 더해졌다. 이탈리아 작곡가이자 바이올린 연주자 안토니오 비발디의 '사계'는 1725년에 발표된 4개의 독립적인 콘체르토 모음인데, 바로크 음악의 가장 유명하고 사랑 받는 예 중 하나이다. 그것은 두 개의 빠른 악장 사이에 느린 악장이 있는 것으로 작곡된 4개의 곡을 포함한다. 비발디는 바이올린 콘체르토를 4편의 시와 어울리도록 작곡했는데, 이 시들은 봄, 여름, 가을, 겨울의 풍경과 소리를 상세하게 묘사한다. [5]비발디의 콘체르토는 자연계의 이미지를 묘사하기 위해 작곡된 곡인 표제 음악으로 알려지게 된 것의 선례이다. 예를 들면 '여름'이라고 제목이 붙여진 곡의 마지막 악장에서는 뇌우의 발생을 음악적으로 표현한다.

5 춤, 악기, 목소리를 겸비한 극적인 공연인 오페라도 바로크 시대에 생겨났다. 오페라는 이탈리아에서 작곡가 야코포 페리로부터 시작되었고 곧 다른 나라 작곡가들에 의해 받아들여졌다. 이 새로운 종류의 음악 공연은 시적인 글을 이야기 형태

300 토플 인강·단어암기 MP3 HackersIngang.com

로 선율적으로 노래할 수 있게 하였다. 오페라 공연에서 배경음악은 관중을 이런저런 감정으로 동요시켜 강한 감정을 떠올리게 하는 데 자주 사용되었다. [7]주로 개인의 집의 응접실이나 교회에서 연주된 콘체르토와 소나타와는 달리 오페라는 돈을 내는 관중들에게 개방된 공공 극장 공연이었다. 그렇기 때문에, 오페라는 대중이 복잡한 악곡을 처음으로 경험하게 하는 것을 도왔다.

6 바로크 시대의 새로운 장르들은 우연적이지 않았다. 새로운 음악 형태가 생겨난 지적인 세계는 굉장히 창의적이었다. 훌륭한 철학자들처럼, 바로크 작곡가들은 인간 정신의 합리성에 대한 믿음을 공유했고, 어떤 이들은 아직도 클래식 음악계의 거장으로 여겨진다. 결과적으로, 그들의 작품은 그들의 죽음이 수세기 지난 후에도 세계의 심포니 홀에서 계속 연주되고 있다. 바흐와 비발디 같은 천재들의 끊임없는 명성과 영향력은 음악사에서 바로크 시대의 중요성을 나타내는 증거이다.

Glossary
악장: 특유의 구조, 리듬, 조를 가지는 확장된 악곡의 부분을 이루는 고유 단위

어휘
exaggeration[igzæ̀dʒəréiʃən] 과장 revolutionary[rèvəlúːʃəneri] 혁명적인 plentiful[pléntifəl] 풍부한
principal[prínsəpəl] 주된 ensemble[ɑːnsɑ́ːmbl] 합주곡 prominently[prɑ́mənəntli] 두드러지게 notable[nóutəbl] 주목할 만한
essentially[isénʃəli] 본래 alternate[ɔ́ːltərnèit] 교차하다 counterpoint[káuntərpɔ̀int] 대위법
sandwich[sǽndwitʃ] 사이에 끼우다 contrapuntal[kɑ̀ntrəpʌ́ntl] 대위법의 simultaneously[sàiməltéiniəsli] 동시에
convey[kənvéi] 전달하다 complicated[kɑ́mpləkèitid] 복잡한 woodwind[wúdwìnd] 목관 악기 depict[dipíkt] 묘사하다
vocalize[vóukəlàiz] 노래하다 narrative[nǽrətiv] 이야기식의 employ[implɔ́i] 사용하다 evoke[ivóuk] 떠올리다
spectacle[spéktəkl] 공연 introduce[ìntrədjúːs] 처음으로 경험하게 하다 accidental[æ̀ksədéntl] 우연적인
intellectual[ìntəléktʃuəl] 지적인 rationality[ræ̀ʃənǽləti] 합리성 persistent[pərsístənt] 끊임없는 testament[téstəmənt] 증거

3 Earth's Core 지구의 핵
p.139

1. (A)   2. (B)   3. (D)   4. (C)   5. (B)   6. (A)   7. (B)   8. (A)

1 지진학자들은 한때 지구의 핵이 완전히 녹아 있다고 믿었다. 그들은 지진에서 방출되는 횡파(S파)가 지구 반대편에서는 감지될 수 없다는 사실에 이 추측의 근거를 두었다. 이는 S파가 액체를 통과하지 못하기 때문이다. 반면, 액체를 통과할 수 있는 종파(P파)는 감지될 수 있었으므로 핵이 녹아 있다고 추측하는 것은 논리적이었다.

2 [1]그러나 이후의 연구는 이 가설에 의심을 불러일으켰다. 1929년에 지진파를 연구하던 덴마크 지진학자 잉게 레만은 P파, 즉 메아리의 간접적인 신호가 내부 경계선의 일부에서 빗나가는 것처럼 보이는 것에 주목했다. 그녀는 핵 내부의 불연속성, 즉 구성의 변화를 이에 대한 원인으로 보았다. 1936년에 'P 프라임'이라고 간단하게 알려져 있는 논문에서 그녀는 지구의 핵을 고체와 액체 층이 있는 것으로 설명했다. 레만이 처음으로 내핵과 외핵의 존재를 입증했기 때문에, 그 둘 사이를 가르는 선은 레만의 불연속면이라고 알려졌다. 레만의 가설은 1970년대에 더더욱 정교한 지진 계측기들이 생기고 지진학 자료가 수집되면서 널리 받아들여졌다. 레만 이후에 과학자들은 핵의 물리적인 특성에 대해 많은 것을 배웠다.

3 [2]지구의 내부는 양파와 같이 겹으로 쌓여 있다. [3]이는 중력이 밀도에 따라 원소를 분류하였기 때문이다. 지각 밑 2,900킬로미터의 지구 깊숙한 곳에는 핵이 있는데, 이것은 밀도가 굉장히 큰 고체로 된 내부와 용해된 외부 층으로 이루어져 있다. 내핵은 반지름이 1,255킬로미터이고 거의 철과 니켈로 이루어졌는데, 이 무거운 요소들은 위에 있는 녹은 금속과 고체 바위의 무게 때문에 극도의 압력을 받는다. 내핵의 온도는 태양의 표면 온도와 비슷하며 4,500℃와 5,500℃ 사이이다. 구성 물질의 압력, 온도, 그리고 밀도는 고체 내핵에서 나올수록 약 반으로 줄어들고, 무거운 금속 또한 외핵의 많은 부분을 차지하지만, 그곳에서 녹은 형태로 존재한다. 규소와 수소 또한 소량 존재한다. 이렇게 더 가벼운 성분들은 외핵의 상한 쪽으로 움직이다가 때때로 맨틀 아래에서 굳을 수도 있다.

4 [4]내핵과 외핵 사이의 이런 차이 때문에 그 둘 사이의 동적인 관계가 생기는데, 지구 핵 내부 힘의 상호작용은 지구 표면에 엄청난 영향을 준다. 내핵과 외핵이 회전하면서, 외핵에 있는 액체가 순환하며 뜨거운 수프와 같은 조합물 안에 온도 변화

를 일으킨다. 일부 열은 윗층으로 새나가는데 결국 대류 또는 전도를 통해 표면으로 가는 길을 찾는다. 이 열 이동은 판구조론의 주된 원인이며, 대륙을 움직이고, 산을 만들고, 지진과 화산의 형성을 일으킨다.

5 또한, 내핵은 외핵에 의해 지구의 윗층들로부터 격리되어 있으므로, 지구의 나머지 부분보다 더 빠르게 회전한다. [5A/D]내핵과 외핵의 회전의 차이는 전류를 일으켜 내핵과 외핵 사이의 경계가 지속적으로 융해, 응고되는 결과를 초래한다. [5C]이 활동은 엄청난 에너지 방출을 초래하고 지구의 자기장이 생기게 한다. 태양에서 우주로 뿌려진 대전 입자의 흐름인 태양풍으로부터 지구를 지켜주는 것이 바로 자기장이다. 그것은 나침반을 이용한 항해를 가능하게 하는 힘이기도 한데, 자기가 남극과 북극에서 더 강하기 때문에 자기를 띠는 나침반의 침을 주어진 극으로 당긴다.

6 비록 지구와 우주에 대한 핵의 영향이 지속되고 있지만, 이는 변하기 쉽다. 지각 운동이 어떤 곳에서는 다른 곳보다 더 강하고 일정한 패턴이나 간격을 두고 일어나지 않듯이, 지구의 자기장은 지역에 따라 강도가 달라지고 시간이 흐름에 따라 변한다. 실제로, 과거에 자기장의 방향이 여러 번 뒤바뀌었다. 이러한 변화는 핵의 깊숙한 곳에서 발생하는 변화에 따른 직접적인 결과이다.

어휘

seismologist[saizmάlədʒist] 지진학자 core[kɔːr] 핵 assumption[əsʌ́mpʃən] 추측 emanate[émənèit] 방출하다
detect[ditékt] 감지하다 reasonable[ríːzənəbl] 논리적인 hypothesis[haipάθəsis] 가설 deflect[diflékt] 빗나가다
discontinuity[dìskɑntənjúːəti] 불연속성 compile[kəmpáil] 수집하다 sort[sɔːrt] 분류하다 crust[krʌst] 지각
radius[réidiəs] 반지름 approximately[əprάksəmətli] 약 constitute[kάnstətjùːt] 구성하다 dynamic[dainǽmik] 동적인
interaction[ìntərǽkʃən] 상호작용 profound[prəfáund] 엄청난, 의미심장한 implication[ìmplikéiʃən] 영향
concoction[kɑnkάkʃən] 조합물 conduction[kəndʌ́kʃən] 전도 convection[kənvékʃən] 대류 intensity[inténsəti] 강도
reverse[rivə́ːrs] 뒤바뀌다

문제 공략하기
p.147

1970년대 중반에 과학자들은 개울에 서식하는 개구리 두 종, 'Rheobatrachus silus'와 'Rheobatrachus vitellinus'를 호주 동부의 열대 다우림에서 발견했다. 이러한 하얀색 또는 크림색 개구리들은 다른 양서류 사이에서는 알려지지 않은 생식 습성을 가지고 있는 것으로 밝혀졌다. 수정 후에, 암컷 개구리는 알을 삼키고 뱃속에 보관한다. 부화 기간 동안 소화가 완전히 중단되고 위액은 분비되지 않는다. 약 한 달 후, 암컷은 부화한 올챙이들을 얕은 수역에 뱉어내고 그곳에서 올챙이들은 천천히 자라고 성숙한다.

HACKERS PRACTICE
p.148

01 (A)   02 (C)   03 (B)   04 (B)   05 (C)   06 (A)   07 (C)   08 (C)   09 1. (C) 2. (B)   10 1. (A) 2. (B)
11 1. (C) 2. (D)   12 1. (C) 2. (A)

01 아즈텍 사람들은 금이나 은보다 코코아 나무 열매를 더 높이 평가하였고, 코코아는 제국에서 통화의 형태로 사용되었다. 그러나 아즈텍의 기후는 너무 차갑고 건조하여 코코아를 재배할 수 없었으므로 다른 지역에서 얻어야 했다. 그들은 다른 민족을 정복하고 코코아로 조공을 요구함으로써 이를 달성하였다. 저지대 지역 사람들은 코코아를 재배하였고 이것은 고무와 무명 같은 다른 품목들과 함께 아즈텍의 수도로 보내졌다.

02 1960년대 후반, 캘리포니아 대학교의 심해 굴착 계획의 일부로 수행된 지중해 해저에 관한 연구는 해저에서 흔히 마주치지 않는 물리적인 특징을 밝혀냈다. 과학자들은 모래, 자갈, 진흙이 해저에 자연적으로 쌓이는 퇴적물이기 때문에 이들을 발견할 거라고 예상하였다. 대신에 그들은 암염, 석고, 해양 현무암과 같은 증발광상을 발견하였다. 이 물질들은 물이 완전히 증발된 지표면에서만 형성된다. 더 깊이 뚫음으로써, 과학자들은 식물이 성장할 수 있는 충분한 빛이 있는 해수면에서만 사는 식물인 청녹조의 화석을 발견하였다. 이는 일부 과학자들로 하여금 지중해가 한때는 얕은 수역이었거나 심지어 언젠가는 건조한 사막이었을지도 모른다고 주장하게 하였다.

03 1543년에 중국 배가 항로를 이탈하여 일본 해안에 닿았다. 배에 타고 있었던 사람들은 3명의 포르투갈 상인들로 머스킷총이라고 불리는 화기를 가지고 왔다. 일본인들은 이 낯선 무기에 호기심이 생겼고 재빨리 장인과 제강소 직공을 소집하여 그것을 연구하고 생산 과정을 습득하도록 하였다. 이미 잘 발달된 야금 공업이 있었던 일본은 그 총을 모방할 수 있었고 곧 전쟁에 도입하였다. 최초로 이 새로운 무기를 결정적인 전투에서 성공적으로 사용한 사람은 군 지도자 노부나가였는데, 그는 일본 전쟁사의 전환점으로 널리 여겨지는 1575년 나가시노 전투에서 3천 명의 보병에게 머스킷총을 갖추게 했다.

04 태평양 연안 지방의 아메리카삼나무('Sequoia sempervirens')는 캘리포니아 북부 해안을 따라 나타나고, 침엽수 나무 과인 Cupressaceae의 한 종이다. 아메리카 삼나무는 평균 150피트 높이로 지구에서 생존하는 가장 큰 나무이며, 일부는 350피트 이상의 높이까지 자라기도 하였다. 개별 나무의 무게는 500톤까지 달하며 평균 지름은 14피트에 달한다. 아메리카 삼나무는 최대 2,000년 정도 살며, 죽기 전까지 계속 성장한다. 그러나 100년에 달했을 때 길이 생장은 상당히 느려지는데, 이는 영양소와 물을 줄기를 따라 올려 보내는 과정이 더 어려워지기 때문이다. 성장 에너지의 많은 부분은 대신 반지름의 확장에 쓰인다.

05 인간의 유대는 일반적으로 부모자녀 관계와 관련된다. 예를 들어 어머니는 대체로 갓난 아기 삶의 초기 단계에서 아이들과 강한 애착을 형성한다. 어머니의 유대는 임신 기간에 시작되어 출산 후 모유 수유 기간 동안 지속된다. 이러한 애착에는 신체적 근거가 있는데, 어머니는 사실상 임신 중, 후에 신체 화학적 변화를 경험하며, 이 변화가 모성적 행동을 촉진한다고 알려져 있다. 시간이 지남에 따라, 감정적 혹은 애정적 유대가 생겨난다. 이것은 어머니와 아이 간의 친밀하고 한결같은 접촉으로 인해 발생하며 이끌림의 감정이 되어, 어머니와 아이가 떨어져 있을 때 어머니는 아이를 그리워하게 된다. 끈끈한 애정적 유대는 아버지와 아이 사이에서도 껴안기, 달래기, 놀기와 같은 활동을 통해 생겨난다. 아버지와 아이의 일생 내내 이러한 유대가 계속해서 강화되며 안전과 편안함의 감정과 밀접하게 연관된다.

06 판게아 이론은 알프레트 로타르 베게너에 의해 1920년 그의 저서 '대륙과 대양의 기원'에서 처음으로 주장되었다. 베게너는 약 2억 5천만 년 전에 초대륙 판게아가 개별적인 큰 땅덩어리들로부터 형성되었다고 주장하였다. 그는 대륙 이동에 관한 그의 이론으로 그 주장을 뒷받침하였다. 대륙은 암류권과 암석권으로 구성된 층인 지구의 외부맨틀에 위치했기 때문에 움직일 수 있었다. 암석권은 암류권에 떠 있는 몇 개의 큰 암석 판으로 구성되는데, 암류권은 걸쭉하게 녹은 진흙 강처럼 매우 느리게 흐르는 뜨거운 맨틀 층이다. 판의 움직임은 대륙을 같이 밀어서 판게아를 형성하게 하였는데, 이는 오늘날 지구에 존재하는 대륙으로 나뉘기 전에 고생대와 중생대에 약 1억 년간 존재하였다. 판게아는 처음에 로라시아, 곤드와나라고 불리는 두 개의 거대한 대륙으로 나뉘었는데, 로라시아는 대략 오늘날의 북반구와 일치하고, 곤드와나는 결국 남반구를 형성하게 되었다. 두 개의 대륙은 지구의 일곱 대륙으로 더 나누어졌다.

07 지중해 세계 최초의 희곡 형태는 종교적 목적으로 행해졌던 의식 공연이었다. 이러한 공연들은 사람들이 역사적 사실로 받아들였던 신화에 바탕을 두고 있었다. 종종 이 신화는 신의 창조력과 관련이 있었고 의식 공연은 특정 신이 행한 일을 반복함으로써 사람들이 신화를 재현하는 길을 제공했다. 신의 행위를 의식적으로 연기해냄으로써, 참가자들은 신과 같이 될 수 있었고 우주를 지배하는 마법을 일시적으로 즐길 수 있었다. 가장 유명한 사례는 기원전 700년 즈음 고대 그리스에 자연신 디오니소스 숭배가 성행하면서 발생하였다. 헌신적인 신봉자들이 신에게 경의를 표하며 춤추고 노래하였고, 이 공연은 항상 숭배자 집단 구성원들의 제창으로 행해졌는데, 이들은 집단으로 합창단을 구성했다. 이 양식은 6세기경까지 지속되었는데, 이때 디오니소스 성직자 테스피스가 합창에서 탈피하여 노래보다는 대담을 통해 신화를 표현해내기 시작했다. 배우의 극적 역할을 창조하고 그리스 극작가 시대의 도래를 알렸던 것은 바로 그의 혁신이었다.

08 혜성은 태양 주위를 타원 궤도로 움직인다. 태양으로부터 멀리 떨어진 혜성은 핵으로 구성된 머리를 가진다. 일반적으로 지름이 10킬로미터 이하인 핵은 혜성이 태양에서 떨어져 있을 때 결빙한 구형의 기체와 먼지로 존재한다. 혜성이 태양 가까이 갈수록, 핵은 가열되기 시작하고 휘발성 기체가 증발하여 '코마'라고 불리는 흩어진 물질로 이루어진 구름을 형성한다. 먼지 입자가 태양의 전자기 방사선을 반사시키고 기체 분자가 자외선을 흡수하면서 코마는 빛을 내게 된다. 태양풍은 핵과 코마로부터 먼지 입자와 기체를 불어, 태양 반대쪽으로 꼬리가 생기게 한다. 혜성의 궤도는 혜성을 태양 가까이로 이끌어서 육안으로는 머리와 꼬리를 모두 감지하는 것을 어렵게 한다. 혜성의 크기와 모양은 바뀌기 시작하며, 비엘라 혜성이 1846년에 그랬듯이 때때로 두 개로 나뉜다. 혜성은 태양에 가까이 갈 때마다 물질을 잃는다. 결국 혜성은 여러 개의 조각으로 나뉘어 지구로 떨어지거나 우주로 날아간다.

09 농업 생산은 멕시코부터 현재의 온두라스까지 뻗어 있었던 마야 문명의 많은 인구를 지탱하는 데 필수적이었다. 종종 도시는 농업 생산에 도움이 되지 않는 지역에 위치했지만 마야인들은 어려운 조건에 대처하는 선진 농업 생산 방법을 개발하였다. 그들은 빗물을 저장하는 댐과 저수지, 메마른 지역의 농토에 물을 대기 위한 수로 체계를 만들었다. 습지에서는 식물 뿌리가 과다한 물에 노출되는 것을 막기 위해 물을 빼고 땅을 높이는 기술을 수행하였다. 숲이 우거진 지역에서는 일부 사람들은 화전 농업을 실행한 반면 다른 이들은 비옥한 목초지를 찾아 주기적으로 이동하였다.

마야인들의 능숙한 농업 기술 덕분에 그들은 제국의 도처에서 교환되고 분배될 다양한 작물을 여러 지역에서 기를 수 있었다. 마야인의 식품은 대부분 주식인 옥수수, 호박, 콩, 고추로 구성되었으나 과일, 카카오, 해바라기 씨, 꿀 또한 적정량 사용되었다. 이러한 음식은 때때로 육류로 보충되었는데, 그것은 수렵과 어로로 획득된 것이었다. 요리에 맛을 내기 위해 마야인들은 양파, 계피, 오레가노, 바닐라, 소금을 포함한 다양한 향신료를 사용하였다. 소모 상품 외에 마야인들은 또한 방직용 목화를 재배하였고 고무액을 받았는데, 이 고무액의 라텍스는 공을 만들거나 심지어 기초적인 장신구나 옷을 만드는 데까지도 사용되었다.

10   홍적세는 가장 최근의 세계적 규모의 빙하시대였고, 몇 개의 빙결 또는 빙하의 확장 기간으로 특징지어진다. 이 시기의 기후 변화는 많은 동식물 종에게 파괴적인 결과를 가져왔다. 지구의 극, 특히 북극으로부터 빙하가 발전하면서 매머드, 마스토돈, 검치 호랑이, 거대한 대륙성 나무늘보와 비버, 사향 황소, 일부 낙타와 말 종 등 많은 큰 포유류가 멸종되었다. 북미에서만 32개 속의 큰 포유류가 사라졌다. 일반적으로, 더 작은 포유류는 멸종 과정에서 살아남았다. 과학자들은 이에 대한 원인을 입증하지는 못 했지만, 일부 생물학자들은 그들이 살아남은 이유를 급속한 성장과 한 번의 짝짓기 시기 동안 많은 수의 자손을 낳을 수 있는 능력의 결과로 본다. 대조적으로, 더 큰 포유류는 성적인 성숙에 도달하는 데 더 긴 시간이 걸리고, 종종 한번에 하나만 혹은 적은 자손을 낳는다. 게다가, 더 큰 육식 동물은 특정 먹이 종이 멸종했을 때 생계 수단을 찾는 데 큰 어려움이 있었다. 반면, 많은 더 작은 포유류는 잡식성이거나 초식성이었다. 생존한 동물들은 극심한 추위를 피하기 위해서뿐만 아니라 빙하가 남쪽으로 확장하면서 옮겨진 식물 지대에 다다르기 위해서 이동하였다. 토양 연구는 보통 북부 지역에서 자라는 전나무와 소나무 숲이 심지어 유럽 지중해 지역과 북미 루이지애나의 북부까지 확장되었음을 시사한다.

11   그리스와 로마인들이 만든 고전적인 조각상과 비교했을 때 고대 이집트의 조각상은 부자연스럽고 왜곡되어 보인다. 고전적인 그리스 조각상은 종종 움직이는 것처럼 자세를 취한 인간으로 다양한 인간의 감정과 움직임의 굉장한 자유를 나타낸다. 반면, 이집트 조각상은 뻣뻣한 자세를 취하는데, 머리와 몸이 앞쪽 이외의 방향은 바라보지 않으며 팔은 옆구리 가까이 놓인다. 얼굴은 표정이 없다. 이집트 조각상의 또 다른 특징은 특이한 비례이다. 이집트인들은 인간의 해부학적 구조에 정통했으나 신체의 일부분만이 현실적인 방법으로 묘사되었다. 목 아래의 신체 부위는 상대적으로 인간 형태에 충실했으나 머리 그리고 때때로 발은 불균형적으로 컸다.

본질적으로, 고대 이집트의 세 번째 왕조(대략 기원전 2690~2575년) 동안의 조각은 특정한 목적을 위해 만들어졌는데, 이는 인간이 어떻게 묘사되었는지에 큰 영향을 미쳤다. 조각상은 종종 신전과 무덤에서 행해지는 의식을 위해 사용되었으며, 왕과 신을 상징하는 조각상은 앞을 보게 할 필요가 있었는데, 이러한 묘사를 정면성이라고 한다. 이는 조각상이 의식을 행하는 이집트인들을 '볼' 수 있게 하였다. 최상류층 남자 조각상 또한 의식 중에 제물을 받기 위해 앞을 바라보았다. 네 번째 왕조 때에서야 하인의 묘사가 장식을 위해 추가되어 삶에서의 지위를 나타내기 위해 곡물을 빻고 빨래를 하는 등 다양한 일에 열중한 모습으로 표현되었다.

12   1725년에 시작된 살롱은 파리 미술 아카데미의 공식 미술 전시회였다. 그것은 곧 프랑스에서 가장 중요한 미술 전시회일 뿐만 아니라 세계에서 가장 성대한 미술 행사가 되었다. 살롱의 일차적 초점은 아카데미 졸업생의 작품을 소개하는 것이었다. 그것은 루브르 미술관에서 열렸고, 처음에는 아카데미 회원들이나 사회 최상류층 사람들에게만 공개되었다. 1737년이 되어서야 전시회가 공개 행사가 되어 매해 두 번씩 몇 주 동안 개최되었다. 모두 수상 작가들인 심사원단이 1748년에 도입되었다. 그들의 주요 책임은 어떤 미술 작품이 전시될 것인지 결정하는 것이었다.

살롱은 프랑스 미술계에 명백한 영향력을 행사하였고 그것의 막대한 힘과 영향력은 후에 좋지 않은 평을 받았다. 심사원들은 보수적인 학문 환경에서 교육을 받았기 때문에 훌륭한 미술의 구성 요소에 대한 그들의 이해는 매우 편협하였다. 그들은 인상주의 작품을 끊임없이 탈락시켰고 예술적 실험으로 명성을 얻는 데 관심이 있었던 미술가들을 화나게 했다. 거절당한 미술가들의 수가 1863년에 특히 많았고, 불만이 대중 매체를 통해 활자화되어 선발 체계의 공정성을 둘러싼 대중의 소동을 불러일으켰다. 이에 대응하여, 나폴레옹 황제 3세가 모든 거절당한 미술가들이 살롱의 별관에서 그림을 전시할 수 있도록 허가할 것을 명령했다. Salon des Refusés(불합격자의 전시회)라는 이 전시는 5월 17일에 많은 대중에게 공개되었으며 아방가르드의 탄생을 상징했다.

HACKERS TEST

* 각 문제에 대한 정답단서는 지문에 초록색으로 표시되어 있습니다.

1 The Founding of Londinium 론디니움의 건설

p.156

1. (C)	2. (A)	3. (A)	4. (C)

1 　43년, 로마 제국을 확장하려고 하던 로마 군인들은 현재 영국으로 알려진 섬 나라 브리타니아에 들어갔다. 그 후, 47년경에 로마인들은 템스 강변의 고요한 땅 위 자연 그대로의 완만한 언덕에 도시를 건설하였다. 오늘날의 런던 지역에 세워진 이 도시는 로마인들에게 라틴어 이름 론디니움으로 알려져 있었다.

2 　론디니움의 정확한 배치는 아마도 좋은 위치 때문이었을 것이다. 그곳에서 강은 바다로 가는 배를 지탱할 만큼 충분히 넓고 깊었으며, 다리를 건설할 만큼 충분히 좁았다. 일부 학자들은 이곳이 원래 군사 전초기지로 여겨졌다고 믿으나, 고고학적 발굴에서 초기 요새는 거의 발굴되지 않았다. 게다가, ¹그곳이 설립 후 1세기도 안 되었을 때 주로 민간 도시로 기능했다는 것을 제시하는 증거가 있다. 옷을 짜는 베틀, 원형극장, 지하 관개 시설, 동전의 발견은 모두 신흥 국가의 상업적 생기를 증명한다. 가죽 세공소, 도기 제조소, 제분소와 다른 공장이 도시 근처에 산발적으로 생겨났고, 도시 중심부의 광장에는 많은 상점이 있었다.

3 　역사문서 또한 신흥 도시 론디니움이 주로 민간 도시였다는 의견을 뒷받침한다. 109년 로마 역사가 타키투스는 론디니움을 '교역과 상인을 위한 분주한 상업 중심지'로 묘사했다. ³그는 또한 60년에 론디니움의 북동부 지역에 거주한 이케니부족의 여왕 부디카가 브리타니아 남동부의 로마 도시에 대항하는 반란을 일으켜 로마 마을을 약탈하고 론디니움을 포함한 전체 공동체를 잿더미로 만들었다고 기록했다. 그녀의 성공은 침입 당시 아마도 도시가 잘 요새화되지 않았다는 것을 나타낸다. 더욱이, 사료에 따르면 부디카의 침입 이후 론디니움의 재건은 로마 속주 브리타니아의 재정 장관이었던 Gaius Alpinus Classicianus의 직접적인 감독 아래 완수되었다. 이 사실은 론디니움에서 문관에게 최고의 권력과 책임이 부과되었다는 것을 나타낸다.

4 　최초에 왜 설립되었는지에 상관없이, 론디니움은 곧 제조와 교역에 종사하는 정착자들을 끌어들였고, 도시는 브리타니아와 본토의 로마 식민지 간의 교역에 중요한 상업 중심지가 되었다. ⁴2세기 중반에 이르러, 론디니움은 작은 지방 도시에서 5만 명에 가까운 사람들로 구성된 도시로 커졌다. 그러나 그 후 도시는 알 수 없는 이유로 쇠퇴하였고, 중세 시대의 론디니움에 대해서는 알려진 바가 거의 없다.

어휘
pristine[prístiːn] 자연 그대로의　rolling[róuliŋ] 완만한　favorable[féivərəbl] 좋은　conceive[kənsíːv] 여겨지다
fortification[fɔ̀ːrtəfikéiʃən] 요새　unearth[ʌnə́ːrθ] 발굴하다　archaeological[àːrkiəládʒikəl] 고고학의
excavation[èkskəvéiʃən] 발굴　loom[luːm] 베틀　amphitheater[ǽmfəθìːətər] 원형극장　irrigation[ìrəgéiʃən] 관개
attest[ətést] 증명하다　vivacity[vivǽsəti] 생기　sporadically[spərǽdikəli] 산발적으로　score[skɔːr] 많음
colonize[kálənàiz] ~에 거주하다　revolt[rivóult] 반란　sack[sæk] 약탈하다　supervision[sùːpərvíʒən] 감독
province[právins] 속주(고대 로마의 지배를 받던 국외의 토지)　utmost[ʌ́tmòust] 최고의　hub[hʌb] 중심지

2 Identification of Minerals 광물 감별

p.158

1. (A)	2. (A)	3. (D)	4. (B)	5. (C)	6. (B)	7. (A)	8. (A)

1 　지구의 고체 물질 중 다수는 광물로 이루어져 있는데, 광물은 반복되는 패턴으로 배열된 원자의 결정 구조를 가진 물질로 정의된다. 가장 정교한 광물은 거의 완벽하게 대칭인데, 이 특성은 반짝이는 색과 함께 그들을 매우 가치 있게 한다. 광물학자들이 광물을 식별하고 이해하도록 하는 몇 가지 구별되는 특징이 있다.

2 육안으로는 다양한 광물들이 종종 똑같아 보인다. 예를 들면, 석영과 다이아몬드는 투명한 형태를 갖고 있고 심지어 유리 같은 비광물과도 헷갈릴 수 있다. 게다가, 불순물이 광물의 색을 포함한 외양에 영향을 미칠 수 있다. 다이아몬드는 굉장히 강하고 유일한 결정 구조를 가지는데, 이는 단단히 접합되어 있는 탄소 원자에 침투할 수 있는 원소가 거의 없다는 뜻이다. 그러나 침투할 수 있는 몇 가지 원소(질소, 수소, 붕소)가 원래 무색인 다이아몬드를 다른 빛깔을 띠게 만든다. 어떤 광물은 색이 같고 [2]광물 속 불순물의 존재가 빛깔을 바꿀 수 있기 때문에 광물의 색만으로는 아주 효과적인 구별 방법이 될 수 없다.

3 더 좋은 방법은 조흔 검사를 이용하는 것이다. 가루 형태일 때의 광물의 색을 조흔이라고 한다. 조흔은 두 가지 방법으로 측정될 수 있다. 광물은 조흔판이라고 불리는 딱딱한 자기 위에 대고 긁거나 가루로 만들 수 있다. 전자가 대부분의 광물에 쓰이는 가장 흔한 방법인데, 쉽고 덜 파괴적이기 때문이다. 조흔판에 남아있는 광물 가루의 색깔은 대개 불순물에 영향을 받지 않는데, 광물의 미세한 가루에서는 불순물이 빛을 강하게 흡수, 투과, 또는 반사하지 않기 때문이다. 결과적으로, 조흔색은 광물의 색보다 더 신뢰할 수 있는 식별 방법이다. 색이 매우 다양할 수 있는 방해석은 언제나 하얀색 조흔을 가진다. [3]철을 기반으로 하는 적철광과 자철광은 종종 비슷한 어두운 회색을 띠어 때때로 시각적으로 구별하기 힘들 수 있지만, 조흔은 확실하게 다르다. 자철광은 어두운 회색 조흔을 낸다. 반면, 적철광의 조흔은 어두운 붉은 갈색이다.

4 광물들의 상대적인 경도도 그것들을 구분하는 유용한 특징이다. 경도를 측정하기 위해 사용되는 등급은 모스 경도로 알려져 있는데, 그것의 고안자이자 독일의 광물학자인 프리드리히 모스의 이름을 딴 것이다. [4]모스 경도는 알려진 광물의 경도 범위를 나타내는 10가지 예를 사용하여 그것들을 1에서 10까지 등급을 매긴다. 가장 아래의 경도 1은 활석인데 분필의 경도들 가진 부드러운 광물이고, 등급의 맨 위는 다이아몬드이다. 띠라서 광물과 심지어 다른 고형 물체도 서로 비교하여 등급을 매길 수 있다. 낮은 등급을 가진 물질은 더 높은 등급의 물질에 흔적을 남길 수 없기 때문에 경도는 검사하기 쉽다. 3.5의 경도를 가진 구리 동전은 활석을 쉽게 긁을 수 있지만, 경도 7을 가진 석영에 흔적을 남기기에는 충분히 단단하지 않다. 반대로, 석영은 구리 동전보다 단단하지만 다이아몬드를 긁을 수는 없다.

5 광물의 다른 구별되는 특징은 벽개이다. 벽개는 광물이 힘을 받았을 때 특정 면을 따라 깨지는 경향이다. 결정 구조 때문에 많은 광물이 깨질 때 매끄럽고 평평한 면이 나타난다. [5A]한 면을 따라 깨지는 광물은 완벽한 벽개를 가지고 있다고 한다. [5D]다른 광물은 여러 개의 면을 따라 깨져서 어떤 표면은 매끄럽고 어떤 표면은 거칠다. 매끄러운 표면이 거친 표면보다 많으면, 그 광물은 좋은 벽개를 가지고 있는 것이다. 반면, 거친 표면이 지배적이면, 그 광물은 나쁜 벽개를 가지고 있는 것이다. [5B]어떤 광물은 심지어 벽개가 없고 깨질 때 부서져서 명백한 면이 없는 들쭉날쭉하고 거친 표면을 남긴다.

6 [7]광물의 특징을 식별하는 것은 광물학자뿐만 아니라 보석 세공인과 소비자에게도 유용하다. [8]전문적인 안목과 신중한 실험은 특정한 광물 결정이 진품인지 모조품인지 판단하는 데 필수적이다. 예를 들어 많은 가짜 원석은 색유리나 플라스틱으로 만들어졌고 진짜 에메랄드나 사파이어와 똑같아 보인다. 원석의 가치를 보장하는 것은 바로 원석의 물리적인 특징을 올바로 판단하는 것이다.

어휘

mineral[mínərəl] 광물 crystalline[krístəlin] 결정의 exquisite[ikskwízit] 정교한 symmetrical[simétrikəl] 대칭의
sparkling[spáːrkliŋ] 반짝이는 distinguishing[distíŋgwiʃiŋ] 구별되는 mineralogist[mìnərálədʒist] 광물학자
quartz[kwɔːrts] 석영 transparent[trænspέərənt] 투명한 impurity[impjúərəti] 불순물
exclusive[iksklúːsiv] 유일한 infiltrate[ínfiltreit] 침투하다 bond[band] 접합하다 boron[bɔ́ːran] 붕소 hue[hjuː] 빛깔
differentiation[dìfərènʃiéiʃən] 구별 streak[striːk] 조흔 drag[dræg] 끌다 porcelain[pɔ́ːrsəlin] 자기
crush[krʌʃ] 가루로 만들다 destructive[distrʌ́ktiv] 파괴적인 transmit[trænsmít] 투과시키다 fine[fain] 미세한
calcite[kǽlsait] 방해석 hematite[híːmətàit] 적철광 magnetite[mǽgnətàit] 자철광 scale[skeil] 등급 talc[tælk] 활석
consistency[kənsístənsi] 경도 scratch[skrætʃ] 긁다 conversely[kənvɔ́ːrsli] 반대로 cleavage[klíːvidʒ] 벽개, 쪼개짐
tendency[téndənsi] 경향 plane[plein] 면 subject[sʌbdʒékt] 겪게 하다 splinter[splíntər] 부서지다
jagged[dʒǽgid] 들쭉날쭉한 apparent[əpǽrənt] 명백한 imitation[ìmətéiʃən] 모조품 fake[feik] 가짜의

1　7세기경, 일본의 지도자들은 대규모의 계획적인 문화 차용 캠페인에 착수하였다. 다수의 관료와 학자들이 문화와 제도에 대해 직접적으로 배우기 위해 중국으로 보내졌다. 그들은 중국의 학문적 지식뿐만 아니라 관료주의적 통치와 조직의 양식을 가지고 돌아왔다. 이러한 문화적인 요소는 문명의 도구로, 심지어 문명의 지표 자체로 간주되었고, 일본의 삶에 활발하게 도입되었다.

2　²일본의 지배력은 전통적으로 다른 부족과 장군에 의해 통치되는 많은 왕국에 나뉘어 있었다. 이는 645년 쿠데타가 코토쿠 황제의 휘하로 권력을 통합한 후에 변하였는데, 황제는 정치개혁을 빠르게 제정하였다. 타이카 개신 칙령으로 알려진 개혁에 의해 중국 관료 원형에 기반한 중앙 집권적 정부가 수립되었다. 따라서 황제는 모든 지방에 대한 최고의 지배권을 행사하였고, 정부 관리는 중국 당 왕조(618~907년)의 시험을 본떠 만든 공무원 시험을 봐야 했다. ³새롭게 통일된 일본의 수도는 나라에 건설되었고, 중국의 수도 장안을 본따 직각의 격자 모양으로 계획되었는데, 북쪽으로는 에워싸인 궁, 중앙 대로와 교차하는 동서 대로, 남쪽으로는 정문 입구가 있다. 이 도시 계획의 상징적인 의의는 관료의 배치와 조화를 이루는 것이었다. ⁴황제의 궁이 북쪽 중심에 위치한 것은 천국이 땅 위에 위치하는 것처럼 그가 국민 위에 있음을 의미하였다. 궁 주변의 넓은 땅은 귀족의 거주지로 남겨졌고, 바깥쪽으로 갈수록 땅은 작은 구획으로 나뉘어 평민들이 차지하였다.

3　아시아 본토로부터의 추가적인 차용 증거는 예술과 건축에 반영되어 있다. 일본 정부는 공식적으로 불교를 국교로 채택하였고, ⁵한국, 중국, 인도로부터 불교 예술 작품을 수입하는 것에 열심이었다. 국부적으로는, 8세기 전에 중국과 한국의 장인들이 일본에서 많은 불교 조각과 그림을 만들었으나, ⁵일본 예술가들이 더 포괄적인 지식을 쌓으면서 중국 양식으로 그들만의 예술에 노력을 쏟기 시작하였다. 일본 궁정은 이러한 활동을 후원하였고 높은 비용으로 수도에 큰 절을 지었다. 이 중 가장 인상적인 것은 토다지 사원으로 752년 거대한 규모로 건설되었다. 그곳의 유명한 예술 작품은 16미터의 비로자나 불상이었다. 이 불상은 청동으로 주조되었으며, 세계에서 가장 큰 목조 건물에 보관되어 있었다. 유명한 불교 승려의 작품과 같은 일본인 조각가들의 작품은 특출한 불교도의 모습을 묘사한 그림 작품과 함께 절에 배치되었다.

4　문학에서는, 중국어가 일본 산문과 운문의 발전에 큰 요인이 되었다. 일본은 그들만의 문자 체계가 없었기 때문에, 중국 문자를 글을 쓰는 데 차용하였다. 이 언어적 차용은 일본인들이 많은 양의 중국 학문에 접근할 수 있게 해주었다. 게다가, 일본 학자들이 곧 스스로 문학 원고를 쓰기 시작하면서 일본의 학문적인 창조성을 촉진하였다. 현존하는 최초의 일본 문서는 8세기 초의 것이다.

5　중국어로 쓰여진 대부분의 산문은 유교 고전 작품 및 공무원 시험과 밀접한 관련이 있다. 정부직을 맡고 싶은 일본인은 누구나 중국 역사와 철학을 배워야만 했다. 그러나 일본 작가들은 또한 중국 문자를 사용하여 그들의 언어로 집필하기도 했다. 중국 문자 체계를 일본어에 적용하는 것은 어려웠다. ⁷따라서 대부분의 일본 시는 자국어를 계속 사용하였고, 중국 문자는 일본 음절, 단어와 어미를 문어로 표현하는 데만 사용되었다. ⁸가장 오래된 일본 시의 예는 759년에 편집된 시집 '만엽집'에서 발견되었다. 그 시는 구조적으로 일본어를 사용하여 지어졌다. '와카'로 알려진 이 전통 시는 계층이나 성별 제한이 없고 슬픔과 사랑 같은 익숙한 주제에 집중된 것으로 보인다. 이는 'kanshi'라는 중국어 어순과 문법을 사용하여 만들어진 시와는 다른데, 최상류층 학자들의 시가 이러했다.

6　본토의 영향은 7세기 훨씬 전부터 시작되었고, 공식적인 사절을 보내는 것을 그만 둔 894년 이후에도 오랫동안 계속되었지만, 3세기 동안 일본의 중국 문화 차용은 의도적이었고 집중적이었다. 이는 아시아에서 최고의 권세를 누렸던 문명인 중국 당 나라의 동시대적 안정성과 진보에서 대부분 기인한 것이다.

　　어휘
　　embark[imbáːrk] 착수하다　deliberate[delíbərət] 계획적인　borrowing[bárouiŋ] 차용　institution[ìnstətjúːʃən] 제도
　　bureaucratic[bjùərəkrǽtik] 관료주의의　administration[ædmìnəstréiʃən] 통치　vigorously[vígərəsli] 활발하게
　　incorporate[inkɔ́ːrpərèit] 도입하다　warlord[wɔ́ːrlɔ̀ːrd] 장군　coup d'état[kùːdeitáː] 쿠데타
　　consolidate[kənsálədèit] 통합하다　enact[inǽkt] 제정하다　reform[riːfɔ́ːrm] 개혁　edict[íːdikt] 칙령

centralize[séntrəlàiz] 중앙 집권화 하다   rectangular[rektǽŋgjulər] 직각의   grid[grid] 격자   enclose[inklóuz] 에워싸다

intersect[ìntərsékt] 교차하다   boulevard[búləvàːrd] 대로   significance[signífikəns] 의의

signify[sígnəfài] 의미하다   nobility[noubíləti] 귀족   occupy[ákjupài] 차지하다   commoner[kámənər] 평민

embrace[imbréis] 차용하다   keen[kiːn] 열심인   commence[kəméns] 시작하다   endeavor[indévər] 노력

sponsor[spánsər] 후원하다   celebrated[séləbrèitid] 유명한   rendition[rendíʃən] 작품   prominent[prámənənt] 특출한

factor into ~을 하나의 요인으로 포함하다   prose[prouz] 산문   verse[vəːrs] 운문   script[skript] 문자

linguistic[liŋgwístik] 언어의   adoption[ədápʃən] 차용   extant[ékstənt] 현존하는   Confucian[kənfjúːʃən] 유교의

syllable[síləbl] 음절   anthology[ænθálədʒi] 시집   compile[kəmpáil] 편집하다   intentional[inténʃənl] 의도적인

intensive[inténsiv] 집중적인   attributable[ətríbjutəbl] ~에 기인하는   concurrent[kənkə́ːrənt] 동시대적인

prestige[prestíːʒ] 세력

문제 공략하기

p.169

감소의 또 다른 원인은 질병이 한 개구리 개체군에서 다른 개체군으로 전파되는 것이다. 수십 년간, 취미 생활자들은 수족관에 넣을 외래 종의 양서류를 수입하였으며, 종종 이러한 애완동물은 적절한 검사를 받지 않은 채 대륙을 건너왔다. **이러한 검사는 질병이 해외에서 들어오지 않도록 보통 법에 의해 요구된다.** 병든 개구리가 일단 수조 안에 넣어지면 빠르게 다른 개구리들을 전염시킬 수 있고, 외래 질병을 치료하려는 시도는 효과가 없을 수 있다. 더 중요한 것은, 병든 개구리에게 노출된 후 방생된 모든 애완동물은 계속해서 다른 양서류를 감염시킬 수 있다. 토착 양서류는 외래 질병에 대한 면역력이 약하거나 없으므로, 질병의 노출은 전체 야생 개체군을 전멸할 수 있다.

HACKERS PRACTICE

p.170

01 3rd ■ 02 2nd ■ 03 1st ■ 04 2nd ■ 05 3rd ■ 06 3rd ■ 07 3rd ■ 08 1st ■ 09 3rd ■
10 3rd ■ 11 1st ■ 12 3rd ■ 13 1st ■ 14 4th ■ 15 1. 3rd ■ 2. 1st ■ 16 1. 1st ■ 2. 1st ■

01 덴마크계 미국인 발달 심리학자 에릭 홈부르거 에릭슨은 출생부터 사망까지 몇 가지 단계를 아우르는 인간 발달 이론을 체계적으로 나타냈다. 대부분의 발달 이론은 유년기에만 적용되지만 에릭슨은 발달이 성인기까지 지속된다고 믿었다. 에릭슨 이론의 각 단계는 한 사람의 인생에서 특정 시기에 일반적으로 나타나는 특정한 갈등에 초점을 맞춘다. 개인이 그 시기를 성공적으로 끝마치기 위해서는 갈등을 해결해야 한다. **예를 들어, 최초의 단계에서 18개월 된 아이는 믿음과 불신이라는 서로 반대되는 것 사이에서 갈등한다.**

02 전세계의 온대 우림과 열대 우림은 계절적인 온도 같은 일부 면에서는 다르지만 어느 정도의 유사점도 지닌다. 모든 다우림의 구별되는 특징 중 하나는 매년 내리는 상당한 강수량이다. 온대 우림의 강수량은 매년 1,400~2,000밀리미터인 반면, 열대 우림은 2,100~7,600밀리미터이다. **이 양은 구름에서 온 비뿐만 아니라 눈, 가랑비, 안개에서 온 물도 포함한다.** 많은 양의 습기는 다우림의 두 가지 유형 모두에서 동식물 종의 굉장한 다양성을 보증한다.

03 미국 원주민들은 수완이 비상하여 그들의 구할 수 있는 천연 재료로 옷을 만들었다. **동물 가죽, 식물 섬유, 조개, 깃털 모두 옷을 만드는 데 사용되었다.** 식민지 개척자들이 신세계에 도착한 후에는 구슬과 자수 같은 유럽식 요소가 더해져서 옷에 독특한 장식 스타일을 창출했다. 여성들은 옷을 만들 의무가 있었고 그들의 일을 꽤 중요하게 여겼으며 실용적인 것만큼이나 아름다운 제품을 만들었다.

04 산호초는 죽은 산호, 살아 있는 산호, 그리고 조류와 다른 살아 있는 생물 분비물로 구성된 무더기이다. 살아 있는 산호는 대양저에 자리잡은 산호 골격에 자신을 묶어 두기 위해 그 분비물을 사용한다. 매년 약 13밀리미터의 비율로 자라는 산호 조직은 일반적으로 거의 2~3미터의 평균 길이에 달한다. **특히 큰 산호인 그레이트 배리어 리프는 호주 북동부 연안에 있는데 길이가 대략 2,000킬로미터이다.** 완전히 자란 산호초는 바다 생물 약 90퍼센트의 중요한 서식지이다.

05 많은 고대 이집트 그림이 왕족이나 부유한 최상류층의 무덤 벽에서 발견된다. 이집트 화가들은 사망한 자들에게 사후에 어떤 일이 일어나는지 보여주는 장례식 장면을 그렸다. 종종, 대상은 심판관과 함께 묘사되었는데, 그는 사람이 살아 있을 때 행했던 공적을 평가하기 위해 참석했다. 이러한 그림은 삶과 죽음의 연속성을 보여주었다. 그 외에도, 이집트 화가들은 때때로 노래하고 춤추는 것 같은 보다 일상적인 활동을 묘사했다.

06 동물은 환경 주기에 주기적으로 반응하는 체내 기제를 가지고 있다. 이 주기는 24시간 간격으로 일어날지도 모르고 보름달 간의 평균 시간에 따를 수도 있다. 또한 계절 패턴에 기반을 둘 수도 있다. 생체 시계라고 불리는 이 기제는 동물이 앞으로 다가올 일을 알아차리게 하는 기능을 한다. 예를 들어, 곰의 시계는 날이 점점 짧아지며 겨울이 다가옴을 나타내는 것을 지각한다. 곰은 동면을 위한 지방을 비축하기 위해 많은 양의 음식을 먹음으로써 신호에 반응한다. **그런 신호가 없다면, 곰은 충분한 지방을 제때에 만들어낼 수 없을 것이다.**

07 19세기 미국 초월론자들의 뚜렷한 특징은 주변의 사회에 대한 경멸이었다. 그들은 미국인을 당시에 우세한 정치사회적 관습을, 그러한 관습이 부도덕할지라도, 생각 없이 따르는 순응자로 보았다. 그들은 신념에 이끌려 노예 제도를 인류에 대한 범죄라고 부르며 강력히 반발하였고, 다른 사람들로 하여금 여권 운동 같은 사회 개혁의 노력에 참여하도록 적극적으로 북돋았다. 그들은 심지어 정의의 이름 아래 시민 불복종의 한 형태로 법을 위반하기까지 하였다. **예를 들어 헨리 데이비드 소로는 불공정한 정부에 세금을 내느니 차라리 감옥에 갔다.**

08 화석 연료 공급이 감소하기 시작했기 때문에 전기 발생도 머지 않아 근본적인 변화를 겪을 것이다. **현재의 석유와 가스 저장량이 얼마나 오래 갈지 아무도 정확히 알지 못하지만 결국 고갈될 것임은 명확하다.** 최근, 온실가스 배출에 의한 지구온난화에 대한 우려가 에너지 생산자들로 하여금 에너지 정책에 대해 다시 생각하고 좀 더 깨끗한 전기 공급처를 찾도록 하고 있다. 대체 에너지 중에서는 태양열이 가장 널리 생산되고 대기 오염을 일으키지 않는다. 태양은 집을 따뜻하게 하고 상업 건물에 동력을 공급하는 재생 가능한 에너지의 소중한 공급처이며 자원을 탐사하고 파내는 비용을 요하지 않는다. 태양 전지판 기술의 혁신 또한 태양열 발전을 더욱 경제적이고 효율적으로 만들었다.

09 고대 로마 문화는 완전히 고유한 것은 아니었다. 많은 부분이 로마 제국의 확장기에 다른 문명, 그 중에서도 특히 그리스와의 접촉을 통해 획득되었다. 기원전 146년 로마의 그리스 정복에 뒤따라, 몇 가지 요소가 로마인들의 삶에 도입되어 받아들여졌다. 이 중 가장 주요한 것이 그리스 종교였다. 대부분의 로마 신과 여신은 그리스 신과 동일시 되었는데, 제우스는 주피터, 아프로디테는 비너스, 아르테미스는 다이애나와 동일시 되었다. **따라서, 이러한 각각의 신에게 상응하는 그리스 신의 속성과 신화가 부여되었다.** 심지어 신전과 종교적 목적으로 지어진 다른 건축물까지 그리스 양식을 본받았으며 시간이 지나면서 로마 도시의 필요를 충족시키기 위해 단지 수정되었을 뿐이다.

10 생물학적 분류법은 생물을 분류하는 방식이다. 현대의 분류법은 스웨덴 과학자 칼 린네가 개발한 체제에 기반을 두고 있다. 린네는 일반적인 것에서 구체적인 것으로 나아가는 계급제로 생물을 분류하였다. 가장 광범위한 수준인 계는 식물과 동물로 나뉜다. 이러한 넓은 분류는 공유하는 신체적 특징에 따라 더 작은 집단으로 구분된다. 예를 들어 그는 유선이 있는 모든 동물을 포유류 강에 배치하였다. **유사하게, 쌍안시와 움켜쥐는 손가락을 가진 생물은 영장류 목에 들어간다.** 그는 가장 구체적인 수준에서는 이명법 체제를 만들어서 각각의 고유한 생물이 속과 종을 나타내는 두 단어로 이루어진 라틴어 이름을 가지도록 했다. 인간은 이명법으로 '호모 사피엔스'이다.

11 초기 천문학자들은 우주의 별을 관찰하기 위해 육안을 이용했다. 그러나 눈의 작은 수정체는 충분한 빛을 모으지 못하고, 더 희미한 별을 포착하고 거리를 재고 밝기를 측정하는 데 필요한 시지각이 부족하다. 이러한 단점을 극복하기 위해, 천문학자들은 별의 형상을 기록하고 모으고 분석할 새로운 기기를 발명했다. **아마도 이러한 기기 중에 가장 잘 알려지고 영속하는 것은 망원경일 것이다.** 최초의 굴절 렌즈 망원경은 1608년 네덜란드에서 발명되었고 상을 형성하기 위해 렌즈를 사용하였다. 대부분 20세기 초에 만들어진 광학 망원경은 전자기 스펙트럼에서 빛을 흡수하여 멀리 있는 대상의 크기와 밝기를 증대시킨다. 1931년에 발명된 전파 망원경은 별의 형상을 만들어 내기 위해 안테나를 통해 천체에서 오는 전파 송신을 모은다는 점에서 광학 망원경과 다르다. 1990년에 나온 허블 망원경은 매우 정확한 측정치를 도출하기 위해 우주의 만곡, 지속적으로 확장하는 우주, 우주에서 빛을 왜곡시키는 현상을 고려한다.

12 낙엽성 나무는 모든 성장과 세포 활동을 중지함으로써 추운 온도에 반응한다. 그들은 영양소를 뿌리로 보내고 잎을 떨어뜨림으로써 이것을 달성하며, 봄이 되어서야 활발한 성장을 재개한다. 반면, 상록수는 겨울 내내 잎을 유지하고 햇빛을 계속 사용하여 에너지를 생성한다. 히말라야삼목과 가문비나무 같은 침엽수의 바늘 같은 잎은 활엽수의 잎보다 작은 표면적과 훨씬 작은 기공을 가지고 있다. 이것은 그들이 물을 흔히 구할 수 없는 겨울 동안 수분 손실을 최소화하도록

해준다. 잎의 짙은 색깔은 태양의 따뜻한 빛을 끌어당기도록 돕는다. 그 색깔은 잎 표면 근처의 온도를 몇 도 증가시킬 수 있다. 잎은 또한 빽빽하게 모여 있고 눈을 모으는데, 이것은 식물을 극단적인 온도로부터 차단하는 담요 역할을 한다. 그러나 너무 많은 눈은 식물에게 너무 무거워서 가지가 부러질 수 있으므로, 침엽수는 여분의 눈을 땅으로 떨어뜨릴 수 있도록 가지가 없는 하나의 줄기와 원뿔 모양의 초관을 가지고 있다.

13 '가내 공업'이라는 용어는 공장보다는 가정에서 이루어지는 직물 생산 같은 일련의 소규모 회사를 가리킨다. 가내 공업은 16세기 영국의 농업 지역과 작은 마을에서 흔했다. **그것은 또한 가끔 도시 지역의 가난한 사람들 사이에서 생겨났다.** 그것은 조직 수준이 낮다는 특징이 있고 농업이나 다른 작업을 위한 시간을 충분히 확보하기 위해서 종종 단시간 근무이고 계절적이었다. 가족 내 모든 사람들이 작업에 참여하였다. 아이들은 간단한 일을 도왔던 반면, 부모는 좀 더 기술적인 세부 작업에 집중하였다. 옷을 전문으로 하는 가내 공업의 경우, 아이들은 실을 준비하고 그것이 엉키지 않도록 한다. 그 후 부모는 실을 자아내고 짜서 완성품을 만들었다. 영국에서 가내 공업은 결국 그것을 대체한 산업 공장의 전조였지만, 많은 개발도상국에서는 여전히 흔하다. 특히 아시아 국가들에서는 주로 농업 지역에서 여전히 가내 공업이 성행하고 있다.

14 부식 동판술은 금속에 디자인이나 그림을 새기는 방법이며 여러 장의 거의 똑같은 인쇄본을 만들어내기 위해 사용될 수 있다. 이를 해내기 위해, 화가는 먼저 금속판에 왁스를 입힌다. 그 후 화가는 끝이 뾰족한 부식 동판술 도구를 사용해 왁스에 디자인을 '긁어서 새긴다.' 디자인이 완성된 후 산을 판 위에 붓는다. 산은 금속의 노출된 부분을 부식시키고, 그려진 선에 해당하는 패인 자국을 만든다. 그 후 왁스를 제거하고 판을 잉크로 칠한 후 표면을 닦아내 금속의 움푹 들어간 선에만 잉크를 남긴다. 마침내 금속 판을 종이로 덮고 고압의 인쇄기에 넣는다. 압력에 의해 잉크가 종이 위에 찍히는데, 이 과정은 한 부식 동판의 많은 인쇄본을 만들어내기 위하여 여러번 반복될 수 있다. **그러나 인쇄 중간 중간에 잉크를 깨끗이 닦아 내고 다시 칠하기 때문에 각 인쇄물은 진본으로 간주된다.**

15 대공황은 미국 역사상 가장 심각한 경기 침체였다. 경제학자들은 1929년 주식 시장 붕괴와 종종 관련시켜 생각되는 이 경기 침체의 주요 원인에 대하여 의견이 다르지만, 한 가지 대중적인 이론은 이 사건이 불공평한 부의 분배 때문이라는 것이다. 광란의 20년대에, 미국은 더 높은 노동자 생산성과 더 낮은 생산비 덕분에 매우 부유한 국가가 되었다. 전반적으로, 제조업 생산은 1920년대에 3분의 1 증가하였다. 이는 회사의 이익을 60퍼센트 이상 증대시켰지만 노동자의 봉급은 8퍼센트 밖에 오르지 않았다. 생산의 급격한 증가에 의한 이익의 대부분은 소수의 부유한 개인에게 돌아갔다. **예를 들어, 기업가 헨리 포드는 평균적인 노동자보다 거의 20,000배에 가까운 연수입이 있었다.** 관련된 현상은 수요와 공급 차의 증가였다. 과잉생산은 소비재를 널리 이용 가능하게 하였지만 서민의 수입이 매우 낮았기 때문에 이러한 상품에 대한 실제 수요는 공급에 발을 맞출 수 없었다.

두 번째 설명은 연방준비은행의 정책에 초점을 맞춘다. **연방준비은행의 역할을 강조하는 경제학자들은 대공황을 완전히 피할 수 있었다고 주장한다.** 불경기 때문에 기업이 부채를 갚기가 어려웠고, 그 결과 많은 기업들이 그들의 대부금에 대한 채무를 이행하지 못해서 은행들이 무너졌다. 1929년과 1933년 사이, 반이 넘는 미국 은행들이 운영을 멈췄다. 이는 자금 공급에 막대한 감소가 있었음을 의미했다. 연방준비은행은 채권을 사서 이 문제를 해결할 수 있었으나 그러지 않았다. 행동하기를 거부함으로써, 연방준비은행은 금리를 오르게 했고, 사람들이 필요한 융자를 받는 것을 더욱더 어렵게 만들었다.

16 모든 포식자는 생태계에서 먹이 사슬의 다양한 단계에서 생물 개체수를 통제하는 역할을 한다. **하지만 특정 포식자의 존재나 부재는 극적인 영향을 미칠 수 있다.** 이러한 포식자들은 그들의 개체수가 나타내는 것보다 훨씬 더 많은 영향을 미치며 그들의 기능은 아치의 종석과 비슷하다. 종석은 아치의 중앙에 놓이는 한 조각의 돌로서 구조상의 무게에서 제일 적은 부분을 차지하지만 종석이 제거되면 전체 구조가 부스러질 것이다. 이와 같은 것은 핵심종에서도 사실이다. 개체수는 적을지라도 그들이 없이는 생태계 생물 다양성이 무너질 것이다.

핵심종 개념은 1969년에 생태학자 로버트 페인에 의해 소개되었고 생물학 논문에서 표준 용어가 되었다. **이 개념은 사실상 생태계와 보존을 다루는 어느 책에서나 발견될 수 있다.** 페인은 태평양 해안선에서 일부러 한 불가사리 종('Pisaster ochraceus')을 제거하고 해안선을 따라 있는 작은 무척추동물 군집으로 실험을 한 후에 그 개념을 소개했다. 그는 불가사리를 제거했을 때 몇몇 생물은 증식한 반면 다른 몇몇은 차츰 사라지기 시작했다는 것을 알아챘다. 이는 불가사리가 말조개 'Mytilus californicus'의 주요 포식자였기 때문이다. 불가사리가 사라지자 말조개 군체가 자라나서 성게와 말미잘 같은 암석 해변의 다른 생물들을 밀어냈다. 실험 이전에는 대략 15종의 무척추동물이 그 지역에 살았다. 그 수치는 불가사리 제거에 의해 2종으로 줄어들었다.

HACKERS TEST

* 각 문제에 대한 정답단서는 지문에 초록색으로 표시되어 있습니다.

1 Teotihuacan 테오티우아칸 p.178

1. (B)　2. 1st ■　3. (B)　4. 3rd ■

1　멕시코시티 북동부의 골짜기는 웅장한 문명의 폐허를 포함하고 있다. 이 고대 사회에 대한 많은 것들은 수수께끼로 남아 있는데, 주 도시를 누가 지었는지, 무엇이라고 불렸는지, 그리고 왜 멸망했는지 정확히 알지 못한다. **고대 사람들이 어떻게 이런 장엄한 건축물을 지을 수 있었는지도 파악할 수 없다.** 그러나 기원전 2세기에서 기원후 750년 정도까지 그 문명이 번창한 것은 알고 있다. 수백 년 후, 아즈텍인들이 결국 중앙 도시를 발견했을 때 그곳은 이미 버려져 있었지만 그들은 폐허의 웅대함에 충격을 받았다. 도시의 많은 종교 유적 때문에 아즈텍인들은 그곳을 테오티우아칸이라고 이름 지었는데, 이는 '신들의 장소'라는 뜻이나. 광내한 유적지에서 발굴된 폐허와 공예품을 이용하여, 고고힉자들은 고대 도시의 모습을 그려볼 수 있었다.

2　고대 메소아메리카에서 굉장히 중요한 곳으로의 테오티우아칸의 지위는 거대 규모로 건축된 의식용 건축물에서 드러난다. 도시 가운데에는 건물의 집합체가 위치했는데, 거기에는 알려진 피라미드 중 세계에서 세 번째로 큰 것이 포함되어 있다. 고고학자들은 그것을 태양의 피라미드라고 부르고 신을 숭배하기 위해 건축되었다고 믿는다. 그러나 발굴 전 그 굉장한 건축물의 꼭대기에 있는 신전이 파괴되어 그 신전이 정확히 어느 신에게 바쳐진 것이었는지 알기 힘들게 되었다. 선명하게 채색된 벽화가 한 때 피라미드 내부의 벽에 칠해져 있었는데, 대부분 테오티우아칸 사람들이 숭배한 재규어, 뱀, 천체와 같은 자연적인 상징들을 나타내고 있다. 다른 주요 숭배 장소로 쓰인 피라미드 건축물은 케찰코아틀 신전이었는데, 이 이름은 한때 메소아메리카 도처에서 찬양되었던 용과 비슷한 깃털이 있는 중요한 뱀을 뜻하는 아즈텍 단어에서 명명된 것이다. 신전 가까이에 있는 방의 발굴로 인간과 동물 뼈가 드러났는데, 어떤 고고학자들은 이 발견을 신성한 공간에서 한 때 시행되었던 번제 의식의 증거로 해석한다.

3　피라미드 근처에 있는 커다란 저택들은 아마 종교적, 정치적인 의무가 모두 있었던 종교 지도자 가족의 집이었을 것이다. 사회 계급에서 영향력 있는 다른 가족들은 도시를 관통하는 중심 대로에 늘어서 있었던 석조 건축물에서 살았던 반면, 농부들은 도시 외곽을 따라 퍼져 있었던 나무 집에서 살았을 것이다. 농업 계층인 이들은 당시 세계에서 가장 큰 도시 중 하나였던 대략 150,000명의 거대한 공동체를 위한 작물을 기르기 위해 매일 주위 밭으로 이동했을 것이다. 도시 전체의 도처에 있는 아파트 건물에 살았던 도공과 보석 세공인 계층도 있었다. **이러한 공동체 거주지 내의 방에서 일상 생활에 사용되는 수많은 수공예품이 생산되었다.** 인간 입상과 화살촉이 이 장소에서 발견되는 흔한 공예품에 속하고, 장인들은 그것을 그 지역의 화산암에서 수집된 흑요석으로 자주 조각했다.

어휘
ruin[ru:in] 폐허　majestic[mədʒéstik] 웅장한　collapse[kəlǽps] 멸망하다　flourish[flə́:riʃ] 번창하다
abandon[əbǽndən] 버리다　awestruck[ɔ́:strʌ̀k] 충격받다　grandeur[grǽndʒər] 웅대함　monument[mánjumənt] 유적
artifact[á:rtəfæ̀kt] 공예품　ceremonial[sèrəmóuniəl] 의식의　construct[kənstrʌ́kt] 건축하다　immense[iméns] 거대한
situate[sítʃuèit] 위치시키다　venerate[vénərèit] 숭배하다　deity[díːəti] 신　atop[ətáp] 꼭대기의
excavation[èkskəvéiʃən] 발굴　dedicate[dédikèit] 바치다　vibrantly[váibrəntli] 선명하게　plaster[plǽstər] 칠하다
astronomical[æ̀strənámikəl] 천문의　revere[rivíər] 숭배하다　feathered[féðərd] 깃털이 있는　exalt[igzɔ́:lt] 찬양하다
mansion[mǽnʃən] 저택　hierarchy[háiərà:rki] 계급제　avenue[ǽvənjù:] 대로　tend[tend] 기르다
figurine[fìgjuríːn] 입상　arrowhead[ǽrouhèd] 화살촉　obsidian[əbsídiən] 흑요석

1. (B)   2. 1st ■   3. (D)   4. (B)   5. 2nd ■   6. (B)   7. (D)   8. 4th ■

1   초원 생태계는 평평한 지대나 부드럽게 경사진 굽이치는 산, 그리고 지배적인 초본류 식물로 특징지어진다. 나무, 관목, 그리고 다른 목본은 초원에 없는 것이나 다름 없고 뜨거운 태양 복사와 거친 바람으로부터의 피난처가 거의 없다. 초원은 대체적으로 적당한 연평균 강수량을 갖지만, 여름에는 때때로 심각한 가뭄이 나타난다. 결국, 식물이 초원 생태계에서 번영하기 위해서는 계절적으로 건조한 조건을 견뎌야 한다. 이러한 생태계에서 살아남기 적당한 초본에는 초원잔디가 있는데, 이들은 생존을 위한 몇 개의 적응 장치를 가진다.

2   초원잔디의 잎은 폭이 다양하지만, 대부분 단지 길고 얇은 잎이다. **그들은 뿌리 조직 바로 위인 식물 기부 근처의 줄기에 붙어 있다.** 잎의 상피 층에는 기공이라고 불리는 작은 구멍이 있는데, 그것은 이산화탄소를 들여보내고 산소를 내보내기 위해 열릴 수 있고 수분을 보유하기 위해 닫힐 수 있다. 이산화탄소는 식물 광합성과 호흡에 필수이기 때문에, [3]기공은 가스 교환을 위해 넓혀져 있어야 한다. 그러나 잎 내부의 기실은 수증기로 가득 차 있고, 이는 구멍이 닫혀있지 않으면 증산작용을 통해 사라진다. 이것은 수분이 대기로 사라지기 때문에 건조한 환경에서 식물에게 위기를 준다. 이 문제를 헤쳐나가기 위해, 초원잔디는 낮과 밤을 구별하도록 진화했다. 태양에서 나오는 열 에너지가 가장 강한 낮에 잔디는 기공을 닫아 수분 손실을 최소화한다. 그 후 공기가 더 차가운 저녁에는 호흡을 위해 기공을 확장한다. 이런 식으로 건조한 시기에도 완전히 건조되는 것을 방지하면서 잔디가 필요한 이산화탄소를 얻을 수 있게 한다.

3   초원잔디의 한 종은 잎맥 사이와 잎맥을 따라 확장된 상피세포를 가진다. 비가 온 후, 세포는 최대 용량으로 부풀어 올라 물에 흠뻑 젖어 있지만, 가뭄일 때는 세포가 오그라든다. 이렇게 오그라드는 것은 물에 젖은 조직과 젖지 않은 조직 간에 부피의 차이를 야기하고, 이로 인해 잎이 똘똘 감겨 잎 표면에 있는 수분을 효과적으로 감싼다. 이것은 잎의 표면을 그늘지게 하여 직접적인 태양 복사열로 인한 증발을 줄이는 데 도움이 된다. 초원잔디의 또 다른 종은 연모로 덮인 잎을 가지고 있는데, 잎이 작은 털로 덮여 있다는 뜻이다. **이 털은 잎 위에 드문드문 나 있거나 빽빽하게 나 있다.** 연모는 태양 광선을 걸러서 표면의 온도를 낮추고, 물을 보유하여 습도를 증가시킬 수 있다. 공기의 습도가 충분하면, 밤새 떨어지는 기온 때문에 식물에 이슬이 맺힐 것이다. 이슬은 반들반들한(털이 없는) 잎의 매끄러운 표면 위에서는 종종 그냥 흘러 내리기 때문에 연모로 덮인 잎은 물방울을 더 오랫동안 보전할 수 있다.

4   초원잔디는 잎을 푸르고 건강하게 유지하기 위한 적응 장치를 가지고 있지만, 상황이 너무 심각해지면 잎을 휴면상태로 변화시킬 수 있다. 초원은 몇 주 또는 몇 달 동안 비가 없는 날씨를 겪을 수도 있다. 이런 상황에서는 잎이 말라버릴 수도 있지만, 많은 초원잔디가 다년초이기 때문에 뿌리 조직은 지하에서 계속 살아남는다. 초원잔디의 뿌리 조직은 상당히 광대할 수 있는데, 뿌리가 깊을수록 식물이 비 없이 오래 살 수 있다. 'Andropogon gerardii'(큰 푸른 줄기)라는 어떤 식물은 늦게 개화하는 커다란 북미 종으로, 식물 생장에 비해 상당히 깊은 뿌리를 가지고 있다. [6]생장 초기에는 잎이 천천히 나오고, 깊고 튼튼한 뿌리 조직을 만드는 데 식물의 에너지의 대부분이 바쳐진다. 이것이 느린 지상 성장과 낮은 번식 속도라는 에너지 불균형의 원인이 된다. 생장에 에너지를 덜 쏟기 때문에, 식물은 어쩔 수 없이 개화기를 줄인다. 반면, 튼튼하게 발달된 지하 부분은 땅속 깊숙이 있는 수분에 닿을 수 있도록 해주고 질소와 흙의 다른 영양분을 위해 경쟁할 수 있도록 해준다.

5   초원잔디는 그들의 적응력 때문에 식물학계 사람들의 주의를 끌었다. 그들의 강인함은 물 보존을 지지하는 환경주의자들에게 찬양 받고 있다. 그 결과, 초원잔디는 최근 들어 잔디밭과 정원의 후보로 더욱 흔해졌는데, 특히 가뭄이 심각한 고민인 지역에서 그렇다. 수분에 의존하는 잔디를 가뭄에 내성이 있는 초원잔디로 바꾸면서 사람들은 원예를 위한 물 사용을 크게 줄일 수 있다. **그렇게 함으로써, 그들은 수도 요금도 절약할 수 있다.**

어휘
prairie[prɛ́əri] 초원의   **terrain**[təréin] 지대   **predominance**[pridámənəns] 지배   **herbaceous**[həːrbéiʃəs] 초본류
moderate[mádərət] 적당한   **adaptive**[ədǽptiv] 적응의   **blade**[bleid] 잎   **epidermal**[èpədə́ːrməl] 상피의
stoma[stóumə] 기공   **retain**[ritéin] 보유하다   **photosynthesis**[fòutousínθəsis] 광합성   **respiration**[rèspəréiʃən] 호흡
evaporate[ivǽpərèit] 사라지다   **transpiration**[trænspəréiʃən] 증산 작용   **pore**[pɔːr] 구멍   **enlarge**[inláːrdʒ] 확장시키다

vein[vein] 잎맥 swell[swel] 부풀다 saturated[sǽtʃərèitid] 흠뻑 젖은 shrink[ʃriŋk] 오그라들다
envelop[invéləp] 감싸다 pubescent[pju:bésnt] 연모로 덮인 foliage[fóuliidʒ] 잎 bristle[brísl] 털 humidity[hju:mídəti] 습도
retention[riténʃən] 보유 glabrous[gléibrəs] 반들반들한 foliar[fóuliər] 잎의 dormancy[dɔ́:rmənsi] 휴면
perennial[pəréniəl] 다년생의 extensive[iksténsiv] 광대한 emerge[imə́:rdʒ] 나오다 imbalance[imbǽləns] 불균형
toughness[tʌ́fnis] 강인함 extol[ikstóul] 찬양하다 advocate[ǽdvəkèit] 지지하다 conservation[kànsərvéiʃən] 보존
horticultural[hɔ̀:rtəkʌ́ltʃərəl] 원예의

3 The Port of Melaka 믈라카 항구 p.183

---

1. 2nd ■   2. (B)   3. (D)   4. (A)   5. 3rd ■   6. (B)   7. (A)   8. 3rd ■

---

1 믈라카 해협의 가장 좁은 지점인 말레이시아에 위치한 믈라카 항구는 세계에서 가장 분주한 국제 수로 중 하나에 자리잡고 있다. 약 600척의 상업용 선박이 매일 그 수로를 지나다닌다. 믈라카는 오백 년 이상의 복잡한 지정학적 역사를 가지고 있으며 다양한 인종 집단이 살고 있다. 게다가, 국제 교역의 중요한 중추 중 하나에 위치하여 특히 향신료 교역에 전략적인 요지가 되었으며, 국제적으로 정치경제적인 세력의 영향을 받았다.

2 국제적인 상업 중심지로서의 믈라카의 장점과 관련된 이야기를 가장 먼저 기록하고 퍼뜨린 사람은 중국의 유명한 해군 제독이자 해양 탐험가 정화였다. 정화는 1405·1433년 사이에 7번의 동남아시아 항해 중 믈라카를 5번 방문하여 그 지역의 물질적인 부와 천연 자원의 소식을 명나라 황제에게 전하고 15세기 중국의 동남아시아 제품에 대한 왕성한 수요를 촉진시켰다.

3 15세기 믈라카는 술탄 만수르 샤의 지배 아래 있었다. 당시, 정화의 함대에 중국인이 믈라카 현지인과 친교를 맺도록 도운 이슬람교도 선원들이 있었다. 믈라카와 중국 명나라의 이러한 관계는 인도에서 생산된 향신료가 중앙아시아를 통해 육로로 운반되기 보다는 믈라카를 주요 중간체류지로 하여 중국으로 쉽게 운반될 수 있었음을 뜻했다. [4]술탄의 세금 정책은 중국의 특권이 있는 지위를 반영했다. 아라비아와 인도 상인들은 6퍼센트의 세금이 붙었고 말레이 지역 상인들은 3퍼센트만 붙었으며 중국 무역업자들은 아예 세금이 붙지 않았다.

4 이슬람 문명의 믈라카 지배는 서양에도 멀리 영향을 미쳤다. 향신료 무역은 유럽인들이 동남아시아에 관여할 주요 동기가 되었다. 예를 들어, 후추와 계피는 그 지역에서 풍부했고 이국적인 풍미로 해외에서 높이 평가 받았다. 다른 다양한 현지의 향신료 또한 높이 평가 받았으며, 그것의 희귀성은 높은 가격으로 팔리게 했다. 15세기에 유럽으로 보내진 향신료는 터키인들이 지배하는 페르시아 만을 거치거나 홍해를 통해 이집트의 알렉산드리아로 먼저 향했다. 따라서, 유럽인들은 중개자 역할을 했던 이슬람 상인들을 거쳐야 했다. 여러 손을 거친 상품의 운송은 최종 구매자에 대한 가격을 높였기 때문에 유럽 국가들은 향신료 해양 교역 항로에 대한 지역 통제 수단을 찾기 시작했다. 이로써 전설적인 동쪽의 향신료 섬은 국제 세력의 경쟁적인 싸움터가 되었다. 1500년 이후, 포르투갈인들의 침입이 권력 관계를 바꿔 놓았고 믈라카 해협을 통해 지나가던 상품의 대부분이 유럽으로 직송되었다.

5 포르투갈인들은 1511년에 믈라카의 통치자를 내쫓고 1641년까지 그 항구 도시를 점령하였다. 점령 초기에 포르투갈 정부는 믈라카의 향신료 교역에 엄격한 독점권을 행사하였으나 1530년에 이르러서는 교역권을 개인 상인에게로 확장하기 시작했다. 곧, 믈라카에서 수백 명의 포르투갈 상인들이 사고 팔고 개인 선박을 이용해 향신료를 운반하였다. [6]16세기 동안 포르투갈은 교역 항로를 비밀로 유지할 수 있었지만 1600년대 해군 강국 네덜란드의 등장이 포르투갈의 지배를 종식했다. 1641년에 네덜란드는 포르투갈로부터 믈라카를 무력으로 빼앗았고 항구는 네덜란드 식민지가 되었다.

6 [7D]포르투갈과 네덜란드의 지배 기간 동안 해외로 교역된 현지 향신료 중에서 후추가 가장 주요 상품이었다. [7B/C]네덜란드의 지배 아래 1670년에 환금 작물의 생산이 8,500톤의 연 교역량으로 최고에 달하였고, 그 후 가격이 하락하기 시작하여 그 지역의 농부들은 대신 목화와 사탕수수 같은 다른 작물을 재배하기 시작하였다. 믈라카는 또한 직물과 쌀 같은 중요 상품의 주요 항구가 되었는데, 이들은 지역의 더 작은 항구에서 믈라카의 붐비는 시장으로 가져온 것이었다.

7 작은 교역 중심지에서 일어나는 짧은 거래와는 다르게, 믈라카의 상인들은 몇 달간 시장을 열었다. 이 관행은 장기 거주자

Chapter 07 Insertion **315**

들의 출현을 낳았다. 외국에서 온 일부 교역자들은 믈라카에 정착하였고 말레이 여성들과 결혼을 하여 지역적 유대를 형성하였다. 이주민들 중에서 중국인 공동체가 절대적인 수에서 지배적이었고 중국 소수 민족은 심지어 오늘날까지도 믈라카에서 가장 큰 소수 집단이다. **상당한 수의 다른 집단은 인도와 포르투갈 선조를 가진 집단을 포함한다.** 믈라카의 국제적인 역사는 건축에서도 분명히 나타난다. 현지와 포르투갈 및 네덜란드의 건축물은 믈라카 도시의 역사적 중심지에 남아 관광객들에게 여전히 인기 있는 특유의 분위기를 제공하고 그것의 국제적인 뿌리를 기념한다.

어휘

geopolitical[dʒì:oupəlítikəl] 지정학상의 millennium[miléniəm] 천년간 artery[á:rtəri] 중추

spice[spais] 향신료 hub[hʌb] 중심지 naval[néivəl] 해군의 admiral[ǽdmərəl] 제독

maritime[mǽrətàim] 해양의 voyage[vɔ́iidʒ] 항해 vigorous[vígərəs] 원기 왕성한 fleet[fli:t] 함대

Muslim[mʌ́zlim] 이슬람교도 local[lóukəl] 현지인 stop-off[stápɔ̀:f] 중간체류지 overland[óuvərlǽnd] 육로로

privileged[prívəlidʒd] 특권이 주어진 trader[tréidər] 무역업자 far-reaching[fà:rí:tʃiŋ] 멀리까지 미치는

cinnamon[sínəmən] 계피 value[vǽlju:] 높이 평가하다 flavor[fléivər] 풍미 abroad[əbrɔ́:d] 해외에 Red Sea 홍해

middlemen[mídlmèn] 중개자 route[ru:t] 항로 fabled[féibld] 전설적인 battleground[bǽtlgràund] 싸움터

expel[ikspél] 내쫓다 occupy[ákjupài] 점령하다 monopoly[mənápəli] 독점

entrepreneur[à:ntrəprənə́:r] 상인, 기업가 outpost[áutpòust] 식민지 commodity[kəmádəti] 상품

peak[pi:k] 최고에 달하다 staples[stéiplz] 중요 상품 bustling[bʌ́sliŋ] 붐비는 absolute[ǽbsəlù:t] 절대적인

minority[minɔ́:rəti] 소수의 cosmopolitan[kàzməpálətn] 국제적인 commemorate[kəmémərèit] 기념하다

문제 공략하기

p.191

최근의 연구에 따르면, 양서류 개체수는 지난 50년간 세계적으로 감소하였다. 전문가들은 서식지 파괴가 부분적인 원인이라는 데 동의한다. 늪이 마르는 것과 강에 댐을 건설하는 것은 양서류가 먹이와 생식을 위해 의존하는 수계를 완전히 바꾸어 버렸고, 숲의 파괴는 이러한 많은 동물로부터 적당한 쉼터를 빼앗아갔다. 기후 변화 또한 가능성 있는 범인으로 분류되어 왔다. 양서류의 얇은 피부는 투과성이 있고 알은 껍질이 없기 때문에 그들은 온도와 습도 변화에 매우 민감하다. 지구 온난화가 번식 패턴을 방해하고 신체적 질병을 가져온다고 가정되어 왔다. 관련된 문제는 최근 몇 십년간의 대기 오존 감소이다. 변온동물인 양서류는 스스로를 따뜻하게 하기 위해 반드시 햇볕을 쬐야 한다. 높은 자외선 강도는 개구리의 왜소 발육증과 면역 문제와 연관이 있다.

HACKERS PRACTICE

p.192

01 (C), (D) 02 (A), (C) 03 (A), (D) 04 (B), (C) 05 (A), (D), (E) 06 (B), (E), (F) 07 (A), (B), (D)

01 1917년 12월 18일, 국회에 의해 채택된 미국 헌법 수정 제18조는 사람들의 권리를 빼앗은 유일한 수정안이었다. 1919년 1월에 승인된 이 법은 취하게 하는 음료의 판매, 수입, 수출을 금지하였다. 수정 조항의 정당성을 입증하는 이후의 법이 1919년 10월 28일에 통과되어 취하게 하는 음료의 알코올 내용물을 구체화하였다.

진보 운동을 지지하는 사회 개혁 단체와 금주 운동을 지지하는 종교 단체는 술집의 폐점을 주장하고 있었다. 금주법으로 알려진 이 운동은 대중의 음주 태도에 경종을 울렸다. 진보와 금주 단체는 금주를 지지하는 다른 이유를 가지고 있었다. 전자는 부가 공유되고 사람들이 평등한 권리를 갖는 사회로의 급진적인 변화를 촉구한 반면, 후자는 보수주의와 절제의 원칙을 진척시키고 싶어했다. 그럼에도 불구하고, 그들의 연합과 미국 대중의 지지가 수정 제18조의 승인으로 이어졌다.

그러나 그 운동이 원했던 결과는 실제로 실현되지 못 했다. 수정 조항은 술 소비가 30퍼센트 줄어드는 것에는 기여했지만, 더 젊은 세대의 미국인들이 결국 법을 거부했고 소비되는 술의 양이 금주 전의 수준까지 다시 올라갔다. 암시장에 불법 주류가 나타났고 알코올의 밀매 또는 밀수가 범죄 단체에 엄청난 이득을 가져다 주었다. 그러나 정부는 음료의 불법 생산과 판매에 세금을 매길 수 없었다. 승인된 지 14년 후, 수정 조항은 폐지되었다.

02 전 세계의 광고는 소비자들의 흥미를 끌고 제품과 서비스를 구입하도록 만들어진다. 성인들은 광고의 강력한 설득력이 있는 메시지에 항상 속지는 않지만, 아이들은 쉽게 속는다. 1991년 심리학자 쿤켈과 로버츠가 시행한 연구에서 아이들은 제품 판촉의 설득적 목적을 이해하는 데 인식 능력이 부족하다는 증거를 제시했다. 그들의 연구는 진실과 거짓을 종종 구별하지 못하는 아이들이 만화 캐릭터와 연예인에게 매혹된다는 점을 광고주들이 이용한다는 것을 보여준다.

광고주들은 6세 이하의 아이들이 현실과 환상을 구별하지 못한다는 것을 알고 있다. 시금치 통조림 상표의 광고 방송에서는 만화 캐릭터 뽀빠이가 나올 수 있다. 아이들은 만화에서 뽀빠이가 시금치를 먹은 후 육체적으로 강해진다는 것을 안다. 그들은 만화에서 보는 것을 방송의 광고 메시지와 연관시킨다. 성인들은 이것을 믿을 수 없다는 것을 알지만, 아이들은 그 메시지를 쉽게 진실로 받아들일 것이다. 이는 광고와 아이들에 대해 미국 정신 의학회(APA)가 시행한 연구에 의해 뒷받침되는데, 이 연구에서는 과장을 인식하지 못하는 것이 아이들을 광고 내용의 심리적 압박에 더 영향 받기 쉽게 만든다는 결론을 내렸다.

APA의 연구는 또한 저항할 수 없는 광고가 물질주의로의 가치 변화를 양성할 수 있다고 하였다. 광고주들은 아이들이 가장 좋아하는 연예인과 만화 캐릭터를 광고에 이용하여 물질에 대한 선입견을 조장한다. 예를 들어, 닌자거북이의 창조자는 가방, 도시락, 시리얼, 칫솔 같은 수백 개의 제품에 특허를 냈다. 1989년에는 제품 매출액이 640억 달러에 달했다.

03   사회 생물학은 특정 행동 양식이 가지고 있을 만한 진화적으로 유리한 요소 내에서 동물의 사회적인 행동을 설명하려는 학문이다. 무리 사냥 같은 행동이나 사회성 곤충들의 벌집 사회가 종종 관찰된다. 조직을 이루는 것은 개체수를 유지하기 위한 노력으로 보여지며 생식과 생존에 관련된 행동 양식을 포함한다. 즉, 동물의 사회적인 행동을 연구할 때 연구원들은 동물 종이 집단 환경 내에서 어떻게 상호작용하는지 관찰한다.

어떤 포식동물 종은 생존을 보증하기 위해 무리 지어 산다. 늑대는 이러한 종 중 하나이며 12~20마리의 가족 같은 무리를 형성한다. 그들의 조직은 방어를 강화하여 사냥하고 이동하는 동안 무리를 보호한다. 무리에서 가장 지배적인 암수인 우두머리 늑대와 그 다음인 2인자 늑대가 주요 구성원이다. 다른 늑대들은 더 계급이 낮지만 그래도 무리의 생존에 기여한다. 낮은 계급의 구성원들은 우두머리의 지도 아래 복종함으로써 무리 구성원들의 생존을 돕는 데 합세한다.

비슷하게, 벌과 같은 사회성 곤충은 집단을 유지하고 생존을 돕는 매우 조직화된 벌집 사회를 이룬다. 하나의 벌집은 2~5만 마리의 벌로 구성되며 구성원들은 기능에 따라 나뉜다. 여왕벌은 알을 낳고 수벌은 여왕과 짝짓기를 하여 알을 수정한다. 일벌은 벌집 짓기, 새끼 기르기, 여왕 시중 들기, 꿀과 꽃가루 모으기, 벌집 지키기 등 다양한 업무를 통해 벌집을 지키고 구성원을 돌본다. 이렇게 조직화되어 각각의 벌은 집단의 생존을 보장한다.

04   낙타와 유사한 동물인 라마는 한때 북미의 토박이였지만 마지막 빙하 시대 때 북미 대륙에서 사라졌다. 라마는 남미에서는 살아남았는데, 그곳에서 안데스 산맥 원주민들에 의해 다양한 목적으로 사용되었다. 6천 년 전만큼이나 일찍 잉카인들은 라마를 길들였고 이 동물과 가까운 관계를 형성하였다.

라마는 잉카인들에게 음식과 옷의 재료를 제공하였다. 어른 수컷 한 마리는 식용 고기 100킬로그램을 산출하였고, 이것은 종종 저장하기 위하여 소금에 절인 후 건조되었다. 무게가 가볍고 영양이 높은 말린 라마 고기는 잉카인 병사와 여행자의 기본 식료품이었다. 라마의 가죽은 판초나 신발 같은 방한복을 위한 양질의 가죽으로 바뀌었다. 예를 들어, 잉카인의 샌들 밑창은 가장 두꺼운 목 부분 가죽으로 만들어졌다. 털의 섬유는 옷감을 만드는 데 이용되었다. 잉카인들은 그것을 'aluascay'라고 불렀고 그것은 일반인들이 입는 옷에 사용되는 일반적인 재료였다.

약 600년에 이르러, 라마는 또한 짐을 나르는 동물로 중요해졌다. 잉카인들은 라마를 물건과 건축 재료를 운반하는 짐을 나르는 동물로 사용했다. 커다란 수컷 라마는 하루에 20킬로미터까지 약 30킬로그램의 짐을 운반할 수 있었다. 라마의 속도는 빠른 건 아니었지만 훈련이 잘 된다는 점이 라마를 그 일에 적합하게 했다. 라마는 상당한 거리를 손으로 물건을 운반해야 하는 부담을 매우 덜어주었다.

05   달의 기원을 설명하려는 하나의 시도는 포획설이다. 이 설에 의하면 달은 태양계 내 다른 곳에서 형성되었고, 우주를 떠돌다가 지구의 중력장에 '포획'되어 오늘날과 같이 우리 행성 주위를 돌기 시작했다. 이 주장의 강점은 지구와 달 사이의 구성 요소 차이를 태양계 내 동떨어진 지역에서 형성된 것으로 설명할 수 있다는 것이다. 그러나 많은 과학자들은 달 크기 물체의 지나가는 속도가 지구의 중력에 영구히 영향 받을 만큼 충분히 느렸을지에 대해 회의적이다.

다른 가능성은 달이 분열에서 기원했다는 것이다. 이 가설은 핵 원자나 생물 세포가 둘로 쪼개질 수 있듯이, 달이 한때 지구의 일부였는데 나중에 분리되었다고 제안한다. 이 설에 의하면, 지구는 형성 시기에 너무 빨리 회전하고 있어서 적도 부근에 불룩한 부분이 발달했다. 마침내, 회전이 계속 되면서 불룩한 부분이 떨어져 나갔다. 이 설의 문제는 현재 달의 궤도가 적도와 정렬되어 있지 않다는 것이다. 그러나 분리설을 지지하는 일부 과학자들은 달이 적도로부터 이동하여 다른 궤도를 따르게 되었을 수도 있다고 주장한다.

세 번째 설은 거대 충돌설로, 태양계가 형성된 후 지구의 구성 요소와는 다른 구성 요소를 가진 더 작은 크기의 다른 행성이 지구와 충돌했다는 것이다. 두 행성에서 물질이 떨어져 나와 합쳐졌고 나중에는 달이 되었다. 이러한 시나리오는 달이 왜 지구의 핵에 존재하는 철과 니켈 같은 고밀도 물질이 아닌 돌로 구성되어 있는지 명백하게 설명해 준다. 충돌이 표면의 파편을 옮겨 놓았을 것이다.

---

06 지구에 생명이 어떻게 생겨났는지에 대해 가장 널리 받아들여지는 과학적인 가설은 '화학 합성'인데, 이는 지구와 대기에 서서히 점진적으로 쌓인 화학 물질의 집적이 유기 화합물의 형성을 촉진했다고 주장한다. 생물 유기체의 기초단위가 된 것은 이 유기적 화합물이었다. 이와 매우 비슷하지만 모순되는 주장은 본질적으로 똑같은 과정이 지구가 아닌 은하계의 다른 곳, 아마도 우주나 다른 행성에서 일어났다는 것이다. 생명의 가능성을 가진 분자 구조는 지구에서 자생한 것이 아니라 운석이나 혜성 같은 외래 천체에서 떨어진 것이다. 이러한 두 번째 주장은 '범종설'로 알려져 있다.

이 과정이 어디에서 일어났던 간에, 과학자들은 생명에 필수적인 분자 화합물이 알려진 원소들의 작은 파편에서 창조되었을 거라고 믿는다. 무기 화합물이 어떻게 합성되어 유기 화합물이 되었는지는 1952년에 스탠리 밀러와 해럴드 유리에 의해 증명되었다. 두 과학자들은 원시 기체인 암모니아, 메탄, 수소와 수증기를 함께 튜브에 섞어 넣고, 전기 불꽃을 더했다. 1주 후, 그 통에는 살아있는 세포 내 단백질을 만드는 데 중요한 아미노산 같은 유기 화합물이 생겨났다. 밀러-유리의 실험은 번개와 원시 기체가 섞여 유기 화합물을 창조했을 수도 있다는 것을 시사한다.

그래도 유기 화합물 자체만으로는 생명이 아니다. 예를 들어 아미노산은 화학 반응으로 창조되지만 생명을 발생시키려면 부가적인 단계가 필요하다. 지금까지 정확히 이런 일이 어떻게 일어나는지를 증명한 실험은 없지만 전문가들은 지구의 초기 생명체들이 원핵 생물(단세포 생물)이었다고 믿는다. 최초의 단순한 세포는 먹이를 위해 환경에 의존하는 종속 영양 생물이었다. 이러한 단세포의 일부는 광합성을 통해 직접 먹이를 생산할 수 있게 진화하였다. 이를 독립 영양 생물이라고 부른다. 수백만 년에 걸쳐 일부 세포의 핵에서 DNA가 형성되었고, 그 이상의 진화는 결국 복잡한 다세포 생물체로 이어졌다.

---

07 인쇄의 역사에서 15세기 중반 유럽의 인쇄기 발명의 궁극적인 영향은 상당했지만, 그것의 혁명적인 효과는 바로 나타나지 않았다. 이러한 지연은 몇 가지 요인 때문이었다. 인쇄기 덕분에 유례없는 속도로 인쇄물을 생산하는 것이 가능해졌음에도 불구하고, 당시 대부분의 사람들은 글자를 몰랐다. 따라서, 읽지 못 하는 사람들에게 책에 나오는 정보를 읽어줘야 했다. 또한, 당시에는 인쇄물의 종류가 제한적이었다. 종교적인 글과 고전의 재생산물은 흔했지만, 새로운 아이디어의 출판은 드물었다. 이 요소들이 합쳐져 판매되는 부수는 별로 많지 않았다.

19세기가 되자, 상당히 더 넓은 범위의 출판물이 인쇄되었다. 미국만큼 이것이 분명히 나타난 곳은 없었다. 더 빠른 인쇄기와 더 저렴한 잉크 덕분에 많은 양의 인쇄물을 생산하는 것이 매우 효율적이었고, 1830년대의 전보 발명이 장거리의 빠른 통신을 가능하게 하였다. 이러한 발달은 뉴스에 대한 사람들의 관심을 불러 일으켰고, 곧 신문이 전국적으로 배부되었다. 1860년대에는 일리노이 주에 400개의 활성화된 신문이 있었고, 일리노이 대중매체의 중심지였던 시카고에는 11개의 자체 일간신문이 있었다.

동시에, 공공 교육이 일반화되어 식자율을 크게 높였다. 신문사는 '하루의 모든 뉴스를 모두가 감당할 수 있는 가격으로' 제공하여 이로 인한 이익을 보았다. 한 부 당 1센트밖에 안 되는 penny newspapers는 전통적이고 좀 더 진지한 정기간행물의 가격의 몇 분의 1에 재미있고 흥미진진한 기사를 보증했다. 게다가, 그들의 페이지는 광고로 가득 차 있었는데, 이 신문들은 연간 혹은 월간 구독료보다는 광고에 의해 자금을 제공받았기 때문이다. 많은 회사들이 광고를 통해 노동자 계층의 고객들과 접촉하기 위해 이 새로운 대중매체를 사용하였다.

소설계에서도 비슷한 발달이 일어났다. 낮은 가격 때문에 dime novels라는 이름이 붙은 소설이 19세기에 대유행이 되었다. 이렇게 저렴하게 제작된 인기 있는 책들은 모험에 대한 선정적인 이야기로 미국이 가장 사랑하는 이야기가 되었고 소설 시장을 새로운 유형의 고객들에게 확장시키는 데 기여했다. 저렴한 출판물의 경향은 유럽에서도 볼 수 있었지만, 이만큼 두드러지지는 않았다. 영국 같은 곳에서는, 사람들이 여전히 정교한 표지의 수제 책을 선호하였다.

1 Assessing Auditory Perception in Infants 유아의 청력 평가   p.202

| 1. (B) | 2. (C) | 3. (B) | 4. (C) | 5. (B) | 6. (D) | 7. 4th ■ | 8. (B)–2~3단락, (D)–5단락, (F)–4단락 |

1   유아는 인생 경험이 상대적으로 부족하여 소리에 대해 심하게 제한된 이해를 가지고 세상에 태어난다. 그러나 소리를 듣는 그들의 능력은 성인의 능력에 비해 약간 덜 민감할 뿐이며 청각 전문가들은 6개월이 되면 아기들이 청력을 완전히 발달시킨다는 데 동의한다. 아동 발달에 청각이 중요하기 때문에 연구원들은 유아의 청각 발달을 평가하는 다양한 방법을 생각해냈다.

2   성인과 달리, 유아는 실험 중에 언어 지시를 따르는 것이 불가능하다. 이는 신생아의 청각 실험을 힘들게 한다. ²그러나 다행히도 성인처럼 유아는 특정한 소리에 대한 자연적인 생리 반응을 보인다. 이러한 무의식적인 반응은 예상치 못한 큰 소리가 존재할 때 가장 분명하다. 유아는 갑작스런 소음에 노출되면 즉각적으로 눈을 깜빡이고 깜짝 놀랐을 때와 같은 신체 반응을 보인다. 초음파 사진은 태아가 자궁에 있을 때에도 이와 같은 방식으로 반응한다는 것을 보여 주었다. 다른 무의식적인 반응은 유아가 흥미를 유발하는 무언가를 들을 때이다. 정상적인 청각을 가진 유아는 일반적으로 엄마의 목소리처럼 흥미로운 소리가 나는 방향으로 머리를 움직일 것이며 이러한 경향은 또한 신생아의 소리 위치 추정 능력에 대한 유용한 정보를 연구원들에게 제공한다.

3   무의식적인 반응에 집중된 다른 실험은 청각 신호가 심장 박동률과 뇌파에 미치는 영향을 검사하는 것을 포함한다. 눈을 깜빡이는 빈도처럼 심장 박동률은 한 사람이 흥분하면 종종 무의식적으로 바뀌며, 단순한 전자식 모니터로 측정될 수 있다. 뇌파는 유아의 두피에 전극을 부착하고 청각 신호가 있을 때마다 간격을 두고 뇌파 그래프를 검토함으로써 측정된다. 뇌간 유발 청력 반응(BEAR)이라고 알려진 이 실험은 귀와 뇌 사이의 신경 활동을 자극하기 위해 딸깍하는 소리를 사용한다. ³전극은 파동 정보를 그래프로 전송하는데, 이것은 유아가 소리를 감지하면 증가하고 감소한다. 그래프가 뇌파의 변화를 나타내지 않으면 유아에게 청력 문제가 있다는 것을 의미한다. BEAR 실험은 예를 들어 혼수상태에 빠졌거나 심각한 정신 장애를 가진 성인의 경우처럼 피실험자가 의사소통을 하지 못할 때의 성인 환자에게도 유용하다.

4   연구원들이 사용하는 추가적인 방법은 조건 반사적인 행동 반응을 실험하는 것이다. 청력학자들은 다양한 소리에 대한 주의력과 관련된 행동에 대해 유아에게 보상함으로써 소리를 구분하는 유아의 능력을 검사하도록 고안된 일련의 절차를 사용한다. 하나의 유명한 방법은 고무젖꼭지, 막대사탕 또는 빠는 행동을 유발하는 다른 도구를 사용하는 것이다. 유아가 빠는 것이 관찰될 때마다 연구원들은 빠는 내내 하나의 소리를 들려준다. 서서히 유아는 그 특정한 소리와 빠는 것을 연관짓기 시작한다. ⁴그러나 시간이 지남에 따라 유아는 소리에 싫증을 느끼고 빠는 것을 멈출 것이다. 이러한 흥미의 상실은 '습관화'라고 알려져 있다. 청력학자들이 유아에게서 습관화를 발견하면, 새로운 소리로 바꾸어 이 과정을 다시 시작할 것이다. 유아가 소리의 변화를 인식하면 새로운 소리를 듣기 위해서 빠는 행동을 보여줄 것이라는 것이 가정이다.

5   신생아부터 4개월 된 유아에 대한 연구는 소리 감지와 위치 추정 능력에 대한 단서만을 제공하지만, 나이가 더 많은 유아의 경우 언어 신호에 대해 반응하는 눈의 움직임을 연구함으로써 유용한 정보를 얻을 수 있다. 그러므로, 인지 심리학자들은 유아의 성장에 따른 시청각적 언어 인지 발달에 매우 관심이 있다. 보고 들을 수 있는 유아는 다른 하나를 강화하기 위해서 두 개의 감각(방식)을 모두 사용할 것이고, 이는 통합 인지로 알려져 있다. 안구 운동 실험은 소리를 식별하는 연구와 초기 언어 이해력을 실험하는 연구를 연결하는 다리로 널리 사용된다. 따라서, 언어음은 유아의 안구 운동 반응을 이끌어 내는 데 사용되는 주요한 도구 중 하나이다. 예를 들어, 연구원들은 개와 공이 그려진 두 개의 그림 카드를 유아 앞에서 손에 쥐고 둘 중 하나의 단어를 말했을 때 유아의 안구 운동을 관찰한다. **만약 유아가 발음된 단어에 일치하는 그림을 본다면 그것은 이해했음을 나타내는 것이다.**

6   유아의 청각 발달을 평가하는 모든 방법의 목표는 초기에 청력 문제를 발견해내는 것인데, 초기의 개입이 장기적인 부정적 효과를 방지하는 데 도움이 될 수 있기 때문이다. 수많은 심리 연구는 청력 결핍을 일생의 대화와 언어 습득 문제, 낮은 학업 성적, 사회적 상호작용의 어려움에서 오는 감정적 피로 같은 연관된 문제와 연결시켰다. 이러한 문제 중 상당수는 초기 치료와 청각 장애 아동을 위한 특수 교육 프로그램을 통해 예방할 수 있다.

slightly[sláitli] 약간 **auditory**[ɔ́:dətɔ̀:ri] 청각의 **verbal**[və́:rbəl] 언어의 **neonatal**[nì:ounéitl] 신생아의

spontaneous[spɑntéiniəs] 자연적인 **involuntary**[inváləntèri] 무의식적인 **blink**[bliŋk] 눈을 깜빡이다

ultrasound[ʌ́ltrəsàund] 초음파 **fetus**[fí:təs] 태아 **womb**[wu:m] 자궁 **generate**[dʒénərèit] 유발하다

attach[ətǽtʃ] 부착하다 **electrode**[iléktroud] 전극 **neurological**[njùərəládʒikəl] 신경의 **disorder**[disɔ́:rdər] 장애

conditioned[kəndíʃənd] 조건 반사적인 **audiologist**[ɔ̀:diálədʒist] 청력학자 **reward**[riwɔ́:rd] 보상하다

attentiveness[əténtivnis] 주의력 **pacifier**[pǽsəfàiər] 고무젖꼭지 **suck**[sʌk] 빨다 **associate**[əsóuʃièit] 연관짓다

tire[taiər] 싫증나다 **habituation**[həbìtʃuéiʃən] 습관화 **cognitive**[kágnətiv] 인지의 **mode**[moud] 방식

discrimination[diskrìmənéiʃən] 식별 **elicit**[ilísit] 이끌어내다 **intervention**[intərvénʃən] 개입

deficiency[difíʃənsi] 결핍 **lifelong**[láiflɔ̀:ŋ] 일생의 **acquisition**[æ̀kwəzíʃən] 습득 **avoid**[əvɔ́id] 예방하다

hearing-impaired[híəriŋimpɛ̀ərd] 청각 장애를 가진

---

② Ancient Greek Vases 고대 그리스 항아리   p.206

p.206

> 1. (C)   2. (B)   3. (B)   4. (A)   5. (B)   6. (D)   7. (D)   8. (A)   9. 1st ■   10. (C)-3단락, (E)-2단락, (F)-4~5단락

1   예술 역사가와 고고학자가 고대 유적지를 탐험할 때, 그들은 문서, 예술 작품, 오랜 과거 문명의 물리적인 흔적을 찾는다. 모든 역사적인 유물 중, 도자기만큼 영구적인 문화적 상징으로 중요한 것은 별로 없다. 고대 책과 벽화는 희귀한 발견이지만, 도자기는 내구성 덕분에 유적지에서 상당히 흔하다. **도자기는 불을 잘 견디며 깨졌을 때도 도자기 파편은 오랫동안 손상되지 않는다.** 그러므로 도자기는 잊혀진 문화의 예술과 사회로의 작은 창문 역할을 한다. 예를 들면, 고대 그리스의 색칠된 항아리는 그리스 예술의 연속적인 역사를 보여준다. 탁월한 질을 가진 이 작품은 수많은 예술가와 수집가에게 영감을 주었다. 이 아름다운 항아리는 생산된 시간과 장소에 따라 양식이 다르다.

2   기원전 10세기에는, 기하학적인 장식이 그리스 항아리를 공통적으로 장식하였다. 수학과 논리에 대한 그리스인들의 몰두는 기원전 750년까지의 도자기에서 아주 명백하게 드러난다. 추상적인 모양과 선이 항아리의 돌출된 부분에 위치해 있는데 가장 흔한 곳은 어깨와 배 부분이며, 종종 반복되는 양식으로 가로로 놓인 아치, 동그라미, 물결 모양의 선이 시종 논리적인 균형을 이루었다. 곡선은 나중에 직선과 삼각형 모양으로 바뀌었고, 물결 모양 선은 교차되는 45도 각으로 연결되는 일련의 지그재그의 집합인 오늬 무늬와 같은 더 날카로운 요소로 대거 대체되었다. 이러한 기술적인 개선과 함께, 대상은 손잡이 사이의 배 부분에 집중되기 시작하였다. 이런 기하학적인 디자인은 연한 빨간색 진흙 위에 진한 색으로 그려져 장식과 배경 사이에 뚜렷한 대조를 나타냈다.

3   기원전 8세기 말이 되면서, [4D]항아리에 무늬와 함께 그림이 나타나기 시작했다. 이집트와 시리아의 동양적인 영향의 결과라고 여겨지는 이 시기는 그리스 도자기의 '동양화 시기'로 알려져 있다. 동양화 시기에 가장 영향력 있는 도공들은 주요 교역 중심지인 코린트에 있었다. [4C]코린트의 장인들은 기름과 향수를 담기 위한 작은 휴대용 항아리를 생산하여 도자기에 대한 해외 수요를 이용하였다. [4B]그들은 동양의 이미지에 매료되었고 사자 같은 이국적인 동물과 불사조 같은 이상화된 괴물을 도자기에 그려 넣었다. [3]그들은 검은 유약을 사용하여 그림을 사실적인 스타일로 칠했고 유약을 파내어 그 아래 연한 색깔의 진흙이 보이도록 선을 긁는 기술을 완성했다. 이 전문적인 기술은 새의 깃털이나 꽃의 정교한 부분에서 볼 수 있듯이 대비되는 미세한 세부 사항을 묘사하는 방법을 나타낸다.

4   그리스 항아리의 진화는 그림이 더욱 더 사실적인 요소를 갖게 되는 향상의 시기인 기원전 5세기에 아테네에서 최고조에 이르렀다. [5]기원전 500년쯤에 일어난 발전은 반면상에서 4분의 3이 정면인 자세로의 변화였다. 이를 달성하기 위해, 아테네의 화가들은 원근법을 사용했다. 원근법은 관찰자에 대한 각도 위치에 따라 그려진 물체가 실제보다 더 짧아 보이게 하는 시각적인 기술이다. 그것은 3차원적 장면이 항아리의 표면 같은 2차원적 공간에 표현될 수 있는 시각적인 관점을 창조하였다. 관점 기술은 겹치는 그림으로 물체의 공간적인 움직임의 느낌을 표현하는 것을 포함하도록 확장되었다.

5   움직임의 더 사실적인 표현은 색칠된 항아리가 단순히 장식적이기 보다는 종종 설명적이었기 때문에 유용했다. 화가들은 그리스 신화에 전해 내려오는 이야기에 등장하는 신과 영웅에 대한 장면을 묘사하였다. 관점의 혁신은 그림이 감정을 전달하는 데 더 표현력과 설득력이 있도록 하였고, 적색상 도자기라고 불리는 새로운 양식이 도공의 표현적인 선택을 더 넓

혀주었다. 코린트 사람들과 달리, 아테네 도공들은 검은 바탕으로 대상의 윤곽을 그렸는데, 이 혁신은 새기는 대신 붓으로 마지막 마무리를 할 수 있었다는 것을 의미하였다. 이러한 변화 덕분에 사소한 세부 묘사를 더 쉽게 할 수 있었고 더 탄력적으로 명암을 넣을 수 있었다. [6]오늘날까지 살아남은 예가 거의 없긴 하지만 일부 적색상 항아리는 화가의 비문이나 서명을 포함하기까지 했다.

6 진화되는 고대 그리스 항아리 그림 방식은 다른 그림 분야에서도 비슷한 시도와 혁신이 일어나고 있었다는 것을 시사하지만, 고대 그리스의 벽화는 오늘날까지 하나도 남지 못 했다. 하지만 다행히도 도자기의 많은 예가 존재한다. 살아남은 수만 개의 항아리 조각과 표본은 수집가와 박물관들의 수요가 많고 종종 높은 가격에 팔린다. 그것은 엄청난 아름다움과 현대 화가들에게 영감을 주는 데 영향력이 있는 요소라는 사실 뿐만 아니라, 고대 그리스 예술을 이해하는 데 있어서의 중요성 때문에도 중시된다.

어휘
remnant[rémnənt] 흔적 **artifact**[ɑ́ːrtəfæ̀kt] 유물 **pottery**[pátəri] 도자기 **enduring**[indʒúəriŋ] 영구적인
mural[mjúərəl] 벽화 **find**[faind] 발견 **fairly**[fέərli] 상당히 **durability**[djùərəbíləti] 내구성
unsurpassed[ʌ̀nsərpǽst] 탁월한 **inspire**[inspáiər] 영감을 주다 **geometric**[dʒìːəmétrik] 기하학의
ornament[ɔ́ːrnəmənt] 장식하다 **obsession**[əbséʃən] 몰두 **horizontally**[hɔ̀ːrəzántli] 가로로 **rectilinear**[rèktəlíniər] 직선의
triangular[traiǽŋgjulər] 삼각의 **alternating**[ɔ́ːltərnèitiŋ] 교차의 **refinement**[riːfáinmənt] 개선 **stark**[staːrk] 뚜렷한
decor[deikɔ́ːr] 장식 **Orientalize**[ɔ̀ːriéntəlàiz] 동양화하다 **portable**[pɔ́ːrtəbl] 휴대용의 **fascinate**[fǽsənèit] 매혹하다
exotic[igzátik] 이국적인 **phoenix**[fíːniks] 불사조 **naturalistic**[næ̀tʃərəlístik] 사실적인 **perfect**[pə́ːrfikt] 완성하다
intricate[íntrikət] 복잡한 **enhancement**[inhǽnsmənt] 향상 **profile**[próufail] 반면상 **frontal**[frʌ́ntl] 정면의
foreshortening[fɔːrʃɔ́ːrtniŋ] 원근법 **optical**[áptikəl] 시각의 **tactic**[tǽktik] 기술 **perspective**[pərspéktiv] 관점
depict[dipíkt] 묘사하다 **innovation**[ìnəvéiʃən] 혁신 **flexibility**[flèksəbíləti] 탄력성 **shard**[ʃaːrd] 조각
command[kəmǽnd] 팔리다 **tremendous**[triméndəs] 엄청난

③ Commedia Dell'arte 코메디아 델라르테 p.210

1. (D)　2. (A)　3. (B)　4. (B)　5. (A)　6. (A)　7. (B)　8. (B)　9. 3rd ▪　10. (A)-6단락, (D)-4~5단락, (E)-2~3단락

1 코메디아 델라르테는 희극과 희곡 요소를 결합한 무대 공연이었다. 문자 그대로 이 용어는 '예술가의 희극'을 의미하고 18세기 영국과 프랑스에서 흔했던 장르에 처음으로 응용되었다. 그러나 이 장르는 사실상 16세기 이탈리아에서 무대 연기를 직업으로 정립하는 데 영향력이 있었던 방랑하는 극 배우 집단에서 발생하였다. 당시에, 이는 고전적인 연극 제작에 매우 혁신적인 접근이었다.

2 [2D]코메디아 델라르테의 구성 요소 중 다수의 유래는 고대 로마와 그리스 연극까지 거슬러 올라갈 수 있고 사랑, 돈, 즐거움, 세대 간 갈등, 질투와 같은 주제를 포함한다. 일반적인 시나리오는 무언가가 두 연인의 앞길을 방해하는 낭만적인 갈등이다. 일반적으로, 남자와 여자 등장인물 한 쌍이 사랑에 빠지지만 전형적으로 여자의 아버지와 같은 나이가 더 많은 인물이 그 관계에 반대하고 관계가 발전되는 것을 방해하려고 한다. **이 반대는 주로 구혼자의 사회적 지위나 부의 결핍에 기초했다.** 이야기가 진전되는 동안 여자의 사랑의 감정이 일시적으로 가라앉지만, 집요한 구혼자는 연장자의 반대에도 불구하고 계속해서 그녀의 사랑을 갈구한다.

3 구혼자는 사랑하는 여인에게 접근하기 위해 대개 하인과 같은 제3자의 도움을 이용한다. [2C]하지만 종종 또 다른 문제가 발전하는데, 일반적으로 아버지가 호의를 보인 구혼 경쟁자의 형태로 등장한다. 이 보조적인 인물은 협력이나 대립을 통해 연결된 등장인물 간의 복잡한 상호작용을 야기한다. 관여된 다양한 관계에 따라 긴장이 조성되고, [2B]이 대인 관계는 종종 부모와 자식, 주인과 종, 부자와 가난한 자와 같이 위계적인 질서로 구성된다. 그럼에도 불구하고, 일반적으로 결말은 비극적이기보다 운명적인 두 연인의 결혼, 모든 등장인물 간의 용서를 포함하는 행복한 결말로 관객에게 긍정적인 감정을 남기는 만족스러운 결말이다.

4 코메디아 델라르테의 기본적인 줄거리는 전통적인 자료와 등장인물에 기반하고 있기 때문에, 그 줄거리는 관객 구성원에

게 매우 친숙했다. 배우들은 오래된 이야기를 본질적으로 재생산하였고, 공연의 많은 부분은 잘 연습된 대사와 대화에서 왔다. 배우들은 종종 상당한 기간 동안 특정한 역할을 맡았으며 특정 등장인물의 뉘앙스와 세부 묘사의 달인이었다. 게다가, 배우의 가장 주요한 요건은 고전 수사학, 즉 설득적인 언어의 구술에 대한 기본적인 이해였다. 결과적으로, [4]코메디아 델라르테의 흥행단은 종종 대사를 암기하고, 줄거리를 짜고, 대사와 동작을 의미 있게 전달하기 위한 전통적인 기법을 연구하기 위해 문학 작품을 참고했다.

5 이러한 기본적인 기술은 역동적인 배우들에 의한 해석의 자유에 의해 향상되었다. 등장인물의 진실된 효과는 문어적, 구어적 전통으로부터 얻은 지혜를 받아들이고 이를 즉흥적인 방식으로 전략적으로 정교하게 만드는 배우의 능력에 달려 있었다. 코메디아 델라르테의 대본은 훨씬 축소되었고 배우들은 세부적인 대사와 장면을 암기할 책임이 없었다. [5]오히려 교양 있는 관객의 주목을 얻기 위해서, 배우들은 즉흥연기를 자주 하였다. 이는 예측할 수 없고 희극적인 요소를 연기에 도입하였다. 혁신의 가능성은 배우들이 지역적인 기호와 환경에 대응할 수 있게 하였는데, 예를 들어, 희극적으로 지역의 추문을 알리거나 시국을 풍자하기 위해 장면을 바꾸는 것을 통해서였다.

6 무대 위에서 배우는 관객에게 명백하게 규정된 역할을 전달하기 위해 의상을 입었으나, 가면과 다른 가장복을 바꿈으로써 그들이 다른 역할을 맡고 연기에 또 다른 역동적인 측면을 더하게 해주었다. 또한 소도구의 사용은 관객과의 의사소통에서 중요했다. 손에 드는 지팡이 또는 인조 곤봉인, 슬랩스틱으로 알려진 물체는 싸움이나 논쟁 중에 과장된 폭력을 표현하는 데 사용되었다. [7]슬랩스틱은 등장인물이나 물체가 세게 부딪쳤을 때 매우 큰 소리를 냈으나, 개인에게 아무런 해도 끼치지 않았다. 본질은 온화하지만 과도한 소리 때문에, 슬랩스틱은 부조리한 내용을 유쾌하게 전달하기 위해 사용되었던 모든 과장된 신체 행동에 대한 은유로서 현대 오락에 들어왔고, 여기서 슬랩스틱 코미디라는 표현이 나왔다.

7 코메디아 델라르테는 16~18세기에 전성기를 맞이하였고 특히 이탈리아와 프랑스에서 인기 있었다. 배우들은 10~12명으로 구성된 흥행단을 구성하여 대중 앞에서 공연하고 종종 함께 이동했다. 그러는 중에, 그들은 일시적으로 쓰는 무대를 만들었다. 공연에서 얻은 이윤은 집단 내에 분배되었다. 이러한 관점에서, 이 집단은 자급자족하였고 각 구성원은 실질적으로 전문적이었다.

어휘

literally[lítərəli] 문자 그대로 apply[əplái] 응용하다 originate[ərídʒənèit] 발생하다 profession[prəféʃən] 직업
innovative[ínəvèitiv] 혁신적인 intergenerational[intərdʒènəréiʃənl] 세대 간 figure[fígjər] 인물
typically[típikəli] 전형적으로 disapprove[dìsəprú:v] 반대하다 impede[impí:d] 방해하다 amorous[æmərəs] 사랑의
subside[səbsáid] 가라앉다 relentless[riléntlis] 집요한 suitor[sú:tər] 구혼자 complication[kàmpləkéiʃən] 문제점
cooperation[kouàpəréiʃən] 협력 antagonism[æntǽgənìzm] 대립 hierarchical[hàiərá:rkikəl] 위계적인
destined[déstind] 운명적인 commit[kəmít] 맡기다 foremost[fɔ́:rmòust] 주요한 requirement[rikwáiərmənt] 요건
rhetoric[rétərik] 수사학 persuasive[pərswéisiv] 설득적인 troupe[tru:p] 흥행단 memorize[méməràiz] 암기하다
argument[á:rgjumənt] 줄거리 fundamental[fʌ̀ndəméntl] 기본적인 craft[kræft] 정교하게 만들다
improvisational[impràvəzéiʃənl] 즉흥적인 satirize[sǽtəràiz] 풍자하다 convey[kənvéi] 전달하다
disguise[disgáiz] 가장, 변장 prop[prɑp] 소도구 baton[bətán] 지팡이 faux[fou] 인조의 club[klʌb] 곤봉
exaggerated[igzǽdʒərèitid] 과장된 benign[bináin] 온화한 absurdity[æbsɔ́:rdəti] 부조리 heyday[héidèi] 전성기
temporarily[tèmpərérəli] 일시적으로

문제 공략하기 p.219

물소와 같은 반추동물은 음식을 소화하는 데 제한적인 능력을 가지고 있고, 영양분을 쉽게 추출할 수 있는 부드럽고 잎이 많은 식물에 의존한다. 반추 초식동물의 소화기관은 매우 크다. 그들의 소화는 오랜 시간이 걸리고, 식사 후에는 혈당이 서서히 증가한다. 따라서, 자극했을 때 느리고 둔감한 모습을 보인다. 코뿔소와 같은 비반추동물은 영양분을 추출하는 데 상당히 더 유능하고, 따라서 높은 영양분의 음식에 의존하지 않는다. 그들은 식물 줄기 같은 섬유질을 먹고 살 수 있는데, 이는 고산성인 위와 장 속의 미생물에 의해 쉽게 분해된다. 위산 때문에 당이 혈류로 빠르게 방출된다.

HACKERS PRACTICE p.220

01 Lithosphere – (A), (C) Asthenosphere – (B)

02 Cross-sectional – (B) Longitudinal – (A), (C)

03 Athens – (B) Sparta – (D), (E)

04 Intraspecific – (C) Interspecific – (B), (E)

05 Acute – (B), (G) Chronic – (C), (E), (F)

06 Contagion – (A), (D) Convergence – (C), (G) Emergent Norm – (B)

07 Core Accretion – (B), (C), (F) Disc Instability – (A), (D)

01 지구의 가장 외각 층은 암석권으로, 해양지각과 대륙지각 그리고 지각과 맞닿은 맨틀의 최상층부로 구성된 암석이다. 해양지각의 두께는 50~100킬로미터인 반면, 대륙지각의 두께는 40~200킬로미터에 이른다. 비록 지각과 맨틀 상층부는 구성 면에서 다르지만, 하나의 덩어리로 움직이기 때문에 암석권이라고 불린다. 지구의 표면에 존재하는 암석권은 가장 차가운 층이며, 따라서 시간이 지남에 따라 부서지기 쉽고 단단한 암석으로 굳어지는 경향이 있다. 부서지기 쉬운 성질은 암석권이 서로 독립적으로 움직이는 거대한 판으로 나누어지게 한다. 암석권 아래 놓여있는 것은 암류권이며, 이는 지표면 아래 100~350킬로미터 깊이까지 뻗어있고 일부 지역에서는 깊이가 700킬로미터이다. 암석권과 암류권의 차이는 움직임에 대해 이 층들이 얼마만큼 저항력을 갖는가이다. 암류권은 맨틀의 약하고 부분적으로 녹은 부분이다. 이러한 성질 때문에, 암류권은 암석권처럼 갈라지지 않고 대체로 부드러운 찰흙처럼 움직인다. 이는 천천히 흐르는 강 위의 배처럼 암석권이 천천히 떠다니거나 암류권을 따라 이동하도록 한다.

02 모집단의 특징에 대한 정보를 수집하기 위한 두 가지 가장 보편적인 기술 연구는 횡적 연구와 종적 연구이다. 횡적 연구는 특정 시점에 주어진 모집단에 존재하는 변수들 간의 관계를 설명하는 것을 목표로 한다. 따라서, 그것은 특정한 특징의 존재와 가능한 연관성을 밝히는 데 유용하지만, 인과관계를 명확하게 규명할 수는 없다. 예를 들어, 한 나라에서 흡연과 폐환의 관계를 규명하고자 하는 횡적 연구는 담배 연기에 노출되는 것과 질병의 발생을 동시에 측정할 것이다. 폐질환으로 조사된 대다수의 사람이 흡연자이면, 그 정보는 흡연과 폐질환 간에 연관성이 있다는 것을 시사한다. 이후에 비슷한 정보가 필요하면, 새로운 피실험자 집단이 조사된다.

반면, 종적 연구는 시간이 지남에 따라 요소들을 반복해서 관찰하여 그들을 상호관련 지으려고 한다. 이러한 연구는 몇 십 년간 지속될 수 있고 따라서 완수하기에 매우 비쌀 수 있다. 일회성 조사와 달리, 종적 연구는 프로젝트가 지속되는 동안 내내 같은 피실험자를 추적한다. 이는 연구의 초기에 측정한 것과 이후의 시기에 발생한 변화를 비교할 수 있게 한다. 따라서 그것은 발달 관계를 확립하는 데 매우 유용하다. 하나의 예는 아동의 행동 형성이다. 유아의 행동적 패턴은 관찰되고 기록될 수 있으며, 그 다음 아동기에 지속되는지 아니면 사라지는지에 기초하여 분석될 수 있다. 그 후 변화와 가난이나 부모의 교육과 같은 외부 변수 간의 관계가 결정될 수 있다.

03 기원전 7세기, 그리스는 수백 개의 작은 자치 도시국가로 구성되었다. 기원전 5세기에 이르러, 두 개의 도시국가가 두드러졌다. 아테네는 정부 형태를 조직하고 폭군이 국민을 억압하는 것을 방지하는 민주 정치를 확립하였다. 스파르타는 과두 정치로 유명했는데, 이는 강한 군대를 통해 설립되고 지원되었다.

기원전 508년경 아테네가 민주국가를 형성했을 때, 이 도시는 정치적인 문제를 결정하기 위해 남성 500명의 시민대표로 이루어진 의회를 만들었다. 여성들은 정부 문제에 참여하지 않았고, 집안 일을 하는 것에 국한되었다. 다른 몇 개의 도시국가들이 민주주의에 소속되면서 이 도시국가는 평화와 번영의 기간을 경험하였다. 아테네는 동맹국의 안전을 지켜주기 위해 강력한 해군을 이용하였고, 작은 도시로부터 공물을 요구했다. 민주주의로서 아테네는 문화적으로 번영하였고, 건축, 문학, 예술로 유명해졌다.

스파르타는 전혀 다른 길을 걸었다. 스파르타는 시민을 통제하기 위해 징벌에 의존하였고, 도시국가들을 정복하기 위해 폭력에 의존하였다. 스파르타는 시민들로부터 전적인 복종을 요구하는 군국주의적, 전체주의적 국가였다. 스파르타에는 통화가 없었고, 사람들이 자유를 찾는 것을 방지하기 위해 주변국과 교역하는 것을 거부하였다. 일곱 살부터 남성들은 언제든 병역 의무를 수행할 준비가 된 전문적인 군인으로 키워졌다. 병들고 약하게 태어난 남아들은 죽게 내버려졌다. 여성들은 교육을 받고 재산을 소유할 기회가 주어졌지만, 아들을 강하고 헌신적인 군인으로 키우는 데 헌신하는 것에만 전념하였다. 스파르타는 최강의 군사력을 가졌지만 문화적, 예술적으로는 뒤떨어졌다.

04 동종 경쟁은 같은 종의 개체가 영역과 자원을 놓고 경쟁할 때 일어난다. 이 경쟁 유형은 같은 종의 조류 사이에서 많이 나타나는데, 왜냐하면 이들의 필요조건이 같아서 먹이와 공간에 대한 경쟁이 특히 격렬하기 때문이다. 하나의 예로는 열대 벌새가 있는데, 꿀을 지닌 꽃이 있는 좋은 지역을 보호하기 위해 같은 종을 쫓아낼 것이다. 조류 한 종의 개체수 밀도가 특히 높아질 때, 한정적인 자원은 공유되어야 한다. 이는 약한 개체가 차선의 지역에서 번식하고 보금자리를 만들도록 강요당하는 결과를 초래한다. 핀란드의 솔새가 좋은 예이다. 솔새의 일반적인 서식지는 전나무와 자작나무로 이루어진 숲인데, 자원이 부족할 경우 덜 강한 개체들은 다른 서식지에서 발견된다.

이종 경쟁은 같은 영역에 살고 같은 자원을 사용하는 두 가지 다른 종 개체 간의 경쟁이다. 만약 공간과 음식이 풍족하다면 경쟁은 약할 것이고 두 종은 공존할 것이지만, 만약 자원이 희소하거나 희소하게 여겨진다면 강한 경쟁이 전형적이다. 일반적으로, 제한된 자원을 가장 효과적으로 채취하는 종이 승리자일 것이다. 약한 종이 새로운 영역을 찾거나 다른 식생활을 발달시키지 않는 한, 강하고 지속적인 경쟁은 멸종에 이를 수 있다. 이종 경쟁은 직접적으로 관련된 종에 영향을 미칠 뿐만 아니라 전체 생태계에도 영향을 미칠 수 있는데 이것은 한 개체군의 변화가 생태계 전체에 파급 효과를 가질 수 있기 때문이다.

05 불면증은 수면 장애 증상이며 충분한 수면을 취하지 못하는 것으로 나타난다. 일부 불면증 환자들은 이른 아침 시간에만 잠에 드는 반면 다른 환자들은 적절한 시간에 잠은 들지만 자정이 지나면 바로 깬다. 연구원들은 급성과 만성, 두 종류의 불면증을 알아냈다. 이러한 종류는 개인이 불면증을 겪는 기간에 따라 분류된다.

급성 수면 부족은 며칠에서 3주까지 지속될 수 있다. 환경 내 스트레스 유발 요인, 겨울의 불충분한 햇빛, 극심한 날씨 조건, 시차로 인한 피로는 모두 불면을 가져올 수 있다. 커피, 알코올, 담배, 약물과 같은 흥분제 또한 단기 불면증을 유발할 수 있다. 불면증을 유발한 흥분제가 일단 확인되면, 상태는 치유될 수 있다. 일반적으로 수면제가 일정 기간 동안 처방되거나 불면을 촉진시킨 요인을 제거하기 위해 개인은 수면 습관을 바꾸라는 충고를 받는다. 그러나 대개 급성 불면증은 치료 없이 자연히 사라진다.

만성 수면 부족은 3주 이상 지속된다. 이것의 원인은 한 개인의 생리학적, 심리학적 조건에 있다. 일차성 불면증은 일반적으로 한 개인의 심리상태와 연관이 있다. 실업이나 가족의 상실, 사고나 폭력으로 인한 부상 같은 주요하거나 충격적인 사건은 지속적인 수면 부족을 가져올 수 있다. 반면, 진행 중이며 지속되는 건강 문제와 같은 생리학적인 원인인 경우는 이차성 불면증이라고 불린다. 신체적 불편과 카페인이나 유사한 성분이 있는 처방약을 먹는 것이 몇 가지 예이다.

만성 불면증은 불면의 시간이 축적되고 시간이 지남에 따라 개인의 건강에 파괴적인 효과를 갖기 때문에 급성보다 훨씬 더 심각하다. 의학 기술의 발전은 오늘날의 연구원들이 생리학적, 신경학적인 측면에서 불충분한 수면의 효과를 실험할 수 있게 하였다. 현재 수면 부족은 호르몬의 분비, 면역 체계 작동, 심장혈관계의 건강에 영향을 준다고 알려져 있다. 성장, 내분비, 신진대사 기능과 에너지 조절에 영향을 주는 호르몬은 수면 중에 분비된다. 이러한 액체가 혈관으로 분비되는 것은 수면이 불충분하거나 지연될 경우 악영향을 받는다. 수면이 부족한 사람은 낮은 면역 반응을 갖는다. 그들은 더 천천히 회복되고 그들의 신체는 감염과 질병에 효과적으로 싸우지 못한다. 마지막으로, 많은 증거들은 수면 부족과 증가된 혈압으로 인한 심장혈관 건강의 관계를 나타낸다.

06 한 개인이 혼자 있을 때와 군중의 일부일 때의 행동에는 상당한 차이가 있다. 사회학자들은 군중에 속한 사람들은 심지어 정치적인 시위나 스포츠 행사에서 보이는 사람들의 폭력적인 행위처럼 행동이 파괴적인 경우에도 자신의 행동에 대한 책임을 덜 느낀다는 점에 주목하였다. 일부 군중 행동은 명백하지 않지만, 그럼에도 불구하고 영향력이 있다. 예를 들어, 사람들은 재정 투자를 할 때 종종 시장 경향을 따르는데, 경제 위기에 그들의 주식을 처분하여 주식 시장 붕괴를 촉진하게 한다. 집단의 행동은 강력한 효과를 가질 수 있기 때문에, 경제학자와 같은 특정 집단의 사람들은 군중 행동을 이해하는 것이 중요하다. 이 행동을 설명하고 예측하기 위한 몇 가지 이론이 사회학자들에 의해 발전되었고, 이 중 세 가지 이론이 가장 두드러진다.

프랑스 사회학자 귀스타브 르 봉은 1895년 출판물 '군중심리학'에서 감염 이론을 제안하였는데, 이는 군중이 개별 구성원을 사로잡는 효과가 있다고 설명한다. 집단의 구성원은 일어나고 있는 일에 대해 주의를 집중한다. 그러나 이 상황을 평가하기 위해 그들 자신의 사고력을 사용하는 대신, 개인들은 자신의 신분을 숨기고 군중의 의지와 감정에 대해 개인의 의지와 감정은 부차적인 것이 되게 한다. 르 봉은 이러한 집단 의식을 '군중 심리'라고 부른다. 군중 심리는 혼란스럽고 본능적이고 일차적인 군중의 충동에 문화적, 도덕적, 개인적인 교육과 관심을 저버리기 때문에 비이성적이다. 르 봉은 군중 구성원들은 야만인이 되고, 전체로서의 군중은 폭도가 된다고 설명한다.

심리학자 고든 올포트의 수렴 이론은 군중이 사람들을 특정 방식으로 행동하게 만드는 것이 아니라 특정 경향을 가진 사람들이 군중에 끌린다고 주장한다. 바꾸어 말하면, 같은 생각을 가진 개인들이 수렴하여 군중을 이루는 경향이 있고, 겉으로 보기에 같은 행동은 군중 경험 후에 일어나는 것이 아니라 군중 형성보다 먼저 일어난다. 수렴 이론의 문제는 겉으로 보기에 매우 다른 배경과 신념을 가진 사람들이 왜 군중을 이루게 될 수 있었는지 설명하지 못 한다는 것이다.

군중 행동의 자생적 규범 이론은 감염 이론과 수렴 이론을 종합하려는 시도였다. 1972년, 사회학자 랄프 터너와 루이스 킬리언은 군중이 비이성적인 것도 아니고 같은 생각을 가진 사람들에 의해 끌려가는 것도 아니며 경험하는 사건에 대하여 자발적이고 이성적인 결정을 내리는 개인들로 구성되어 있다고 주장하였다. 행동은 전염되는 것이 아니라 이성적인데, 왜냐하면 사람들은 만약 다른 모든 사람들이 무슨 일을 하고 있다면 그 행동이 틀릴 수는 없다고 생각하기 때문이다. 따라서, 군중은 용인할 수 있는 행동의 개념을 단순히 재정의한다. 군중이 클수록 그것의 주장은 더 보편적인 것으로 보여진다.

07 목성 형성에 대한 지배적인 이론은 목성이 핵 형성과 기체 증대라는 두 단계 과정에 의해 형성되었다는 것이다. 소용돌이치는 먼지와 기체로 된 원반인 태양성운에서 얼음과 암석의 충돌은 물질이 모여서 커지게 했으며, 결과적으로 미래 행성의 핵이 된 고체 덩어리를 형성하였다. 추가적인 고체 물질이 원시 행성의 표면에 충격을 가하자 부피, 압력, 온도가 모두 증가하였다. 이러한 요인이 결합하여 핵에서 에너지가 방출되게 하였고, 이 에너지는 처음에 성운 기체가 원시 행성으로 떨어지는 것을 막았다. 목성 원시 행성의 핵 형성은 고체 덩어리가 결정적인 부피(기체 증대를 위한 최소한의 부피)에 도달하기 전까지 대략 50만 년의 기간 동안 계속되었다.

결정적인 부피에 도달하자, 성운 기체의 표면으로의 점차적인 이동이 뒤이어 일어났고, 핵을 감싸고 있는 기체 층의 형성으로 이어졌다. 기체 성분의 부피가 고체 성분의 부피에 도달하고 이를 능가한 후, 기체 증대의 가속화가 시작되었다. 핵 형성 이론의 이 두 번째 단계는 목성의 거대한 크기의 원인이었다. 이렇게 빠른 증대는 기체 탈주로 알려졌으며, 이 탈주는 원시 행성의 궤도 근처에 충분한 기체가 있는 한 계속되었다. 목성의 경우, 그 크기를 고려한다면 이용 가능한 기체가 충분히 있었을 것이다. 해왕성과 천왕성 같은 다른 외곽 행성에서는, 성운 기체의 이용 가능성이 더 적었을 것이다.

핵 증대 외의 다른 주요한 이론은 표면 불안정 이론이다. 일부 천체 물리학자에 따르면, 표면 불안정은 많은 행성을 빠르게 형성시켰을 수 있으며, 목성과 같은 크기의 행성이 단지 몇백 년 안에 완전히 형성되었을 수도 있다. 우주의 시간 관점에서 이는 사실상 자연 발생적이라고 여겨지고 단지 하나의 단계만을 거쳤을 것이다. 이러한 표면 불안정 이론의 원리는 성운 자체의 중력이라고 가정된다. 중력이 불안정했다면 기체와 먼지 부분이 나뉘어서, 자체의 중력을 갖는 기체 행성을 형성했을 수 있다. 표면 불안정 이론은 1950년대 초기에 처음 제안되었으나, 이 이론은 거대한 핵의 형성과 모순되어 보였기 때문에 별로 받아들여지지 않았다. 회의론자들은 먼지와 다른 고체 조각들이 거대한 기체 행성의 중심부에 도달하기 전에 뜨거운 기체 안에서 분해되었을 것이라고 주장하였다. 그러나 이 이론은 몇 가지 새로운 가설 때문에 최근에 주목을 받기 시작하였다. 1990년대 후반에 과학자들은 목성이 매우 작은 핵을 가졌거나 아예 핵이 없다고 주장하였다. 그러나 이러한 주장은 매우 불확실하다. 다른 비슷한 모의 실험은 목성의 핵이 기존에 생각되었던 것보다 두 배 크다고 주장하였다.

HACKERS TEST

각 문제에 대한 정답단서는 지문에 초록색으로 표시되어 있습니다.

1 Dinosaur Diets 공룡의 식습관 p.230

1. (A) 2. (B) 3. (D) 4. (C) 5. (C) 6. (D) 7. 2nd ■ 8. Direct – (B), (D), (E) Indirect – (C), (G)

Hackers TOEFL Reading Intermediate

1 공룡이 실제로 무엇을 먹었는지에 관한 질문은 수십 년 동안 순고생물학자들을 몰두하게 하였고, 비록 종합적인 합의는 나오지 않았으나, 화석 기록을 통해 공룡의 섭식활동에 대해 정보를 제공하는 흔적을 얻을 수 있다. 공룡의 식습관에 대해 연구하는 방법은 두 개의 일반적 영역, 즉 직접적인 영역과 간접적인 영역으로 나뉜다. 화석이 된 공룡 내부에 남겨진 음식물과 화석화된 배설물과 같은 다른 물리적인 증거를 연구함으로써 과학자들은 멸종 전에 공룡이 어떤 종류의 음식을 섭취했는지에 대한 직접적인 지식을 얻을 수 있다. 다른 방법으로, 과학자들은 간접적인 단서를 연구하여 이 흥미로운 파충류의 식습관에 대해 추측할 수 있다.

2 특정한 공룡이 어떤 음식을 먹었는지에 대한 명백한 증거는 얻기 어려운데, 섭취와 직접 관련된 화석은 드물기 때문이다. **대부분의 화석 기록은 공룡의 식습관에 대한 아무런 직접적인 단서도 제공하지 않는 뼈 조각으로 이루어진다.** 그러나 때때로 운 좋은 발견이 탐색과 포획에서 섭취와 배설까지 섭식 과정의 모든 단계에 대한 정보를 드러낸다. [8D]이러한 특별한 발견 중 하나는 고비 사막에서 두 마리의 공룡, 즉 육식성 공룡 벨로키랍토르와 초식성 공룡 프로토케라톱스가 포개져 있는 형태로 나타났는데, 그들의 뼈대 전체가 온전한 상태였다. 프로토케라톱스의 턱을 발톱으로 꽉 쥐고 있는 벨로키랍토르의 위치는 그들이 죽었을 때 벨로키랍토르가 다른 공룡을 먹고 있었다는 것을 드러내는데, 이는 두 공룡이 포식자−먹이 관계였다는 것을 암시한다. 과학자들은 이 배치가 단지 우연히 일어날 수는 없다고 믿고, 이 화석화된 유해를 벨로키랍토르가 육식이었고 프로토케라톱스는 먹이의 일부였다는 명백한 증거로 여긴다.

3 더 설득력 있는 것은 먹자마자 죽은 공룡의 잘 보존된 시체이다. [8B]침엽수의 잎, 열매, 다른 식물 물질들이 일부 공룡의 위에서 발견되었고, 이는 명백한 초식 식단을 보여준다. 유사하게, 화석화된 공룡의 흉곽에서 도마뱀이 발견되었고, 이는 일부 종이 다른 파충류를 먹었다는 것을 증명한다. 더 놀라운 뜻밖의 사실은 다 자란 어른 코엘로피시스의 체내에 있는 미숙한 코엘로피시스 표본의 위치이다. 하나의 가능성은 작은 공룡이 임신한 어미의 산도 내부에서 알에서 부화했다는 것인데, 과학자들은 이 이론이 성립하기에는 작은 코엘로피시스가 너무 크다고 결론지었다. [3]그러므로, 코엘로피시스는 육식뿐만 아니라 동족을 잡아먹는 행위를 했을 것이다. 그러나 어린 공룡이 산채로 잡혔는지는 여전히 알 수 없다. 직접적인 단서는 또한 배설물을 통해 발견될 수 있다. [8E]분석, 즉 화석화된 배설물은 때때로 변하지 않은 채 공룡의 소화기관을 지나간 음식물을 보여준다.

4 [8C]분석과 음식물 증거가 제공하는 희박한 직접적인 단서를 보완하는 것은 개별 신체 부위로 특히 이와 턱이 있는데, 소비 패턴에 대한 간접적인 단서를 제공한다. 이러한 종류의 화석화된 유해는 위에서 언급한 예외적인 경우에 비해 더 보편적

Chapter 09 Category Chart **327**

이고, 일부 공룡의 뼈 구조는 상세히 기록되어 있다. 예를 들어, 이빨을 갖춘 완전하거나 거의 완전한 턱 뼈가 수각류 공룡 골격에서 복원되었다. 큰 이는 길어지고 구부러져서 끝이 뾰족하게 되었으며, 미세한 톱니 모양으로 살을 자르고 뼈를 으깨는 데 이상적이었다. 대조적으로, [4]초식공룡으로 추정되는 공룡의 이는 종종 무딘 표면과 거친 톱니를 가진 직각 모양으로, 특히 식물을 움켜잡고 자르는 데 적합했다. 거대한 용각류 공룡 같은 일부 공룡의 이는 갈퀴의 이처럼 넓은 간격으로 배열되었다. 이 간격은 아마 공룡이 더 단단한 섬유질의 줄기와 가지를 부러뜨리지 않으면서 잎과 같은 물질을 잡아 당기는 것을 가능하게 했을 것이다.

5   고생물학자는 또한 공룡 발자국을 공룡이 먹이를 탐색할 때 어떻게 움직였는지에 대한 단서로 여긴다. 발자국으로부터 결론을 도출하는 것은 매우 추론적인 접근이 요구되지만 가능한 시나리오가 만들어질 수 있다. 예를 들어, [6]호주에서 수천 개의 빽빽하게 밀집한 발자국이 발견되고 연구되었다. 현장에서 수백 마리의 작은 공룡들이 만든 수많은 발자국과 한 마리 거대한 수각류 공룡의 발자국이 있었다. 발자국 사이의 거리를 측정함으로써 연구원들은 작은 공룡들이 다양한 방향으로 달려가며 갑자기 흩어졌다는 것을 알아냈다. 그들이 수각류와 같이 접근하는 포식자처럼 위협적인 존재로부터 달아나고 있었다는 것을 가정하는 것이 가능하다. [8G]비록 이 발자국들이 과학자들에게 결정적인 설명을 제시하지는 않지만, 간접적인 단서는 공룡의 섭식에 관한 정보를 조합하는 데 필요한 개념적인 틀을 형성하는 데 도움이 된다.

어휘
occupy[ákjupài] 몰두하다   paleobiologist[pèilioubaiáləʤist] 순고생물학자   comprehensive[kàmprihénsiv] 종합적인
consensus[kənsénsəs] 합의   firsthand[fə́ːrsthænd] 직접적인   speculate[spékjulèit] 추측하다   intriguing[intríːgiŋ] 흥미로운
indisputable[ìndispjúːtəbl] 명백한   defecation[dèfikéiʃən] 배설   exceptional[iksépʃənl] 특별한
interlock[ìntərlák] 포개지다, 맞물리다   carnivorous[kɑːrnívərəs] 육식의   herbivorous[həːrbívərəs] 초식의   intact[intǽkt] 온전한
claw[klɔː] 발톱   clutch[klʌtʃ] 꽉 붙잡다   arrangement[əréindʒmənt] 배치   carcass[kɑ́ːrkəs] 시체   conifer[kóunəfər] 침엽수
rib cage 흉곽   startling[stɑ́ːrtliŋ] 놀라운   revelation[rèvəléiʃən] 뜻밖의 사실   immature[ìmətʃúər] 미숙한
specimen[spésəmən] 표본   birth canal 산도   cannibalistic[kænəbəlístik] 동족을 잡아먹는   fecal[fíːkəl] 배설물
coprolite[kɑ́prəlàit] 분석   feces[fíːsiːz] 배설물   complement[kɑ́mpləmənt] 보완하다   sparse[spɑːrs] 희박한
straightforward[strèitfɔ́ːrwərd] 직접적인   theropod[θíərəpɑ̀d] 수각류 공룡   elongate[ilɔ́ːŋgeit] 길어지다
terminal[tə́ːrmənl] 끝의   finely[fáinli] 미세하게   serrated[sérətid] 톱니 모양의   flesh[fleʃ] 살   presume[prizúːm] 추정하다
blunt[blʌnt] 무딘   sauropod[sɔ́ːrəpɑ̀d] 용각류 공룡   rake[réik] 갈퀴   fibrous[fáibrəs] 섬유질의
paleontologist[pèiliəntáləʤist] 고생물학자   track[træk] 발자국   indication[ìndikéiʃən] 단서   speculative[spékjulèitiv] 추론적인
conclusive[kənklúːsiv] 결정적인   conceptual[kənséptʃuəl] 개념적인

2 Architectural Materials 건축 재료   p.234

1. (D)   2. (B)   3. (B)   4. (C)   5. (B)   6. (B)   7. (B)   8. (B)   9. 3rd ■
10. Before the Nineteenth Century – (B), (F)   After 1800 – (A), (C), (G)

1   [10B]고대 건축가들은 전형적으로 가공되지 않은 소재를 사용하였고, 이 경향은 19세기까지 계속되었다. 1800년 이후, 가공된 재료가 더 중요한 역할을 하기 시작하였고, 많은 현대 건물들은 가공된 재료로 건축되었다. 이 변화는 기술적 진보와 건축 재료에 대한 변화하는 인식에서 비롯되었다.

2   고대에 사용되었던 건축 재료의 범위는 제한적이었다. 목재는 가능한 곳에 일부 구조적인 목적으로 사용되었는데, 특히 들보와 지붕의 다른 부분에 사용되었다. [2/10F]나중에 목재는 문이나 칸막이 같은 상대적으로 작은 품목을 제외하고는 대부분 돌로 대체되었다. 실제로, 중세와 근세 초기에는 간단한 주택을 제외한 거의 모든 유럽의 건축물이 석공술로 만들어졌다.

3   석조 건축은 돌이나 벽돌을 모으고 쌓음으로써 이루어졌다. 가끔, 석공들은 단순히 하나의 돌 위에 다른 하나를 얹었다. 다른 때에는, [3]편하게 쌓기 위해 돌을 네모나게 만들거나 진흙으로 벽돌을 만들었다. 회반죽은 때때로 틈을 메우거나 돌을 일시적으로 붙이기 위해 사용되었지만, 대단한 구조적인 힘은 없었다. 기둥, 들보, 아치, 벽은 모두 이런 방법으로 설계되었고, 중력을 통한 압축이 건물에 안정성을 부여했다.

4 ⁴ᴮ산업사회 이전에 금속은 일반적으로 하찮은 목적을 위해서만, 가장 흔하게는 난간이나 창문 같은 작은 장식적인 요소를 위해 사용되었다. ⁴ᴬ이 금속의 제한적인 사용은 그것이 대량으로 생산하기에는 비쌌다는 사실에서 부분적으로 기인한다. 철과 강철을 생산하는 기술이 존재하긴 했지만, 저렴한 대량 생산의 수단이 부재했다. 또한 건축가들 사이에서는 건축 재료로 석공술을 강력히 선호했기 때문에, 결과적으로 구조적인 건축에서 금속은 대부분 다리와 온실에 한정되어 있었다. ⁴ᴰ금속은 인간이 만든 것이고 미적인 매력이 적은 것으로 보았기 때문에 건물을 위한 건축 재료로 열등하다고 여겨졌다.

5 ⁵/¹⁰ᶜ19세기에는 큰 변화가 일어났다. 예를 들어, 금속을 건물에 이용하는 것에 대한 경제적인 우려와 심미적인 편견이 서서히 사라지고 있었다. 뉴욕의 제임스 보가더스 같은 일부 건축가들이 건물에 주철을 사용하는 것을 공공연하게 지지했다. 1850년대에 보가더스는 건물 정면에 주철을 광범위하게 사용했다. 주철은 거의 모든 모양으로 형성될 수 있기 때문에 보통 대리석과 돌로 세밀하게 조각되는 화려한 외양을 쉽게 흉내낼 수 있었다. **이는 건물 정면이 전문적인 석공이나 조각가 없이도 세워질 수 있다는 것을 의미했다.** 건물의 성공에 이어 보가더스는 구조적인 재료로 초점을 바꾸어 건물 전체의 틀을 잡기 위해 금속을 이용하기 시작했다.

6 매우 무거운 건물을 지탱하는 목적으로는, 주철이 장기적으로 부적합하다는 것이 드러났다. 주철은 탄소와 같은 불순물을 포함한다. 강하기는 하지만, 불순물은 그것을 부서지기 쉽게 만든다. 장력이 약해서 높은 수위의 힘에 노출되면 부러질 수 있다. 이 특성은 1800년대에 몇 개의 다리가 붕괴된 후 발견되었고, 무거운 건물을 지탱하기 위한 주철의 사용은 19세기에 중단되었다.

7 대부분의 불순물이 제거된 철인 연철은 일시적인 해결책을 제공하였다. ⁶주철과 달리 연철은 연성인데, 균열되지 않으면서 더 많은 힘을 받을 수 있다는 뜻이다. 그러나 이것은 생산하는 데 시간과 비용이 많이 든다. 더 실용적인 재료는 강철이다. ¹⁰ᴳ강철은 1850년대부터 생산하기 쉽고 저렴해졌으며, 주철과 연철의 이로운 특성이 혼합되어 있다. 주철처럼 주형에 부어 어떤 형체로든지 만들어질 수 있고, 연철처럼 무거운 짐을 안전하게 지탱할 수 있다. ¹⁰ᴬ19세기 후반에는, 강철이 건축 용도의 주된 금속으로서 모든 형태의 철을 대체했다.

8 거의 동시에, ¹⁰ᶜ건축가들과 기술자들은 콘크리트를 건축 재료로 사용하기 시작했다. 처음에 콘크리트는 석공술처럼 보이게 제조되었는데, 이는 금속이나 다른 가공된 재료처럼 일반적으로 신성한 건물과 시립 건물에의 사용에는 사람들이 반대했기 때문이다. 1900년대가 되어서야 가공된 재료가 숭배되는 교회의 벽이나 다른 역사적인 건물을 장식했고, 광범위하게는 석공술이 20세기에 계속 선호되는 재료였다. 반면, 산업이나 상업 건물에는 강철과 콘크리트가 표준이 되었고 현대 고층빌딩에도 널리 이용되었다.

9 금속을 값싸게 생산하는 기술적 능력과 서서히 건축가들과 설계자들이 인정한 콘크리트 같은 가공된 재료가 건물 풍경을 바꾸었다. 특히 도시 환경에는 구조적, 미적 목적 모두를 생각하면서 만들어진 것을 포함하여, 19세기 후에 건축된 금속과 콘크리트 건물의 수많은 예가 있다.

어휘
timber[tímbər] 목재 beam[bi:m] 들보 partition[pɑːrtíʃən] 칸막이 virtually[vɜ́ːrtʃuəli] 거의 assemble[əsémbl] 모으다
stack[stæk] 쌓다 mortar[mɔ́ːrtər] 회반죽 seal[si:l] 메우다 temporarily[tèmpərérəli] 일시적으로
compaction[kəmpǽkʃən] 압축 stability[stəbíləti] 안정성 superficial[sùːpərfíʃəl] 하찮은 preference[préfərəns] 선호
inferior[infíəriər] 열등한 prejudice[prédʒudis] 편견 erode[iróud] 사라지다 openly[óupənli] 공공연하게
advocate[ǽdvəkèit] 지지하다 extensively[iksténsivli] 광범위하게 ornate[ɔːrnéit] 화려한 meticulously[mətíkjuləsli] 세밀하게
inappropriate[ìnəpróupriət] 부적합한 impurity[impjúərəti] 불순물 brittle[brítl] 부서지기 쉬운 tensile[ténsəl] 장력의
expose[ikspóuz] 노출되다 phase out 중단되다 temporary[témpərèri] 일시적인 ductile[dʎktəl] 연성의
fracture[frǽktʃər] 균열지다 mold[mould] 주형 load[loud] 짐 frown[fraun] 반대하다 sacred[séikrid] 신성한
municipal[mjuːnísəpəl] 시립의 venerate[vénərèit] 숭배하다

1　본성과 양육이라는 두 개의 주요한 화제가 인간 감정에 대한 연구를 지배한다. 생물학적 결정론자들은 감정이 본성에 의해 결정된다고 믿는다. 그들은 인간 감정의 태생적이고 자연적인 원인을 강조한다. 사회적 결정론자들은 감정이 양육에 의해 결정된다고 믿는다. 그들은 감정 발달에 있어서 환경의 역할을 강조하는 경향이 있다.

2　생물학적 또는 유전학적 결정론은 사람의 유전자가 한 사람이 어떻게 행동하고 시간이 지남에 따라 어떻게 변하는지 결정하는 요인이라는 이론이다. [10C]이 유전학적인 관점에 따르면, 뇌는 태생적으로 다양한 감정을 표현하는 것과 밀접한 관계가 있으며, 신체적인 요인이 생의 다양한 단계에서 감정의 차이를 설명할 수 있다. [1]예를 들어, 사춘기에 남성과 여성은 각각 테스토스테론과 에스트로겐의 생성에 변화를 경험한다. [10F]이는 생리적인 변화로, 순수하게 생물학적인 감정 변화를 가져온다.

3　[10E]생물학적 접근의 증거는 완전히 다른 문화권에서 자라난 사람들의 공유된 감정 특성에서 찾을 수 있다. [2]1976년 저서 '언마스크, 얼굴 표정 읽는 기술'을 위해 신경심리학자 폴 에크만과 월리스 프리슨은 표정에 관한 광범위한 비교문화 연구를 수행했다. 에크만과 프리슨은 파푸아뉴기니의 고립된 종족을 인터뷰하였고 종족 사람들이 완전히 생소한 다른 나라 사람들의 사진을 보여주었다. 심리학자들은 참가자들이 특정한 감정과 표정을 확실히 식별할 뿐만 아니라 그 감정이 유발된 상황도 묘사할 수 있다는 것을 발견하였다. 이는 저자들로 하여금 인간의 여섯 가지 기본 감정(화, 혐오감, 두려움, 행복, 슬픔, 놀람)과 이 감정들의 신체적 표현이 사람들 사이에 보편적이라고 결론 짓게 하였다.

4　[3D]생물학적 결정론자들이 인간 감정의 보편성에 감명을 받은 반면, 사회적 결정론자들은 그 다양성에 관심을 갖는다. [3A]생물학적 설명에 대한 반대론은 성장하는 어린이들의 심리적 패턴과 행동 양식에 상당한 차이가 있을 수 있고 실제로 있으며, 이러한 변화가 경험적 요인에 의해 설명될 수 있음을 강조한다. [10B]사회적 결정론자들은 육아, 가난, 교육, 폭력에의 노출 같은 변수를 아이의 감정 상태에 미치는 주요한 영향이라고 지적한다. 게다가, 그들은 유전학적 결정론자들의 견해를 위험하다고 여기는데 이는 논리적인 결론 면에서 인간의 책임을 인간의 행동으로부터 분리시키는 것 같아 보이기 때문이다. [3B]특정한 방식으로 한 사람이 태어난다는 이 가정은 부당한 행동에 대한 즉각적인 방어를 제공한다고 그들은 주장한다. 예를 들어, 쉽게 화를 내는 아이는 부적절한 행동에 대해 그 혹은 그녀의 타고난 공격적인 성격 탓으로 변명하는 것을 배울 수 있다.

5　따라서, 사회적 결정학파의 대부분의 지지자들은 조건화 요소로서의 환경을 강조하는 행동주의자다. [10A]행동주의자의 관점에 따르면, 개의 공격으로 신체적인 고통과 정신적인 충격을 경험하는 아이는 거의 확실히 개에 대한 공포를 형성할 것이다. **두려워하는 경향은 그 동물에 대한 경고를 반복적으로 들었을 때도 나타날 수 있다.** 대조적으로, 그 동물과 긍정적인 만남만을 가진 아이는 개가 짖는 소리를 기분 좋은 소리로 인식할 것이며 동물에게 접근해도 불안한 감정을 느끼지 않을 것이다. 따라서, 자극에 대한 감정적인 반응은 오로지 본성의 결과만이 아니라 성장하는 아이가 겪는 경험의 결과이기도 하다.

6　또한 문화적 차이는 양육 가설의 핵심이다. 일부 나라에서는 국가가 강렬한 감정 반응을 불러 일으키지 않을 수도 있으나, 애국적 전통이 강한 나라에서는 사람들이 종종 국가를 듣는 것에 대해 슬프게 반응하는데, 이는 애국심에 기반한 강렬한 반응을 설명한다. 이러한 감정적 반응이 즉각적으로 나타나고 무의식적으로 일어난다는 사실은 하품과 재채기처럼 자연적이라는 것을 나타낸다고 보일 수 있으나, 이는 사실상 단순히 자극에 대한 신체적인 반응이 아니라 매우 섬세한 '문화적 각본'의 결과이다. [6]이 각본은 모든 사회에서 발생하며, 사람들에게 언제 그리고 어떻게 감정을 적합하게 표출하는지를 가르치는 데 책임이 있다. [7]비슷하게, 어떤 감정은 문화적으로 결정되는 것으로 보인다. 예를 들어, 미크로네시아의 이팔루크 족은 '화'에 대한 직접적인 용어가 없고 '용인된 화'라고 대략 번역되는 'song'이라는 감정이 있다. 그것은 영어 단어 anger에서 발견되는 분노나 공격성이라는 감정과는 아무런 관련이 없고, 오히려 엄격한 도덕적 비난의 감정을 전달한다.

7　각 견해를 지지하는 자료가 매우 설득력이 있어서, 대부분의 심리학자와 생물학자는 유전학적인 요인과 환경적인 요인이

모두 인간 감정 발달에 기여하는 것으로 인정한다. 따라서, 전문가들은 이제 감정적인 기질의 형성에 있어 본성과 양육 간의 복잡한 상호작용을 분석하고 이해하는 더 적절한 과제에 초점을 맞춘다.

어휘

nurture[nə́ːrtʃər] 양육 determinist[ditə́ːrminist] 결정론자 intrinsic[intrínsik] 태생적인
puberty[pjú:bərti] 사춘기 testosterone[testástəròun] 테스토스테론 estrogen[éstrədʒən] 에스트로겐
isolated[áisəlèitid] 고립된 tribal[tráibəl] 종족의 identify[aidéntəfài] 식별하다 disgust[disgʌ́st] 혐오감
universal[jùːnəvə́rsəl] 보편적인 objection[əbdʒékʃən] 반대 substantial[səbstǽnʃəl] 상당한 experiential[ikspìəriénʃəl] 경험의
variable[vɛ́əriəbl] 변수 unwarranted[ʌnwɔ́ːrəntid] 부당한 adherent[ædhíərənt] 지지자 trauma[tráumə] 정신적 충격
encounter[inkáuntər] 만남 national anthem 국가 robust[roubʌ́st] 강한 patriotic[pèitriátik] 애국적인
intense[inténs] 강렬한 unconsciously[ʌnkánʃəsli] 무의식적으로 yawn[jɔːn] 하품 sneeze[sni:z] 재채기 rage[reidʒ] 분노
aggression[əgréʃən] 공격성 stern[stəːrn] 엄격한 disapproval[dìsəprú:vəl] 비난 temperament[témpərəmənt] 기질

*각 문제에 대한 정답단서는 지문에 초록색으로 표시되어 있습니다.

1. (C) Vocabulary
2. (B) Inference
3. (C) Fact
4. (D) Negative Fact
5. (D) Vocabulary
6. (D) Reference
7. (B) Fact
8. (C) Rhetorical Purpose
9. 1st ■ Insertion
10. (C)-3단락, (D)-4단락, (F)-2단락 Summary

11. (D) Vocabulary
12. (D) Fact
13. (D) Vocabulary
14. (B) Negative Fact
15. (A) Sentence Simplification
16. (B) Inference
17. (B) Rhetorical Purpose
18. (D) Fact
19. 3rd ■ Insertion
20. (A)-2~3단락, (B)-4단락, (D)-5~6단락 Summary

▮1 Olmec Civilization in Mesoamerica 메소아메리카의 올멕 문명

1 현재의 중앙아메리카와 멕시코 남부의 위치와 대략 일치하는 메소아메리카에 기원전 1200년 즈음 아메리카 최초의 중요한 공동체가 나타났고, 500년 남짓 이후 결국 쇠퇴하기 전까지 수 세기 동안 번성했다. 올멕 문명은 현재의 도시 베라크루스의 위치인, 산 로렌초에 중심을 두었고, 새로운 이주민들은 멕시코 만에서 내륙 쪽에 있는 열대 저지대에 거주지를 설립했다. 이것은 주요 강들을 따라 생겨난 유럽과 아시아의 고대 문명들과 뚜렷한 대조를 이룬다. 몇몇 연구원들이 가설을 세운 것과 같이 올멕인들이 북쪽에서 시작하여 멕시코 만을 통해 산 로렌초 지역에 들어왔는지, 아니면 ²고고학적 기록에서 분명하게 보이듯이 육지를 걸쳐 남쪽에서 왔는지 여부는 아마도 논란의 여지가 있을 것이다.

2 둘 중 어느 경우이든, 기원전 900년 즈음, 올멕 문명은 번성했고 넓은 지역에 걸쳐 올멕 문명의 특성의 전파가 일어났다. 올멕족이 태평양 연안 방향으로 영토를 확장했다는 것은 명백하고, 현존하는 조각들을 보면, 그들이 종교를 통해 문화를 퍼뜨렸던 것으로 보인다. 발견된 물건들은 옥으로 만들어지고 재규어 얼굴의 모양으로 만든 의식용 가면을 포함한다. ³성직자들이 의식적인 행사에서 자신들을 성스러운 고양이로 변형시키고 신성한 힘과의 결합을 보여주기 위해 이러한 가면을 썼던 것으로 생각된다. 이 주장에 대한 증거는 높이 올린 흙으로 된 언덕 위에 있는 사원들을 포함한 요새화 된 제사센터에서 가면들이 발견된 것에서 비롯된다. 게다가, 올멕인들은 깃털이 달린 뱀 신뿐 아니라 불, 비, 그리고 곡물의 신들을 묘사하는 작은 형상을 만들었는데, 그것들은 모두 그 지역의 일반적인 신학적인 상징이 되었다.

3 올멕족의 또 하나의 중요한 특징은 석조 건축과 석조물에 대한 그들의 기량이었는데, 이는 이스터 섬의 거대한 석상들을 다소 연상시키는 커다란 두상 조각뿐 아니라 높이가 30미터가 넘는 피라미드의 건축에 분명히 나타났다. 아마도, 오직 머리만이 사람의 진정한 본질을 포함하고 있다는 메소아메리카에 널리 퍼져있는 생각 때문에 몸의 나머지는 무시되었을 것이다. ⁴ᴮ지금까지 17개의 두상이 발견되었고, 가장 큰 것은 3미터의 높이, 4.5미터의 둘레, 그리고 8톤의 무게에 육박한다. ⁴ᴬ그것들은 현무암 바위로 조각되었는데, 이것은 산에서 채굴되어 해상에서는 커다란 뗏목을, 육지에서는 통나무 굴림대를, 혹은 두 가지를 병행해 100킬로미터까지 운송되었다. ⁴ᶜ그리고 올멕인들이 오로지 석기로 조각했다는 점을 고려하면, 이러한 기념물들을 창작하는 데 필요한 노력과 시간의 양은 대단했을 것임이 틀림없다. 따라서, 지배적인 견해는 석조 두상들이 통치자 또는 운동선수나 전사들과 같은 올멕 사회에서 존경받는 다른 인물들을 나타냈다는 것이다. 이것이 사실이라는 것을 증명할 수 있는 자료가 현재는 없지만, 고고학자들은 무너져 파묻힌 석조 조각물을 발견했는데, 이는 올멕 문명 내부 또는 외부의 몇몇 경쟁 상대들이 고의적으로 그 기념물들을 파괴했다는 것을 시사한다.

4 게다가, 올멕족들은 경제와 농업 활동에 있어 매우 유능했던 것처럼 보인다. 인접한 고원지대와의 무역과 거래가 광범위했고, 교역은 적어도 코스타리카까지 남쪽으로 확장되었다. 올멕족들은 그들의 도자기와 고무를 옥과 흑요석으로 교환했

다. 이러한 지역적 상품들 중 어느 것도 그 지역에서 자연적으로 발생하지 않았기 때문에 전문가들은 이렇게 알고 있다. 하지만, 올멕족들이 식품을 거래했다는 확실한 증거는 없는데, 이는 토종이 아닌 식품들의 흔적이 고고학자들에 의해 발견된 적이 없기 때문이다. 분명한 것은 그들이 생계를 위해 옥수수에 크게 의존했던 성공적인 농업 전문가들이었다는 것이다. 그들은 성장을 위해 요구되는 배수가 잘되는 조건에서 그들의 선택 작물이 잘 자라나도록 하기 위해 낮은 습지를 일련의 배수로를 가진 높은 지층으로 능숙능란하게 개조했다. 일단 수확이 되면, 곡식은 종종 빻아져서 토르티야로 바뀌었는데, 이는 휴대하기 쉬운, 비교적 부패하지 않는 납작한 빵의 한 종류이다.

5 [8]올멕 문명의 다양한 요소들은 올멕 문명의 기이한 붕괴 이후에도 그 지역에서 지속되었고, 따라서 올멕이 다음 천 년의 문화적 업적을 위한 기초를 수립했다는 이론을 세우는 것은 타당하다. 몇백 년 후 남쪽의 마야 문명 발생과 북쪽의 대도시 테오티우아칸의 출현은 모두, 어떤 이유에서든 여기저기 산재한 일련의 마을들 외에는 그 사이의 기간 동안 잠복 상태였던 올멕 문명의 일종의 부활 덕분이다. [7]올멕족과 이러한 그 다음의 문명들 사이의 정확한 관계를 안다는 것은 현재 불가능하지만, 종교, 건축, 그리고 천문학과 수학에 대한 공통적인 집념에서 그들의 유사점은 너무 확실해서 무시할 수 없다.

어휘
correspond to ~와 일치하다 **emerge**[imə́ːrdʒ] 나타나다 **millennium**[miléniəm] 천년 **hypothesize**[haipáθəsàiz] 가설을 세우다
diffusion[difjúːʒən] 전파 **enlarge**[inláːrdʒ] 확장하다 **ritualistic**[rìtʃuəlístik] 의식의 **feline**[fíːlain] 고양잇과의 동물
divine[diváin] 신성한 **earthen**[ə́ːrθən] 흙으로 된 **deity**[díːəti] 신 **theological**[θìːəládʒikəl] 신학적인
masonry[méisnri] 석조 건축 **reminiscent**[rèmənísnt] 연상시키는 **approach**[əpróutʃ] 육박하다
circumference[sərkʌ́mfərəns] 둘레 **basalt**[bəsɔ́ːlt] 현무암 **boulder**[bóuldər] 바위 **extraordinary**[ikstrɔ́ːrdəneːri] 대단한
revered[rivíərd] 존경받는 **verifiable**[vérəfàiəbl] 증명할 수 있는 **obsidian**[əbsídiən] 흑요석 **subsistence**[səbsístəns] 생계
marsh[mɑːrʃ] 습지 **bed**[bed] [지질학] 지층 **imperishable**[impériʃəbl] 부패하지 않는 **persist**[pərsíst] 지속되다
theorize[θíːəràiz] 이론을 세우다 **dormant**[dɔ́ːrmənt] 잠복 상태인 **obsession**[əbséʃən] 집념

2 Lightning 번개

1 대기는 전하로 가득 차 있다. 하늘이 평온하고 맑을 때에는 중성 전하가 우세한데, 이는 양성자와 전자가 다소 고르게 분산되어 있기 때문이지만, 뇌우가 쏟아질 때에는 양전하와 음전하가 분리되어 응축된다. 때때로 구름 속의 전하는 매우 빠르게 움직여, 엄청난 에너지를 방출시킨다. 이러한 격렬한 에너지 분출이 우리가 번개라고 부르는 것이다. 번개에 대한 많은 과학 연구는 번개 형성의 배후 기제와 뇌우가 발생하는 동안 안전을 향상시키기 위한 방법에 초점을 맞춘다.

2 번개 형성의 결정적인 기제는 전하 분리이다. [12]이것은 구름의 아랫부분에는 음전하(전자), 구름의 윗부분에는 양전하(양성자)가 축적되는 것으로 특징지어진다. 이는 상승 기류와 온도 차 때문에 가능해진다. 상승 기류는 상승하는 공기에 의해 야기되는데, 이것이 대부분의 뇌우가 날씨가 따뜻할 때 발생하는 이유이다. 이것은 또한 대부분의 낙뢰가 여름에 일어나는 이유이다. 상승하는 공기는 고도가 증가하면서 차가워지고 어는점에 도달하면 응결하는 물방울을 운반한다. 이렇게 차가워진 물방울은 구름의 윗부분 근처에서 얼음 결정으로 변한다. 더 많은 물방울과 얼음 결정이 상승하면서 충돌하기 시작하여 더 큰 얼음 덩어리를 형성한다. 일단 그것이 충분히 무거우면 떨어지는데, 하강하면서 주변의 물과 얼음을 더 많이 모은다. 이러한 충돌의 결과로, 더 가벼운 입자는 음이온을 잃고 양전하가 된다. 결국, 더 큰 입자는 음이온을 얻는다. 이 과정은 구름의 아랫부분에 강력한 음전하 지대가 형성되는 결과를 낳는다.

3 전하 분리가 강력할 때 전자는 불안해지지만 [14D]번개가 치기 위해서는 전자가 대량으로 방출되어야 한다. 같은 전하는 밀어내고 반대 전하는 끌어당기기 때문에, [14A]번개가 칠 가능성이 가장 높은 방법은 전자가 축적된 지역이 양으로 대전된 지역에 반대되게 놓이는 것이다. 예를 들어, [14C]뇌운이 땅 위를 맴돌 때 구름 속의 전자는 땅의 전자를 지표면 아래로 '밀어서' 땅이 양전하를 띠도록 한다. 번개는 전자가 '계단형 선도' 내에서 구름을 떠날 때 개시된다. 때때로 지름이 몇 센티미터도 안 되는 계단형 선도는 전자가 거의 빛의 절반 속도로 통과하는 길이며, 지그재그 모양으로 보이게 하는 구별되는 단계로 하늘을 가로질러 이동하기 때문에 이렇게 명명되었다.

4 우리가 보는 번개는 사실상 하나의 깜박거리는 벼락처럼 보이는 일련의 타격이다. 전자는 공기 통로를 만들어 통로의 원천에 있는 잉여 전자가 소진될 때까지 구름과 목적지 사이를 계속 이동한다. 양전하 지역은 항상 땅을 향하고 있는 것은

아니어서, 번개는 어느 방향에서나 나올 수 있다. 번개는 구름 내부에서 이동할 수 있고 구름에서 구름으로 이동할 수 있다. 그것은 또한 구름 위 수직으로 높이 뻗어서 대략 해발 50킬로미터에서 시작되는 대기 중 대전된 입자 층인 전리층을 향할 수 있다. 아마도, 그 고도에서의 산소가 희박한 공기는 더 적은 분자가 가열되도록 할 것이고, 전달된 전기 에너지는 반짝이는 붉은 빛의 기둥을 만들어 낼 것이다. [16]이러한 'Red Sprites'는 50~90킬로미터 고도 사이에서 발생하며 항공기에서 관찰된다.

5 번개는 뇌우에서 전혀 희귀한 현상이 아니며 큰 폭풍은 초당 백 번만큼이나 번개를 발생시킨다. 멀리서 보면, 번개 폭풍은 멋져 보이지만 구름에서 땅에 걸친 번개는 특히 파괴적인 결과를 초래할 수 있다. [17]번개를 끌어당기는 지점은 전기 에너지 발생지점으로부터 꽤 멀 수 있고, 길이가 100킬로미터 이상인 낙뢰도 가능하다. 이것은 심지어 폭풍 바로 아래에 위치한 물체도 완전히 안전하지는 않음을 의미한다. 일반적으로, 물체가 땅 위로 더 높이 돌출될수록 번개를 맞을 확률이 더 높다. 뇌우가 일어나기 쉬운 지역에서는, 번개가 사람과 건물을 위태롭게 하는 것을 방지하기 위해 알루미늄이나 구리로 만들어진 피뢰침을 흔히 세운다. 그것들은 건물의 옥상처럼 가장 높은 곳에 설치되어, 그곳에서 번개 에너지를 끌어당겨 안전하게 땅으로 전도한다.

6 과학자들은 번개가 어떻게 형성되고 어떻게 번개를 위험한 진로로부터 다른 곳으로 돌릴 수 있을지에 대해 여전히 알아가는 중이다. 피뢰침은 효율적이긴 하지만 완벽하지는 않다. [18]때때로 번개가 피뢰침이 아닌 물체에 떨어질 수 있기 때문에 새로운 기술이 필요하다. 결과적으로, 최소한 실험실에서는 전자 방출을 위한 계획된 통로를 만들어내는 자외선 레이저로 전망 있는 연구가 현재 수행되고 있다.

어휘

electric charge 전하 neutral[njú:trəl] 중성의 prevail[privéil] 우세하다 proton[próutɑn] 양성자 electron[iléktrɑn] 전자
disperse[dispə́:rs] 분산시키다 thunderstorm[θʌ́ndərstɔ̀:rm] 뇌우 segregate[ségrigèit] 분리시키다
concentrate[kɑ́nsəntréit] 응축하다 tremendous[triméndəs] 엄청난 expulsion[ikspʌ́lʃən] 분출 crucial[krú:ʃəl] 결정적인
accumulation[əkjù:mjuléiʃən] 축적 updraft[ʌ́pdræft] 상승 기류 altitude[æltətjù:d] 고도 solidify[səlídəfài] 응결하다
ascend[əsénd] 상승하다 collide[kəláid] 충돌하다 pellet[pélit] 덩이 descend[disénd] 하강하다 particle[pɑ́:rtikl] 입자
repel[ripél] 밀어내다 thundercloud[θʌ́ndərklàud] 뇌운 hover[hʌ́vər] 맴돌다 stepped leader 계단형 선도
flicker[flíkər] 깜박거리다 ionosphere[aiɑ́nəsfìər] 전리층 approximately[əprɑ́ksəmətli] 대략 presumably[prizú:məbli] 아마도
thin[θin] 산소가 희박한 luminous[lú:mənəs] 반짝이는 aircraft[έərkræft] 항공기 devastating[dévəstèitiŋ] 파괴적인
project[prɑ́dʒekt] 돌출하다 lightning rod 피뢰침 conduct[kəndʌ́kt] 전도하다 divert[divə́:rt] 다른 곳으로 돌리다
path[pæθ] 진로 promising[prɑ́misiŋ] 전망 있는

p.256

1. **(B)** Inference
2. **(A)** Vocabulary
3. **(C)** Fact
4. **(D)** Vocabulary
5. **(A)** Rhetorical Purpose
6. **(A)** Fact
7. **(B)** Sentence Simplification
8. **(C)** Negative Fact
9. **1st ■** Insertion
10. **(A)**-3단락, **(C)**-5단락, **(E)**-4단락 Summary

11. **(D)** Fact
12. **(A)** Rhetorical Purpose
13. **(D)** Fact
14. **(A)** Vocabulary
15. **(B)** Inference
16. **(B)** Vocabulary
17. **(C)** Reference
18. **(C)** Negative Fact
19. **1st ■** Insertion
20. **(A)**-4단락, **(C)**-5단락, **(F)**-3단락 Summary

1 Discovery of Pluto 명왕성의 발견

1   태양계의 다섯 행성인 수성, 금성, 화성, 목성, 그리고 토성은 고대 시대부터 알려져 왔지만, 태양계의 두 행성인 천왕성과 해왕성뿐 아니라 이전에 행성에 속했던 명왕성은 육안으로는 알아볼 수 없다. 따라서, [1]이러한 천체들이 관찰되기 전에 첨단 천문학 장비가 개발되어야 했다. 18세기의 가장 위대한 천문학자였던 윌리엄 허셜 경은 처음에 실수로 천왕성을 혜성이라고 밝힌 후에 1781년 천왕성을 발견했고, 해왕성은 1846년 영국, 독일, 프랑스 천문학자들에 의해 발견되었는데, 천왕성의 궤도의 변칙이 그들로 하여금 미상의 천체가 천왕성에 중력의 힘을 가하고 있다는 결론을 내리도록 이끌었던 이후였다.

2   그러나 명왕성의 존재는 20세기 초까지 알려지지 않았다. 태양계 외곽에 있는 명왕성의 존재에 관한 첫 번째 그럴듯한 증거는 천왕성의 궤도 패턴의 주기 변화 분석에 의해 나타났고, 그 분석은 해왕성의 중력 하나만으로는 편차를 설명하기에 충분하지 못했다고 밝혔다. 따라서, 다른 천체가 틀림없이 그 행성에 힘을 가하고 있을 것이라고 추론되었다. 과학자들은 즉시 불일치의 원인이 되는 천체에 대한 탐사를 시작했고 잠정적으로 그것을 제 10행성이라고 이름 지었다. 그들 중 한 명은 퍼시벌 로웰이었는데, 화성을 연구하기 위해 애리조나 주에 천문대를 세웠던 부유한 아마추어 천문학자였다. [3]1900년대 초, 로웰은 제 10행성을 찾기 위한 탐사에 관심을 돌렸고, 천왕성의 궤도에 관한 일련의 복잡한 계산을 시행한 후, 미상의 천체가 발견될 수 있을 거라고 믿은 하늘의 한 구역을 알아냈다.

3   로웰은 그의 탐구를 성공하지 못한 채 1916년에 사망했지만, 천문대의 다른 천문학자들은 이 중요한 연구 과제를 이어갔다. 그들 중 한 명이었던 23살의 클라이드 톰보는 체계적으로 하늘의 여러 구역의 연속된 사진을 며칠 간격으로 찍고 나서 깜빡이 비교기라고 불리는 기계를 이용하여 그것들을 분석했는데, 깜빡이 비교기는 각 쌍의 이미지가 빠르게 번갈아 나오게 하였다. [5]기본적으로, 그것은 그가 두 사진간의 차이를 비교하고 발견하기 위한 방법이었는데, 하늘에서 위치를 바꾼 천체들을 알아차리고 발견하기 쉽도록 만들었다. 그의 연구는 1930년에 성공했는데, 이때 그는 제 10행성의 예상 위치와 일치하는 빛의 움직이는 흔적을 알아냈다. 그 후의 수개월 동안의 망원경 분석으로 그 천체의 궤도를 찾아냈고 그것의 존재를 확인했으며, 그것은 나중에 지하 세계의 그리스 신의 이름을 따 플루토라고 이름 지어졌다.

4   단지 한 가지 문제가 있었다. [6]명왕성은 훨씬 더 희미했고, 따라서 로웰의 계산이 예측했던 것보다 훨씬 더 적은 질량을 가지고 있는 것으로 여겨졌다. 사실, 새로 발견된 천체는 천왕성의 궤도의 변칙을 일으킬 만큼 충분히 크지 않았다. 결과적으로, 명왕성은 여전히 엄청나게 중요하고 가치 있는 과학적 발견이지만, 로웰과 톰보가 찾고 있었던 천체는 아니었다. 제 10행성이 여전히 발견되길 기다리고 있을 것이라고 확신하고, 톰보는 사진 비교의 고된 연구를 계속했고, 이후 14년 동안 수백 장의 사진을 분석하며 많은 시간을 들였다. 역설적이게도, 수십 년 후 명왕성의 존재와 위치를 예측하기 위해 사용되

었던 계산은 해왕성 질량의 잘못된 추정에 근거한 것이라는 것이 알려졌다. 더 정확한 측정이 1989년 보이저 2호의 근접 비행에 의해 이루어진 후, 해왕성의 중력은 사실상 천왕성 궤도의 편차를 설명하기에 전적으로 충분했다는 결론이 내려졌다. 이것은 제 10행성이 환영이었다는 것을 의미했고, 잘못된 추정을 근거로 한 로웰의 계산이 행성이 발견될 것이라고 예상했던 곳과 같은 위치에서 명왕성이 발견되었다는 것은 단지 우연의 일치였다.

5 태양계에 대한 인류의 지식이 확장했기 때문에 명왕성은 행성으로서의 지위를 잃었다. 2000년대에, 천문학자들은 카이퍼 띠에 있는 다수의 커다란 천체들을 관찰하여 목록을 만들기 시작했는데, ^{8A/D}카이퍼 띠는 해왕성 너머에 펼쳐져 있고 1992년에 처음 발견된, 태양계의 멀리 떨어져 있는 도넛 모양의 지역이다. 이러한 천체들 중 다수가 명왕성의 것과 비슷하거나 더 큰 질량을 가지고 있다. 따라서, 전문가들에게는 태양계가 수십의, 혹은 수백이나 되는 작은 미지의 행성들을 포함한다고 인정하거나, 그 단어(행성)의 정의를 한정하고 개선하거나 하는 선택이 남게 되었다. 그들은 후자를 선택했고, 2006년, 국제천문연맹은 자격을 제대로 갖춘 행성은 태양을 공전하고 궤도의 주변이 깨끗한 구형의 천체로 제한한다고 선언했다. 즉, 행성은 궤도 지역을 비슷한 크기의 어떤 천체들과도 공유하지 않는다. ^{8B}새로운 정의가 명왕성과 카이퍼 띠에서 발견된 다른 천체들을 제외했으므로, 왜소행성이라는 새로운 용어가 특별히 그것들을 위해 만들어졌다.

어휘

the naked eye 육안 comet[kάmit] 혜성 irregularity[irègjulǽrəti] 변칙 exert[igzə́:rt] 가하다
gravitational[græ̀vətéiʃənl] 중력의 seeming[síːmin] 그럴듯한, 외관상의 deviation[dìːviéiʃən] 편차, 이탈
discrepancy[diskrépənsi] 불일치 tentatively[téntətivli] 잠정적으로 observatory[əbzə́ːrvətɔ̀ːri] 천문대
successive[səksésiv] 연속된 alternate[ɔ́ltərnèit] 번갈아 나오다 speck[spek] 흔적, 자국 faint[feint] 희미한 mass[mæs] 질량
arduous[άːrdʒuəs] 고된 flyby[flái bài] 근접비행 illusion[ilúːʒən] 환영, 오해 coincidence[kouínsidəns] 우연의 일치
assumption[əsʌ́mpʃən] 추정, 가설 overturn[òuvərtə́ːrn] 번복시키다 acknowledge[æknάlidʒ] 인정하다 refine[riːfáin] 개선하다
full-fledged[fùlflédʒd] 자격을 제대로 갖춘, 완전한 comparable[kάmpərəbl] 비슷한

2 Memphis as the Capital of Ancient Egypt 고대 이집트의 수도 멤피스

1 세계에서 가장 오래 된 문명 중 하나인 이집트는 장대한 나일 강의 강둑을 따라 5천 년도 더 전에 자리 잡았다. ¹¹기원전 약 5500년에서 기원전 3100년까지의 이집트 역사 기간은 선왕조시대라고 불리는데, 그 당시 고대 이집트가 두 개의 지역으로 나누어졌기 때문이다. 남쪽 지역은 나일 강의 상류 직선 유역에 가까웠기 때문에 상이집트라고 불렸고, 나일 강이 삼각주로 펼쳐지고 지중해와 만나는 북쪽의 하류 지역은 하이집트라고 불렸다. 이 지역들은 처음으로 나라가 통일되었던 기원전 거의 3100년까지 서로 다른 왕들에 의해 통치되었다. 전통적으로, 이 일(통일)은 메네스라는 이름을 가진 상이집트의 파라오의 공으로 여겨지는데, 그는 하이집트를 흡수하자마자, 나일 강에 그가 설립한 새로운 도시인 멤피스에 수도를 세웠다.

2 ¹²일부 이집트학자들은 이러한 전설적인 이야기에 의문을 갖고, 상하 이집트 왕의 상징을 둘 다 지닌 나르메라라는 이름의 한 통치자의 고대 장식용 조각품이 통일된 이집트의 최초의 파라오로서 통치했던 것은 사실 그였다는 것을 보여준다고 주장한다. 다른 학자들은 메네스와 나르메르를 같은 사람으로 간주한다. 개국 군주의 정확한 신원에 상관없이, 이후 천 년의 대부분에 걸쳐 이어졌던 연속적인 여덟 왕조 동안, 멤피스가 이집트의 정치적, 문화적, 종교적, 그리고 경제적 수도의 역할을 했다는 데에는 의심의 여지가 없고, 근처에서 발견된 묘지의 엄청난 크기에 근거하여, 일부 역사가들은 최대 십만 명만큼 많은 인구에 달하는, 그 당시 세계에서 가장 큰 도시였을 것으로 생각한다. 이집트의 선도하는 도시로서의 멤피스의 지속은 그것이 제공했던 다수의 중요한 이점의 결과로 간주할 수 있다.

3 관리의 편리함이 멤피스에 수도를 설립하게 된 주된 동기였을 것이다. 사실상, 새로운 수도는 초기에는 왕족 통치자들의 활동 중심지로서 주된 역할을 했던 것으로 여겨지고, 이후 고왕국의 제 3왕조 시대 동안에 멤피스는 왕족이 거주하는 곳도 되었다. 멤피스가 통치하기 좋은 곳에 위치해 있었던 한 가지 이유는 그것이 나머지 왕국과 소통할 수 있었던 편의성이었다. 나일 강은 이집트의 소통을 위한 중요한 중추였고, 선박은 나라 곳곳에 메시지를 전달하기 위해 남북을 계속해서 횡단했다. ¹³나일 강에 있는 멤피스의 위치는 외진 지역들로 왕실의 메시지를 제때에 보내는 것을 가능하게 했다. 공지사항들은 불법적인 행위와 그것들의 처벌에 관한 명령에서부터 인구 중 이해관계에 있는 일원들의 불만과 고충으로 야기된 법

의 변화들까지 모든 것을 포함했다.

4 그 지역의 계절에 따른 가뭄과 홍수에 더 잘 대응하기 위한 바람으로 그 위치가 선택되었다는 것을 암시하는 증거도 있다. 나일 강은 상류 고지대 지역의 장마 때문에 매년 홍수가 있었다. 이집트인들은 작물을 관개하기 위해 이러한 홍수를 매우 필요로 했다. 하지만 너무 적은 비는 작물이 자랄 수 없었기 때문에 가뭄과 기근으로 이어졌고, 과도한 비는 마을을 파괴하는 홍수를 야기했다. 삼각주 가장자리의 30킬로미터 정도 남쪽에 위치했던 멤피스는 비옥한 충적토로부터 이익을 얻을 만큼 가까웠고 홍수의 일부를 자연적으로 피할 수 있을 만큼 먼 상류에 있었다. 더욱이, [15]성직자들에 의해 전해 내려온 구전 역사에 따르면, 메네스는 특히 댐을 이용해 멤피스를 나일 강으로부터 분리시켰고 일련의 수로를 이용해 그 지대의 물을 빼냈는데, 이것은 여분의 피난처를 제공하고 주민들이 그들이 홍수로부터 안전하다는 것을 알고 편안하게 도시에 거주할 수 있도록 했을 것이다.

5 마침내, 멤피스는 국제적인 무역에 있어 그것의 전략적인 위치로 인해 더 부유하게 되었고, 통치자들이 실용적이고 일상적인 일들을 위한 재료뿐 아니라 즐거움을 위한 사치품에도 꾸준히 접근할 수 있도록 했다. 고고학자들은 북동쪽으로 300킬로미터 이상 떨어져 있는 레바논에서 수입한 것이 틀림없는 삼나무로 만들어진 커다란 문과 지지대를 발견했다. **이러한 물건들은 꽤 건조한 기후와 이 특정한 나무의 부패에 대한 자연 내성 덕분에 존속해왔다.** [18A/B]금은 중앙아프리카의 누비아에서 얻었고 포도주는 소아시아에서 들어왔다. 배를 이용한 무역을 쉽게 해주었던 지중해와 나일 강으로의 근접성에 더하여, 멤피스는 페니키아와 메소포타미아에 있는 무역 상대국들과 도시를 연결해주는 중요한 육상 무역 노선의 역할을 했던 동쪽 사막의 건조한 강바닥으로부터 이익을 얻었다. 게다가, [18D]몇몇 고고학적 유적지에 있는 옥의 존재는 멤피스가 동아시아와 같이 먼 문화들과의 간접무역에 침여했었다는 것을 보여준다.

어휘
mighty[máiti] 장대한, 웅장한 **reach**[ri:tʃ] (강의) 직선 유역 **fan out** 펼쳐지다 **delta**[déltə] 삼각주
assimilate[əsíməlèit] 흡수하다, 동화하다 **found**[fáund] 세우다, 설립하다 **question**[kwéstʃən] 의문을 갖다 **account**[əkáunt] 이야기
bear[bɛər] 지니다 **founding monarch** 개국 군주 **consecutive**[kənsékjutiv] 연속적인 **span**[spæn] 걸쳐 이어지다
longevity[lɑndʒévəti] 지속, 장수 **ascribe to** ~의 결과로 간주하다 **headquarters**[hédkwɔ̀:rtərz] 활동의 중심지, 본사
governance[gʌ́vərnəns] 통치 **ease**[i:z] 편의성 **artery**[á:rtəri] 중추, 동맥 **traverse**[trǽvə:rs] 횡단하다
grievance[grí:vəns] 고충 **irrigate**[írəgèit] 관개하다 **famine**[fǽmin] 기근 **alluvial soil** 충적토 **drain**[drein] 물을 빼내다
occupy[ɑ́kjupài] 거주하다 **cedar**[sí:dər] 삼나무 **acquire**[əkwáiər] 얻다 **overland trade** 육상 무역 **jade**[dʒeid] 옥
archaeological[ɑ̀:rkiəlɑ́dʒikəl] 고고학적인

MEMO

MEMO

MEMO

|H|A|C|K|E|R|S|

TOEFL
READING
Intermediate

본 교재 인강 · 지문녹음 및 단어암기 MP3 · iBT 리딩 실전모의고사 **해커스인강**(HackersIngang.com)
토플 보카 외우기 · 토플 스피킹/라이팅 첨삭 게시판 · 토플 공부전략 강의 · 토플 자료 및 유학 정보 **고우해커스**(goHackers.com)

해커스 어학연구소